Becoming Israeli

THE SCHUSTERMAN SERIES
IN ISRAEL STUDIES

Editors
S. Ilan Troen
Jehuda Reinharz
Sylvia Fuks Fried

The Schusterman Series in Israel Studies publishes original scholarship
of exceptional significance on the history of Zionism and the State of Israel.
It draws on disciplines across the academy, from anthropology, sociology,
political science and international relations to the arts, history and literature.
It seeks to further an understanding of Israel within the context of the
modern Middle East and the modern Jewish experience. There is special
interest in developing publications that enrich the university curriculum and
enlighten the public at large. The series is published under the auspices of
the Schusterman Center for Israel Studies at Brandeis University.

For a complete list of books in this series, please see www.upne.com

Anat Helman
Becoming Israeli: National Ideals and Everyday Life in the 1950s

Tuvia Friling
A Jewish Kapo in Auschwitz: History, Memory, and the Politics of Survival

Motti Golani
Palestine between Politics and Terror, 1945–1947

Ilana Szobel
A Poetics of Trauma: The Work of Dahlia Ravikovitch

Anita Shapira
Israel: A History

Orit Rozin
The Rise of the Individual in 1950s Israel: A Challenge to Collectivism

Boaz Neumann
Land and Desire in Early Zionism

Anat Helman
Young Tel Aviv: A Tale of Two Cities

becoming

Anat Helman

Israeli

National Ideals
& Everyday Life
in the 1950s

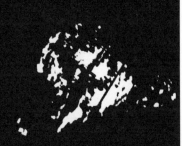

Brandeis University Press ▪ Waltham, Massachusetts

BRANDEIS UNIVERSITY PRESS
An imprint of University Press of New England
www.upne.com
© 2014 Brandeis University
All rights reserved
Manufactured in the United States of America
Designed by Eric M. Brooks
Typeset in Arno Pro by Passumpsic Publishing

University Press of New England is a member of the
Green Press Initiative. The paper used in this book meets
their minimum requirement for recycled paper.

For permission to reproduce any of the material
in this book, contact Permissions, University Press
of New England, One Court Street, Suite 250,
Lebanon NH 03766; or visit www.upne.com

Hardover ISBN: 978-1-61168-556-5
Paperback ISBN: 978-1-61168-557-2
Ebook ISBN: 978-1-61168-558-9

Library of Congress Cataloging-in-Publication Data
available upon request.

5 4 3 2 1

Contents

Preface

IN THE SUMMER OF 1949, a member of a kibbutz
— an Israeli agricultural collective community — wrote an essay for the local
bulletin. He complained about too much noise and disorder in the communal dining hall during mealtimes and listed some behaviors that members
of the kibbutz, both workers and diners, could adopt to improve the situation. After the founding of the state, Israeli kibbutzim faced economic, demographic, social, and ideological difficulties; as the writer well knew, noisy
and chaotic meals were neither the kibbutz's gravest problem nor its most
urgent, and yet he found the topic worthy of attention and remedy. He ended
his essay with a somewhat apologetic statement: "Small matters should not
be disregarded," he wrote, because all the big and important issues "are composed of such 'small matters.'"[1] Following this cue, the chapters of this book
focus on various ordinary, supposedly trivial, daily matters that accumulated
alongside other components in creating a larger entity: Israeli culture during
its formative years.

Whereas the kibbutzim were collective communities, the moshavim were
Israeli cooperatives of individual farms. In 1951 the chair of the moshavim
movement listed four areas of organized cultural activity: (1) "the culture of
language" — implementing the use of Hebrew among the new immigrants
while teaching them "the basic values of the regenerated life in the State of
Israel"; (2) "the culture of the soil" — familiarizing new immigrants with the
country, taking them on hikes, training them in agricultural labor, and teaching them the country's folk songs; (3) "the culture of manners" — proper
daily behavior, for example refraining from shouts and blows during arguments; and (4) "culture and lifestyle: combining the good and the excellent
in each ethnic lore into one wholeness."[2] The list, presented by the writer as
a program in process, actually portrayed the aspired-for ideal: a culture run
in the national tongue, infused with national values, prioritizing agriculture
and direct contact with the land, composed of well-behaved citizens from
different ethnic backgrounds, merging harmoniously into a unified entity.

This book shows how this dominant cultural ideal met reality, how norms and practices interacted in Israeli daily life.

Note that the chair of the moshavim movement assumed that longtime Israelis (Jews who had arrived in Palestine during the prestate era and their offspring) could and should mold the new immigrants, who flocked to the country after the founding of the state and doubled its population, into the preferred cultural form. Longtime members of moshavim wished not only to impart Hebrew and agricultural skills but also to change the new immigrants' worldview and to initiate them into the ideology and lifestyle of socialist Zionism. Regarding the newcomers' cultures, skills, and ambitions as insignificant, longtime Israelis aspired to guide them to assimilate into their own dominant culture.[3] As political philosopher Michael Walzer remarks, although socialist Zionists were committed to democracy, once in power their leaders "operated with a sure sense that they knew what was best for their backward and often recalcitrant" constituents.[4]

Historians and sociologists portray a hegemonic Israeli culture that reflected the values of socialist Zionism and was promoted vigorously by the ruling party, Mapai; they argue that although some Israeli segments did not adopt these values, still the hegemonic status of the national culture, like the political domination of Mapai, wasn't seriously challenged during the first decade of the state and thus it reigned supreme.[5] According to philosopher Antonio Gramsci, parliamentary regimes do not have to rely on the state apparatuses of force as long as the ruling group achieves moral authority and public legitimacy. Rather than using force, the ruling group can lean on its economic power and propagate its own definition of reality among all other groups in society. The latter adopt the ideology — which actually represents the interests of the ruling group — as the "natural" and permanent order of things. Hegemony is thus a wide agreement with and a general support of the existing social order. Hegemony depends on successful persuasion, and it is spread by various agents such as the family, the educational system, the media, and other cultural and religious institutions.[6]

Whether viewed with admiration or censure, the national culture of 1950s Israel is an example of a successful hegemony, a historical case in which the ruling group's ideology was persuasively and effectively circulated among the citizens.[7] While consenting with this well-established general assessment, this study nonetheless aims to investigate the scales and the manners in which hegemonic values were informally practiced in commonplace circumstances. We should keep in mind that hegemony is not a concrete entity but rather a continuous process; the examination of lifestyles and behavioral patterns alongside written texts reveals how hegemonic ideologies are constantly interpreted, translated, modified, contested, or ignored by their multiple "users."[8] Thus, by focusing on several public spheres of social interaction, this book reconstructs and analyzes various forms in which national ideals were applied, lived, and experienced by ordinary Israelis on a daily basis.

In order to decipher daily practices and communications, let us apply the concepts of *strategy* and *tactic* suggested by Michel de Certeau. In his influential *The Practice of Everyday Life*, Certeau reveals how ordinary people, rather than being passive or docile, take part in composing culture by utilizing and manipulating presentations. Instead of stressing the violence of order as it transmutes into a disciplinary technology, Certeau's goal is to bring to light "the clandestine forms taken by the dispersed, tactical, and makeshift creativity of groups and individuals already caught in the nets of 'discipline,'" their procedures composing a "network of antidiscipline."[9] The "consumers" of culture do not produce the initial image, but rather their manner of using it hides a process of "secondary production." Certeau employs the word *strategy* to indicate a relationship in which a subject of will and power can be isolated from an environment (such as political, economic, and scientific rationality); the word *tactic*, on the other hand, describes heterogeneous elements, combined by various decisions, acts, and manners rather than a discourse. Many everyday practices and ways of operating are tactical in character, and these multiform and fragmentary acts conform to certain rules.[10] The location of streets, determined by a municipal plan, can serve as an example of a strategy, whereas the routes taken by local taxi drivers, who know best how to navigate those streets, can be defined as tactical. Scientific and political definitions of sex and gender roles are strategic, while the different manners in which men and women actually position their legs when they sit in public, often automatically and unconsciously, are tactical.

Historian Roger Chartier notes that a certain gap exists between dominant norms and real-life experiences. Alongside the institutional mechanisms of power, he argues, we should keep in mind that an elite's intention to discipline bodies and to mold minds does not determine the ways in which its models are actually appropriated by individuals and groups. Chartier applies the word *appropriation* to describe a creative and differentiated process that continually generates cultural meanings. "High" culture and "popular" culture are not two separate entities because popular practices are tied to —

though not dictated by—dominant models and norms, whether the latter are accepted and imitated or challenged and negated. Popular culture is neither totally dependent nor totally independent, and cultural meanings are created by the very tension between creative appropriation and the limits of confining conventions. Cultural research should therefore investigate both how practices are controlled by dominant norms and how they negotiate with, or ignore, these controls.[11] Hence, this book describes appropriations of cultural products, various "tactics" employed by users within the limits of dominant norms and official institutions ("strategies"). It portrays how, during the first years of sovereignty Israeli identity emerged from a combination of a self-conscious elite culture and the array of informal habitual practices and conventions shared by many Israelis.

[handwritten marginalia: now Israel is not known]

The State of Israel was founded on May 15, 1948, and spent its first months in a total war. Although the last battles took place in March of the next year, by early 1949 the result of the War of Independence[12] was already determined in Israel's favor, and cease-fire agreements were gradually signed with the Arab states. The Sinai campaign, launched in October 1956, disrupted the routine of the previous years while improving Israel's international status and boosting its military confidence. It is considered by several historians as the completion of the War of Independence and as the end of the first stage of Israel's statehood.[13]

"War is the greatest of all agents of change," wrote George Orwell. "It speeds up all processes, wipes out minor distinctions, brings realities to the surface."[14] It is this dramatic nature of war, and not necessarily the militant leanings of historians and their subject matter,[15] that makes wars effective markers on historical time lines.[16] Moreover, an examination of everyday practices might profit from viewing mundane periods of relative "normalcy," continuous phases of routine (or at least attempts to regain a routine) between climactic events, such as the interwar period in 1949–1956 Israel. Focusing on a short period including eight years gives the study a snapshot quality, a synchronic bias relative to most historical writing:[17] whereas daily life in 1950s Israel is reconstructed and discussed in detail in this book, long-term developments can only be mentioned succinctly, although several issues examined here originated in prestate Palestine and some had older roots and precedents in Jewish history.

As will be explained in the opening chapter, 1950s Israel was marked both by technical statism—namely, centralized state institutions and policy—and by a sort of ideological and ethical centralism, expressed in ardent official attempts to interfere in and influence various spheres of life, to unify the nation, and to stimulate a feeling of respect for the state. The early years of Israeli sovereignty are therefore convenient for the study of cultural codification, due to the distinctness of institutional strategies in many areas of Israeli life. Indeed, most research on the period tends to focus on, or gravitate toward, institutional and formal policies, activities, and discourse, and many studies dwell on the violence of order and disciplinary technologies in 1950s Israel.[18] Yet the creative network of antidiscipline practiced in daily life by Israeli groups and individuals has been studied so far only by a handful of scholars.[19] The present study seeks to redress this imbalance, so even as it traces and notes the strategies,[20] above all it reconstructs dispersed and makeshift tactics. By arranging assorted details and contemporary perspectives into a larger mosaic, the study portrays how Israelis took an active, though often informal, part in composing their emerging national culture. They did so neither solely nor primarily in a set discourse but rather in their mundane customs and commonplace behaviors.

The qualitative description of daily practices may sometimes seem anecdotal, and many of the historical sources themselves are highly subjective and impressionistic; yet we should beware not to erroneously transfer the methodology of intellectual and political history onto the cultural history of daily life. Whereas the former's engagement with historical documents involves a clear hierarchy of "authority" and "reliability," the latter depends on a wider and less hierarchal range of evidence.[21] When, for instance, we try to ascertain the number of movie theaters operating in 1950s Israel, we must of course look for the most trustworthy quantitative sources, such as municipal and government census records. However, when we try to reconstruct the *experience* of moviegoing, which is subjective by definition, then even the most tendentious description clumsily scribbled by an anonymous consumer could be as relevant for our study as the most eloquent account produced by an accomplished and well-known member of the elite. Cultural historians tend to doubt whether behavior could be induced from the discourse that aims to justify it. We therefore treat all descriptive sources, both "high" and "low," as partial and argumentative and constantly juxtapose discourse and practice. Rather than rank our sources, we try to accumulate enough evidence of various kinds to trace regular tendencies and recurring patterns, and to verify findings by assessing overlaps and contradictions.[22]

Luckily for the historian of everyday life, alongside the manifest strategies of statism and centralism, 1950s Israel was characterized by abundant documentation of daily tactics. Ample textual and visual primary sources depict, often in detail, the daily lives of Israeli citizens.[23] This keen interest in every mundane feature was probably generated, or at least enhanced, by the newness of statehood. Sociologist Colin Campbell argues that the emergence of a new set of attitudes and behaviors arouses much comment and debate, unlike attitudes and behaviors that have become a taken-for-granted part of life.[24] Similarly, firstborn children are often photographed more frequently than their younger siblings, especially during their early years: everything the firstborn does is an exciting novelty for the parents, whereas the same feats performed later by younger siblings are treated more casually.[25] In addition to attention stimulated by mere novelty, Zionists viewed the Israeli state as a momentous historical achievement. After centuries of Jewish yearnings for Zion and after decades of ardent Zionist settlement, activity, and struggle, a Jewish state was finally established. The founding of Israel was viewed by Zionists as a historic opportunity and as the beginning of a new phase.[26] *Nothing* in the new state was taken for granted; every element was noticed, described, discussed, praised, or rebuked. Anything that was built, founded, or materialized during the first years of the Israeli state was announced with pathos as the first of its kind "after two thousand years of exile."[27]

With marked institutional strategies on the one hand, and plentiful sources for reconstructing daily tactics on the other, the ground is thus set for the exploration of common customs and concepts in 1950s Israel. As hundreds of visual and textual primary sources are collected, some topics gradually come to the fore by their sheer frequency of occurrence. Among many topics that appear repeatedly and insistently in historical documents, and therefore suggest themselves as worthy of closer scrutiny, seven spheres of daily social interaction have been chosen.[28] This series includes three representative public spaces — the bus, the movie house, and the kibbutz communal dining hall; two major forms of human interaction — language and manners; and two central subjects of Israeli public opinion and reference — the economic rationing policy and the army. Each chapter could be treated like a different drawing on a transparency: when put on top of each other, the various lines accumulate into a dense, detailed picture of common public customs and sensibilities.

Although this study mentions Israelis of all walks of life, it focuses particularly on longtime Jewish Israelis. During the prestate era, Zionists distinguished between the pioneering elite and other Jewish immigrants, but after the state was founded and new immigrants were pouring into the country, a hidden unofficial alliance was formed among longtime Jewish residents, enveloping both the middle classes and former manual laborers. Socialist Zionist ideals remained hegemonic on the political, rhetorical, and official levels, yet the middle class flourished economically and many longtime Israelis gradually joined its ranks, their working-class past and socialist political affiliations notwithstanding. Longtime Israelis (*"vatikim"*) and their offspring thus became the state's new, wide, and heterogeneous dominant social layer.[29] On the other hand, Arab citizens, some of the new immigrants (especially, though not solely, those who came from Muslim countries), and ultra-Orthodox Jews often lacked either the essential ability and power or the required concepts and language to communicate effectively with the rest of the Israeli collectivity. According to sociologist Baruch Kimmerling, during the first years of the state these groups remained outside Israeli hegemony.[30]

Since the author is not proficient in Arabic, Yiddish, and other languages spoken by these latter groups in the early years of Israeli statehood, and since they rarely documented their own daily lives at the time, treatment of this subject from within their own viewpoints requires different methodologies and deserves a separate research. Yet in addition to technical and disciplinary limitations, there is the fact that these groups, as Kimmerling and others argue, were often not included within hegemonic culture. And since this study investigates informal daily correspondence with national hegemony, it is interested mainly in Israelis who *did* share the hegemonic culture to a large degree and even took part in shaping it: How did *they* interpret, distribute, modify, contest, or ignore familiar hegemonic notions? How were hegemonic ideals translated, practiced, and communicated in the hectic flow of daily life, by the people who were well acquainted with these ideals?

By reconstructing commonplace daily patterns and deciphering the intricate relations between strategies and tactics, this study aims to view the first years of statehood from a new angle. It seeks to show how Israel's public culture was formed not only by ideological discourse, political decisions, and governmental policies but also, and to a large extent, by the manners in which many Israelis actually lived their lives, communicated with each other, and related to hegemonic national ideals.

Popular depictions present 1950s Israel either nostalgically, as a heroic age of national revival after two thousand years of exile, or iconoclastically, as a despotic age of repression. The present book, however, reconstructs a daily struggle that set grand projects and good intentions alongside socioeconomic strife and cultural conflict. Media scholar John Fiske defines the culture of everyday life as "a culture of concrete practices which embody and perform differences,"[31] and indeed, by analyzing daily practices and informal social interactions we can assemble a more detailed, multifaceted, and accurate picture of Israeli society. "Accurate"—mind you—does not necessarily mean "tidy": as we shall see, contradictions, confusion, and disarray were central components of Israeli culture in the 1950s.

Acknowledgments

I WOULD LIKE TO express my gratitude to Ezra Mendelsohn, Yael Reshef, Hagit Lavsky, and Emmanuel Sivan, who kindly read the book's manuscript and provided me with constructive criticism and invaluable advice.

I also wish to thank a team of excellent research assistants — Erez Hacker, Shira Meyerson, Arik Moran, and Noah Benninga — for tracing and gathering thousands of textual and visual historical sources. These documents were collected at the National Library in Jerusalem, the Bloomfield Library at the Hebrew University, the Central Zionist Archives, the Israel State Archives, the IDF Archives, the Pinhas Lavon Institute for Labor Movement Research, the Jabotinsky Institute Archive, the Steven Spielberg Jewish Film Archive, the JNF Photo Archive, the National Photo Collection, the Tel Aviv–Jaffa Municipal Historical Archives, the Jerusalem City Archive, the Haifa Municipal Archives, the Afula Archive, the Nahariya Archive, the Yad Tabenkin Archive, the Religious Kibbutz Movement Archive, and the local archives of Afikim, Kiryat Anavim, Hazorea, and Alonim. Thanks are due to the archivists, librarians, and employees in all these institutions.

It was a real pleasure to work once again with Brandeis University Press and the University Press of New England. I am grateful to Sylvia Fuks Fried and Phyllis Deutsch, Lori Miller, Eric Brooks, Amanda Dupuis, Barbara Briggs, and an anonymous reviewer, whose suggestions were extremely useful. Special thanks to Jason Warshof, whose attentive and creative editing job went far beyond style and technical matters.

This study is part of a wider research endeavor on everyday culture in 1950s Israel, which was generously funded by the Israel Science Foundation. Images were purchased with a research grant from the Levi Eshkol Institute for Social, Economic and Political Research in Israel.

Introducing Israel in White

IN FEBRUARY 1950, an Israeli daily newspaper published a cartoon titled "Israel — The Land of Wonders." It showed three local symbols — a camel, a cactus, and a palm tree — all draped in snow.[1] The wondrous juxtaposition depicted in the cartoon referred to the days during the previous week when Israel, characterized by a subtropical Mediterranean climate, was covered in snow. Normally January, the coldest month of the year, witnessed an average temperature of 55 degrees Fahrenheit in Tel Aviv, located in the country's coastal plain, and 47 degrees in Jerusalem, located in the eastern mountain region.[2] Snow fell occasionally, during particularly cold winters, in the latter region, as well as in the northern mountain region of the upper Galilee, but the snow of 1950 was exceptional: it fell for a number of days and not only in the higher, cooler areas, but all over the country, even, albeit lightly, in parts of the southern Negev desert. During three days in February, temperatures all over Israel broke the known record after eighty-five years of meteorological measurements (at one point as low as −8.6 degrees),[3] a record that has not been broken since.

Unsurprisingly, the weather — ordinarily a marginal topic in Israeli newspapers — filled front pages, as reporters and journalists described excitedly the effects of snow in the towns and the countryside.[4] Yet beyond the rarity of the specific event, its portrayal in the local media discloses much about the general political, demographic, economic, social, and cultural conditions in 1950s Israel.

Located geographically in the Middle East, Israel was politically and economically isolated from its Arab neighbors. During 1949 Israel signed cease-fire agreements with the Arab states, but the war's end did not bring about peace, and security remained a central and costly national concern. Israelis were terrified by constant infiltrations and by the armament of the neighboring Arab states; they were concerned over the unsupportive policy of the superpowers and the United Nations, and uncertain about the state's ability to

An extraordinary sight
in Israel's coastal plain:
orange groves in the snow.
National Photo Collection
(Government Press Office),
D235-084. Photo by David Eldan.

survive for long. Not until after the Sinai campaign would Israelis acquire a
new sense of security, resistance, confidence, and power.[5]

Thus, the snow of February 1950 fell all over the conflicted Middle East.
Israeli newspapers reported about the cold spell's effect not only on Israel
but also on Egypt and key cities, cut off by the snow, in Lebanon, Syria, Iraq,
and Jordan.[6] Nor were the Palestinian war refugees ignored by the Israeli
media, with several newspapers mentioning their plight. They quoted Arab
sources regarding sixty-two people, mostly children, who died in the refugee
camps, and related the suffering of other refugees in the Arab states, unpro-
tected from the harsh cold in their provisional tents and shacks.[7]

Whereas the Palestinian refugees, some of whom fled and others of whom
were deported during the war, were confident of their eventual repatriation
following the hostilities, Israel deemed the Arab League responsible for the
refugees' fate and expected the Arab governments to resettle them in their
countries.[8] Hence, an Israeli newspaper reporting about the distress of the

refugees in Jordan, and about the Arab states' plea through the Red Cross for international help, added, "Various propagandists and politicians try to exploit the disaster for inciting against Israel, and repeatedly raise the problem of the Arab refugees in order to gain political capital."[9] Under international pressure Israel consented to some "family unifications," and around thirty thousand Palestinian refugees were allowed to gradually cross the border and join their families in Israel.[10] In February 1950, however, a scheduled border crossing was delayed and postponed because some of the hundred appointed returnees were stuck on the snow-blocked roads and did not reach the crossing point in East Jerusalem.[11]

The Arab community of Palestine, numbering about 1.3 million in 1947 (800,000 of them in the area that would become Israel), was dispersed, dwindled, and devastated by the 1948 war. About 160,000 non-Jews (mainly Muslim Arabs, alongside Druze and various Christian minorities), 15 percent of them internal refugees, remained in the State of Israel. Eighty percent of this population lived in villages, without sufficient resources or any elected local authorities.[12] Cut off from the Palestinian collectivity and missing their former leadership, Israeli Arabs were not included in the Israeli collectivity either, in spite of their Israeli citizenship. They were isolated and closely supervised, governed by a special military rule, which enacted emergency defense regulations inherited from the British Mandate period. Established during the war, this military rule eventually enveloped those areas densely populated by Arab citizens. The necessity and morality of a military rule, imposed on the Arab population within a democratic state, was disputed and debated by the Israeli public, in the political system, and within the army itself.[13]

During the 1950s Israeli Arabs, who had become a minority in their native land, were excluded from the culture of the Israeli Jewish majority. Their politics at the time focused on survival, not least in the economic sphere.[14] Most Israeli Arabs, especially Bedouins, were among the country's poorest residents.[15] After the escape of most of the urban Arab elite in 1948, the local Arab economy was based solely on agriculture, which was plagued by insufficient land (a rapidly growing population in the villages, on the one hand, and confiscation of Arab land by the state, on the other), a lack of state resources and encouragement (these were channeled to Jewish agriculture), and the mobility and employment limitations imposed by military rule.[16] With few exceptions, Arabs only started to be hired as workers by Jewish employers during the latter part of the decade.[17]

[handwritten margin note: Israel becoming a state made Arabs living there extremely poor]

Registering the Bedouins
in the Negev, 1949.
JNF Photo Archive, d5-011.
Photo by Fred Chesnik.

The Negev desert was accorded the status of "the country's untapped frontier," and efforts were made to "make the desert bloom" — to settle it in order
to strengthen Israel's hold on the region.[18] The Bedouins in the Negev were
put under military rule within a restricted area, while the fertile Negev lands
were settled by Jews.[19] On February 7, 1950, newspapers reported that the
Negev Bedouins were suffering from a lack of food and blankets needed to
keep them warm in their tents, and that a six-year-old Arab girl died in northern Israel when the snow-covered roof of her family's house collapsed.[20]

In a transit camp, four other Israelis, new Jewish immigrants from Yemen,
were also killed by the snow. The large building that housed the camp's dining hall, serving five thousand immigrants, caved in under the snow's weight.
Due to the unusual cold, many of these immigrants had decided that day to
remain in their huts and tents rather than walk to the dining hall, yet others lined up inside the hall, waiting to be served. Most residents escaped
the crumbling structure, but in addition to those killed, five were injured.[21]
One journalist described these casualties as yet another portion of affliction
endured by "our Yemenite brethren," who paid the highest price for immigrating to Israel, the land of their ancient yearnings. This instance of natural
destruction, he wrote, should urge settled Israelis to do their best to house
and absorb those new immigrants still living in the transit camps.[22]

Indeed, the mass Jewish immigration to Israel was defined by the government as the state's primary mission. About 650,000 Jews lived in Israel

in May 1948, and after one decade the number had jumped to more than 1.8 million.[23] This mass immigration was characterized both by its rapid pace (between 1948 and 1951 the population of Israel doubled) and by the unusual ratio of newcomers to longtime residents. While 85 percent of the Zionist immigrants before 1948 were Ashkenazim (Jews of European origin), after 1948 fewer than half of the new immigrants came from Europe (mainly survivors of the Holocaust) and America, and more than half arrived from Asia and North Africa. Whereas most Jewish immigrants during the Mandate era were young adults, more than half of the newly arrived immigrants were older people and young children.[24]

The prestate Zionist community, forged by the experiences and events of the "founding generation," was relatively homogeneous: in 1948, natives constituted more than 35 percent of the population, and among those born elsewhere, 65 percent had lived in the land for more than a decade. By 1953, however, natives constituted only 29 percent of the Israeli Jewish population, and more than 70 percent of the citizens born elsewhere had lived in the country for less than five years.[25] It became harder to find a common denominator among the longtime Israelis, the newly arrived immigrants from Europe, and the Jews from Muslim countries who were starting to arrive. The ancient Hebrew past could provide the required unifying myth, and hence the mass immigration was often described in messianic terms, with the ingathering of the exiles to the newly founded state linked to momentous events from the biblical past.[26]

Messianic rhetoric notwithstanding, the new immigrants, many of whom were dispossessed refugees, had to be physically accommodated. To solve this problem, arriving immigrants were put in camps, where they were expected to spend a relatively short period of several weeks going through initial processes of registration, documentation, and medical examination. However, since permanent housing was not available, immigrants remained in the camps for months, some for years. The transit camps (*ma'abarot*) were, in effect, places of residence composed of tents, tin huts, sheds, and canvas huts. These camps were crowded, lacked sanitation facilities and proper water supply, and lacked adequate food and clothes; some camps didn't have access to roads, telephone lines, and public transportation. The institutions responsible for absorbing the immigrants usually didn't have the means to supply necessary services,[27] and the stormy weather of February 1950 hit this vulnerable population hardest.[28] As soon as heavy snow started falling, newspapers reported on concerns for the safety of those residing in tin

Tents at the Pardes Hanna transit camp, December 1950.
National Photo Collection (Government Press Office), D200-045. Photo by Teddy Brauner.

shacks, tents, and mud huts in deserted Arab villages,[29] namely the new immigrants. When snow kept falling in subsequent days, some new immigrants were evacuated from their temporary dwellings. In the northern region, longtime Israelis took into their homes children who had resided in transit camps. In Jerusalem many residents—both new immigrants in temporary dwellings and longtime Israelis whose houses were still damaged by the war—were evacuated to hotels, and the municipal social services department managed to bring blankets and warm clothes to new immigrants in a neighborhood cut off by the snow. In the Tel Aviv vicinity, scores of families were evacuated from their tents and shacks and rehoused in various public buildings. In the southern city of Beer Sheva, forty-five mothers and their newborns were moved from the new-immigrant dwellings into the warmer local school building.[30] As one journalist put it, "While the children of Israel had fun with snowballs and snowmen, their eyes shining with excitement from the rare substance, there were other children, deprived by fate, whose hands turned blue from the cold, whose eyes watered, whose thin garments could not supply any warmth. The meager residences of some families were destroyed, leaving them roofless in the snow and the storm and the frost."[31]

A journalist who visited a transit camp in the Galilee reported that the

Skiing outside the "Zion"
cinema in Jerusalem,
February 1950. JNF Photo
Archive, d178-175. Photo by
Verner Braun.

huts were withstanding the weight of the snow and not leaking. Yet while
the camp's European inhabitants enjoyed the snow, which reminded them of
their countries of origin, the new immigrants from North Africa remained in
bed, trying to keep warm under the blankets.[32] When concerns were voiced
regarding the frost's dangerous effects on the new immigrants' health, the
people considered particularly at risk were those "from Eastern countries,"
who were unaccustomed to, and unequipped for, cold weather.[33] The new
immigrants from Europe certainly experienced the snow differently from
those who arrived from warmer climates. "Snow sleds, brought by the European new immigrants, made their appearance in Safed." In Jaffa, a former
Arab city now populated mainly by new immigrants, "scores of people were
seen wearing furs." In Haifa, people skied down the slopes of Mount Carmel
in ski gear brought from Europe, and similar attempts were made by some
European new immigrants in Jerusalem.[34] Reporting from Safed, one journalist mentioned that "The new immigrants enjoyed themselves most. For
the first time, they had the upper hand over the longtime Israelis and were
able to prove their vast experience and knowledge of snow and its ways. They
wore warm coats and fur hats, went around town in their sleds, and affected
the whole town with the same chant: 'just like overseas.'"[35]

The snow itself was comically defined as yet another new immigrant
in Israel, and was described as having been transported to the country by
its recent inhabitants.[36] If European newcomers felt at home in the snow,

immigrants from Yemen were taken aback. Reporters related that Yemenites in camps in the coastal plain and in the Galilee mountains, seeing snow for the first time, shouted excitedly: "Manna is falling from the sky."[37] A journalist for the newspaper of the religious Zionist party elaborated on this Yemenite encounter with snow:

> The immigrants from Yemen are staring with surprise at the freezing white carpets. The transformation from the heat storms of Yemen to the present cold storms is far from easy, even more so when they hit the dwellers of the camps, living in tents, lightly dressed and used to walking barefoot. One reporter narrates how he encountered a Yemenite in a transit camp, walking barefoot in the snow, soaking wet and shaking from the cold.
>
> Where are your shoes?
>
> I'm saving my shoes for the Sabbath.
>
> This reply reveals the wonderful religious naïveté of the Yemenite Jews. They walk barefoot in the snow, endangering their health, suffering from the cold and yet they refrain from wearing their shoes, which are reserved for the holy Sabbath day.[38]

Such descriptions of the Yemenites' reaction to the snow, mingling patronizing superiority with real appreciation, reflected a typical view of this ethnic group among longtime Israelis, the majority of whom came from Eastern Europe during the Mandate era and who created an ideal-type Yemenite as representative of the old Oriental Jew: illiterate, naïve, and primitive, yet authentic, devout, and hardworking. Israel's first prime minister, David Ben-Gurion (1886–1973), said of the new immigrants from Yemen that two thousand years separated them from Israeli society, especially the attitude of men to women and children. He maintained that the feelings of the immigrants should be understood and their customs respected, yet the cultural gap should be filled by gentle persuasion and by organized education.[39]

Art historian Yael Guilat argues that this available, familiar, functional Yemenite model, which was being molded in Zionist culture for decades, served the Israeli elite as a "boundary marker" vis-à-vis the mass wave of newcomers from Muslim countries. Accessible and approachable, the model facilitated the absorption of the recently arrived immigrants of the 1950s.[40] Still, cultural differences between longtime Ashkenazi Israelis and new immigrants from Asia and North Africa often resulted in misunderstandings, mistrust, mutual prejudices, and conflict. New immigrants from Europe, who came from cultural and linguistic backgrounds similar to most longtime Israelis,

A boy with a tea can on his way to the Rosh Ha'ayin camp's kitchen in 1950. Traces of snow can still be seen around the tents. National Photo Collection (Government Press Office), D400-007. Photo by David Eldan.

usually adapted to their new life and acculturated to Israeli society faster and more successfully than did arrivals from Asia and North Africa.[41] Hungarian-born British writer and journalist George Mikes visited Israel in late 1949 and wrote: "Many people are afraid — though few speak their mind — that the Yemenites, with the North Africans, will soon give a Middle Eastern character to this Middle Eastern country. The Yemenites are treated well; nobody thinks of refusing them right of entry. But some people think of 'keeping them in their place.' Intermarriages are rare and these people are regarded by many as poor relatives and not as brothers."[42]

Indeed, historian Orit Rozin describes the complex attitude of longtime Israelis toward the newcomers as consisting of a sense of duty and obligation, mixed with, and abated by, recoiling disdain and at times even disgust.[43] The plight of the new immigrants during the cold winter of 1950 brought this ambivalence to the fore, and one journalist confessed that tucked in his warm bed at night, he suddenly remembered that thousands of newcomers were spending the same cold night in tents and shacks. He tried to console his guilty conscience by recalling that he too, once upon a time, spent his nights in a tent in a kibbutz. However, he admitted, how could his memories from the pioneering past console today's refugees and immigrants, exposed with their large families to the storm? Before the founding of the state, recollected the journalist, the country's Jews had demanded that the gates be opened for the immigration of their brethren, but after the state had been founded and the gates opened, "it seems as if we have become indifferent to the fate of the newcomers." The journalist feared that "we [longtime Israelis] have alienated ourselves from the new immigrants, enclosed ourselves within the homes that we had built with our sweat, within our accustomed habits."[44]

Receiving the mass immigration was a momentous task indeed, and doubly challenging for a young state facing a postwar recession. The first years of Israel's statehood were marked by dire economic hardships and crises, though this situation was followed after 1954 by rapid economic growth. Due to the overall security threat, significant resources had to be channeled to defending the state, in addition to resources allocated for absorbing the mass immigration. Such high expenses increased both the national debt and local inflation. Led by the labor party and influenced by postwar centralist economic tendencies, in 1949 Israel's government started rationing all vital commodities and fully controlled their prices. It imposed egalitarian distribution of the limited supplies by requiring longtime Israelis to restrict their consumption. During its first two years, the rationing regime (*tzena* in Hebrew) seemed to have achieved its main goals—prices were stabilized, the new immigrants were fed, and local investments and production increased. However, public support for the rationing regime soon waned, and the system would be considerably diminished in early 1953.[45]

Nineteen fifty, meanwhile, was a bleak economic year: an acute lack of foreign currency plagued and disabled the entire economic system. Feeding and providing for the population—both longtime Israelis and newcomers —became a struggle, although successful new agricultural settlements were raising hopes for future improvement.[46] It is no wonder that reports about the effects of the snow worriedly spotlighted locally grown food. Vegetables were in short supply as it was, and the destruction of tomatoes, lettuce, potatoes, and kohlrabi by snow and frost meant even scarcer amounts and diminished rations. Citrus groves and banana plantations were also harmed.[47]

The snow revealed other symptoms of the postwar recession, such as hastily built houses, with foundations that flooded, roofs that flew off, and cracked walls. No more gasoline stoves could be found in the market, not to mention the rarer and more expensive electric heaters. Boots, too, were hard to come by and in Jerusalem long lines, occasionally violent, gathered outside shoe stores.[48] Although the new immigrants were particularly exposed to the perils of the sudden cold, most longtime Israelis were also affected during those years by the shortages and lived in spartan conditions. Socioeconomic stratification was determined to a large degree by seniority in the land and by ethnicity, as longtime Israelis gradually improved their socioeconomic status by taking advantage of the conditions of immigration. Yet

יצור הירקות
בכפר הערבי
(באביב 1950)
33.000 דונם
46% 15.180 עגבניות לרסק
14% 4.720 במיה
8% 2.720 בצל
3% 1.070 שום דונם
71%
3.060 מלפפונים 9%
1.900 קישואים 6%
1.880 קטניות 6%
1.230 תפ"א 4%
1.270 שונות 4%
29%

A poster depicting the vegetable output of Arab farming in Israel during 1950 (Arab total farming provided less than 5 percent of the country's produce), part of an exhibition of locally grown vegetables held in Tel Aviv in June 1950. While the country recovered from war and absorbed mass immigration, agricultural settlement and development was considered one of the young state's central projects. National Photo Collection (Government Press Office), D401-066. Photo by Fritz Cohen.

the general economic crisis of the early fifties and the government's central-ized policy, despite areas of discrimination in distribution, prompted relative economic equality, as compared with the disparities during the prestate era and the following decades.[49]

In spite of the grave economic difficulties, about three hundred new ag-ricultural settlements were founded in Israel during the first three years of statehood, and by decade's end local agriculture had achieved impressive re-sults and met almost the entire food demand of Israel's increasing popula-tion.[50] Moshavim—cooperatives of individual farms—became the main form of agricultural settlement after the founding of the state. Many new im-migrants were settled in moshavim due to the availability of land, the prom-inence of the pioneering ideology, the housing these settlements provided, and their potential for increasing food production for the population.[51] Still, more than 70 percent of Israelis did not farm the land but rather re-sided in towns and cities. State authorities intended to "spread" the popula-tion throughout the country, especially along its volatile border areas, and new development towns were established, populated with new immigrants.

However, most Israelis gravitated to the larger cities — Jerusalem, Haifa, and especially Tel Aviv.[52]

Newspaper coverage of the cold weather during February 1950 also focused on these three central cities,[53] and discloses the vulnerability of Jerusalem in particular. Israel's announcement of west Jerusalem as the state's capital in 1949 involved political risks and implications, as it defied UN resolutions. Transferring the government ministries from Tel Aviv to Jerusalem was progressing slowly: its symbolic significance for Zionism notwithstanding, war-devastated Jerusalem was a poor city, inconveniently distant from the thriving demographic and economic center of the coastal plain.[54] Mikes compared his impressions of ancient Jerusalem and new Tel Aviv: "Jerusalem is beautiful; Tel Aviv is ugly. Jerusalem is dignified and sacred; Tel Aviv is noisy and commercial. Tel Aviv is bursting with activity; Jerusalem is half dead. Tel Aviv is dedicated to a great and promising future; Jerusalem is a monument of a magnificent past. Tel Aviv is an American town; Jerusalem is much more European and yet Oriental at the same time. Jerusalem is the capital of Christianity, Judaism and Islam; Tel Aviv is the real capital of Israel."[55]

Jerusalem's weaknesses were exacerbated and exposed during the snowy days of 1950: "Jerusalem has now been badly damaged by four consecutive days of economic standstill. The city's merchants and businessmen alone complain about damages of hundreds of thousands of pounds. Transport companies and their workers have suffered a considerable loss. Places of entertainment, the poor peddlers and daily hired workers have lost all. Those who are dependent on daily pay have remained penniless."[56]

Access to the snow-covered capital was so difficult that a parliament meeting had to be postponed: despite the decision to move both the parliament and the cabinet offices to Jerusalem, many parliament members remained in Tel Aviv, their rout to work temporarily blocked.[57] From the outset, some government officials and clerks, as well as their spouses, were reluctant about "leaving swanky Tel Aviv and settling in gloomy, dull, historical Jerusalem."[58] The cold weather further detracted from Jerusalem's unappealing image: "Government workers who were relocated from Tel Aviv to Jerusalem are starting to slowly adjust to their new location and to come to terms with the harsh command [that they live there], in spite of the difficult living conditions. Still, they can't adjust to Jerusalem's cold climate, including the interiors of the government's offices."[59]

Some writers blamed the government for the disabling effects of the snow. "Where's the Government?" — declared a headline in a politically unaffiliated daily newspaper. The writer complained that the government had not announced how it intended to help the immigrants who were hit by the cold.[60] In a newspaper associated with the middle class, an article rebuked the authorities for their "negligence" and called on the government to take care of the settlements and the camps.[61] The Jewish nation is ancient, wrote a journalist in another newspaper representing the middle class, but the Jewish state is a mere "baby" and clearly unprepared for climatic surprises, so one stormy day can cut off all the state's institutions, its transportation system, and its communication lines.[62] The newspaper of the opposition right-wing party, Herut, quoted a student saying that the government's helpless response to the snow was "typical of the government's work in general."[63] The same paper also published an article by a religious writer who claimed that the snow and the preceding cold spell were God's punishment for the socialist rule in Israel.[64]

While the claim of God's judgment and intervention remains disputable, the Israeli multiparty political system was indeed led during those years by the labor party Mapai, which won all general national elections and headed the coalition governments. Its authoritative chairman, David Ben-Gurion, served as prime minister and as minister of defense until 1963, apart from a fourteen-month hiatus when he retired from politics and settled in a kibbutz in the Negev.[65]

The prime minister consolidated and championed Israel's centralist ethos (*mamlakhtiyut* in Hebrew[66]). Whereas "statism" indicates centralized *state* institutions and policy, Ben-Gurion's centralism stressed the all-encompassing functions of the state and especially the civil obligation *to* the state. This approach was meant to draw respect toward the authority of the state and its laws, to excite Israelis with a feeling of public commitment, and to unify the nation. Ben-Gurion regarded the state as the only political and symbolic entity that could bind together the fragmented Jewish people. From its onset the Zionist movement aimed to create a strong, brave, and active "new Jew," the utter opposite of the stereotypical weak and passive "old Jew" of the Diaspora (the latter's image was often influenced by antisemitic notions). The centralist ethos was, in turn, intended to constitute a "new Israeli" and to shape the mass of new immigrants — described by Ben-Gurion as "a mixture of human dust, with no language, no education, no national roots, tradition or vision"[67] — into proper Israelis.[68]

Centralism was thus supposed to unite the diverse Jewish people, and to create a new Israeli culture, one that would erase the remnants of any exilic

Eleanor Roosevelt having tea with David Ben-Gurion at his residence in
Tel Aviv, February 1952. National Photo Collection (Government Press Office), D778-022.
Photo by Fritz Cohen.

traits. This aspired-for culture, a continuation of the prestate pioneering legacy, blended modern and Eastern European elements. A proper acculturation of the newcomers, especially of the young generation, was conceived
as a national goal, a necessary step in creating a unified nation and securing
its modernity. The formal terms in use were *melting pot* and *merging of the exiles.* In the 1950s the multicultural reality of the young Israeli society was not
accompanied by any multicultural ideals or agendas; the latter would take
shape only decades later. The purpose was not to integrate all immigrants'
cultures into a new entity but rather to assimilate newcomers into the dominant culture of longtime Israelis. The pressure to assimilate was weighty, and
many new immigrants — especially young ones — succumbed to it and tried
to imitate and adopt local norms, customs, and habits. Furthermore, some
newcomers internalized the dominant viewpoint about the inferiority of Diaspora cultures, growing ashamed of their original ethnic culture and trying to conceal it. Other new immigrants — especially older ones — reacted
to the pressure of the melting pot by turning their backs to it, secluding and
segregating themselves within their original ethnic cultures.[69]

After the founding of the state, the centralist ethos was supposed to extend the prestate pioneering ideology unto the entire Israeli population. Agriculture and manual labor were still viewed as vital for developing the land, but now Ben-Gurion broadened the notion of "pioneering" to envelop all sections of society and to cover whatever mission, task, or occupation could benefit the state.[70] He believed that civil commitment was vital for accomplishing the goals of sovereignty, and aimed to create a direct link between the citizen, who would work willingly for the sake of the national collectivity, and the state institutions, which defined the national targets and supplied the means to achieve them.[71]

Yet the promotion of the centralist ethos was an attempt to counter an actual relaxation and dwindling of the pioneering spirit.[72] After the climax of achieving sovereignty and the concentrated effort of the War of Independence, the first years of statehood were experienced as an anticlimax and a grinding gray routine. Pioneering seemed to have lost some of its former "trendy" appeal. Ben-Gurion and other leaders, who tried to motivate the people into a new, important phase of national dedication, were bitterly disappointed and frustrated by the decline of the pioneering spirit in Israel. Between late 1953 and early 1955, Ben-Gurion, withdrawing from politics and living on a new kibbutz in the Negev, worked, at least part time, as a shepherd; the masses, though, did not follow his example and did not rush to settle the Negev.[73] Nonetheless, although most Israelis did not live as pioneers, the centralist ethos did manage to win general public agreement, and thus its main values achieved a hegemonic status on the ethical and rhetorical levels.[74] This hegemony was achieved and maintained by the combination of statism and centralism: Ben-Gurion's civic ideals supplied the main contents, while state-ruled institutions served as disseminating agents. It is also noteworthy that some of those who disagreed with Ben-Gurion on partisan and ideological grounds still shared his belief that the state had the means, the right, and even the duty to educate and mold society "from above."[75]

The editor of the religious Zionist party's newspaper combined the statist and centralist approaches in discussing the responsibility of both state institutions and the citizens at large for dealing with the extreme weather of February 1950.[76] Religious Israelis were divided into different ideological, cultural, and political segments, and whereas the Haredim (ultra-Orthodox) included a moderate non-Zionist religious group and an extreme anti-Zionist group, religious Zionists intentionally combined Judaism with modern Hebrew nationalism.[77] No one is to be blamed for the sudden cold, wrote the editor, but both the government and individual Israelis must make every effort to relieve the suffering of the camp dwellers. The grave damage caused by the weather should not be aggravated by human neglect and inefficiency. While government offices should salvage the agricultural fields, citizens should open their homes and lodge their poor brethren. Let not the sudden cold that hit our country, he summed up, cool our spirits and paralyze us: "A warm home for our suffering brethren and quick repairing actions by the government — these are the duties thrust upon us in this special winter time of emergency, cast down by the heavens."[78]

The media coverage of the exceptional winter of 1950 also mentioned several everyday characteristics, to be discussed in detail in the following chapters: these included jokes about the rationing regime, use of military notions in civilian life, and the archetypical traits of Israeli natives. Several descriptions of the surprising snow referred humorously to the daily reality of rationing. "Great Joy among All the Children of Israel, as They Are Given Plentiful Snow without Any Rationing," declared one headline. A journalist mentioned that the way to get rid of the snow was to declare it "a rationed product,"[79] because rationed products were always scarce or missing. People in the white street were reported to be devising apt metaphors for the snow — "sugar without rationing," "feathers of a white chicken with no coupons."[80] A local joke claimed that a dealer in the black market almost had a stroke when he first saw the city's roofs covered with snow: he thought that his (illegal) sugar had been stolen.[81] Likewise, we shall see later, in the third chapter, how the hardships of the economic recession, of scarcity, shortage, and rationing, were molded into jokes, a common tactic for venting, and thus alleviating, frustrations.

The fourth chapter of this book portrays the cultural militaristic presence in Israeli daily life. The IDF — Israel Defense Forces — was established in 1948, and during the war a hundred thousand soldiers were eventually mobilized. When the war ended, it was clear that Israel could not maintain such a large army, and a reserve system was designed, combining the regular army, the reserve army, and a smaller framework of professional soldiers.[82] Due to Israel's volatile security situation, the IDF became a central national institution, "an army of the people," which carried out civilian assignments, such as settlement and education, as well as military tasks.[83] When, for instance, the aforesaid dining hall roof in a transit camp collapsed from the snow, killing four people and injuring five, soldiers stationed in a nearby settlement took part in the rescue efforts.[84]

The snow of 1950 was frequently discussed using martial images and ref-

A snowball fight in Tel Aviv in 1950.
National Photo Collection (Government Press Office), D225-046. Photo by David Eldan.

erences. Some reporters depicted Jerusalem's plight as yet another "siege," although merely a minor siege imposed by "Commander Snow" when compared to the much longer and more painful siege during the war.[85] Haifa was described as put under a "snow curfew."[86] When members of parliament were transported by bus from Tel Aviv to Jerusalem through the blocked roads, the "operation" went well, apart from one MP, whose window wasn't shut and who was consequently "shot" with a snowball.[87] "No News on the Weather Front," announced a headline when the snow kept falling,[88] and Israelis were characterized as waiting for a "cease-fire."[89] Friendly snowball fights were naturally depicted in military terms: "harsh battles" among joyful "soldiers," streets turning into "battlefields" and rooftops into "fronts," where children "fired" and "bombarded" with snowballs.[90] Referring to Israel's victory in the War of Independence, one journalist wrote, "We cannot be defeated by guns and weapons, but we can certainly be defeated by proper snow and mud."[91] Journalists were probably relieved to knowingly use the military terms, painfully learned during a traumatic war, in a relatively benign context.

For most of the country's natives, the snow was a first-time experience,[92] and some native children in Tel Aviv, unaccustomed to the cold, fainted on their way to school and required medical treatment.[93] Israeli natives were nicknamed "Sabras" (*tzabarim*) after the fruit of the common local cactus. The title indicated the natives' rough and prickly exterior and their sweet interior. Once the main pool of potential new pioneers was eradicated in the Holocaust, the Sabra replaced the pioneer as the ultimate national hero. Moreover, the Sabras' share as fighters in the War of Independence was prominent, and thereafter they were showered with national feelings of gratitude and admiration.[94] Sabras constituted about one third of the Israeli population and were depicted both formally and in popular culture as cheerful and disobedient.[95] Historians and sociologists define the Sabras who grew up in the Land of Israel in the 1920s and 1930s as a generational group with its own specific style. These Sabras could be recognized by their distinct form of speech and their Hebrew accent, their special body language and typical dress. The Sabra was perceived as the extreme opposite of the stereotypical Diaspora old Jew: healthful, brave, active, tough, group-oriented, deeply rooted in his native land, direct, informal, spontaneous, uncomplicated, and anti-intellectual.[96] Mikes wrote that the Sabras "are Israelis as young Frenchmen are French." He continued: "Few young Frenchmen would ponder over the question why they were born in Lyons and not in Santiago or Reykjavik; nor would they, in normal circumstances, meditate on various emigration schemes. They are French and that's that; the sabras are Israeli and that, again, is that."[97]

It should be noted that not *all* Jewish Israeli natives adopted the Sabra lore and style. The "salon youths" were urban youngsters who did not join the organized youth movements and instead followed the rising American youth culture, its music and its fashions. Members of Israeli youth movements were highly appreciated and applauded in Israeli society for their devotion to the centralist ethos and their dedication to national goals. Americanized teenagers, on the other hand, were frowned upon as unideological, and references to them as salon youths, or "golden youths," were sarcastic, meant to indicate their inactivity, decadence, and vanity.[98]

As will be indicated in the book's last chapter, the Sabras were also known for their inflated self-confidence and arrogance, and the journalists who reported on the 1950 snow amusingly accentuated this trait. They described Sabras who looked down on the snow, belittled its importance, and voiced disbelief that any snow abroad might be heavier than the snow that fell in Israel.[99] One journalist rendered the scene as follows:

> For once in their cocksure lives the "Sabra" brats came down a peg and
> showed distinct signs of inferiority—for that alone, it was worth hav-

ing the snow. There was the snow — centimeters deep — and they didn't know what to do with it, beyond making snowballs. So the immigrant kids from Europe had their big hour. They taught the Sabras how you can easily turn a small snowball into a big one simply by rolling it; and how to make snowmen with hats and pipes and swords. At first, the Sabras were meek and awkward — refreshing sight. Naturally, by evening, they were trying to teach the boys from Warsaw how to make a snowman, with improvements.[100]

This last quotation, published in the *Jerusalem Post*, was written originally in English, whereas most other quotations presented in this chapter were originally written, published, and read in Hebrew. The next chapter explores the daily linguistic reality, located between a national melting pot policy, on the one hand, and the implications of mass immigration, on the other.

The Language of
the Melting Pot

"THE VERY FOUNDATION of each and every nation is its national tongue," wrote the Hebrew writer Yehuda Burla in 1954. Born in Jerusalem to a Sephardi family, Burla considered linguistic unification during these years of mass immigration an arduous task. Some comfort could be found in the younger generation, the children of Israel, who would absorb the language in a natural, organic manner, but, he wrote, "it is much harder to root out a foreign tongue from the mouth of an adult and plant the national tongue instead." Nonetheless, this too must be accomplished, because the use of "the languages of the Diaspora" in newspapers, books, and the theater in Israel hinders the creation of a people. The government, suggested Burla, should consult thinkers, writers, linguists, teachers, and publishers, and create laws that limit the use of foreign languages, on the one hand, and facilitate the learning of Hebrew, on the other.[1]

One year later the Galician-born linguist Naftali Herz Tur-Sinai, first head of the Academy of the Hebrew Language, said that Hebrew expresses "the special character of our land." The heritage of the past was molded in the language, and it will also determine the future "development of our thought" and literary creativity.[2] Burla and Tur-Sinai's words reflected and enhanced strongly held beliefs concerning the centrality of Hebrew in the Jewish national revival and its role in connecting the Jewish people anew to their historic land. Both men held that the state and its elites were responsible for implementing the linguistic ideal and ensuring the actual leading position of Hebrew in Israel.

Language often plays a central role in national movements.[3] Moreover, the literary scholar, translator, and poet Benjamin Harshav defines the revival of Hebrew as the greatest achievement of the Jewish people in the modern era. It wasn't just a resurrection of a "dead" tongue and the transformation of a religious and written language into a secular and spoken one, he writes, but — most important — the creation of a whole new sociocultural foundation. Harshav lists three stages in the revival of Hebrew: during the nineteenth century, mainly its last quarter, Hebrew was revived in Europe in the field of literature; during the first four decades of the twentieth century, Hebrew was turned into the basic language of the Jewish Zionist society in Palestine; and after the founding of the State of Israel, Hebrew was turned into the basic language of the state and all its institutions and systems.[4]

Hebrew served for centuries mainly as a sacred language of religious Judaic ritual, and the first stage of its revival occurred in the Diaspora. Members of the Jewish Enlightenment movement, the Haskalah, approved ideologically of Hebrew as a "pure" language, like German.[5] Emanating from Berlin, the Haskalah gradually spread in Eastern Europe, where, later in the nineteenth century, Hebrew was used by poets, writers, and journalists. The language, often secularized by its nonreligious usage, was celebrated for its aesthetics, its past, its ability to convey information, and sometimes for its importance as a national means of communication. The Zionist community in prestate Palestine extended these cultural and political European trends, but whereas in the Diaspora a lively culture was conducted in written Hebrew while Jews kept speaking other languages (including local Jewish dialects), in the Land of Israel Hebrew was intentionally transformed into the language that ruled all domains of life. This second stage of linguistic revival included standardization, homogenizing of dialects, and introduction of Hebrew into the schools.[6]

Still, for more than twenty years the Zionist efforts to implement Hebrew as a national tongue had very limited success, and in the first years of the twentieth century, the use of Hebrew in speech was still confined to schoolchildren and a very small number of zealots. After 1903, however, following the arrival of a new wave of immigrants in Palestine and further consolidation of the Hebrew school system, the situation changed dramatically. By the eve of World War I, Hebrew had become the spoken language among ever-expanding social circles within the Zionist community in Palestine. In spite of the continued presence of other languages, the role of Hebrew increased steadily in daily life, and it gradually became a constitutive element in the Jewish settlers' self-image. Still, the position of Hebrew as a daily means of communication was far from secure. The Jewish population remained multilingual, and in order to fulfill all the communicational needs of a modern society, the newly revived language had to expand and go through vast processes of standardization. Its use was not evenly distributed but rather concentrated in certain social circles and geographic locations, and its diffusion among the population was periodically impaired by waves of immigration.[7]

The British law from the Mandate era announcing English, Arabic, and Hebrew as the country's three official languages was never revoked after Israel's founding, but an order from 1948 canceled the priority of English, and in practice Hebrew became the main language in official use by the state.[8] Statehood heralded in some ways a continuation of prestate linguistic processes, but it also posed new challenges: the revival of Hebrew could be further institutionalized through the authority of the sovereign state, but the size and pace of immigration since 1948 were unprecedented; spreading the knowledge of Hebrew and ensuring its use among a mass of new immigrants was indeed, as Burla put it, an arduous task. While the establishment of the state strengthened the position of Hebrew in public life, the mass immigration weakened its position in private life. Thus, the number of Hebrew speakers in absolute figures increased from 511,000 in 1948 to 861,000 in 1954; but the *percentage* speaking Hebrew as their only or "first" language decreased steadily during these same years, mainly in the adult population, from 65 percent in 1948 to 50 percent in 1954.[9] Receiving the newcomers and accepting them into Israeli society was regarded by the state and by longtime Israelis as a national responsibility, and linguistic acculturation played a prominent role in this ambitious project.[10]

How was the hegemonic ideal concerning the importance of Hebrew as a unifying national language realized in daily practice? Let us examine official strategies and common tactics with respect to two interrelated issues: the knowledge and use of Hebrew and the cultural status of foreign languages.

As mentioned in the preface, in 1951 the chair of the moshavim movement listed four areas of organized cultural activity conducted by longtime moshavniks among the new settlers: "the culture of language," "the culture of the soil," "the culture of manners," and "culture and lifestyle." The culture of language, which headed his list, was defined in broad ideological terms: the activity was not directed solely for facilitating Hebrew use in daily life but also for granting the immigrants "notions about the basic values of the renewed life in the State of Israel."[11] Teaching Hebrew was clearly not just a technical task, designed to enable communication, nor a legal requirement of new citizens,[12] but rather was regarded as part of a larger educational mission, as a prime condition for comprehensive acculturation and national integration.

The Jewish National Council, the main national Jewish institution in Mandate Palestine, had a special department in charge of teaching Hebrew and acculturating the new immigrants. In 1950 this department, soon to be

An interval between classes in a Tel Aviv ulpan, April 1951.
National Photo Collection (Government Press Office), D463-101. Photo by David Eldan.

named the Department for Language Instruction, was integrated into the state's Ministry of Education and Culture. Special institutions for intensive Hebrew study for adult immigrants with a secondary or university education, named *ulpanim* (academies), were founded near immigrant camps. In 1951, for instance, a journalist reported that 238 students ages twenty to sixty, including professionals and artists from seventeen different countries, had completed their studies in one ulpan during the past year and were "exultant about joining the Hebrew family linguistically-spiritually in such a short while."[13] Five years later another journalist called the ulpanim an original invention for teaching a language from scratch and "our first melting pot." He mentioned that the United States had its own melting pot characterized by its might, incredible wealth, and unprecedented freedom. The Israeli ulpanim, for their part, replaced American abundance and patriotism with their spirit of volunteerism and the intensive Israeli atmosphere cultivated by the teachers.[14]

In the ulpanim, new immigrants were also taught Bible, Jewish and Zionist history, local geography, as well as local folk songs and folk dances. Some of the ulpanim were funded by the Histadrut (General Federation of Hebrew Workers), the powerful organization of workers' unions, which also

Teenage guide in the Gadna ("youth battalions") helping a new
immigrant from Iraq with her homework in the Castel transit camp,
March 1954. Central Zionist Archives, PHKH\1287591. Photo by Yaron Mirlin.

sponsored courses on the history of the local labor movement.[15] The Histadrut was led by ministers from Mapai and operated in practice as an agent
of the government. Thus, the leading party could use its affiliation with the
organization of workers' unions and indoctrinate newcomers with certain
political and partisan leanings.[16]

The ulpanim targeted professionals, mainly highly educated immigrants
from European countries, while less educated immigrants had to settle for
Hebrew evening courses, which were gradually opened in most immigrant
camps. These latter courses, in improvised schools, had both much lower
standards and much worse physical conditions than the ulpanim.[17] Teachers
were unqualified and untrained, and often they themselves were new immigrants who taught what little Hebrew they knew to newer immigrants, without any suitable books. It took a couple of years before enough new teachers
were properly trained and qualified to teach the mass of newcomers.[18] Despite these various shortcomings, the Histadrut, urban municipalities, agricultural local councils, and kibbutzim all regarded Hebrew classes for new
immigrants as their top cultural priority.[19] Furthermore, members of youth
movements and other volunteers went to the camps and taught Hebrew,
sometimes in the new immigrants' homes. In addition to teaching Hebrew,

the volunteers attempted to "eradicate ignorance" by reaching unschooled women mainly from Muslim countries, "many of whom held a pencil and paper for the first time in their lives."[20]

While immigrant children were supposed to study Hebrew in their kindergartens and schools,[21] young men and women were expected to learn Hebrew during their army service. Assimilation could be achieved to a certain degree through the mere experience of serving in the army, but the IDF also conducted intentional activities in the cultural field. The greatest achievement of its educational system during the 1950s was teaching Hebrew and providing general education for new immigrant soldiers. Hebrew was taught in most army bases by recruited teachers and by female soldiers, who were specially trained for the task. A 1952 order demanded soldiers be taught Hebrew until they were able to converse freely on daily matters, write a letter to their commander, understand a simple lecture, and read a vowelized newspaper. The IDF officers in charge of education aimed to supply soldiers with sufficient linguistic skills and general knowledge so that they could assimilate into civilian life after their release from the army. Soldiers who were about to finish their army service without sufficient mastery of the language were sent to a special school for Hebrew founded by the army, where they spent their three final months of service.[22]

Special columns for explicating Hebrew terms and correcting common mistakes were published both in Hebrew newspapers aimed at new immigrants (such as the vowelized military bulletin issued by the IDF) and in non-Hebrew local newspapers like the *Jerusalem Post*. The vowelized paper for immigrants, *Omer*, regularly printed long lists of Hebrew words ("mob," "delicacy," "tiresome," and many others) translated to Yiddish, Arabic, Romanian, French, Hungarian, and English.[23] Audiences could hear Hebrew on the theater stage. The established Hebrew theaters included in their repertoires some plays "in easy, comprehensible language" suitable for new immigrants and occasionally performed in new immigrants' settlements. A special organization for bringing theater to the transit camps (Telem) was founded in 1952.[24]

Teaching and disseminating Hebrew among the new immigrants was tied to ideological and cultural indoctrination, and thus Hebrew instruction books for beginners promoted hegemonic national values.[25] One such book from 1956, for example, followed a story line about a group of new immigrants in Haifa who study Hebrew together. When discussing the native Sabras, the immigrants claim that they are "different from other Jewish children," as most of them are blond, tall and jovial, laughing and dancing, disobedient and independent, no fools, healthful, hardworking and brave, deeply rooted in Israel, which they love.[26] The new immigrants were taught, through the instruction of Hebrew, what the ideal Sabra was supposed to be like and how to view Israeli natives through an idealizing prism. The message that prestate immigrations were worthier than the present-day mass immigration was also instilled in the story: when the students discuss their various reasons for immigrating to Israel, the teacher tells them that while some recently arrived immigrants have never heard about Zionism, "almost all of the arrivals" in the first waves of Zionist immigration were pioneers, and thanks to their endeavor the State of Israel now exists.[27]

Without contesting the contribution of the pioneering elite to practical Zionism and the founding of the state, it should be clarified that during all the prestate waves of immigration the pioneers had remained a select minority.[28] Teaching the newcomers that "almost all" longtime Israelis, to whom they should be grateful, were part of the pioneering past fortified and enhanced a social hierarchy in which the former were placed lower than the latter. Moreover, the prestige of pioneering was preserved exclusively for prestate settlers, whereas new immigrants who were settled in new moshavim were considered "reluctant pioneers."[29] In a like fashion, when the national theater performed before new immigrants in Beer Sheva in 1951, it chose a play about the War of Independence that showed "the immigrants the story of the bravery of the Israel Defense Forces and the pioneering settlements, thanks to whom they [the immigrants] reached their destination of rest and security."[30] The play was meant to teach the newcomers about the heroic turning point in local history as well as engender gratitude for longtime Israelis, who paved the way for them.

In the immigrant camps, children from religious families were often educated by nonreligious teachers. The enraged religious parties protested and instigated a major crisis in the coalition government, and in 1950 the issue was investigated by a special committee, which recommended that longtime Israelis be more sensitive and patient about the new immigrants' cultural and religious heritage. The committee reported that in some immigrant camps, secular teachers and guides cut off the side locks of Yemenite children, sometimes using the danger of lice as an excuse, but usually as part of a wider secularizing endeavor.[31] The talented cartoonist Friedl (Stern) seized on the educational venue as a means of secularizing new immigrants. In her 1949 cartoon "Evening Classes for the Immigrants," the teacher has written the

"Evening Classes for the Immigrants," by Friedl. *Ashmoret*, August 11, 1949.

Hebrew word "to cut" on the blackboard, and she demonstrates the word by cutting the beard of an elderly religious pupil.

In 1955 the "Operation of Language Instruction for the People" was launched in order to teach basic Hebrew to the entire adult Jewish population in Israel, to supply newcomers with basic knowledge about the country and its culture, and to "kindle the spirit of volunteering and naturalization in the people for the sake of merging the exiles in Israeli society." The "operation" was carried out by volunteers who taught evening lessons in ulpanim, school classrooms, and private houses, using new books and applying novel methods for teaching adults. At the same time, the national radio network broadcast Hebrew lessons for beginners, and learning Hebrew was propagated in movie newsreels, a central visual medium in 1950s Israel, which lacked television broadcasting. The Histadrut was one of the operation's sponsors, and so Hebrew lessons were also conducted in factories and other workplaces. All in all, more than three thousand volunteers taught Hebrew to sixty thousand people, most of whom were new immigrants.[32]

The Operation of Language Instruction for the People is a telling example of the hegemonic centralist ethos in action: it was sponsored by formal national organizations, and in addition to teaching Hebrew to the new immigrants, it attempted to awaken the volunteerist mood among longtime Israelis and urge them to act. Although the state was in charge of education, citizens were called to take an active role in the assimilation of new immigrants.[33] Sociologist Baruch Kimmerling views the teaching of Hebrew as part of a wider mechanism, operated by longtime Israelis of European descent during the early years of the state, designed to sustain their hegemonic status vis-à-vis the new immigrants.[34] This conspiratorial phraseology might be misleading: the thousands of longtime Israelis who volunteered to teach

Hebrew to adult new immigrants were probably not just intent on enhancing their social status but also trying sincerely to assist the state and their fellow countrymen.[35] The operation's *goal* was to aid newcomers and help them integrate into Israeli society, but it did inadvertently reveal and accentuate the distinction between longtime Israelis — the volunteering teachers — and their charges, the new immigrants.[36]

This distinction was visually depicted in a recruiting poster calling on the public to "Take Part in the Operation of Language Instruction for the People."[37] The text addressed potential teachers, and the image portrayed one such volunteer lifting the heavy burden of foreign languages from the bent back of a suffering new immigrant. Whereas the immigrant figure was "dressed" in a foreign Roman text, the teacher was clad in a Hebrew-lettered text. Furthermore, the latter's deeply rooted locality was indicated by the "tembel" hat, which by the mid-fifties was regarded as the quintessential sartorial symbol of the Israeli native.[38]

All these institutional and voluntary strategic efforts bore fruit, and in 1956 the statistician and demographer Roberto Bachi published "a statistical analysis of the revival of Hebrew in Israel." He wrote of the 861,000 Hebrew speakers in 1954 Israel, versus 34,000 Hebrew speakers in 1914 Palestine: "Hebrew is the only or the main language for all people born in Israel to old settlers' families, and this language gains at an amazing speed among children and youth of new immigrants."[39]

Indeed, if we examine daily behavior, we find a wide adoption, especially among the younger generation, of the ideology concerning the importance of Hebrew as Israel's national tongue. As would be expected, children were quicker to learn Hebrew than their parents, and thus a six-year-old boy rebuked his mother, an immigrant who was not speaking Hebrew well. After finding the local Hebrew channel on the newly bought radio set, he said to her, "You see, such a box as this, only two weeks in the country — and it already speaks Hebrew; and you still don't."[40] Another new immigrant boy was speaking to his mother in his recently acquired Hebrew, but as the neighbor's daughter entered the room, he switched to Yiddish and introduced her to his mother: "This is my bride." When asked later why he had suddenly switched to Yiddish, he replied, "One mustn't lie in Hebrew"[41] — a view that perhaps preserved Hebrew's ancient position as a sacred language.[42] A three-year-old was sick and sighed, so her father told her that a little girl should not sigh like an old granny. "But I'm sighing in Hebrew!" she retorted.[43]

Although anecdotal, children's perspectives often reflect local norms and are therefore a useful source for reconstructing widespread notions. The sayings just quoted, for example, testify that Hebrew was seen by children as the proper, legitimate, youthful, and truthful (moral) language. In a similar fashion, during a physicians' strike in 1956 one physician gave the nurse in his clinic some instructions in Russian, "in order not to break the strike,"[44] as if using a non-Hebrew language didn't really count.

By 1948, 80.9 percent of Palestine-born Jews spoke Hebrew as their only language in daily life, and another 14.2 percent used it as a first among two or more languages. The few Palestine-born Jews still using languages other than Hebrew had grown up before the development of the Hebrew school system. The Hebrew schools' influence was enhanced by the use of Hebrew in kindergartens, youth movements, and informal children's play. After the founding of the state, Hebrew became dominant not only among the children of longtime Israelis but also among Israeli-born children of new immigrants, who benefited from educational institutions and the army.[45]

Whereas many Zionist immigrants in the Mandate era arrived in Palestine with some knowledge of Hebrew, the proportion with previous knowledge of the language decreased sharply after 1948, strongly affecting their daily use of the language. Bachi found that the use of Hebrew in family life, at work, in social contacts, and in reading newspapers and books was systematically higher among immigrants with previous knowledge of Hebrew. He also found that immigrants with a stronger educational background had higher rates of Hebrew learning in Israel, but also deeper ties with their non-Jewish languages. Woman adult immigrants, especially older women, showed lower percentages of learning, knowledge, and use of Hebrew than did men.[46]

So despite a generally successful dissemination of Hebrew, the actual acquisition of the language lagged somewhat behind the ideal. The scope of Hebrew evening courses for adults took a while to catch up with the unprecedented pace of mass immigration,[47] and even when Hebrew classes were supplied, they were not always in demand. In 1950–1951 it was found that only 12 percent of the new immigrants took advantage of Hebrew courses.[48] We remember that the chair of the moshavim movement listed "the culture of language" as a top cultural goal. However, in practice only a minority of the new immigrants who were settled in moshavim went to evening classes, with many claiming to be too tired to attend after a hard day of manual labor. Although the moshavim movement insisted that all books be kept in Hebrew, daily life was run in the original languages of the immigrants. Furthermore, although the moshavim movement formally upheld the melting pot ideology, in practice new immigrants were settled away from urban centers, in small communities based on countries of origin, and thus they were cut off from longtime Israelis and their culture, and could hold on to their original languages.[49] A settler in one moshav, for instance, related that although the residents, who had arrived from four different countries, lived together peacefully, the local social life — five years after the moshav's founding — was still conducted in Hungarian, Polish, Slovakian, or Romanian.[50]

One problem diagnosed as early as 1949 was that most new immigrants in the transit camps were from "countries where Yiddish was not spoken, while most of the camps' workers did not speak the languages of the new immigrants."[51] Most longtime Israelis who served as the new immigrants' guides, teachers, nurses, and clerks were Ashkenazim. And whereas longtime Israelis and new immigrants from the same Eastern European countries of origin shared some common ground, a wider cultural and linguistic gap divided longtime Ashkenazi Israelis and newcomers from Muslim countries. European culture served as the educational paradigm, and while some immigrants from Muslim countries tried to assimilate into it, hiding or even discarding their original cultures, others reacted by doing the opposite, fencing themselves within their original cultures.[52] This linguistic gulf between newcomers and longtime Israelis may help explain why immigrants from Muslim countries learned Hebrew faster than European immigrants, a fact that was usually attributed merely to the basic similarity between Arabic and Hebrew, or to the immigrants' previous knowledge of Hebrew through religious ritual.[53]

Although in the 1950s the dissemination of Hebrew among new immigrants was prioritized, the Hebraization project included other targets as well. Eliezer Ben-Yehuda (1858–1922), a leading figure in the revival of Hebrew, founded the Hebrew Language Committee, which coined new words and published them in pamphlets during the Mandate era. In 1953 the committee was replaced by the Academy of the Hebrew Language, which, following in its predecessor's footsteps, prescribed standards for all aspects of modern Hebrew and coined greatly needed words.[54] Linguistic activities conducted by Zionists during the prestate era were now continued and fortified under the sovereign state's authority: new Hebrew names were given to geographical sites (Jalil became Gliliot, Majidel became Migdal Ha'emek, Ein Sabha became Ein Naftali, and so on), new immigrants were pressured to replace their original foreign names with Hebrew ones, and official representatives of the state (for instance Foreign Office workers, IDF officers, and members of the Olympic delegation) were ordered by ministers to take Hebrew names.[55]

Hebrew was placed on a national pedestal. Writers, educators, and journalists connected linguistic quality (as opposed to mere knowledge and technical use of the language) with literary creativity and general cultural achievement. Hebrew was supposed to be practiced using correct grammar, and richness of expression and style was highly valued by the elite. Different institutions held courses for improving and enriching the Hebrew of Israelis who had already mastered the language.[56] As one journalist put it, striking roots in the land could be accomplished only in the national tongue, and this applied as well to longtime Israelis, "those for whom Hebrew had already become not just the language of daily life but also, and more crucially, the language of their thoughts and imagination."[57] But the actual nature of this "language of imagination" was contested, as in the mid-1950s a group of young poets nurtured a new poetic style. Defying the leading Hebrew poets of the former generation, they objected to "stylistic embellishments" and "pathos" and instead espoused a direct and simple expression of personal experience in a freely flowing speechlike rhythm.[58] Thus, even within the cultural elite, Hebrew was constantly evolving.[59]

On the level of daily practices, Hebrew's vitality brought about some phenomena that were not prescribed by the elite, who favored correct language, whether simple or embellished. The Hebrew that was written, read, and spoken in everyday life included abbreviations[60] and slang[61] (as well as translations of foreign slang and dialects[62]), grammatical mistakes and stylistic flaws,[63] insertion of foreign notions; some required words were still missing from Hebrew, while others (such as words for *reconstruction* and *air-conditioning*) had been invented but still not adopted into common usage.[64] Thus, although the centrality of Hebrew, promoted on the strategic level, was largely echoed in daily tactics, Hebrew was appropriated by many users in manners dissimilar to those advocated by formal ideology and elite culture.

The particular style of Hebrew spoken by the Sabras was gradually making its way into the center of Israeli popular cultural.[65] Cultural researcher Itamar Even Zohar writes that native Hebrew assumed a position of a noncanonized, nonofficial system, hence its absence and exclusion from the written literary corpus and the theater.[66] Literary style was closely bound to classical traditions of Hebrew, and even personal letters were usually written in a normative manner that deviated sharply from ordinary speech. Most scholars and teachers were not native speakers of Hebrew, but rather learned the language from written texts and regarded other sources of Hebrew as illegitimate. The elite's attitude was accepted by many natives, who were corrected by their teachers and regarded their own spoken Hebrew as "mistaken."[67] Moreover, when performing onstage, even Sabras adopted the non-Sabra Hebrew pronunciation of their elders.[68]

Yet its peripheral status in formal culture belies native Hebrew's centrality in popular culture: although it was still considered a "lower" and "thinner" Hebrew than the ideal canonized style, it was widely regarded by Israelis as the "juicy" authentic local version of the language, and its use was seen as a badge of belonging and assimilating. It was often quoted in the media in parentheses, thus maintaining its nonofficial status, and was treated by the founding generation with a mixture of disdain and fondness.[69] Significantly, in the early 1950s the young linguist Haim Rosen introduced the term "Israeli Hebrew"; he and his colleague Haim Blanc were the first to study and analyze the innovations of spoken native Hebrew in linguistic terms and with no corrective attempts. They regarded the unconscious creativity of speakers and various non-Hebrew influences as integral elements in contemporary "living Hebrew," and described them as being as natural and legitimate as the basic grammar and vocabulary of traditional, canonical Hebrew.[70]

Native Hebrew probably received more attention after 1948 due to its association with the Palmach, the military units that bore the main share of fighting during the Arab-Jewish strife that began in late 1947 and later played a major role in the War of Independence. Since its founding in 1941, the Palmach was surrounded by a heroic aura and symbolized youth, pioneering, and committed love of the land. During the 1940s the Palmach became the body most associated with the Sabras and with the local new Jew. Although the Palmach was dismantled when the IDF was established in June 1948, during and after the war it was immortalized in songs, drawings, and tales that were filled with nostalgic admiration.[71] Palmach lore was tightly connected to the native Hebrew spoken by its members and characterized, inter alia, by laconic distortions of formal grammar and prolific use of Arabic words, such as *Ahlan, dir balak, majnun,* and many more.[72]

Sociologist Dan Horowitz writes that since Hebrew became a central cultural bond in Israel's immigrant society, Sabras' mastery of Hebrew as a mother tongue helped them find their way into Israeli elite, as did their familiarity with local institutions and culture.[73] Yet it wasn't merely the Sabras' proficiency in Hebrew, but more precisely the *kind* of Hebrew they actually spoke — its specific style and pronunciation — that gave secular Ashkenazi

Sabras an audible cultural edge over other social groups who knew Hebrew well but spoke it differently (e.g., members of the founding generation, some new immigrants from Muslim countries, Sephardi natives).

By contrast, Israelis who did not know Hebrew often used their mother tongues. In 1954, 60 percent of the population (especially adult men) reported the use of more than one language in daily life. Bachi found that Hebrew was used to the largest degree to satisfy work needs, to a somewhat lesser degree to satisfy cultural needs, to an even lesser degree to satisfy social needs, and to the least degree within the family. Many immigrants thus used Hebrew at work but conducted their social intercourse and their family life in their original languages.[74] When spoken privately at home, foreign languages sometimes changed their role and their position. As children were quicker to adopt Hebrew than adults, a family's original language could turn into a second language alongside the national tongue. Judeo-Spanish turned from the daily spoken language of the Sephardi families who immigrated to Israel into the language of their special heritage and lore.[75] As for Yiddish and other languages, these tongues sometimes became parents' "secret language" vis-à-vis their Hebrew-speaking offspring.[76]

Using Hebrew alongside other languages was one thing; refraining from Hebrew altogether was another. If learning Hebrew could reflect and enhance acculturation and assimilation,[77] then refusing to learn the national language could reflect, or even demonstrate, disappointment and dissatisfaction among new immigrants. In the early 1950s sociologist Shmuel Noah Eisenstadt conducted pioneering research about the new immigrants. In a chapter titled "The Types of Immigrants," he described some families and their life in Israel, including the languages they used. An immigrant from Morocco and an immigrant from Romania, whose families struggled in Israel, both expressed their increasing depression by not bothering to learn Hebrew. Similarly, members of a family from Poland, who were extremely dissatisfied with life in Israel, spoke Polish and Yiddish at home. On the other hand, a couple from Tripoli who came from a Zionist background were happy in Israel, so even as they still spoke Italian and Arabic at home, the wife was learning Hebrew and the husband spoke Hebrew with his friends. A couple from Morocco and their children were finally starting to acclimate themselves after the husband had found work, but previously they were deeply depressed and "intentionally spoke only Arabic and French."[78]

Refusing to learn Hebrew could be a personal and spontaneous expression of one's fatigue and despair, but it could also serve as an intentional social manifestation, namely a resistance to comply with dominant expectations and hegemonic demands. Some immigrants described linguistic compliance or defiance as a purposeful choice, and therefore opting to speak foreign languages in public *could* serve as a demonstrative act.[79] The ideological importance attached to Hebrew, far beyond technical considerations, turned any linguistic choice into a potentially expressive and meaningful behavior for speakers and listeners alike.

Despite the priority given to Hebrew, the Hebraization project was not conducted fanatically, as state institutions acknowledged various practical needs in an immigrant society during a transitional period. Even in the prestate Zionist community, the enthusiastic embrace of the national language was somewhat tempered by a toleration of language diversity in the spheres of commerce and leisure, and an approval of certain languages in bureaucratic settings, foreign-language classes in schools, and organizations committed to engaging with Palestinian Arabs.[80] This allowance for foreign languages increased when the young state faced mass immigration.[81] In the immigrant camps and the transit camps, political and partisan meetings were conducted either in Hebrew, when aimed at the camp's general population, or in Yiddish, Berber, Arabic, or other pertinent tongues.[82] Newspapers in foreign languages — both local and imported — were sold alongside Hebrew ones.[83] We lack exact figures regarding the distribution of Israeli newspapers, but it was estimated in 1950 that alongside about 200,000 copies of Hebrew dailies, almost 70,000 copies of dailies in foreign languages were issued, among them the English *Jerusalem Post*, two newspapers in German, and dailies in Hungarian, French, and Arabic.[84] In 1954 seven dailies in foreign languages, besides numerous weeklies and monthlies, were distributed.[85] In addition to the broadcasting of Hebrew lessons, the national radio aired news bulletins and other programs in foreign languages.[86] Musical and theatrical shows were performed in Romanian, Hungarian, German, English, Arabic, and Yiddish.[87] Posters announcing these performances were sometimes issued in the appropriate foreign languages,[88] and the activities of some *landsmanshaften* (immigrant organizations according to places of origin) were published in Hebrew side by side with the specific language of the organization.[89] In former Arab cities, such as Jaffa and Beer Sheva, signs in Arabic still adorned some buildings, gradually joined by shop signs in the various languages of new Jewish immigrants.[90]

This toleration of foreign languages in 1950s Israel did not reflect a multilingual ideology but rather a limited, often reluctant, acceptance of a multi-

A new barbershop serving immigrants in Ramle in 1949 has a sign in Hebrew, Romanian, and Bulgarian. National Photo Collection (Government Press Office), D197-039.

lingual reality. As we shall see, on the strategic level official permissions to use foreign languages were granted by institutions unwillingly, conditionally, provisionally, and selectively. If we follow the patterns of these permissions, we can trace a sort of hierarchy in which some languages were considered more "legitimate" and justifiable than others. On the tactical level, the hegemonic linguistic ideal of "only Hebrew" was either obeyed or partly realized or challenged or simply ignored. But on this level, too, feelings about different foreign languages were at play and influenced the manners in which Israelis treated and utilized different tongues. Significantly, the strategic linguistic hierarchy and the tactical one were not identical. This leads us to a closer look at the ideological and cultural positions of four languages in particular — Arabic, English, German, and Yiddish.

Arabic, one of the country's three official languages according to the unrevoked British Mandate law, was the language of Israeli Arabs, Druze, and other minorities. Whereas some Jewish new immigrants from North Africa spoke French or Italian, many others spoke Arabic in various dialects, as did Jewish immigrants from Asian Muslim countries.[91] The attitude to this tongue among Israeli policy makers, most of whom came from European backgrounds, was indecisive: Arabic was taught in some of the leading

Jewish teachers are taught Arabic as part of the teachers' course in Nazareth, July 1949. The first Israeli minister of education, Zalman Shazar, and his wife, Rachel Katznelson-Shazar, attend the class. (Shazar would become Israel's third president in 1963.) National Photo Collection (Government Press Office), D230-122.

Jewish high schools, and it was appreciated for its military intelligence and public relations functions. On the other hand, as a non-European language Arabic carried no Western prestige and, furthermore, it was strongly and unfavorably associated with the hostile Arab states.[92]

The Hebraization project did not include the country's Arab citizens, who were expected to speak Arabic. Relatedly, in 1951 Aharon Cohen, an expert on Middle East affairs, wrote about the sorry state of education in the Israeli Arab sector. Among other things, he mentioned the urgent need to improve the teaching of Hebrew in Arab schools, because Hebrew was required in order for Israeli Arab citizens to enjoy higher education.[93] Israeli Jews, on the other hand, were demanded to replace Arabic with Hebrew. This distinction between Arabs and Jews was reflected in the work of the National Censorship Committee for Films and Plays. In early 1950s the Censorship Committee decided to allow the screening of Arab films that passed its censorship (mostly produced in Egypt before 1948), in areas populated by Arabs, such as Haifa, Nazareth, Ramle, Jaffa, and Acre, on the condition that every Arab film would be accompanied by a local Israeli newsreel with Arabic narration.[94] While seeking to meet the demand for entertainment, the committee also wanted to ensure that films in Arabic included no hostile anti-Israeli political messages and that these films be screened only within the regions inhabited by Arabs. Although the Censorship Committee did not prohibit theatrical and musical shows in Arabic, their performance in front of *Jewish* audiences was regarded unfavorably, on the grounds that it reduced the new immigrants' need to learn Hebrew and thus hindered their acculturation.[95]

Although some new immigrants from Muslim countries, especially young ones, hurried to forsake their mother tongue, both longtime Israelis and new immigrants could remain strongly attached to Arab culture and yearn for its musical, poetic, and cinematic products.[96] As early as 1949, a left-wing journalist wrote that music broadcast on Arab radio stations, well loved by Israelis originating from Muslim countries and constantly heard in their enclaves, further alienated these Jews from the new Hebrew culture. Interestingly, he was not referring to new immigrants but rather to longtime Israelis from Yemen and other Muslim countries, who remained economically deprived and culturally cut off from the dominant norms embraced by European Jews in the prestate era.[97] Like most members of the Ashkenazi elite, the journalist viewed Arab culture as a socioeconomic disadvantage, a temporary setback in the hegemonic Western-oriented cultural project.[98]

According to historian Liora Halperin, one prestate-era argument in favor of Arabic study in Hebrew schools was that Jews needed to get in touch with their Semitic roots in order to return to an authentic Hebrew identity.[99] Anthropologist Yael Zerubavel describes the use of Arabic words and dress items among European Zionist settlers as an attempt to embody a local identity. Still, she notes that the cultural trend of adapting Arab features was by no means welcomed by the entire Zionist community and, furthermore, that while traditional Arab culture was viewed as a connection to the Jewish past, it was also regarded as primitive.[100] The association of Arabic with authentic locality was manifested, as we saw, in the slang used by Palmachniks and Sabras.[101] However, Zerubavel remarks that Palmachniks' drawing on Arab culture remained ambivalent, suggesting both sameness to and difference from the Arabs.[102] Indeed, while selective adoption of Arab trappings and their incorporation into a modern setting could enhance one's cultural status, the Arab culture as an entirety was looked down upon by many Ashkenazi Israelis. Those who were born into Arab culture, whether Israeli Arabs, longtime Sephardim, or Jewish new immigrants from Muslim countries, did not enjoy much social cachet.[103]

If Arabic stood for the Semitic East, English, according to Halperin, represented for the Zionist community in Palestine a strengthened commitment to democratic values, civic pride, and European modernity. During three decades of British rule, Jewish municipalities, parties, and organizations corresponded with British officials in English. English was the language of administration and law, as well as a linguistic gateway to individual and collective success. Still, accounts make clear that students in Zionist schools learned next to nothing in their English studies.[104] Unsuccessful teaching of English continued after the state was founded: 24 percent of the 2,183 Israeli high school students who took their matriculation exams in 1954 failed the English component (scoring an average of 59.1 percent), compared with only 13 percent who failed in history.[105] While an order from 1948 canceled the previous legal obligation to use English in all formal documents, the Mandate era law, as noted, was never repealed and English was still used in Israeli signposts, coins, and stamps. On the formal level English was associated in particular with Britain, and therefore ads for English lessons stressed that their excellent and certified teachers were English, or "just returned from England."[106] Yet precisely because English was associated with Britain, it was sometimes treated by longtime Israelis — who had experienced Mandate era British rule — with reluctance and resentment.[107]

On the informal level, meanwhile, English was associated particularly with the United States and its appealing mass culture.[108] Whereas French could lend local advertised products an air of good taste, elegance, and sophistication, English was supposed to confer modernity, efficiency, comfort, abundance, and vitality. Specific Israeli products and firms were named after enticing American locations: Broadway, New York, California, Florida, and Miami.[109] English titles and words appeared in ads for cars and bicycles, domestic appliances and electronic devices, restaurants and cafés.[110] English was omnipresent in shop signs and posters, usually alongside Hebrew.[111] English words, in parentheses, were also interspersed in Hebrew texts and speeches, thus creating a novel slang: *comfort, risk, review, interview, star, private* (car), and *babysitting*, to name a few examples, all American words or words connected with American enterprises and values.[112]

Israeli sports, like other fields of mass cultural consumption, were affected by American role models and the direct involvement of American Jewish athletes and coaches, such as Nat Holman ("Mr. Basketball"), who developed local basketball clinics, and Irving Mondschein, who trained local physical education teachers and coached the Israeli Olympic track-and-field

This special bus for tourists carries the patriotic Hebrew sign "See the scenery of our country!" However, the company's name, Sightseeing Ltd., is transliterated in Hebrew letters rather than translated into actual Hebrew. National Photo Collection (Government Press Office), D446-100. Photo from 1950 by Fritz Cohen.

team. The American word *managers* was adopted in Hebrew (*managerim*) when referring to local boxing, and the humor column in a local sports magazine was titled *Knock-Out*. American influences notwithstanding, soccer (known, of course, as "football") remained Israel's most popular spectator sport, and therefore technical British English terms remained in formal and popular use, for example *cup final, offside,* and *pendel* — a Yiddishized form of *penalty*.[113]

The use of American English was most noticeable among the "salon youths," but adults, too, were known for using English expressions and trying to follow American lifestyles. Critics sarcastically quoted the appearance within Hebrew of certain English words, such as *weekend* and *darling*, in order to portray bored, snobby, immoral, and socially alienated Israelis. These Israelis' fondness for English-language songs and paperbacks was rebuked as affected, shallow, pretentious, and unpatriotic.[114] The craze for American periodicals and paperbacks, wrote a nationalist journalist, was "another step in the spreading of wretched Americanization," which was destroying the

Hebrew nature of Tel Aviv and other towns.[115] As we shall see in the sixth chapter, the general preference for American popular culture was also apparent in patterns of cinema-going. While on the strategic level British English was favored and employed technically and somewhat warily, on the tactical level American English was favored and adopted enthusiastically in daily leisure and consumerist contexts, to the dismay of the elite.

If English evoked mixed feelings in 1950s Israel, German — treated by most of the Jewish community of Palestine with trepidation after the Nazis came to power in 1933 — was doubly sensitive.[116] Following World War II and the Holocaust, German, for many Israelis, became the most detested and repelling tongue. The National Censorship Committee for Films and Plays unconditionally banned movies and theater performances in German, but still it received many letters from citizens complaining about the use of German in musical concerts. The committee therefore disallowed performing songs in German too, thus trying to pacify Israelis "who cannot forget that this is the language of the people that only a couple of years back annihilated one third of the Jewish people with unprecedented barbarity."[117] The ban on German songs, however, was attacked by figures ranging from professional musicians to academics and intellectuals to Foreign Minister Moshe Sharett himself.[118] Although the Censorship Committee allowed a few special exceptions, it maintained its general prohibition on German public performances, even after the 1952 reparations agreement heralded a new phase in Israel's relations with Germany.[119]

The split among policy makers over the performance of German songs revealed a broader disagreement on societal values. Whereas the ban on German films and plays was accepted without protest, intellectual and cultural elites (many of whose members spoke German) were horrified when the committee forbade singing Schubert and Mozart in their original language. It could be argued, along these lines, that German movies had been banned in Jewish Palestine since the 1930s,[120] and that the committee was merely continuing a familiar pattern, whereas the musical prohibition was a novel, unwelcome addition. But perhaps another factor was also at play. Movies were a popular genre, associated with the masses, who presumably had to be edified and protected, while classical music was consumed by educated, discriminating connoisseurs, who supposedly needed no such protection.[121] We can also discern a disagreement regarding institutional intervention and regulation. Some of those who disagreed with the committee's ruling claimed it had no legal right to ban the use of any language, whereas the Home Office, the body in charge of the Censorship Committee, argued that its censoring authority was not limited to matters of "security, morality, and religion" but also included "any factor that might hurt public sensibilities."[122]

German, a language historically associated with the Haskalah, was used in Israel not only by recently arrived immigrants but also by longtime Israelis of German origin.[123] Whereas new immigrants were treated more leniently in this respect, longtime residents were expected to have learned Hebrew by then and were frowned upon.[124] Whereas German was banned on the strategic level, many of its speakers — who associated it not with recent horrific events but rather with a lengthy tradition of high culture and learning — ignored strategic messages and kept using the language in their daily and professional lives, formal regulations and public pressure notwithstanding.[125]

Since the early days of the Haskalah, writers compared the alleged "purity" of Hebrew and German with the eclectic hybridity of Yiddish, the vernacular language of many Ashkenazi Jews. Writers were torn between their hope to spread the Enlightenment ideas in the "pure" language of Hebrew and their practical desire to be understood by potential readers. Other early exponents of the Haskalah aspired to replace the "corrupted jargon" of Yiddish with pure German, but eventually, in Eastern Europe, they often resorted to Yiddish despite its so-called impurity.[126] Yiddish gained a higher status during the late nineteenth century and the first decades of the twentieth century, when it was employed not only in daily speech but also as an expressive written language of poetry, prose, theater, and journalism.[127]

Thus, when written Hebrew was being revived in Eastern Europe during the last quarter of the nineteenth century, it had to compete with a parallel renaissance of Yiddish culture. Moreover, the Bund and other Jewish socialist groups (including one Zionist faction) promoted Yiddish as the proper national language.[128] Most Zionists viewed Yiddish not merely as vying with Hebrew for the role of national language but also as embodying the old Jew and epitomizing the multiple defects of the sordid diasporic lifestyle. In Mandate-era Palestine, as Hebrew was gradually gaining ground in the Zionist community, Yiddish — the native tongue of most Eastern European immigrants — was still seen as the main threat to the emerging national language.[129]

But in the immigrant society of young Israel, Yiddish had become only one among numerous languages in use. By the time a sovereign Jewish state was established, and the elite could determine and implement an effective language policy, Yiddish, whose users had been murdered in their millions during World War II, had ceased to pose a real threat to Hebrew. Indeed, after the Holocaust, the radical negation of the Diaspora and the rabid language war of previous decades were mellowed and modified; the extinguished culture of the Diaspora was covered with a new shade of nostalgia and guilt. Whereas in the 1920s it had been decided after a heated public debate not to open a Yiddish chair at the Hebrew University, in 1951 a Yiddish department was established.[130]

Yiddish was commonly associated by Israelis with the ultra-Orthodox community, known in Hebrew as the Haredim.[131] After the Holocaust and the founding of the Israeli state, the reduced and dwindling Haredi community faced a demographic, economic, organizational, and ideological-religious crisis.[132] Firmly maintaining its tradition was thus part of the community's attempt to defend its cultural existence when confronted with a threatening tide of nationalization and secularization. This community feared that Yiddish, its daily language, was disappearing.[133] Still, as we have seen, religious Israelis were divided into different ideological, cultural, and political segments. A minority of anti-Zionist ultra-Orthodox Jews, for instance, objected on religious grounds to the use of Hebrew in any nonritualistic contexts, and insisted on maintaining Yiddish alone as their daily tongue.[134] On the other hand, religious Zionists combined Judaism with modern Hebrew nationalism,[135] including the ardent adoption of Hebrew as a spoken tongue. In late 1951 the religious Zionists' periodical attacked the Orthodox yeshivot (seminaries), claiming that they supported no pioneering work and committed the "sin" of speaking Yiddish: "It is totally unacceptable that educational centers in this country nurture an obsolete Diaspora tongue."[136] Many nonreligious Israeli Jews, especially the young, conceived of the Haredim as internal aliens, as fifth columnists, fanatics who were trying to compel religion on a secular majority. If Zionists were attempting to create a new Jew, then the Haredi population was seen as holding on obstinately to the deplorable ways of the old prenational diasporic Jew.[137] Yiddish thus reinforced for most Israelis the negative image of the Haredim, alongside their blatant religiosity and their separatist lifestyle.

Yet Yiddish was associated in 1950s Israel first and foremost with the mass of new Eastern European immigrants who arrived after the founding of the state and tended to stick to their mother tongue.[138] The prevalent connotation of Yiddish and newcomers was revealed in children's expressions. Thus, a six-year-old boy, for instance, spoke Yiddish to his newborn brother. Asked by his aunt why he didn't speak to the baby in Hebrew, he replied, "Newcomers are spoken to in Yiddish."[139] When a six-year-old girl was asked whether she would like to live in America, she answered, "No, I am a Sabra, and I don't want to be a new immigrant in America and speak Yiddish."[140] It was generally accepted that recently arrived immigrants would speak Yiddish until they learned Hebrew, but continued use of Yiddish after the first years was perceived by longtime Israelis as a sign of unsuccessful acculturation.[141]

A provisional attitude was also taken by the National Censorship Committee for Films and Plays. After the state was founded, Yiddish performances by local and visiting artists drew large audiences consisting of both new immigrants and longtime Israelis, and in early 1951 a Yiddish theater was established in Jaffa.[142] After lengthy deliberations,[143] the Censorship Committee decided that visiting artists could perform in Yiddish but must add to their show a section in Hebrew, while new immigrants could continue performing in Yiddish "but must prove that they are making some efforts to learn Hebrew" within one year after their arrival.[144] Theatrical performances in Yiddish were thus limited but not entirely forbidden. Indeed, during the early 1950s additional Yiddish theaters were founded in Israel, performers continued using the language for longer than a year, and a Hebrew section was not always included in the show as required.[145] Yet Yiddish, a Jewish tongue, was treated leniently by the Censorship Committee, both due to post-Holocaust sensibilities and in order not to offend Yiddish-speaking Jews in the Diaspora, especially in the United States.[146] Historian Rachel Rojansky suggests that Israeli policy makers approved of the preservation of Yiddish high culture that appealed to small educated sectors, but at the same time opposed popular Yiddish culture that appealed to broader sectors and was perceived as an obstacle to instilling Hebrew.[147]

As Rojansky demonstrates, David Ben-Gurion treated Yiddish as the language of the Diaspora, and therefore as a thing of the past, although personally he knew Yiddish and rather liked it.[148] Other members of the founding generation shared a similar mind-set in which anti-Yiddishness mingled with emotional fondness for the language, even if their Zionist transformation required that they discard the language in favor of Hebrew as part of the negation of their former Diaspora lives. But no such affection was harbored by this generation's native offspring, who were unfamiliar with the Diaspora, its culture, and its language.[149] The Zionist secular education of the young generation proved excessively effective — so much so that the antidiasporic ideal of the founding generation became the cultural reality of the Sabras, who felt completely alienated from a traditional Jewish lifestyle and treated it with contempt.[150] Thus, many Sabras felt an unequivocal aversion toward Yiddish. For them Hebrew, particularly in its native style, conveyed a deeply rooted locality of youth, energy, and practical heroism, while Yiddish embodied the exact opposite: an old, decadent, weak, and discordant Jewish mentality.[151]

We tend to think of the tactical level as more flexible than the strategic level, but the case of Yiddish in 1950s Israel exemplifies the opposite. The formal institutional policy was cautiously tolerant, leaving Yiddish some leeway alongside the obvious priority of Hebrew. In the informal domain of daily life, on the other hand, attitudes were more extreme and polarized: while some new immigrants and the Haredim kept using Yiddish (instead of Hebrew, as prescribed by the hegemonic national ideal), other Israelis vented unmitigated hostility toward this Jewish language and the culture it stood for.

Whereas the ideology and the actions on the strategic level were meant to unite all Israelis, old and new, within the equalizing effect of the national tongue, behavioral patterns and practices could sometimes increase social heterogeneity. Nonetheless, Bachi noted that the variety of foreign languages actually strengthened the position of Hebrew. While in 1948 some 70 percent of the non-Hebrew speakers in Israel were using one of three languages — Yiddish, Arabic, and German — two years later these languages accounted for only 50 percent of the non-Hebrew speakers. Hebrew thus became the only possible "lingua franca" among the increasing mixture of many languages, each serving one or a few groups of immigrants.[152]

The use of Hebrew by itself, however, did not guarantee one's status, which depended on other social and ethnic factors as well.[153] In 1949, for example, a young Arab patient entered a clinic and the Jewish physician talked to her in Arabic. When the patient replied in Hebrew, the doctor asked, "How do you know Hebrew?" "Why shouldn't I?" she replied. "After all I'm a 'Sabra.'"[154] The Israeli Arab patient, a native who spoke Hebrew and tried to belong, was not considered by the physician (and the readers of the supposedly funny anecdote) to be a real "Sabra": the coveted title was reserved for native Jews alone.

In the following year a journalist visiting Jaffa harbor heard dockworkers speaking Yiddish, Arabic, Turkish, Polish, and Romanian. Finally he met a dark-skinned young worker who spoke Hebrew and assumed that he was a Jewish immigrant from a Muslim country. However, the man turned out to be a Syrian-born Druze, who with his seven friends of the same background had served in the IDF reserves. They were now all permanent workers in the harbor. First they were paid a lower salary, "like the Arab workers," and only after sending letters of complaint to the prime minister's office did they finally get a raise. Still, they were given only the "lower" tasks, with no chances of future promotion. Neither could they return to Syria, where they "would be killed." This was the confession, summed up the journalist, "of a man, perhaps of a population, who wants to live as a citizen of the state."[155]

As these examples reveal, the barrier between Israeli minorities and Jews was not merely linguistic. The trauma of the recent war and the ongoing hostility posed by the Arab states complicated Jewish-Arab relationships within Israel, as did mixed emotions of fear, revenge, and scorn occasionally expressed by Jewish new immigrants who had fled assaults in Yemen, Iraq, and other Muslim countries.[156] In addition to physical and technical limitations imposed by the military rule, Israeli Arabs were hardly included in the Israeli cultural national project. Knowing Hebrew could facilitate Arab citizens' technical integration, but it did not suffice to grant them full membership in the Israeli collectivity, which was informally perceived as essentially Jewish.

The linguistic field in 1950s Israel was, in many aspects, a continuation of earlier processes. Some — as we saw — were a direct sequel to Zionist policies and activities from the Mandate era, while others originated in nineteenth-century developments. Yet all these precedents and tendencies were poured into a new set of circumstances. The familiar multilingual reality of Jewish existence and the primacy of Hebrew were now joined by the demographic and linguistic conditions of mass immigration, the new tools of national sovereignty, and the encompassing role of Hebrew as the only unifying option. Thus, Bachi ended his statistical analysis by stating that, in the long run, the struggle for Hebrew was won already, "with the systematic and continuous conquest of the youth and the disappearance of any other language which could compete with Hebrew in Public life or as a common mean of communication between the variety of foreign born at present living in Israel."[157] Despite the heterogeneous and partial manners of its application, the hegemonic ideal regarding the national tongue was largely accomplished.

Indeed, as early as 1950 a journalist reported that "the sounds of our language can be heard in every corner of the Latin Quarter" in Paris. Hebrew could be heard in the hotels, he complained, where Israeli envoys behaved ostentatiously, and in the cafés, where profiteers conferred secretly; Hebrew was heard even in the Paris jailhouse.[158] The use of the national language overseas confirmed that it had truly taken root. Ironically, the language that was expected to tie the nationalized new Jews to their homeland — the same Hebrew that was laboriously revived, learned, and ingrained in Israel — was being exported abroad by wandering Israeli Jews.[159]

The Humorous Side
of Rationing

IN 1952 A THREE-YEAR-OLD Israeli girl toppled
a tray of rice, put to dry in the sun by her neighbor. This was during the years
of austerity, and the neighbor had to gather back each and every grain. A
supposedly minor incident became one of the girl's earliest memories. Six
decades later she still remembers it as a dramatic event, and although she
cannot recall the details (was she scolded by her neighbor? reprimanded by
her parents?), she associates this guilt-ridden episode with the word *austerity*
and with the harsh economic circumstances of those years.[1]

Israel's severe shortage in foreign currency, hampering the import of food
and other vital products, as well as the steep increase in prices during the
War of Independence and the inability to grow enough food for a rapidly
growing population, led the government to launch an austerity (*tzena*) policy in April 1949. In general terms, rationing is an intentional interference
with the dynamics of the free market, a supervised division of vital goods
and services. The government limits the amount that each citizen can consume by determining a set ration and by fixing compulsory prices. Rationing
was only one of many intervening economic steps taken by Israel's statist
government, led by the labor party Mapai, and it was influenced by similar
statist policies then embraced in many postwar European countries. The austerity policy was based partly on local precedents: rationing was declared by
the British government during World War II and later by the sovereign Israeli
state during the War of Independence. The austerity policy was meant to de-
crease consumption, increase production, and ensure that the entire population, including needy new immigrants, received the food and other goods
they needed.[2]

At first, as noted in an earlier chapter, the austerity policy was accepted
willingly by the Israeli public, who viewed it as a necessary step, a temporary and inevitable restriction of consumption, and a means of achieving important national goals in the long run. However, the policy gradually met
with growing objection and discontent.[3] Historian Orit Rozin describes how

during its first nine months food rationing seemed successful, but by January 1950 the government was struggling to supply sufficient quantities of protein and began to cut ration sizes. The dire shortage of raw materials and products meant that even basic items were hard to find, long lines were gathering at shops, and the quality of available products was deteriorating. Black market activities were on the increase, and the government reacted with stricter enforcement, intrusive inspections, and invasive supervision. But to no avail: the system was eroded by consumers' noncompliance.[4]

On the eve of the 1952 general elections, the General Zionists, a political party representing Israeli bourgeoisie, used the unpopularity of the rationing regime to attack Mapai's centralist economic policy. And sure enough the General Zionists won twenty seats (an increase of seven seats from the previous elections). Now the second largest party in parliament after Mapai (with forty-five seats), it joined the new coalition government, influenced the new economic policy, presented itself as a source of expertise on the economy, and took all the credit for putting an end to the rationing regime,[5] which was considerably diminished in early 1953 (and formally canceled in 1959). By 1954 Israel was starting to recover from its economic crisis. But was it recovering *thanks* to the austerity policy or *despite* it — and only because it was ending?

At the time Mapai's economic policy was attacked from both the left and the right. Whereas the pro-Soviet party Mapam demanded more direct interference in the economy and harsher steps for social equalization, the General Zionists and the right-wing Herut party claimed that only a freer market would attract investors and allow enterprise and growth.[6] Economic historians, for their part, are divided regarding the Israeli rationing regime, its necessity, and the degree of its success.[7] Without attempting to judge the matter on economic terms, we should nonetheless distinguish between two kinds of criticism that were voiced at the time: the ideological and political disapproval of the rationing policy (including the charge that Mapai was guilty of corruption and favoritism, and conducting an unfair distribution of the scarce goods), and a criticism that existed within Mapai and its supporters — not of the economic policy itself but rather of specific technical shortcomings in its implementation.

The centralized economy and the rationing of goods and services can be described as a concrete strategy. Among the daily tactics practiced by Israelis during the years of austerity were inventive methods of making do with less, writing letters of complaint or advice to the Ministry of Rationing and Distribution, and trading on the black market.[8] Yet this chapter focuses on one aspect in particular: the use of humor. Humor, as Rozin mentions, was one of the ways Israeli society dealt with the hardships of rationing, a safety valve into which consumers could channel some of their frustrations.[9] Comic aspects of the grim economic situation were often formed into written satire, verbal jokes, and cartoons.

Beyond amusement, scholars list potential psychological, social, and political effects of humor, in particular during times of trouble, when it can help expose evils, relax fears and address anxieties, create solidarity, boost morale, and raise hopes for a better future.[10] Jewish humor, formed most notably in Eastern Europe in conditions of inferiority and animosity, is often described as a therapeutic agent and a creative means of dealing with hardship and suffering.[11] "Although entertainment is the primary, the recognized, goal of telling jokes," writes author Emil A. Draitser, the subjects of these jokes might be "most important to the tellers, even if they don't realize it." Moreover, he writes, "the implicit assumptions of a culture lie at the foundation of a joke," and by analyzing and interpreting jokes, we can deduce certain behavioral patterns and expose deeply held popular beliefs.[12] Further, according to other thinkers, historians can use humor to reveal "most directly the mood of the time,"[13] because jokes and cartoons capture an immediacy missing in more serious and labored historical sources.[14]

It is perhaps no wonder that rationing, which considerably affected many components of daily life during the first years of statehood, became the butt of satire and an obvious model, reference, and metaphor in Israel's popular culture. As we remember, the rare snow of 1950 was described jestingly in terms of rationing, points, and coupons. Similarly, an entertainment program from 1950 was titled *Laughter without Rationing*.[15] The famous Yiddish performers Dzigan and Schumacher included in one of their satirical sketches a brilliant new economic plan to save the country: "Talking needs to be rationed." In this plan, money will be saved by getting Jews to talk less — in effect, an austerity program for Jewish verbosity. The valuable time of listeners would thus be freed up for them to become more economically productive.[16] Austerity was even embodied in the national folk dance festival of 1951, when one troupe performed a dance titled "Rationing," in which each dancer wore only one boot.[17] Assorted visual, verbal, and textual humorous expressions hereby provide us with many details about the experience of austerity in daily life, and reveal what Israelis thought and, equally important, what they *felt* about the rationing regime.

The satirical troupe Li La Lo presents a sketch on food control, 1949. Note
the pessimistic charts, predicting further deterioration in food quantity in 1951.
National Photo Collection (Government Press Office), D720-084. Photo by Fritz Cohen.

Humor often targeted the minister and the ministry in charge of the austerity program. When the austerity policy was launched, a special rationing and distribution ministry was founded, headed by Dr. Dov (Josef) Yosef (1899–1980). A Canadian-born Zionist activist and a prominent lawyer, Yosef immigrated to Palestine in 1918 and served as military governor of Jerusalem during the War of Independence. In the 1950s he was minister of agriculture, transportation, justice, trade and industry, development, and health. From 1949 until the closure of the Ministry of Rationing and Distribution in late 1950,[18] Yosef was the subject of numerous rationing jokes; many of these were puns and are, sadly, untranslatable.[19] Jokes depicted Yosef as a miser and as the architect, and thus the perpetrator, of scarcity.[20] One ribbing held, for instance, that Yosef employed a rationing advisor from Scotland[21] — the Scots representing stinginess in Israeli lore. When the Ministry of Rationing and Distribution was closed and Yosef was appointed minister of transportation, someone suggested transferring the jokes from the former ministry to the latter as well.[22]

Although many "Dov Yosef austerity jokes" were rather mild, the blaming of the minister (and thereby the government) for the dismal economic situation could be politically charged. In occupied Norway, for comparison, many

Food ration cards issued to new immigrants and demobilized soldiers, 1949. National Photo Collection (Government Press Office), D720-061. Photo by David Eldan.

jokes about the wartime shortage described the Nazis and their Norwegian collaborators as responsible for the country's plight, while in the Soviet bloc an abundance of jokes depicted widespread poverty as the fault of Stalin and the Eastern European governments.[23] In both these latter cases, however, such jokes could only be cautiously whispered, whereas in democratic Israel jokes about Dov Yosef were openly published in the newspapers. Open accusations, albeit through humor, can certainly affect people and influence their opinions, yet their very publicity has a paradoxical taming effect. As will be discussed further at the end of this chapter, underground "illegal" jokes have a sharper, subversive political edge.

Rationing can be implemented by a rigid and direct distribution of goods. Alternatively, each product can be granted a set point-value (according to its cost and its scarcity), and each consumer receives a set number of points, usually in the form of standard coupons, thus allowing consumers more freedom of choice within the limitations of rationing. Israel's policy makers used Britain as their central model in devising the local austerity policy,[24] including the points and coupons system, which became the focal point of many jokes and cartoons.[25]

It was said, for instance, that the rain wasn't falling in winter 1951 due to the large number of points required for buying a raincoat.[26] A cartoon showed two men, each owning only ten points, pooling their resources to buy one pair of boots for twenty points, and marching together under the same umbrella.[27] Another cartoon portrayed a lady bringing the shoemaker one shoe for mending, while leaving the other shoe on her foot: "I will bring you the other shoe when I get my new coupon book," she tells him.[28] Yet another cartoon depicted two cats meeting at the garbage bins, with one of

A 1949 cartoon by Friedl: "They are already eating coupon A28." *Ashmoret*, August 9, 1949.

הם כבר אוכלים תלוש 28A

them saying she was teaching her kittens to become vegetarian "in case they start distributing mice for points as well."[29] A newborn was seen in a different cartoon, flown by a stork to an Israeli moshav, with a coupon book tied to his small neck. "This is where you'll be living," says the stork, "so take good care of your points."[30]

Rationing humor, as with other daily examples, was frequently derived from observations made by young children, whose naiveté could be refreshing. Little girls who heard everybody talking of "points" for clothes and shoes assumed that it meant spotted fabrics ("polka dots"), because the Hebrew word is the same for "points" as it is for "dots" and "spots" (*nekudot*). Thus, a five-year-old girl did not understand why people were complaining about clothes: she thought "dotted dresses and shoes were pretty"; and a three-year-old girl was worried that everyone had already bought the spotted fabrics, leaving her and her mother "only plain fabrics."[31] A four-year-old girl overheard a conversation about beauty spots and asked, "Are they selling beauty, too, for points?"[32] The same word, *nekudot*, is also used in Hebrew for periods to end a sentence. Thus, when an eight-year-old was asked by his father why the letter he had written wasn't properly punctuated, he replied that "Mom has already used all my *nekudot*."[33]

A nine-year-old boy heard on the radio that every couple who weds would receive 250 extra points for clothes. "What a pity," he lamented, "that the marriage-age law has already been passed." This referred to recent legislation approved by the Israeli parliament forbidding early teenage marriage.[34] A six-year-old asked to go to an amusement park—an unrationed service—and when told he'd be taken the next week fretted that "by then it might require points."[35] A two-year-old was congratulated on her new shoes and asked how much they cost: "One shouldn't ask how much it cost," she corrected, "but rather how many points." When this same girl's grandmother castigated her for peeling off a piece from her new shoe, she said, "That's nothing, it's only one point."[36] A four-year-old who wanted a little brother was advised to ask his mother to buy him a brother at the hospital. "We don't have enough points," he replied.[37] Children were clearly attuned to the material difficulties endured by their families, and seem to have shared in their elders' concerns. Yet these difficulties, when filtered through a youthful perspective, could supply comic relief. Even truly sad situations could be eased somewhat by childlike innocence. Trying to comfort her five-year-old, a mother told her that Grandfather had gone straight to heaven, where he would enjoy plenty and lack for nothing. "What?" asked the amazed child. "Is there no austerity in heaven?"[38]

Annoying and distressing facets of shortage, such as the scarcity and low quality of food, the endless lines, the corruption of officials, and trade on the black market, had all been molded into jokes in Europe earlier in the twentieth century; and since all shortages share characteristics, some witticisms became stock jokes, assuming local variations as they traveled through space and time.[39] Draitser explains that "as a bit of communication, a joke dies unless the teller and the hearer share common ground." Jokes cannot be understood when taken out of their original social and psychological setting.[40] Even when comprehended, humor has a short life span; if dated or out of context, jokes can seem boring, childish, and anything but funny.[41] This is why, for the appreciation of Israeli rationing humor from the early 1950s, some background details (shared and even taken for granted by contemporaries) are necessary.

Israeli jokes and cartoons depicted scarcity from absurd angles, mainly highlighting specific goods that had become desirable, such as manufactured ice (most Israelis could not afford refrigerators and used iceboxes), poultry and eggs, meat and fish, coffee and drinking glasses.[42] Thus, a cartoon depicted an Inuit family watching an Israeli tourist packing their igloo into his suitcase. "He is probably interested in our style of architecture," they say,[43] unaware that the Israeli is actually after the ice. During summer 1951 local production couldn't meet demand, and people had to stand long hours in line to get ice for their iceboxes.[44] A few months later a comic declaration announced that this week the citizens of Israel will be receiving meat twice:

once in the newspaper, another time on the radio.[45] The newspapers and the radio did publicize the products to be distributed each week, but the joke suggested that the announcements were not fulfilled, and that they became the *only* meat Israelis were likely to get. Likewise, a man in a comic strip sees a shop sign that reads "No fish today," so he takes a rod and goes fishing, only to draw from the sea an identical sign: "No fish today."[46] According to one joke, a man who once called his wife "my gem" is calling her now, when beef has become extraordinary, "my cow."[47] The portions of meat served in restaurants were so thin that, according to one cartoon, a waiter was warned not to walk past the fan, lest the meat be blown off the plate.[48] A seven-year-old was quizzed in math: if a man eats four eggs a day, how many eggs would he eat in three days? "Is he crazy?" asked the boy. "Who eats four eggs a day?"[49] A teacher who in her math question mentioned a woman buying margarine and chocolate received a similar reply from her pupil: he understood the math, he said, but did not understand where the woman could possibly find any margarine and chocolate.[50]

Passing by a synagogue in 1950, a father asked his five-year-old daughter what the worshippers ask from God. She responded, "They ask him to give them lots of coupons."[51] The following year a six-year-old was asked what she would wish from a falling star. "I don't know what I would wish for," she said, "but you, Mom, would probably wish for drinking glasses."[52] During the same summer of 1951, when a shortage in drinking glasses was strongly felt, a cartoon showed a couple under their wedding canopy, the bridegroom trying unsuccessfully to break the glass underfoot, as is customary in Jewish weddings. "Darn it!" he exclaims. "It's a plastic cup . . ."[53] An old granny was pictured telling her young grandchildren stories about the past: "And in those days, children, people used to drink a beverage called . . . coffee."[54] According to another cartoon, coffee had become such a prized possession that it had to be kept in a safe.[55] In a cartoon panel titled "An Exhibition during the Austerity," hungry people are shown salivating before pictures of food. In the next panel the food within the pictures has disappeared, presumably snatched by the ravenous visitors.[56] The shortage in vital foodstuffs and other products was an unpleasant daily reality that caused many difficulties and tensions,[57] but casting frustrations into humorous shapes could provide some comfort.

By the time rationing of shoes and clothes was declared in summer 1950, Israelis had already experienced the consequences of food rationing for more than a year and were familiar with the system's flaws. In addition to

A 1949 cartoon by Friedl: "And now, dear lady listeners, Mrs. Gesundheit will lecture to you about the austerity menu . . ." *Gesundheit* means "health" in German. Yet the famished Mrs. Gesundheit is so weakened by hunger that she must be helped into the radio studio by two nurses. The cartoon picks at the futility—perhaps even hypocrisy—of formal advice given to the public. Friedl, a woman cartoonist, portrayed the complacent policy makers as plump and healthful men while embodying the sad effects of austerity in a woman. *Ashmoret*, August 11, 1949.

complaining directly about the new austerity decree, people used irony and sarcasm to vent aggression.[58] One week after the announcement of the rationing of clothes and shoes, a daily newspaper published a cartoon of a middle-age, middle-class man coming home in tattered clothes. His disheveled, glum wife greets him at the door with the news, "I have bought a few modern pictures"; and indeed, the wall is decorated with framed pictures showing various items of dress.[59] Dress, in the cartoon, is thereby portrayed as being attainable through artistic representation only, not concrete reality. The cartoon also warned Israelis about the predictable scarcity of clothes, and perhaps by doing so humorously, it attempted to prepare them somewhat for this additional forthcoming hardship.[60]

A cartoon published several months later showed two stereotyped black Africans wearing nothing but loin covers and jewelry, talking underneath two palm trees in a desert landscape. One of them questions his friend amazedly: "And after converting to Judaism, you plan to immigrate to Israel? Did you not hear that there is rationing over there and that people walk about naked"?[61] The Israeli cartoonist was implying that even African "savages"[62] were better off than present-day Israelis: the former were naked as part of their tradition and climate, whereas the latter were forced into nakedness by rationing. Another cartoon portrayed a young woman, who wraps a tangled string around her body, explaining to an astonished friend, "This is how I overcame the difficulties of dressing."[63]

Shortage, as noted, affected not only the quantity of goods but their quality as well, and some puns targeted the deteriorating taste of food.[64] Perhaps the most notorious food product, which became the symbol of the entire austerity diet, was the "fillet," a type of frozen cod imported from Scandinavia. The fillet, often the only available source of protein, was described in jest, but also in earnest, as particularly unpalatable.[65] It stood for another unpleasant feature of the austerity diet — its monotony.[66] A satirical piece in the spirit of the Pesach story described the fillet as "the national food of our ancestors from the War of Independence." Like the biblical manna, the fillet "has all the tastes in the world, and is eaten by the babe in his cradle, the bride and the groom at their wedding, and the aged in his armchair."[67] When a local newsreel presented the growing Israeli fishing industry, the narrator assured the audience that among the various types of fish caught in the Mediterranean Sea "there is no fillet whatsoever!"[68]

Products besides food also worsened in quality.[69] In January 1949 the Israeli government launched a program for manufacturing cheap furniture, clothes, and shoes. The subsidized products, branded "Lakol" ("for all"), were at least 30 percent cheaper than equivalent products sold on the free market. Lakol was supposed to continue the success of the Utility program, implemented in Palestine by the British government during World War II.[70] However, the Lakol program was neither as successful nor as popular as its predecessor. Lakol items were of poor quality and an old-fashioned style, and despite vigorous promotion by the government, consumers remained unconvinced.[71] A rhyme from 1949 ironically depicted a Lakol sofa: at night it serves as a table, in the day as a bed, in the morning as a closet, and in the evening as a chair; most important, this "remarkable" item is inexpensive.[72] The unpopularity of Lakol products was reflected in contemporary slang: unattractive girls were described using the terms "austerity face" and "Lakol figure."[73]

Humor tackled yet another daily hallmark of the shortage: the line.[74] Many commercials in the rationing era presented their products and services as devoid of the familiar shortcomings of austerity, such as monotony or low quality; but in late 1949 a shoe merchant from Haifa chose to do the exact opposite and phrase his newspaper ad as follows:

"Pelota"[75] — the national sport in Cuba . . .

In Canada it's ice hockey, in the United States it's baseball, in England it's cricket, and the national sport in Israel is . . . the line! Just think of the number of lines you have to stand in every day; and your poor feet — what about them? It's time you paid attention to them and got orthopedic shoes from [our] special department. . . .[76]

Cartoons depicted lines as inescapable. Thus, a man was drawn as trying to choose among five possible lines — to the haberdashery, the butcher, the drugstore, the fish distributor, or the movies.[77] Some of the people waiting in the long lines for ice in summer 1951, claimed a journalist, passed the time by reading newspapers, which told them happily that the ice scarcity was over and that there were no more lines for ice. . . .[78] Indeed, while people were waiting in these long lines, the local newsreels declared that the ice shortage was over.[79] Things got even more hectic on holidays. A satirical feuilleton in the Haredi newspaper, titled "Our Nerves Are Not Made of Steel," portrayed a "day of horrors" on the eve of the Jewish New Year, as a mother instructs the whole household how to provide for the holiday. The four-year-old daughter is sent to the milk line and commanded to "start screaming straight away, or else no one will take notice of you." The ten-year-old son is sent to the ice line, and ordered not to let anyone push him, and to choose a block of ice that isn't melting. Another daughter is sent to hold a spot for the father in the clothing line. Another son is sent to buy vegetables in the market, and another daughter to the line for the socks distribution. Alas, eventually all the children return home empty-handed, and all the mother has managed to bring for the New Year's meal is the notorious fillet.[80]

Children plainly noticed and fully accepted the ubiquity of austerity lines. A three-year-old asked her mother why people stand in line at the post office if no tomatoes or cucumbers were being distributed there.[81] A boy of the same age returned from a holiday celebration and said excitedly, "There were lots and lots of people there, just like in the line for fish!"[82] A four-year-old saw a string of ants on the floor, moving toward a morsel of meat that had fallen from the table. "Look, Mom," he said, "the ants are also lining up for the meat."[83] A boy of the same age was climbing onto his mother's lap. When she asked him what would have happened if she had four children, he replied, "Then we'd arrange a line."[84] When another four-year-old went past the synagogue on the Jewish New Year and saw the many worshippers, he said to his mother, "See? Even in the synagogue there's a line."[85] A six-year-old was told by his mother that she was going to the hospital to buy him a little brother. When he first visited after she gave birth, he asked, "Mom, did you wait in line for long?"[86] Adults were frustrated by having to wait long hours in lines for every basic product, but children typically accepted lines as an integral, "natural" part of life. Quoting this childlike viewpoint accentuated the omnipresence of lines in Israeli daily routine, but it simultaneously lessened their obnoxiousness.

As we shall see in other chapters, Israeli lines were neither orderly nor quiet and they frequently involved arguments and shoving, which themselves became fodder for jokes and puns, as were the lines' length.[87] A cartoon from summer 1951 showed a long line at a shop doorstep, including a mannequin with a sign "Back Soon" holding somebody's place in line.[88] That same summer a girl was standing in a line with her mother, and when a passing woman asked what was being distributed, the girl replied, "Sore feet."[89] Other humorous comments were made about people being drawn to lines, even if they neither needed nor wanted whatever was distributed, as if the line itself generated curiosity and attracted the public.[90]

Israeli consumers often reacted to rationing simply by breaking the law and buying goods on the growing black market.[91] The black market — namely, illegal trade without coupons and for higher prices than those set by the government — undermines the whole rationing system by eroding fixed prices and, at the same time, further aggravating the scarcity of supplies.[92] Public participation in the black market could serve as an indication of consumers' levels of compliance with the rationing regime. The British case, for comparison, reveals a gap between public denouncement of the black market, on the one hand, and patterns of informal and private behavior, on the other. During World War II black market profiteers were harshly condemned by the British public as "traitors," but still a black market endured, and it grew after the war was over.[93] Even in wartime Germany, in spite of Nazi propaganda and cruel punishment, the black market thrived as scarcity intensified.[94] In Israel, too, alongside formal denouncements of the black market, it continuously expanded.[95]

Humorous references to the black market could be classified into two

Lining up in Tel Aviv. National Photo Collection
(Government Press Office), D720-097. Photo by Hans Pinn.

main categories: those targeting the black market and its profiteers, and those stressing the black market's ubiquity. The former were published mainly, though not solely, in media affiliated with the ruling Mapai party, and by attacking any activity on the black market they directly supported the rationing policy. The latter were published in media affiliated with different parties, including Mapai; they did not attempt to justify the black market, but by presenting it as encompassing the entire population and detailing the reasons for its existence (e.g., lack of proper distribution, the endless lines), they seem to have condoned it to a certain degree.[96]

The jokes and cartoons attacking trade on the black market contained negative depictions of profiteers and illegal traders, as well as specific forms of fraud, such as faking sick notes in order to obtain special portions of poultry.[97] A local joke referring to butchers who overcharge for meat claimed that their biblical ancestors made a calf of gold, whereas they make gold from a calf (veal).[98] One cartoon showed several Arabs and Jews, all of suspicious appearance, bringing horses, donkeys, and dogs into a shed, then exiting with dubious sausages for sale on the black market.[99] Cartoons of this sort were sometimes of a clear partisan nature, and they resembled election campaign materials and formal state posters rebuking black marketeering.[100]

In targeting black market activity, the government applied a series of measures aimed initially at black market dealers and later at black market consumers as well. Inspectors set up checkpoints where they rummaged through passengers' personal items. They pursued and caught merchants, ritual slaughterers, shopkeepers, and others engaged in illegal trade. Informers were used, and inspectors also searched consumers' homes. The public was outraged by this latter measure, which shocked even those who were considered staunch supporters of the government and its policies.[101]

Whereas the black market, which involved illegal activity, could not be openly supported even by those who opposed the rationing regime, the harsh measures adopted by the government to crack down on offenders drew open and wide criticism. This anti-inspection mood was reflected in cartoons, some of a partisan nature (claiming that the ruling party discriminated in favor of certain sectors while persecuting innocent populations) and others showing vicious supervisors cruelly hounding poor and desperate citizens.[102] One such cartoon showed two inspectors who were supposed to "Fight the black market! Arrest the profiteers!" Yet one of them was telling the other, "I only hope that my wife won't find out that I'm the man who arrested her racketeer vegetable vendor."[103] Such material indicated the pervasiveness of the black market and the inevitable hypocrisy and futility involved in fighting it.

Whereas trade on the black market was illegal, one legal path for Israelis to better their lot was through relatives abroad, especially in the United States, who sent them packages. "Packages from America" became a well-known notion and "an uncle from America" a desirable asset. A four-year-old asked his grandmother for some chocolate, and when she told him there wasn't any, he pondered for a while and said: "You know, Granny, we have to make Uncle Pinieh (who sent the family packages from America) the prime minister, then we'll have lots of nice things like those in the packages."[104] When a five-year-old was quizzed on what the biblical Jacob gave his young son Joseph (referring to the coat of many colors), he replied, "A coat from America."[105] A cartoon from 1951, poking fun at Israeli Jews' reliance on their American relatives, showed a local couple, disguised as shabby beggars on a bench, being photographed. "Now," says the wife to her husband, "we'll surely get a package from America."[106] The following year a cartoon portrayed this dependent relationship from the American standpoint. It presented a formerly

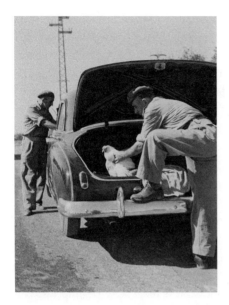

Supervisors search cars for contraband food, brought to town for sale on the black market, 1949. Taken by the government's photographer, this scene might have been staged as a warning. National Photo Collection (Government Press Office), D720-067. Photo by Fritz Cohen.

wealthy American who went bankrupt and became a penniless beggar because he had sent too many gifts to his Israeli relatives ("it started with small packages, but went on to a refrigerator and a car . . .").[107]

In addition to goods sent in packages, relatives could send scrips to be used in Israeli shops. A humorous description titled "Sa'adia's American Aunt" was published in 1952 in the vowelized newspaper issued for new immigrants by Mapai. It reported how a rich American tourist who visited Israel decided to donate a scrip worth one thousand dollars to needy people, but wished to remain anonymous. Hence, her Israeli acquaintance sent her the addresses of his cleaner, his laundry woman, his peddling shoemaker, and other destitute people he knew, and all subsequently received scrips. The article portrayed a poor Yemenite family who entered a store with a scrip, while the surprised vendor wondered who could have sent these people a scrip from America.

The Yemenite family was described as "colorful" and uneducated (they couldn't read the English list of goods made available by the scrip, and they pronounced the word erroneously as "strip"). The tourist's decision was characterized as "an American folly," and "everyone was surprised" when scrips started pouring into the hands of Yemenites. "This is how Sa'adia Shalom son of Yehieh [an unmistakable Yemenite name] won an American 'aunt,'" reported the story.[108] Thus, even as the newspaper's readership was composed of new immigrants, it presented the dominant viewpoint of longtime Israelis and their stereotypical notions concerning Yemenite Jews. Moreover, by portraying a scrip in the hands of a poor Yemenite family as a comic absurdity, it revealed that scrips were usually seen (and expected to be seen) in the hands of other Israelis, perhaps middle-class Jews of European descent.[109] As we saw in the previous chapter, American influence could be noticed in popular Israeli culture even when formal culture remained aloof. "Packages from America" further enhanced the attractive image of the USA as the land of plenty and as a model for unimagined prosperity.[110]

In 1952 Friedl drew her dream of wondrous plenty for the new year ahead: a fully stocked refrigerator (at a time when food was scarce and refrigerators a rare luxury item), lavish apartments for rent (when even humble accommodations were hard to find), plenty of room on the bus (when traveling conditions were hard, as we shall see in the fifth chapter), low-price nylon stockings and a wide choice of shoes (when both products were in shortage and expensive).[111] The cartoon did not express realistic hopes but rather a total fantasy. The utter hyperbole in Friedl's portrayal, easily recognized by residents of 1950s Israel, shed comic light on the period's hardships and thus helped readers come to terms with reality.

Indeed, during the years of shortage and rationing, such luxuries as portrayed in Friedl's cartoon were viewed not only as "unrealistic" but also as somewhat immoral. Luxuries had been frowned upon since the Mandate era because they seemed to contradict and subvert the culturally hegemonic ethos of pioneering. Rozin maintains that the Israeli rationing policy was not meant to reinforce ascetic lifestyles but was rather chosen for practical reasons, mainly involving the absorption of the mass immigration. Moreover, one of the goals of austerity was to allow for future economic growth. Still, once implemented, the policy was also described as "proper" in moral terms[112] and, by the government, as a continuation of the War of Independence. In order to build the state and secure the peace, the national economy must be stabilized and therefore citizens should comply and sacrifice their personal comfort.[113] Thus, the government harped grandiloquently on the traumatic memory of the recent war: "Our sons had not spilled their blood in order to gain luxuries, but for the sake of the state and the great immigration, and we shall not allow material licentiousness to squander what had been won for such a dear price. The people in Zion shall support its government in times of need and they shall enjoy future prosperity. The need of the hour is economizing. No waste. No luxury."[114]

Whether ascetic ideals were truly adopted by Israelis or not, these ideals were often invoked in support of the austerity policy. "Excessive extravagance" was rebuked as unsuitable for "these times," not only because it hindered economic recovery but also because it reflected inequalities within a state that tried to promote civil solidarity.[115] The rationing policy equalized Israeli society more than ever before or after, but it preserved and even fortified the line between the upper middle class and the majority of the population.[116] Criticism expressed through imagery sometimes focused on the issues of inequality and lack of solidarity, presenting rich and hedonistic Israelis' complaints about rationing as nothing but signs of corruption and hypocrisy.[117] A cartoon from 1950, for instance, showed two pampered dogs, dressed in dainty outfits, one of them prophesying to the other, "You'll see; soon we'll have to go naked due to these points."[118] Since the prestate era, spoiled pet dogs had been a local symbol of a decadent lifestyle, a testimony of lack of social solidarity, with the implication being that the owners cared more about their dogs' welfare than about that of their human brethren.[119] Thus, during the rationing regime, with many humans lacking adequate clothing, the cartoon admonished a social sector that could afford to dress its dogs.[120]

Writing on 1950s East Germany, historian Judd Stitziel notes that the regime's efforts to fulfill its citizens' needs achieved mixed results, not only due to the country's economic shortcomings "but also because the party was unable to control and regulate needs, desires, and perceptions of scarcity and affluence even within official institutions, let alone among the population at large." Consumer desires seemed to be at odds with available materials and productive capacities.[121] Control over consumers' desires was even more limited in a democracy like Israel. Rozin writes that during the years 1949–1951, the government of Israel learned the limits of its power. It realized that it could not enforce a policy that the public was unable and unwilling to endure. The public's perception of the policy as discriminatory contributed decisively to the system's failure, as did the government's failure to capture and prosecute the black market sharks.[122] In both 1950s East Germany and Israel, the state presented rationing and its inconveniences as temporary steps to be followed by growing wealth and abundance. But Germans were still disillusioned in the 1960s, as the promised socialist utopia continued to recede into the future, whereas by 1954 Israelis were starting to feel the effects of economic recovery.[123]

The economic situation and the economic policy dictated what Israelis could consume, but the expanding black market certainly weakened the effect of rationing, and the government's inability to eradicate or even diminish it hastened the cancellation of the austerity regime; nonetheless, for many consumers, using the black market was not necessarily an act of deliberate defiance and ideological resistance but rather a technical act of putting private needs and interests before national priorities. Rozin shows that even people who supported the rationing program on the ideological and political level succumbed in their daily lives to their unmet needs and traded on the black market out of what they regarded as necessity.[124]

The economic strategy could also be negotiated through complaints and demonstrations. When clothes and shoes were rationed in summer 1951, more than a year after the rationing of food, the government lost the remnants of public trust, and traders of clothes and shoes launched a general protest strike and closed down their shops. Surprised by this harsh reaction, the government established a special committee to investigate the new rationing decree, and the committee's conclusions prompted an increase in the ration size.[125] Whereas in authoritarian regimes complaints and demonstrations are clear acts of resistance, and are punished accordingly, in democratic regimes the same practices can be part of an open process of negotiation.[126] They are not risky for their participants, and they can affect the strategy and change it from within, without challenging the structure of power itself.

Within this range of possible tactics, what were the roles of humor? Noticeably, austerity humor in Israel was *not* necessarily a subversive humor. In the Soviet Union, by comparison, clandestine jokes about the country's economic plight and other political issues were considered by the citizens as an act of rebellion. And rightly so: in the 1930s the sentence for telling certain jokes was up to ten years' imprisonment.[127] Under Stalin's regime, comedy became a means of coping with oppression and "coming to terms with lingering questions of guilt, complicity and responsibility."[128] The importance of political humor in the entire Soviet bloc was reflected in an abundance of jokes *about* political anticommunist jokes and the high price one might pay for voicing them.[129] In undemocratic societies, where people cannot declare their opinions freely, humor becomes a rare outlet and a channel for maintaining some political awareness.[130] This was apparent in Nazi Germany, where political jokes became sharper and darker, more bitter and sarcastic, as matters turned from bad to worse. Since even jokes uttered in private might result in concentration camp punishment, Germans would check around to ensure no potential informant was present before emitting these "whisper jokes" (*flusterwitze*). Underground jokes provided a welcome emotional release from Nazi pressure and restrictions.[131]

In Israel, by contrast, opinions could be expressed openly and satirists who arrived from nondemocratic regimes had to adapt to their newly acquired political freedom. When satire has to overcome censorship, it must remain vigilantly sharp and elegant, but when political humor no longer puts one's survival at risk, it becomes either softer (attempting solely to improve reality rather than change it) or blunter (particularly aggressive in order to make its uncensored points noticeable).[132] Thus, jokes and cartoons that attacked the government's policy in 1950s Israel did so directly,[133] and similar messages were presented openly and brusquely in election slogans and newspaper articles.[134]

Yet interestingly, most of the jokes and cartoons quoted in this chapter were not published by the opposition but rather by newspapers and publications issued by, or affiliated with, Mapai and supportive of the government. They did not use humor or satire as a means to attack the centralist economic policy per se. Some backed the policy by attacking those who undermined it, and thus became a tool of propaganda; others tried to lighten the daily burden of want by focusing on the situation's absurd and funny aspects. Humor could somewhat relieve consumers' predicament by allowing them to vent anger and frustration about specific manifestations of the rationing system, its conduct, and its familiar and unpopular consequences. Austerity jokes that attacked the rationing policy challenged Mapai's strategy by presenting alternatives, but austerity jokes that implied support for the policy, and attacked only its side effects, could indirectly strengthen the strategy by mellowing the harsh consequences of rationing.

Humor can be molded into predictable, safe jokes. It can steer away from provocative and unexpected ideas and avoid committing taboos, instead affirming the social order by exploiting variations on widely familiar themes.[135] Whereas political satire can be violent and radical, social satire can focus charmingly and gently on issues of daily activity without threatening the social respectability of its creators and users.[136] Moreover, even political antiregime jokes can inadvertently help the regime: if operating as a safety valve, they allow aggressions to be vented that might otherwise have been channeled into active resistance and overt opposition.[137] Curiously, it was rumored in Nazi Germany that anti-Nazi jokes were actually invented by the Ministry of Propaganda in order to measure the pace of their distribution, and a similar rumor in the USSR attributed anti-Soviet jokes to the

KGB.[138] Such rumors reflected the fear of omnipresent dictatorship but also the assumption that political jokes can paradoxically work for the benefit of the rulers.

Writing about French satire during World War I, historian Allen Douglas describes humor that does not fit neatly into a clear opposition of hegemonic discourse and subversive practices. Targeting some topics but significantly ignoring others, satire could provide its consumers with a new language and order, and thus enhance hegemony, even when its producers presented their work as insubordinate.[139] Israeli austerity humor, too, cannot be pigeon-holed as either hegemonic or subversive. Sometimes it served as an opposi-tional tool, but often it wasn't meant to target the system but rather to lighten the harsh economic reality. As Draitser notes, humor expresses serious anx-ieties in lighter terms and has an attractive ability to alleviate frustrations.[140]

Israeli austerity humor is also hard to catalog as either strategic or tacti-cal, testifying to the fluidity between these two spheres. When a young child said something funny about her family's material situation, it was part of in-formal uncharted daily behavior; but when she was quoted in a newspaper, her naïve saying was somewhat institutionalized and incorporated into the strategic level. When said in situ, funny utterances were certainly of a tacti-cal nature, but when printed the same utterances were absorbed into formal culture.

Kathleen Stokker, a scholar of Norwegian language and culture, writes that the humor created in Norway during the Nazi occupation played a part in consolidating local resistance, but it also implanted and fortified myths about Norwegian resistance, presenting it as more immediate, total, effec-tive, and successful than it really was.[141] Austerity humor might have played a comparable myth-promoting role in Israel. Economic historian Nahum Gross mentions that the rationing policy was an economic means, not an end unto itself, a brief phase and one of many centralizing economic mea-sures; still, it won enormous attention both from contemporaries and histo-rians.[142] Perhaps, as it became the focal point of local humor, rationing drew outsize public notice and was engraved deeper into collective memory than it might have been otherwise.[143]

Whether spoken, printed, or drawn, austerity jokes revealed the *emotional* daily experience of rationing in a vivid, direct, and stark manner. Both ver-bal and visual humor required inventiveness, as did the practical daily cop-ing with shortage, scarcity, coupons, and lines.[144] Whereas in Soviet Russia and Nazi Germany joke tellers could pay dearly, in 1950s Israel humor was a safe way of letting off steam. Unlike trading on the black market, austerity jokes permitted Israelis to complain and protest within the hegemonic framework, to voice their displeasure while maintaining their good repute and self-esteem as loyal and law-abiding citizens.

"A People in Uniform"

NEWLY INDEPENDENT NATIONS usually promote a heroic vision of national identity, with themes of struggle, liberation, and sacrifice.[1] Israel was founded during a total war, and when the war ended, the cease-fire agreements did not bring about peace. Since its earliest days as an independent state, Israel had to prepare itself conceptually as well as strategically to withstand a continuous violent conflict.[2] Sociologist Moshe Lissak mentions the two main options for democratic societies engaged in lengthy military conflicts. The military, as an authoritative and hierarchical institution, can be sharply separated from the democratic civil society; this is achieved by a professional army of volunteers. The second option is mandatory conscription. In this case the social and ideological breaches between the military and civilian sectors are intentionally reduced and their institutional borders are deliberately blurred.[3]

Israel opted for mandatory conscription and could be described as a "nation in arms" (or in the Hebrew version: "a people in uniform"), because the civilian and the military meet at numerous points, on both the private and the public levels. The state's founding fathers sought to use the IDF to promote the processes of state formation and social integration, and thus the boundaries between the state's security and civilian spheres were deliberately kept porous.[4] The War of Independence placed security and the army at Israel's political and social center. Army service during the war was a basic element in the mythos aimed at building national identity and unity. The IDF, its commanders, and its soldiers were set as focal points of the national centralist idealism, over and above ideological, political, and partisan disagreements.[5]

As we have seen in previous chapters, the IDF played a central role in Israeli society and fulfilled various nonmilitary functions. The military and the civilian spheres were neither sharply separated nor clearly demarcated. Civilians were part of the army during their regular and reserve service, and regular soldiers were not confined to military bases; they were visible all over the country, performing educational and settlement tasks.[6] Attempts were made to maintain the army's unity and prestige, to consolidate the soldiers' identification with the army's goals, and to nurture the civilians' affection for the army.[7] A military pamphlet from 1956 reminded IDF soldiers that outside the camp they were seen by citizens as the representatives of the army; in order to maintain and enhance public respect and fondness for the army, soldiers were instructed to keep a neat appearance in addition to behaving politely.[8] It is noteworthy and indicative of its special structure and status that the IDF was not just respected and admired among the Israeli public but also liked. As an actual "army of the people," it inspired familial warmth rather than distant awe.[9]

Such informality—atypical for most national armies—was probably related to the mandatory conscription in a small country, as opposed to an army of professional soldiers. It was also a legacy from the Palmach era. As an underground force, in the 1940s the Palmach had to hide its training and other activities from the British authorities. Its secrecy and lack of resources affected its military style. The motto "Every squad commander is a general" reflected the initiative and resourcefulness expected of all soldiers, the close and casual relationship between commanders and their men, and the absence of formal ranks. The Palmachniks relied on mobility, flexible maneuvering, nocturnal guerilla tactics, and their intimate, direct knowledge of the country's landscape. Despite being a military organization, the Palmach held no ranks or insignia and practiced no military salutes or ceremonies. Ben-Gurion's decision to disperse the Palmach (and all other prestate militias) for the sake of a unified national army met with much resentment, and the informal spirit of the Palmach was never quite absent from the IDF. Soon the security needs of Israel, with constant Arab infiltrations through the vulnerable borders answered by Israeli reprisal attacks, required elite infantry units, where all soldiers were encouraged to show initiative and commanders and men held informal relationships. Thus, only a few years after its dispersal, Palmach notions and style once again dominated the IDF.[10]

Ben-Gurion regarded the IDF as a central unifying force in the young state. The IDF's involvement in founding, populating, and defending new frontier settlements, and in helping absorb the new immigrants in transit camps, enhanced its status within Israeli society. At the same time, within the IDF military service became a main tool for achieving the melting pot goal as it forged "new Israelis" according to the centralist ideal. Different segments of Israeli society met during their army service and, as mentioned in

A Bedouin and a military policeman, February 1950. National Photo Collection (Government Press Office), D585-045. Photo by Fritz Cohen.

a previous chapter, many young immigrants learned Hebrew during their army service.[11] Ben-Gurion regarded the IDF's educational role as crucial and expected its officers to turn the immigrant "rabble" into cultured civilians by uprooting any remaining exilic traits and replacing them with the new national values. For young immigrants who strove to assimilate into Israeli society, army service could offer an opportunity to adjust quickly, by learning Hebrew and by acquiring local myths, symbols, and norms.[12]

The IDF hence became a major agent of acculturation among the new immigrants. It stood above partisan disagreements and was conceived as a symbol of national unity, democratic principles, and equal opportunities. Due to the IDF's crucial socializing role and its centrality for the formation of Israeli national identity, the exclusion of Israeli Arabs from military service had far-reaching consequences for their status.[13] While some minorities such as Druze and Circassians were gradually conscripted and Bedouins were allowed to volunteer, most Arabs were not recruited to the IDF. The government didn't want to put them in a situation in which they would be forced to fight against their own people and even members of their own family, and also feared that they might turn their military training and weapons against the state. Without going through the unifying military experience, Israeli

Arabs remained socially, culturally, and also economically marginalized.[14] Moreover, unlike most Israelis, whose national identity included fondness and admiration for the army, many Israeli Arabs met the armed forces in the frustrating and humiliating circumstances of the military rule.[15]

In democracies, public opinion and the media have gradually emerged as influential components of politics, including military politics.[16] Sociologists and historians often describe Israeli society as "militaristic." Stressing the impact of militarism on strategic, economic, political, and ideological levels, they also determine that Israel was and still is marked by "cultural militarism." However, a closer look at this claim shows that these writers are actually basing their conclusions on the institutional-political or the formal-ideological sphere, actual service in the army, or the field of intentional cultural creation and production.[17]

Militarism, notes Lissak, includes a wide range of customs, interests, notions, and activities that accompany armies and wars but are not necessarily tied directly to military goals.[18] Following military historian Mordechai Bar-On, the term *militarism* is used in this chapter according to the nonjudgmental definition in the *Oxford Compact English Dictionary*: "The spirit and tendencies characteristic of the professional soldier; the prevalence of military sentiments or ideals among a people; the political condition characterized by the predominance of the military class in government or administration; the tendency to regard military efficiency as the paramount interest of the state."[19]

Several studies on Israeli militarism, by contrast, embrace a judgmental viewpoint or tend to dwell on the predominance of the military in the state and its policies,[20] while this chapter focuses on the second phrase in the *Oxford* definition, namely "the prevalence of military sentiments or ideals among a people." The *ideological* debates about militarism within early Israeli society have been studied before. Bar-On concludes that in the 1950s most Israelis, under feelings of siege, isolation, and defense, justified the use of force, but at times (the reprisal attacks of the mid-1950s, for instance) military policy met some controversy; the communist party and other minority groups, including two pacifist movements, voiced antimilitaristic principles.[21]

This chapter, as implied, does not discuss the explicit ideological facet of cultural militarism, which was transformed into words and set into conscious doctrines. It does not describe militaristic principles imparted through Israeli educational institutions and the activity of the Gadna ("youth battalions").[22] Nor does it probe other formal cultural expressions: military

Agricultural work conducted under guard in Moshav Nitzanei Oz ("buds of strength") in 1954. Founded in 1951 as a Nahal settlement, the moshav was located on the Jordanian border and the outskirts of Tulkarem, an Arab town with a large population of war refugees. Central Zionist Archives, PHKH\1279202. Photo by Yaron Mirlin.

parades on Independence Day and other public occasions, the army's entertainment troupes, whose songs and performances won huge popularity, and the army's active involvement in cultural activities all over Israel.[23] Rather, it reconstructs unorganized military presence in civilian daily life and examines the indirect effects of military sentiments on linguistic practices.

After the War of Independence the military remained strongly present in Israeli daily life both in concrete ways and as an ideological and mental reference. The volatile situation, especially frequent infiltration by Arabs into Israeli territory, required military defense in settlements along the borders.[24] Jerusalem, now divided between the Israeli western city and the Jordanian eastern city, was clearly scarred by the war,[25] but military presence was experienced in other Israeli cities and towns as well.[26] Soldiers in the special "Nahal" units, which combined military service with agricultural settlement, spent part of their service living and working in established kibbutzim.[27] During the rainy winter of 1951, the soldiers enthusiastically accepted their role of helping out in the transit camps. For their part, the immigrants were

A soldier playing with a young new immigrant from Yemen in a transit
camp, December 1950. National Photo Collection (Government Press Office), D237-041.
Photo by David Eldan.

impressed by the army's efficiency (they were less impressed by the civil authorities), and public esteem for the IDF soared.[28]

On Pesach 1949 the Merchants Association organized a shop-window
competition in Tel Aviv, and among the winning themes were "our battles
in the past, the present, and the future," "military victories," and "the trium-
phant army."[29] Military issues, such as types of weapons and the perceived
forthcoming war (the "second round"), were molded into children's board
games and collectible cards.[30] The public was intentionally involved in the
army's affairs, such as when the IDF asked Israeli artists to suggest designs for
military honors and medals, or when citizens were called to lodge "lone soldiers" (those who had no family of their own) during the holidays.[31] During
the fall maneuvers of 1950, the public enjoyed hearing the "strange and amusing" recruiting code words on the radio; one daily newspaper announced a
competition in which readers were challenged to write a five-hundred-word
story containing at least one hundred recruiting code words (out of 141 such
slogans in use).[32] Local newsreels constantly and proudly showed army units
engaging in military exercises, sporting activities, and parades in their camps,
located "somewhere in the land."[33]

Many soldiers wore their uniforms on leave as well as on duty, and "soldiers on leave" became a common sight in Tel Aviv, Tiberius, Nazareth, and other towns, their image woven into local lore.[34] The Committee for the Well-Being of the Soldier was initially formed during World War II to benefit the soldiers in Britain's Jewish Brigade, and it was reestablished when the IDF was founded. The committee founded "soldiers' homes," which served as clubs and cultural centers in several towns.[35] The position of town officer, too, was instituted to help soldiers who were on leave: town officers "will remind Private Shoshana Pnini that 'Ofir' movie theater in Tel Aviv is showing a high-quality movie and willing to let her in for a reduced-price ticket and without waiting in line; they will advise Lieutenant Eli Friedman to walk around the corner to Noah's Arc café, where he could get a plate of vegetables, sour milk, cheese, jam, margarine, bread and tea" for a very reasonable price.[36]

Soldiers often mixed with citizens in the movie theater. As we shall see in the sixth chapter, moviegoing was an extremely popular form of entertainment in televisionless 1950s Israel. At the movies, soldiers waited in a separate priority line, as they did for the bus,[37] and since the 1948 eruption of war, numerous movie theaters discounted soldiers' tickets by 15 to 30 percent.[38] As early as 1949, however, some Israelis seem to have begun questioning the special benefits accorded to soldiers at movie theaters, cafés, and generally while waiting in line. The army bulletin published a bitter article claiming that as soon as the war had ended some Israelis were thus belittling the soldiers' value: "Disrespect is shown not only in financial matters, but also toward the important role of the soldier and his harsh living conditions. When soldiers arrive in town in the evening, they walk to the head of the bus line, as is customary. But people who have never smelled the odor of gunpowder, men with white collars and leather briefcases, women wearing the latest fall fashion under their parasols, start shouting: 'Soldier or not, on leave or on duty, stand in line like everyone else. Your legs are younger.'"[39]

The perhaps surprising objections to soldiers' privileges surfaced in other areas as well in the years after the war. One such complaint involved the fairness of soldiers standing at the head of civic rationing lines for basic provisions, which they collected for their families. Meanwhile, on the movie ticket issue, the army's formal response was that soldiers should stand in separate lines and get reduced-price tickets but that they should not abuse this privilege by purchasing tickets for civilian friends. With regard to lines for the bus and for foodstuffs, soldiers who served in faraway posts should be given priority because their time in town was limited, whereas soldiers who served in town should stand in line with civilians.[40] In 1956 the IDF modified its former policy by instructing soldiers to form a separate line in movie theaters (unless a separate box office was provided for soldiers), alongside the civilian line, and to be served "according to the principle of 'one civilian — one soldier.'"[41]

The public response to the norm that favored soldiers over civilians[42] derived from the image of the soldier in early Israeli society. On the explicit ideological level, apart from the communist party, all Israeli parties supported IDF soldiers unreservedly. Even a weekly that regularly criticized the security establishment and the policy of military rule expressed a warm and admiring opinion of the soldiers.[43] If the Palmachnik was celebrated for his brave self-sacrifice, the postwar hero was identified with the IDF parachutist and pilot, epitomizing a manly, fearless, and adventurous spirit.[44] The city of Ramat Gan, for instance, "adopted" the entire parachuting corps. In practice this meant providing various forms of entertainment and free visits to movie theaters for parachutists who visited or lived in the city.[45]

In 1950 the public relations branch of the Ministry of Defense organized a radio campaign aimed at creating "an atmosphere of public understanding of security issues." In a country where many citizens were called to serve in the reserve forces, the broadcast was intended to hail the contribution of individual voluntarism to national security.[46] Six months later an exhibition titled *When a People Volunteers* was held in Tel Aviv, presenting the history of Jewish defense in Palestine from the beginning of the twentieth century up until the War of Independence and the present-day IDF.[47] Newspapers, meanwhile, published favorable textual and visual descriptions of army units and soldiers.[48]

However, even elements within the IDF were cautious about military propaganda among soldiers and civilians. In 1950 the national postal service consulted with a commander in the Adjutant General Branch about whether a new stamp being issued contained a faithful representation of the rifle used in "our War of Independence." The commander sent back a sketch of an IDF rifle but also added a significant remark: "Allow me to hope that this proposed stamp does not herald a whole series of militaristic stamps?"[49] Whereas the Hebrew word for "military" (*tzvaii*) was used as a neutral adjective, the foreign term (*militaristi*) employed by the commander in his letter was categorically negative: he clearly objected to weapons as suitable topics for national Israeli stamps. A year later we find similar reservations in an internal correspondence among commanders from the Supply Corps and the Adjutant General Branch. Two commanders voiced their discontent when encountering an army base where decorations for Independence Day included photographs of Israel's president, prime minister, and the IDF chief of staff. One of them remarked that "this provincial and tasteless decoration provoked harsh criticism from soldiers and officers alike." Another wrote that the chief of staff's photograph should never be used as a decoration, because "such visual glorification is very dangerous and makes us seem a bit like Soviet Russia."[50]

The positive image of the Israeli soldier promoted by the IDF and the media was thus an intriguing combination of manly ability and strength with easygoing kindness. Israeli soldiers were described as "people of peace, prepared for battle."[51] On Independence Day of 1952 and 1955, staged color photos on the cover of the army bulletin conveyed this curious blend. They showed a soldier armed and aiming his weapon, but located in a blooming field of flowers and with a flower-covered helmet. The written slogans on the respective covers, "To Crash Every Attacker and Enemy" and "Be Ready for Battle," enhanced the courageous facet of the soldier's image but clarified that the Israeli combat soldier was a defender, not an attacker. The benign background and pastoral association mitigated the aggressive side of the fighter and reassured the viewers of his domestic amiability.[52]

The ultimate recruitment — the military one — was used as a literal and visual metaphor for recruitments into other kinds of national assignments. The military model was familiar and close (historically and physically), and despite the war's traumatic impact, it was more glorious and dramatic than the gray and grinding tasks of the early 1950s. Voluntary activities and organizations thus adopted and employed military concepts.[53]

Demonstrating this tendency, a newspaper's greeting for the Jewish New Year in 1950 portrayed the national tasks of mass immigration and settlement with "the people" drawn as a crowd marching determinedly, military-style, forward.[54] The complex yet apparent associations of war and sports have been amply documented, and it is therefore unsurprising to find military-style marching illustrating posters for sporting events in 1950s Israel.[55] Less easily predicted is the use of the military march and the word *corps* by the Ministry of Agriculture to recruit families to grow vegetables in their private gardens. Under the title "Join the Corps of the Vegetable Growers," the illustration shows a family of smiling parents, a boy, and a small girl marching left-foot-forward in a straight row, carrying their garden equipment as if it were weaponry.[56]

A 1949 cartoon by Dosh: "A recruitment of nurses has been announced."
The nurses carry their medical tools in a military fashion as they storm the
immigrants' camp. *Ashmoret*, December 8, 1949.

The advertising field provides another illuminating example of soldiers'
general attractiveness in Israeli society. In 1949 locally manufactured cigarettes named "Example" (Dugma) were advertised with an image of a marching soldier — "An Exemplary Soldier."[57] Another local brand of cigarettes was
actually named "Sergeant" (Samal).[58] Chocolate ads used images of combat
soldiers and pilots to promote their products,[59] and two female soldiers illustrated an ad for a locally manufactured juice.[60]

Military uniforms generated trust among civilians, trust that could be
abused. In 1949, it took police detectives and the military police a couple
of months to capture and arrest a thief known as "the Lieutenant from Beer
Sheva." The thief would dress up as a lieutenant, "infiltrate" civilian society,
and declare that he had just arrived from Beer Sheva without making any
sleeping arrangements. Usually someone offered the fake lieutenant a bed
for the night, and by the next morning he was gone, along with various stolen goods.[61] Army officers were obviously treated as trustworthy guests, especially so soon after the war.

Seven years later another con artist struck in the form of a twenty-nine-
year-old private, who forged his soldier card and introduced himself to a
teacher from Jerusalem as a lieutenant and a parachutist. The teacher let him
stay at his house, from which the private stole items. After his arrest, he admitted the forgery and the theft. In his testimony the teacher stated that the
private, whose real name was Tzvi Markus, had introduced himself as "Tziki
Sela" and told him that he had just returned from a military exercise and had

nothing to do; he told the civilian that both his brothers had died in the War of Independence and his third brother was an IDF colonel. The teacher then asked him over since, as a former captain in the army, "I was glad to be able to host in my house a man who had parachuted so many times."[62] The incident discloses 1950s Israel's cultural militarism in a nutshell: in order to gain the victim's confidence, the younger man presented a typical Sabra nickname (Tziki) and second name (Sela, which means "rock" in Hebrew) rather than giving his real name. He then faked the supreme military pedigree: two dead war heroes as brothers, a colonel as a third brother, and he himself a parachutist, the most daring and therefore most prestigious military role.

Alongside public admiration and gratitude toward the IDF and its soldiers, several sources reveal concerns regarding the soldiers' cultural level and morality. During the first years of statehood, as it absorbed new immigrants indiscriminately, the IDF became a heterogeneous army. Only six hundred out of an overall six thousand male recruits in the years 1950–1952, for instance, were high school graduates, and most of them served in the Nahal or in professional units, which required knowledge of Hebrew and a high school education. Although the army enabled more social mobility than any other Israeli institution, it too reflected and reinforced social disparities, like the fact that 43 percent of Israeli natives graduated from high school, compared with only 9 percent of the immigrants from Muslim countries. In the exams for military leadership (officer suitability), 30 percent of the Israeli natives won a suitable grade and another 14 percent won a sufficient grade. Among the new immigrants from Muslim countries, only 5.2 percent won a suitable grade and another 6.4 percent won a sufficient grade. Most of the soldiers who served in the infantry and other combat corps during those years were new immigrants from poor economic and educational backgrounds. Only 37 percent of these soldiers mastered Hebrew properly, while 18 percent knew no Hebrew at all. A 1954 report mentioned absenteeism as a major problem, and many privates suffered from lack of motivation and ideological commitment. The socioeconomic difficulties of the recruits and their low educational level affected IDF functioning during its first years,[63] and apparently these factors also affected the public image of the soldiers.

Soldiers were generally and traditionally regarded as "craving the stimulating and the titillating,"[64] and by 1951 a serving female soldier mentioned "the low cultural level of our army" as a well-known fact.[65] Another female soldier wrote about women's unequal and meaningless army service, mentioning "the low morals and frivolity of the army," where "girls are insulted

Soldiers waiting for a ride in
the Negev, 1956. National Photo
Collection (Government Press Office),
D296-079. Photo by Moshe Pridan.

by obscene talk and jokes and by a humiliating attitude."[66] Other sources —
both within and outside the army — mentioned soldiers engaged in illegal
activities such as desertion, stealing food and supplies from the army, black
marketing, and molestation.[67] Thus, without undoing the decisively positive
formal image of the IDF soldier,[68] informal culture sometimes contained un-
complimentary facets and revealed anxieties.

Cultural militarism was frequently expressed in Israeli Hebrew. In 1956
the London Ballet gave a performance in the Ramat Gan stadium. In return
for many free and reduced-price tickets for soldiers, the organizers received
IDF help in building a big stage, erecting a safety fence around the stadium,
and supplying spotlights and military policemen as guards. The journalist
who reported on these preparations called it "a military-artistic-commercial
operation [emphasis added]."[69] After 1948 the word *operation* (in Hebrew,
mivtza[70]) was widely used in Israel to describe nonmilitary successful deeds,
such as the creation of new transit camps for immigrants or the vaccination
of Bedouins in the Negev.[71] Sports conferences held by the leading Israeli
clubs were referred to as effective "operations," and an account of an organized nighttime swim across the Sea of Galilee in 1955 was headlined "A Daring Moonlight Operation."[72] Women too, claimed an article in a left-wing

women's magazine, can perform "strong athletic operations."[73] As we recall, the Ministry of Education and Culture titled its activities associated with spreading Hebrew among the new immigrants the Operation of Language Instruction for the People.[74] When theater companies performed before immigrants in the Negev, the deed was termed "an important cultural operation,"[75] and a music critic described performances given in the transit camps in 1953 as "a well-organized Hanukkah operation."[76]

When criticizing the aggressive behavior of Israelis, one writer suggested announcing a permanent "Operation Courtesy,"[77] and the Tel Aviv municipality named its attempts to fight urban noise and squalor "Operation Silence" and "Operation Cleanliness," respectively.[78] In 1955 a local weekly and a local cosmetic firm announced a joint beauty contest under the title "Operation Smile."[79] After 1954, with rationing effectively over and the Israeli economy starting to recover and even thrive, *operation* was employed informally and in parentheses to indicate sales on goods.[80] This use of the word became widespread, eventually losing the parentheses.

Other military terms were also borrowed for nonmilitary contexts, as we already encountered in the descriptions of the snow in 1950.[81] When a seven-year-old was told that the injection she received protected her body from germs, she said, "I see: it's the Body's Defense Forces."[82] A student in a bus line tried to convince a policeman that students should stand in the special soldiers' line because they were the "Israel Science Forces."[83] The editor of a women's bulletin attacked Ministry of Rationing and Distribution workers for not quelling the black market. "A proper civil servant," she wrote, "should be like a faithful soldier, who never leaves his post, even if he learns that his general was murdered."[84] Even the private familial sphere was described in military terms, with a women's column advising its readers to accept their husbands' demands as a compliment rather than an insult: more demands mean greater authority, "extra demand, extra role, and extra rank!"[85]

Military terms were habitually used in the supposedly far-removed field of cultural and leisure activities. Thus, the National Censorship Committee for Films and Plays sent a special "squad" to visit movie theaters and mark films for adult viewing,[86] and Independence Day celebrations in the transit camps included "a squad of artists: musicians, presenters, singers and dancers, all who were recruited for the occasion."[87] When a satirical theater troupe was about to perform in an open-air theater in the northern town of Nahariya, it requested that the organizers make ample arrangements to stop "infiltrators" from viewing the show without buying tickets.[88] During preparations for the 1950 Folk Dance Convention, the head choreographer stood "on the control tower," and the entire "camp of dancers" was placed "under the command" of a sports coach.[89] The strict director of a fashion show was depicted as "behaving like a master sergeant."[90] No explanations or clarifications were provided in these cases, nor were they needed: all these military terms were widely known and understood by longtime Israelis, while newcomers were taught military words as they were learning Hebrew.[91]

Long before the founding of the state, Zionists borrowed military terms such as *battalion* and *legion* to describe central national missions. The Zionist settlement project, for instance, was referred to as the "conquest of the desert" and the attempt to engage Jewish manual workers as the "conquest of labor."[92] However, after the War of Independence, more specific, detailed, and informed military notions were in common daily use and, as we saw, employed not only to elevate grand, collective national enterprises but also to illustrate contained achievements and describe mundane matters.[93] Whereas the use of military notions in prestate society was gravely earnest, their customary employment in Israel was often lighthearted and ironic. This regular application of detailed military terms indicated a firsthand civil acquaintance with the army, alongside a certain waning of its awe-inspiring halo. As the military became closer, more accessible, and more familiar to many Israelis, its veneration from afar was replaced by a more intimate regard.

Although linguistic style is difficult to translate, it should be mentioned that in addition to lexical and allegorical borrowings, Israeli Hebrew and its texts were sometimes affected by military style, which seeped into various civic fields. Classic examples include texts divided into concise and laconic subarticles, a common use of acronyms and abbreviations (including the omission of necessary pronouns), and the employment of military slang in nonmilitary contexts.[94]

It is not surprising to find military terms in the local bulletins of the kibbutzim. Nahal soldiers, as noted, spent half their service in the kibbutzim, kibbutz natives were prominent in all the voluntary IDF combat units, and by 1956 half of the combat pilots in the air force were kibbutzniks, even though the entire population of the kibbutzim constituted only 5 percent of Israel's Jewish population.[95] Given such extensive involvement and experience with the army, it seems almost natural to see the word *operation* in kibbutz bulletins to describe the communal distribution of clothes, the cleaning of the kibbutz yard, and the arrangement of weddings.[96] Military notions and slang were also used to describe kibbutz activities such as hikes, holiday celebrations, and theatrical and musical productions.[97] Particularly ripe for funny military descriptions were the annual preparations for the Purim masquerade. In 1956 the announcement of the celebration in one kibbutz was a detailed comic imitation of a military order. While the illustrations were of masks and clowns, the text, titled "Operation Order," was divided into articles and subarticles listing "Background" ("Land," "Enemy," "Our Forces"), "Target," "Method," "Administration" ("Equipment," "Food," "Timetable"), and "Code Word." The announcement ended with the martial cry "Move!"[98]

The regular use of borrowed military terms is rather more surprising in the Haredi Hebrew newspaper. About four hundred Haredi men were exempt from military service so that they could study in religious seminars, and the Haredi community objected strongly to any woman — whether religious or not — serving in the army.[99] Yet while the extreme anti-Zionist Orthodox community separated itself politically and culturally from the Israeli state,[100] most Haredim, whose leaders were part of the coalition government, were much more sympathetic to the national cause. According to sociologist Menachem Friedman, military heroes were admired by the Haredi youths.[101] The word *operation* was thus employed in the Haredi newspaper in both negative and positive connections: when the writer condemned greedy financial speculation, the term "Operation Optimism" was applied sarcastically, and the nationalization of religious holidays in contemporary Israel was called "Operation Secularization"; but when applied to the work of IDF rabbis, "Operation Pesach" was meant as a term of praise.[102]

An article in the Haredi paper describing the celebration of the Lag Ba-Omer Jewish holiday on Mount Meron in 1952 praised the army (an impressive military parade was an important part of the festivities, as was the reading by the IDF chief rabbi), and described the entire holiday as a grand "recruitment" to "Operation Meron."[103] On the other hand, an article about Independence Day the next year expressed disapproval of the celebrations' secular and hectic nature and rejected the military arrogance they expressed. Although the article rebuked excessive military pride, parts of it were indeed written in a military style.[104] A satirical portrayal of the faulty local telephone service included the sentence "So here I stand again like a soldier on guard."[105] Other articles used military words and slang, mostly without providing any explanations,[106] as if the Haredi readership were expected to be familiar with military notions even without personal experience.

Military terms were used in earnest in articles concerning the "cultural war" between the Haredi community and the forces of secularism. Hence, the building of a secular institution in the heart of a religious Jerusalem neighborhood was described as a "citadel" intended to "conquer more territory" from the Haredim.[107] The Israeli Haredi minority, seeking to maintain its religious way of life against a tide of secular national culture, "fought back" against worthless secularized and nationalized interpretations of Jewish holidays and used "the same weapons" when presenting their own, religious and meaningful, versions of these holidays.[108] Assuming that his readers encountered numerous violations of religious rules, as well as daily expressions of secular immodesty (such as Israeli young women wearing very short pants[109]), a rabbi called on the Haredim to unite their forces, "as we see the strike platoons of the aggressive secularism."[110]

This customary use of military terms in the Haredi newspaper may indicate that many Haredim were partly involved in the majority national culture rather than totally insulated within an enclave subculture.[111] It may also suggest that cultural militarism was so prevalent in Israeli society that it covered all Jewish subgroups, both those deeply involved in military life, like members of the kibbutzim, and those whose position was more distant and whose sentiments were more ambivalent, like the Haredim.

Israeli cultural militarism thus reflected the mutually porous borders between the civilian and the military sectors, a dynamic also exemplified in the sartorial field. Among their major roles, military uniforms are meant to tell soldiers apart from civilians, but khaki had been a favorite color in Israeli dress since the 1940s, and after the War of Independence, Israeli soldiers and civilians often wore very similar attire.[112] In the summer of 1949, the IDF bulletin described a strange phenomenon on the streets of Israeli towns: "Many of the people passing by are dressed in half-uniforms, [military] caps with no insignia, military shirts. On the other hand, it's hard to find two soldiers dressed in the very same uniform." The writer explained that "today's citizens are yesterday's soldiers," who had received khaki clothes when discharged from their army service. Besides, he continued, "khaki clothes have always been the national dress of Israelis" — evoking memories of the prestate era, suiting the local climate, and fitting the conditions of the rationing regime.[113] In late 1949, no wonder, the IDF uniform committee required that military uniforms be sewn "with a special khaki fabric, which will be strictly forbidden to civilians." The committee insisted on a special uniform shape as well, "because most civilians in our country tend to wear khaki during the larger part of the year, and it is often hard to differentiate a soldier from a civilian."[114]

Watched by her sons, a member of Kibbutz Nirim on the southern border cleans her rifle, December 1955. National Photo Collection (Government Press Office), D295-039. Photo by Moshe Pridan.

Khaki garments were not the only tangible reminder of the recent war. While studied before,[115] the commemoration of the War of Independence and its role in Israeli collective memory bears mention here because of its central role in Israel's cultural militarism. The war was no doubt traumatic (resulting in the death of 1 percent of the country's Jewish population), but it was also the heroic high point for Israeli Jews, considered a crucial episode of dedication and sacrifice.[116] In Israeli culture the War of Independence was depicted as a momentous event that forged all its participants — old and new Jews, religious and secular, men and women — into a unified national entity.[117] This centrality of the war in Israeli national identity magnified the gap between Israelis who arrived before and during 1948, experiencing the war firsthand, and those new immigrants who arrived after its end. The latter were treated as if they had missed the nation's formative event, and to some degree this positioned them as perpetual outsiders. Moreover, they were expected to feel grateful to their predecessors for founding and securing the state "for them" before they had arrived.[118]

While singing the praises of the recent past, the IDF attempted to boost the positive image of the soldiers of the present. The prestige of any country's military is based on societal approval,[119] and the state's propagation of a public image for the IDF was the main strategy in the specific context of *cultural* militarism. From the outset this component could not be enforced but rather entailed persuasion, as is often the case in a well-managed hegemony. Israeli Arabs were not capable of engaging in resistance at the time, but those who were not recruited to the army and those whose experiences of the IDF were trying were unlikely to adopt the strategic propaganda and could only ignore the army's glorification. Most Jewish Israelis, on the other hand, adopted the positive image of the IDF. Fear and awe toward an army can be forced on a population, but not so fondness: only combined strategies and tactics, alongside the fact that mandatory military service meant most Israeli families had "representatives" serving in the army, could engender the warmth toward IDF soldiers shared by many civilians on the tactical level.

We have also seen how military terms were widely appropriated among different sectors in various civilian spheres. This constant use of military notions and expressions might have enhanced the militaristic character of Israeli society, but these terms may also have been "civilized" by their daily unmilitary use, gradually eroding their military essence and further obliterating the already porous border between the military and the civilian. Some might assume that the pervasiveness of cultural militarism in daily life would mean a political militarism was not far behind. This question lies beyond the scope of this chapter, as it leads us back to the institutional-political and formal-ideological spheres, but let us keep in mind that connections between the cultural and the ideological realms are far from straightforward. Take, for instance, the ironic comparison between the fashion show director and a master sergeant: did it elevate the fashion show or belittle the army? Did such a humorous analogy encourage militaristic ideology or trivialize it? Because they don't lend themselves easily to historical investigation, indirect influences between daily tendencies and political ideology are seldom proven and remain largely, as in this case, in the province of conjecture.

5 Taking the Bus

A YOUNG JOURNALIST, an Israeli native who had recently fought in the war, wrote in 1951 about his bus trip from Tel Aviv to Jerusalem — a distance of about fifty miles — as "a daring operation." Getting from his street to the central bus station in Tel Aviv and thence to Jerusalem took him five hours and included "a great deal of bitterness and anger, striking sun, dreadful crowdedness and lengthy delays in endless lines." He knew that "we are poor and have no foreign currency" to invest in transportation ("we" meaning the State of Israel, which subsidized the cost of travel), but still he wondered whether the bus companies were neglecting the well-being of their customers for the sake of a profit.[1]

Israel of the 1950s was in some respects still a developing country, but it aspired to be a modern, Western state. From the outset Zionists intended to import Western modernity into the underdeveloped Middle East, elevating the latter from its lowly condition. Zionists conceived of their movement as modern and tried to create a democratic, technologically advanced, and well-informed society.[2] After the founding of the state, Israel was acutely isolated within its immediate Arab surroundings; this local seclusion might have further intensified Israelis' yearning to be part of the big Western world that lay beyond its narrow geopolitical borders.[3] Some gaps between the lofty aspirations and daily reality were experienced in the field of public transportation, and can be demonstrated in two pairs of drawings.

As shown on the opposite page, in 1949 one of the major bus cooperatives, Egged, advertised its service with an image of a confident, cheerful driver and a bus blending nicely into the flow of traffic. "Travel Safely," read the headline.[4] Yet, in fact, road accidents involving buses were on the increase — so much so[5] that the well-known cartoonist Arieh Navon suggested "securing" buses by following each one with an ambulance and a black funeral car.[6]

A 1954 Egged ad, shown on page 88, promised direct lines to Haifa, Tel Aviv, and Jerusalem whenever a passenger chose, journeys during which "you can sit comfortably." The illustration showed an orderly, solid, spacious

Egged ad from 1949: "Travel Safely."

Cartoon by Arieh Navon, 1950: "Following the Frequent Road Accidents."

כך נוטעים ב.א.ג.ד "ישיר
סע בנוחיות בישיבה
ובשעה הנוחה-לך

Egged ad from 1954:
"This Is How We Travel
in 'Egged' Direct."

vehicle with a poised driver and serene, content customers.[7] One month later, Friedl illustrated a journalistic item about a nightmarish bus trip from Tel Aviv to a nearby suburb. As shown on the opposite page, the driver of this dense and rocking vehicle seemed neither as intelligent nor as handsome as his colleague from the ad, and the cramped passengers—most of whom were standing—looked decisively discontent.[8]

Being the main means of human transportation in 1950s Israel, the bus served as a cardinal public space. Following Michel de Certeau's example, investigation thus turns from particular destinations to time spent by travelers in their vehicle.[9] Earlier in the century, observers in Western society had noticed the democratizing cultural effects of public transportation, in which crowds of strangers from all classes, men and women of different ages, were seated next to each other. All passengers paid the same fare and experienced the same comfort or discomfort. The new modes of transportation brought about new behavioral norms and conventions, reflecting local characteristics and circumstances.[10] After introducing Israeli public transportation and describing conditions of travel, this chapter dwells on common patterns of human interaction on the Israeli bus, a scene where national hegemonic ideals of democracy, equality, and the ingathering of the exiles were put to a daily test.

The Mandate era in Palestine was characterized by a spectacular development of transportation: roads grew more than sixfold in length, and the number of licensed vehicles increased by thirty-eight times. Although the relative growth of the roads was not rapid as compared to the population increase, by 1948 the country was served by a fairly thick, though unevenly dis-

Horrific bus trip, illustrated
by Friedl, 1954.

tributed, road network. The new road network, with its convergence in Tel
Aviv, reinforced the centrality of the coastal plain region.[11] Palestine became
the Middle East's most motorized country: in 1935 there was, on average, one
automobile per 100 inhabitants in Palestine, compared with one in 192 in Cy-
prus, one in 365 in Syria, one in 600 in Iraq, one in 648 in Egypt, and one in
650 in Jordan. It was estimated that one third to one half of the automobiles
in the country were located and used in Tel Aviv.[12]

Many roads were damaged or destroyed during the 1948 war; on the
other hand, the new state's population doubled within a few years, and
newly founded settlements had to be connected to the transportation grid.
The length of the roads was doubled within one decade,[13] yet out of 27,000
motorized vehicles operating in Israel in 1950, about 3,000 had been added
during the previous year. The government's investment of its limited foreign
currency in vehicles, tires, and fuel without equivalent investment in transportation infrastructure sometimes drew public criticism: traffic congested
the roads, and accidents were on the increase.[14]

Passengers waiting for the bus in Moshav Beerotaim, **1951.** National Photo Collection (Government Press Office), D252-100. Photo by Fritz Cohen from July 1951.

In 1952 the local ratio of automobiles per inhabitants was similar to that during the Mandate era—11.1 cars for every thousand people (compared with 57.2 cars in the United States, 3.1 in Lebanon, and 1 in Egypt).[15] Two years later the number of cars per thousand Israelis had risen to 26.4.[16] From 1949 to 1955, the total number of automobiles doubled,[17] but so did the country's population, and the increase in buses lagged behind that of other automobiles. Indeed, bus activity appears to have increased by only 3.7 percent between 1951 and 1955.[18] In 1955, 40 percent of the automobiles in Israel were trucks, 34 percent were private cars, 22 percent were motorcycles, and only 4 percent were buses. More than 80 percent of the country's automobiles were operating in cities and towns, where about 61 percent of the population was residing, especially in Tel Aviv. Although Jerusalem was the country's formal capital, in 1954 Tel Aviv was home to 21 percent of the Israeli population and 45 percent of the country's automobiles.[19] The roads leading into the city were the busiest in Israel,[20] although in other parts of the country, too, according to a visitor from the United States, "Automobiles and trucks fill the roads. There is an atmosphere of energy and vitality."[21]

In 1949 five bus companies were operating in the state, transporting 190 million passengers annually in 806 vehicles. In late 1951 three of the companies merged into Egged (Eshed), and during the following year Egged and the two other cooperatives — Dan and Hamekasher — transported 318 million passengers in 1,573 vehicles.[22] Unsurprisingly, bus transportation was more concentrated in urban centers,[23] but smaller settlements too were gradually connected by new lines to the main three cities.[24] Despite the relatively slow increase in bus activity in the early 1950s, the bus companies dominated local passenger transportation, since the struggling train system offered no real alternative. Some of the bus companies' expenses were subsidized by the state, and ticket prices were supervised by the government.[25]

A six-year-old Israeli defined the Sabbath as "a day on which one is not allowed to take the bus, only private cars."[26] Indeed, public transportation halted its operation during the Jewish Sabbath, namely from Friday afternoon until Saturday evening, because automobile travel violates the sanctity of the Sabbath according to Rabbinic Judaism. The exception was Haifa, a harbor city with a large population of industrial workers and a strong socialist municipal leadership, as well as a large Arab population. In Haifa public buses continued to operate on the Sabbath, albeit on a limited scale, a municipal compromise between the demands of the secular population, who wanted to enjoy their free day on the beach and in soccer matches, and the religious minority, who wanted to minimize the public violation of the Sabbath.[27] Elsewhere in the country, Israelis — the vast majority of whom did not own private cars and many of whom could not afford a taxi — had to stay put, walk, or hitchhike.[28]

Debates about public transportation on the Sabbath revealed the persisting gap between the values of religious and secular Israeli Jews. The latter depicted the stoppage of buses on Saturdays as a return to the traditional lifestyle of the sordid small Jewish town in the Eastern European Diaspora, unfit for a modern democratic state and a large, varied and not necessarily wealthy population. A particular difficulty was posed by the need to transport players and fans to soccer stadiums: Saturday was the only free day of the week, and therefore the only day when soccer league matches could be held. The religious Jews, for their part, not only demanded that all public transportation cease on the holy day but also that the bus companies be more precise in terminating service before the commencement of the Sabbath. They scorned the hedonistic Sabbath enjoyed by nonreligious Jews as hollow, meaningless, and worthless.[29]

The bus cooperatives were "national," therefore, not merely because they were state-subsidized and because every price increase required government approval[30] but also in that they upheld public observation of the Jewish Sabbath. They likewise accommodated travelers with special timetables on occasions such as Independence Day and May 1—the international workers' day, celebrated by a large and politically dominant Israeli sector[31]—and provided transport to cultural events such as a week of concerts in a northern kibbutz during the Pesach holiday.[32]

Moreover, ads for Egged often portrayed the country's largest bus company as not merely an efficient transport service but also a central and integral part of the country's history, its landscape, and its national missions. Its buses were illustrated driving amid the typical iconic scenery of new agricultural settlements, dotting a vast virgin land. Egged published its greetings to the Israeli people on the Jewish New Year, Pesach, and Independence Day.[33] In one such greeting from 1950, the text read, "With all the loyal supporters of the state and its founders, we celebrate the third Independence Day, after a two-year journey of Israel to its renewed independence. Hail to the holders of the steering wheel of authority and to all the state's citizens from Egged."[34] Four years later Egged used the same illustration, showing a line of buses driving between waving national flags, with an agricultural settlement in the background, as shown on the opposite page.

This time, however, Egged inserted a different text, commemorating the War of Independence and encasing itself in the tale of unrelenting bravery. Its drivers "have not let go of the wheel" for the past twenty-five years and were among "the breakers of the siege in rough routes." Egged promised to "maintain this tradition and keep serving the country's residents in all ways and at all times," and sent its greetings "to the government of Israel and to the Israel Defense Forces."[35] When advertising new routes to new settlements, Egged assumed an educational national role: "Do You Know the Country?" asked the headline, and the illustration and text provided a detailed description of a new pioneering hamlet, which could now be reached and visited.[36]

Moving from the strategic formal presentation of the bus and its national roles to the tactics of its daily operation, a reconstruction of typical bus trips in 1950s Israel, both longer intercity journeys and internal urban routes, uncovers three main components that molded the experience: the line at the

Egged's 1954 greetings
for Independence Day.

bus stop or station, the physical circumstances inside the bus, and the behavioral patterns of drivers and passengers.

Israelis, who during the years of rationing had to spend many hours in lines for ice and other distributed products, were also forced to waste time in line for the bus, especially in Tel Aviv, Haifa, and Jerusalem. These long bus lines did not end with the termination of rationing, and became a well-known Israeli characteristic, a topic of complaints, cartoons, and jokes.[37] A man, asked why he walked to work, supposedly replied that "I have no time to wait for the bus." Another local joke claimed that the Jews of Iraq would have to wait longer in line before they immigrated to Israel, because rather than fly in airplanes, they would be transported by bus.[38] A jokester said he intended to disguise himself in the forthcoming Purim masquerade as a bus: "How? Simply, everybody will wait for me and I won't arrive."[39] A six-year-old explained to his father that a clock was fixed in the bus station "so that people would know how many hours they wait in line."[40] The slow increase in the number of buses, compared with the rapid increase of the population, was apparent in the length and duration of the lines.[41]

Line at a Tel Aviv bus stop, 1951.
National Photo Collection (Government Press Office), D218-087. Photo by Hans Pinn.

Writing about the cultural history of the automobile in the West during the first decades of the twentieth century, Guillermo Giucci mentions that there were "less glossy aspects of speed: Anxiety, irritation, frustration. Speed left people nervous and grumbling." As the dependency on automobiles increased, stressed travelers reacted to delays and mechanical failures with growing impatience and anger.[42] Israel was no exception. The long wait tried customers' nerves and was aggravated by the heat, the pounding sun (as most of the stops and stations were unroofed), and swarming flies. When buses eventually arrived in urban stops, they were often full and could either take in only a few more passengers or simply continued past the stop. Passengers had to wait for the second or third bus before they managed to squeeze themselves into the vehicle, while the line grew longer. The crowdedness of the line occasioned verbal conflicts and physical shoving, which would reach their climax when the bus arrived and passengers tried to push and elbow their way in. Sometimes people gave up after being "fried in the sun" and either walked to their destination or, if they could afford it, took a taxi.[43] In some cases the line for the bus became a scene of petty criminal activity, such as pickpocketing, or of violence. A policeman in civilian clothes, for instance, was beaten by five youths in Jerusalem after he tried to prevent them from gate-crushing.[44] War invalids, for whom waiting in long lines was particularly difficult, demanded to be allowed into the buses without waiting, but their request wasn't granted.[45] As we recall, serving IDF soldiers were prioritized in bus lines, a privilege that did not go entirely uncontested.

In many cases the strained wait was accompanied either by moans about the bad service, which united the impatient passengers in their shared grievances against the bus company, or by arguments *between* the customers about their place in the line. A journalist described how people in the line protested ("What a nerve! And here people are being roasted in the sun!") when the driver let in some of his friends, according to a widespread local custom, and thus the bus arrived at the station with these favorites already seated.[46] Another journalist related how a crowd of passengers, frustrated by the heat, the flies, and the buses that arrived at the station with cooperative members' "relatives and friends," poured its ire on one bus driver who happened to pass by.[47] Waiting for the bus at uncovered stops on rainy days was also met by complaints and curses, in Hebrew and other languages.[48]

The writer and editor Shlomo Grodzensky, who visited Israel in late 1949 (two years before migrating from the United States with his family), recorded "a taste of waiting on line for a bus" in Tel Aviv's central bus station:

Tel Aviv is most unpleasant in those rush hours. There are many lines of people waiting for buses going to the various colonies in the vicinity. All the antagonisms boiling beneath the surface in this harassed community of many "nations" and languages emerge as you stand on line. A new immigrant, fat, pasty faced, with prominent gold teeth is moralizing to an old Yemenite woman (in a funny Germanized Yiddish) whom she accuses of gate-crashing. The old lady is embarrassed and somewhat helpless at the impertinence of "western civilization." She knows that she has only one advantage over her "white" adversary. "Don't speak Yiddish, speak Hebrew." The new immigrant is slightly ill at ease — but she continues to scold the Yemenite woman. But the latter has her daughter with her — a young woman, authentically Yemenite, but dressed with crude "elegance," lip-sticked and all. She shoots back in self-confident fluent Hebrew, assures the lady rather disdainfully that nothing is further from their minds than taking an unrightful place on the line — and advises her to keep her shirt on. Temporary silence follows. Then the young Yemenite turns to her mother and tells her, in Hebrew, in the loudest possible voice, so that all shall hear a bit of news. A new immigrant was just caught by a

A bus stop in Jaffa, 1949.
National Photo Collection (Government Press Office), D840-022. Photo by Zoltan Kluger.

policeman trying to pick someone's pockets. She adds a few reflections on the Ashkenazim who accuse the Yemenites of stealing—but who are the pickpockets caught by the police? New immigrants. The mother is somewhat frightened by her daughter's boldness but she too mumbles something about the new immigrants, who don't want to work, only to steal.[49]

Whereas studies of social tensions in young Israel tend to focus on Ashkenazi long-timers versus new immigrants from Muslim countries, Grodzensky provides us with a more multifaceted grid: the longtime Israelis in his report are Yemenites while the newcomer is Ashkenazi; the latter may be armed with her self-image as a more "civilized" person, but the former flaunt their seniority in the land and their control of the national tongue, and fight back by employing the stereotype of the new immigrants as unproductive and immoral.

With the arrival of the bus came the peaking of all the tensions in the line. This active, noisy episode could be seen as a transitional phase between the uncomfortable wait in the line and the uncomfortable stay inside the vehicle. A resident of Beer Sheva described the scene thus: "Here comes the heavy bus to the iron rail of the platform, and after an hour's wait the chaos and agony begin: People step on each other's feet, shouts and yells are uttered, the carrying of bags, baskets, tattered suitcases, and so forth."[50]

Often, wrote one journalist, "elbows sharpen whose owners have lost their patience, and regularly clenched fists hit angrily; in some stops the fist-fighter even wins the day." He was astonished to see his own acquaintance push and shout his way into the bus in Tel Aviv's central station. He himself was still standing outside in the line, resigned to waiting for the next bus, when this acquaintance, already seated, talked with him through the window. "That's nothing," he said, "you should have seen how things look in the line for the bus to Lod in the afternoon. There things are not so simple. There you get fists and teeth and sometimes even knives. But one should learn how to get along."[51] Lod (Lydda) was an Arab city conquered by the IDF in 1948 and populated mainly by poor new immigrants from Muslim countries and by Arabs.[52] The account of its bus line as more violent than the standard line (to Jerusalem, in this specific case) reflected Lod's violent reputation.

The central bus station in Tel Aviv was notoriously crowded and hectic.[53] In 1954 a station attendant had a fatal stroke while arguing with a passenger. Drivers from his cooperative reacted violently and had to be controlled by policemen. Egged, which labeled the attendant's death "a murder," closed down its service for a couple of hours during the day of his funeral, despite requests from the minister of transportation not to do so. An investigation later concluded that the attendant had suffered from serious heart disease, as the cooperative well knew, and therefore should not have been employed in such a job.[54] Clearly filling such a role in Tel Aviv's central bus station necessitated strength and good health. Two years later a municipal committee recommended a different approach that entailed filling the post with women: women workers were already doing a good job as cleaners in the station lavatories, and the committee assumed that female attendants could better respond to female passengers, and hoped that customers in general would behave more civilly toward them.[55]

A journalist who was waiting for a bus in Tel Aviv's central station in 1954 described how "the line suddenly stormed forth, like potatoes rolling out of a sack, in a technique known only to the old-timers of the neighborhood." The infuriated driver shut the door in her face, and she was left to wait for the next bus.[56] "I was the first in line," another observer had narrated from the same site two years earlier, "but miraculously, probably due to the beating I had received, I was last to enter the bus. Needless to add, I had to stand in

Depiction of the central
bus station in Tel Aviv by
artist Shimon Tzabar, 1951.
Dvar hashavu'a, February 15, 1951.

the bus. I was unable to pave my way through this noisy and cluttered crowd, using my elbows and my fists, unable to jump daringly over those who stood in line and crawl wondrously to the window seat. . . . But such feats are a daily matter and are not worth mentioning."[57]

The need to wield physical force to ride the bus was treated in a 1952 cartoon showing a woman who comes home and is surprised to see her skinny husband taking boxing lessons from a husky fighter. "Don't be afraid, Rebecca," he calms his wife. "I'm just getting ready to take the bus."[58] That same year, in a Jewish New Year greeting, a newsreel addressed both drivers and passengers, and requested that they mount the buses quietly, patiently, and politely.[59]

Some people, wrote a kibbutz member humorously in 1955, probably suffer from an inferiority complex and therefore claim Israel is a small country. While in their vast countries of birth every train trip could take days, in tiny Israel there are no long distances. Not so, he claimed: one long journey in an Egged bus proved to him that the country must actually be big. Whereas the trip from Haifa to Safed was comfortable enough to allow passengers to read newspapers and catch a nap, they then had to wait until five o'clock in the afternoon for the bus from Safed to Alma, a six-year-old moshav in the upper Galilee. That bus started on its way only at a quarter to six, after the driver, looking very pleased with himself, kept cramming passengers and packages into the already loaded vehicle, and goaded the customers to squeeze themselves in further: "There's still room! Egged takes everyone. Get in, friends. Sir, move on. Come on, a bit more, we'll be leaving soon." Until he finally announced, "Don't come in! Be careful . . . the door."[60]

The overcrowding in the buses, both on long-distance journeys and within the cities and towns, was documented in photographs as well as in textual descriptions.[61] After all the seats were taken, passengers were closely packed in the narrow aisle, crushing not only those who were standing but also the passengers on the seats near the aisle. No wonder the window seats became such a coveted prize, worth shoving, shouting, and hitting for. Why, mused a Jerusalem resident during the years of rationing, is the vendor who overcharges for goods arrested while the bus driver can lawfully sell him, in practice, only half the seat he had paid for and, moreover, risk his life by over-packing the vehicle?[62] A 1951 comic strip titled "The Cello's Progress" shows a man ascending a bus with his cello case, then trying to shield the cello as he stands huddled in the aisle, and eventually descending the bus with a shrunken fiddle-sized instrument.[63] George Mikes wrote humorously: "Buses are small, overcrowded and they never move. The driver has to col-lect fares — as in the United States — and he is busy giving change, handing out tickets and quarreling with people. The buses are so full, in any case, that they would be unable to move even if the driver could spare a few minutes for driving them."[64]

The discomfort of being crammed in was exacerbated by the bus's fierce rocking, sudden halts, and the heavy summer heat. Passengers, who com-plained about the stench of sweat, alighted from the bus "tired, crumpled, and covered by the sweat of the man who stood pressed to me."[65] Bus jour-neys, summarized one journalist, have become utter hell: "People board the vehicle tidy and clean and descend crumpled and filthy, sometimes in-jured by the shoving and pushing."[66] Another journalist decided in 1954 to trust the newspaper's announcement regarding improvements to the trans-portation system and risk a bus journey from central Tel Aviv to a nearby suburb. Alas, the short-distance trip took thirty-six excruciating minutes. Af-ter a long wait and a violent entry, the bus kept collecting passengers along the way:

And the bus, already cramped, screeching and groaning, continued on its wretched voyage like a donkey pulling his yoke. In great comfort — as promised in the newspapers — the thronged passengers sweated, brushed each other, swayed right and left like a living chain with every shake of the bus. Everything went as usual: A nice young man ruined my hairdo with his sack, a babe in his mother's arms left his shoe marks as a souvenir on my skirt, a fat old lady pressed her bag into my ribs, and the flowers I was

An Egged bus in 1954.
Compare this old vehicle
to a local tourist bus in the
illustration on page 39.
National Photo Collection
(Government Press Office),
D534-076.

carrying were almost totally crushed, but who can notice such trifles in these troubled days? Especially as everybody knows that cramped buses are a thing of the past?[67]

Still another journalist described the bus as a craggy, rusty "box" that had probably not been washed for more than a year, and wondered how this stolid box could have won the modern title "autobus."[68]

In 1956 the Tel Aviv sanitation supervisor wrote that uncleanliness in the public buses might become a health hazard, and that bus companies should clean the vehicles' exterior and interior, wipe the doors and windows, the handles and seats, and wash the floor, on which he had occasionally found vomit.[69] The unhygienic nature of bus rides was evident in an ad for a locally manufactured carbolic soap. The illustration showed a rather calm bus interior with a driver, a woman passenger, and a family with a child. Yet the text recommended using the soap "after a long drive, when you return home covered with dust and sweat," since it "cleans the skin well and disinfects it from germs that transmit infectious diseases."[70] Like other Israeli public spaces, the bus was dirtied with the shells of sunflower seeds, eagerly consumed by passengers (the old-time habit of cracking and eating seeds was rationalized during the rationing era, when seeds were praised for their healthful oils).[71] Noise was another aspect associated with the bus, reportedly produced by the drivers and passengers' chatter, as well as the vehicle itself.[72] A bus passenger in Jerusalem related how a particular ride became unbearable because the springtime *khamsin* (hot and dusty wind) was joined by the shuddering, agonizing squeal of the bus's breaks, putting "everybody's nerves on edge."[73]

Some conditions of the ride were reflected in the signs decorating the bus interior, sarcastically portrayed in the *Jerusalem Post* in 1950: "It is symptomatic of their altruism that bus co-operatives should provide ample and comprehensive reading matter gratis to all those who travel in their vehicles. In the front of every bus, there is a notice forbidding passengers to talk to the driver; near to it there is one forbidding passengers to spit and, presumably added to protect him from the unnerving effect of even dumb insolence, there is another, forbidding passengers to stand anywhere near the driver at all." Two other signs were mentioned: one saying "Please step inside the bus" and another advising the passengers not to push their heads through the windows ("appreciating that discomfort may well drive some passengers to desperate if not to suicidal action").[74]

The human factor was, of course, central to the Israeli bus experience. The passengers accused the drivers of behaving badly and vice versa. In fact, the relationship between bus drivers and passengers was sometimes depicted as one of mutual hatred.[75] For the drivers' part, many had been truck drivers for a couple of years before joining the bus cooperatives, and their constant demands for a salary increase were opposed both by the public and, significantly, the Histadrut, which considered their pay quite sufficient as it was.[76] In 1950s Israel, bus driving was considered a secure, well-paid, and hence coveted job.[77] Some complaints about bus drivers focused on crude technical failures, such as shutting a passenger's finger in the door, or on immoral conduct, such as keeping a recovered ring rather than returning it to its owner.[78] "I have seen cattle trucks driven better," wrote a man who once worked in the London transportation system. "I am certain that 90 per cent of the present bus drivers would never pass a London Bus Driver's Test."[79] Drivers were also described as smoking in the bus, although they were supposed to enforce the regulation that forbade the practice.[80]

A young bus driver who announced the final stop in a Jerusalem neighborhood was told by a passenger that drivers on this route usually ended at the next stop. The new driver replied impatiently ("I want those other drivers to come here and tell me so") and then refused to submit his name and driver's number to the passenger.[81] Another driver in Jerusalem refused to repay a customer who changed his mind and descended the vehicle.[82] A bus driver in Tel Aviv shouted violently at one passenger.[83] Another driver couldn't provide the customers with basic information about the route and, when asked about this failing, replied, "It's none of your business."[84] The insolent drivers, concluded one journalist, look down on the passengers from the Olympic height of their seat, and abuse the customers while at the same time demanding an increase in ticket prices.[85]

Rude bus drivers were no novelty but rather an established phenomenon from the prestate era.[86] In 1949 the locally famous author, dramatist, and poet Avigdor Hameiri met a Jew who had just returned to Israel from overseas, where the first reproach he had heard about the young state concerned its bus drivers. Hameiri did not wish to generalize — "I am familiar with some bus drivers who maintain their patience even with our local hordes." Yet most of the Israeli bus drivers, he claimed, are much worse than the infamously coarse wagoner of the Eastern European shtetl. "They sit at their wheels like a contemporary 'Fuhrer,' destined by a bothersome fate to transport a useless live cargo, fit for the garbage." Whenever he ascended the bus, confessed Hameiri, he felt as if he had returned to the Siberian prison camp (where he was incarcerated during World War I) and expected to be treated by the driver like a black slave by a cruel white mistress.[87] One year later a journalist described one such bus driver, who uttered all his orders in a quiet, fatigued, scornful tone:

> Sometimes he turns his gaze and looks angrily at those who huddle and shove behind his seat. His small green eyes try to save his mouth from the angry curses he would like to discharge out of his body. . . .
>
> His serious expression never alters. It has always been, and will be forever, angry at the whole world but particularly at that scoundrel impolite people, that dreadful race of annoying and small-minded busybodies, those prodding ants and kicking mules — the passengers.
>
> This driver of ours has been sitting on his bus "throne" for a quarter of a century. His wrinkled brow and face can tell of years and months, weeks and days, nights and hours of fussing and drudging, serving this despised hurrying bunch. He is beyond amazement. He is beyond irritation or a smile toward one of these detested beings.[88]

If distinguished writers and self-confident journalists felt the wrath and contempt of bus drivers, new immigrants and Arabs were treated even worse. A 1952 bus ride from Tel Aviv to a transit camp was depicted in the immigrants' newspaper as a voyage of strife and offense. All the permanent drivers on this line apparently treated their passengers with disdain, stating that the latter deserved their tattered bus and would have probably felt uncomfortable in a nicer vehicle. On one certain trip, when a passenger inquired after the line's destination, the driver replied, "To the zoo!" Some indignant passengers tried to protest against the insult, but it was a twelve-year-old Yemenite girl who asked smilingly, "So you, mister driver, must be the zoo-

Election posters on a bus in Nazareth, January 1949.
National Photo Collection (Government Press Office), D132-065.

keeper?" The delighted passengers burst out laughing, and the amazed driver could only reply by swearing at them all and continuing to drive wildly.[89]

Natan Hofshi was a Zionist who immigrated to Palestine in 1909 and became a devoted pacifist. In 1954 he wrote of a driver who intentionally misled a middle-age Arab couple when they boarded his bus in Haifa: the driver told the couple they would have to walk "some distance" from the bus stop to their village, even though he knew the distance was actually more than ten miles. The driver cynically told Hofshi that "two Arabs, walking not far from the border in the dead of night," will probably get arrested and beaten by a military patrol.[90]

The drivers, commonly depicted by their clientele as "impolite, rich, monopolistic, and inconsiderate," replied to their detractors that their difficult and demanding task was unappreciated: they had to deal with the passengers' complaints, guard their safety while driving, forbid smoking, prevent passengers from jumping off the running city bus, goad them to make room for those still waiting at the bus stops, and heed countless rings and calls to stop.[91] Treated by the passengers as the only target of their anger and suffering, the poor driver (who served as conductor and supervisor as well as motorist) "reaps all the oaths in the world in all the languages of the world spoken in our multilingual country."[92] The drivers compared their strained relationship with their customers to the lot of Israeli policemen, who themselves had to deal with a heterogeneous crowd from various countries, whose behavior required patience in the short term and education over the long term.[93]

Yet the Dan cooperative, running the buses in Tel Aviv and its vicinity, acknowledged that some steps could be taken to improve the service. Charging "round" figures for tickets rather than amounts requiring small change, for instance, removed much anger and many disputes.[94] Dan's drivers had become infamous for their obnoxiousness,[95] and in 1952 the cooperative publicly announced an "Operation Courtesy" among its drivers,[96] indirectly admitting that such an "operation" was called for. Although complaints against bus drivers neither ceased nor faded, by 1954 they were compared favorably to taxi drivers, who allegedly behaved even worse.[97]

The drivers' characterization of Israeli passengers as difficult came against the nostalgic depiction of the prestate era, when the whole Jewish community in Palestine was homogeneous and, therefore, the driver, who understood all passengers and was understood by them all, could also serve as a fatherly guide. Nowadays, claimed the drivers, due to the ingathering of the exiles and multilingual reality, the driver was expected to understand multiple tongues, customs, and habits. If he did not accommodate all needs and requests, he was shouted at and cursed. The customers, conceded the bus drivers, were absolutely right to complain about overcrowded buses, but the driver too was affected by such grave conditions: his nerves were shot and his desperate cries to squeeze into the bus or to stop boarding were ignored, leaving him frustrated and voiceless.[98] Some customers, maintained the drivers, pestered, nagged, and talked rudely to them.[99] The cursing at drivers (in a variety of languages) that began during the unnerving wait at the bus stop often continued inside the bus. While the drivers screamed or begged the customers to crowd in, the latter, "whose sweaty faces express despair and revulsion, groan and curse the driver, the Dan company, the government and the whole state."[100]

Passengers ordered the driver not only when to stop but also when to drive on, and often argued with him about whether they should or should not enter a full bus and whether it was possible or impossible to fit. Another common dispute concerned the age of children: parents swore that their offspring were younger than five and therefore should not pay for a ticket, whereas the drivers doubted such claims ("Come on, lady, this child is old enough to get married!").[101] Drivers also had to keep an eye on passengers who entered through the back door without paying.[102] Yet not all driver-passenger interactions were quarrelsome. Despite the sign forbidding passengers to talk to the driver, sometimes long and friendly conversations emerged between them, with the driver telling jokes and passengers reading to him aloud from their newspapers.[103]

A particularly common violation on the bus involved disregard for the "No Smoking" sign.[104] A journalist who rode from Tel Aviv to the Jezreel Valley in early 1950 argued with and ridiculed the policeman who ordered him to stop smoking and wrote down his details. As soon as the policeman got off the bus, the journalist and other passengers lit up their cigarettes once again. Why, asked the journalist, do the police trouble with the smokers, rather than deal with more serious flaws in public transportation, such as the overloading of buses, the inability to keep to schedules, or the frequent episodes of "rudeness and brutality"?[105] During the following year the police tried to enforce the prohibition on smoking, but some passengers refused to comply and were arrested. In one case a passenger even beat the policeman who ordered him not to smoke on the bus, and later hit another policeman in the police station.[106]

Police officers sought to enforce other rules aboard the bus. Natan Hofshi, who tried to promote an equal and peaceful coexistence of Arabs and Jews, related in 1954 how he witnessed Jewish policemen removing a twelve-year-old Arab girl from the bus who had forgotten her identity papers, which Arabs under the military rule were ordered to carry everywhere, and sending her back home to Nazareth. The Arab bus driver, one Arab passenger, and the writer himself (interestingly, it was interference by the last that provoked the policeman's anger) pleaded in vain for the girl's sake; the other Jewish passengers in the bus remained "indifferent and impatient," whereas the Arab passengers "sat quietly, forced into silence, but their eyes speaking for them."[107] The bus in this Nazareth–Haifa route included both Arab and Jewish passengers, but the Jewish policemen had more authority than the Arab driver. Hofshi's depiction reveals the inequality engendered by the military rule both in the official technical sense (only Israeli Arabs had to carry their identity papers at all times) and the unofficial behavioral level: the Arab passengers' "forced silence" in this case stands out when compared with the loud protestations and constant grumblings of Jewish passengers under slighter provocations.

If Jewish passengers in Israeli buses clashed with figures of assumed authority—drivers and policemen—they certainly bickered among themselves, especially when boarding, packing into, and getting off the bus. Fat people, who necessarily took up extra space, invoked discernible attention and occasional hostility.[108] Like the exchanges conducted while waiting in the line, conversations inside the bus could express social tensions and take antagonistic turns. In late 1949, in a bus going to Ramle (another Arab city occupied in 1948 and settled with Jewish new immigrants), passengers were conversing and spicing their speech with Yiddish. Among other topics, they complained about the Israeli state and discussed discrimination directed against them. One of the passengers claimed that longtime Israelis and the Sabras grab everything for themselves. "Why don't they give us a few more buses, so we won't have to be crammed in here like in a train to Auschwitz? And why don't they let one of us earn his livelihood from driving a bus?" The conversation was held internally among new immigrants but heard by longtime Israelis who were occupying the same compact space, and sure enough, a young Sabra sitting next to the writer was enraged by the harsh, provocative words. She told her neighbor what she really felt about the new immigrants: she couldn't stand these ugly people, whose appearance was repulsive, who spoke Yiddish and spat in the bus; they seemed to her like "a totally different race"; they didn't wish to adapt to the country but ridiculed and spoiled it instead.[109]

This recorded conversation—actually two parallel conversations—is quite revealing. The new immigrants chose to exemplify their socioeconomic and professional marginalization[110] with the case of bus driving, a desired job "grabbed" by longtime Israelis with ample connections. But longtime Israelis shared compact buses with new immigrants and, moreover, the newcomers' complaints were uttered aggressively and loudly enough, perhaps intentionally, so that longtime Israelis who were present could hear them. The immigrants applied the charged association of the Holocaust by comparing the Israeli bus to a train to Auschwitz,[111] and the young Sabra (a new Jew) reacted by differentiating herself from the newcomers (old Jews) in racial terms. The forceful, unpleasant opinions aired in the bus completely contradicted formal rhetoric concerning the ingathering of the exiles, the melting pot ideal, and the presentation of the Israeli state as a vessel of deliverance from Diaspora wretchedness. Perhaps the informal situation of the bus ride enabled, and the discomfort of the journey prompted, both sides to vent their true adverse feelings. The bus was a space in which longtime Israelis and newcomers, Jews and Arabs, the poor and the middle classes, actually met on a relatively equal footing. Even if the meeting resulted in the emission of mutual hostilities and disappointments, it was—unlike the usual segregated aspects of daily life[112]—an all-Israeli encounter.

Sociologist Irving Goffman notes that in public streets and other relatively open spaces, people at different locations may observe and be observed by a slightly different set of others, while inside a limited space there exists a stronger copresence: people sense that they are close enough to be perceived in whatever they are doing, and consequently have to maintain greater social alertness.[113] The bus, an enclosed public space where travelers have to stay immobile for a while, differs from the street, where mobile strangers momentarily cross each other's path, and is characterized by special performative conventions.[114] Whereas in some cultures passengers in public transportation refrain as much as possible from staring at, speaking to, or conversing with each other, in Israel, as in other Mediterranean societies, passengers tended to communicate freely, without formal introductions.[115]

An account from 1950 details how two or three passengers often represented the core of a conversation, with others listening or throwing in occasional remarks. To begin with, a thin man rose from his seat and complained in Yiddish about the hardship of finding work. A longtime Israeli, a manual laborer who had arrived in the country fifteen years earlier, said that work can be found for all who seek it. He asked his fellow passenger whether he had worked at all during the past decade in the transit camps. Offended, the man showed his scuffed hands to all the passengers, proof he had worked. Meanwhile, a soldier gave the child sitting next to him a big piece from his chocolate bar, and the child's mother, somewhat horrified by the size of the offering, ordered her son to thank the soldier. A red-haired teacher, while speaking about various matters, instructed a youngster sitting between two women with baskets to offer his seat to an old man, and then instructed another young passenger, who entered through the back door, to pay the driver.[116]

Two years later a listener (the term *eavesdropper* is unsuitable, since no attempt was made to maintain privacy) was taken aback by the immorality exposed by the conversations he had overheard on the bus. One young man, trying to impress the girl who sat next to him, boasted of being a smuggler. Two school headmasters carped about the low quality of their teachers. Some members of a kibbutz discussed shoes they had bought without rationing coupons. On this last point, the listener had never expected to hear such words from members of the kibbutzim,[117] who were presumed to provide a national example. In 1956 an Orthodox rabbi suggested replacing chatter conducted in the bus about news, business, and other mundane and petty matters with preplanned meaningful discussions about the Torah.[118]

Sometimes passengers were connected not merely by chatter, whether trivial or meaningful, but more tightly still by the experience of shared laughter. Audible mirth was triggered by deliberate comic utterances or at the expense of fellow passengers.[119] In 1951, for instance, the vowelized Hebrew newspaper, read by new immigrants, tactlessly reported of a man who mistakenly thought the bus had arrived in Haifa, whereas the bus driver had only announced this destination shortly after departing Tel Aviv. This passenger rose hurriedly and was about to exit, but the other passengers burst out laughing: "The immigrant looked around amazedly, and did not understand why people were laughing. Someone explained to him that Haifa is still far away. The new immigrant was embarrassed, realizing that he was the cause of laughter. He went back to his seat with a blushing face." The anecdote, presented as a comic story, was related in simple Hebrew, and some words were explained for the benefit of the readers. It ended with the writer's insensitive conclusion: "This reminded me of one of our [longtime Israelis'] children. When asked if he wants to go to America, he replied, 'No, I don't, because there I'll be a new immigrant.' "[120] Another anecdote regarding linguistic diversity on the bus (and implying the informal language hierarchy discussed in chapter 2) was published that same year:

> A very large-sized Jewish woman enters [the bus in Jerusalem], filling at least one and three quarters seats, if not two whole seats. A Jerusalem Jew looks at her with huge respect and wants to tell her something, but she doesn't understand Hebrew. "I speak," she says, "only Spanish, Ladino, English, French, German, and . . . also Yiddish." This "also" arrives at the very last minute, and generates general laughter. The Jerusalem Jew can finally address the lady who admits she speaks five languages before confessing her "crime" — she speaks Yiddish. . . .[121]

Sociologist Erich Goode defines "casual crowds" as strangers who gather inadvertently in the same place, united only by their physical proximity. Sets of institutionalized rules and normative conventions govern behavior in such places. Goode notes that casual crowds have no prior common identity, yet certain incidents, such as a scuffle, might generate among its members a sense of a common identity.[122] It could be argued that due to the harsh conditions in Israeli buses, some sort of "scuffle" became a daily occurrence and united the passengers in a strange combination of intimacy and resentment. All passengers shared the discomfort of the public transportation, and this bond was further consolidated by joint laughter or by shared displeasure aimed at the driver and the bus company. A clear manifestation of solidarity among bus passengers occurred during the years of rationing. As we recall, the objection to invasive rationing supervision was widespread among Israelis, and so when inspectors boarded buses, looking for chickens and eggs smuggled from the countryside to the cities, many passengers joined in a collective "hens' clucking," thus helping the culprits conceal real chickens.[123]

However, the rough camaraderie engendered in the bus was rarely chivalrous and did not necessarily include the courtesy of offering one's seat to weaker and frailer fellow passengers. Israeli impoliteness, to be discussed in detail in the book's last chapter, was apparent on the bus, where, according to several witnesses, children and young men did not offer their seats to the elderly without explicit requests and goading.[124] Whereas one young journalist described how he himself always felt obliged to offer his seat to older women,[125] another journalist claimed that young passengers didn't give up their seats even to pregnant women.[126] As clearly instructed to IDF soldiers, civil politeness entailed giving up their seats to older people and women,[127] yet in reality an old man was photographed in summer 1953 sitting in the aisle of a crowded bus on a folding chair, which he had brought with him for the ride.[128]

Despite the nerve-wracking, noisy, sweaty, uncomfortable, and occasionally violent experience of riding buses in young Israel, the buses did transport Israelis to their various destinations. On these rides, the passengers were bound by their shared ordeal. As we saw, encounters in the bus could be antagonistic, but they could also be interesting or amusing.[129] Only rich Israelis could bypass the public transportation system and afford private cars and taxicabs. This fact turned the bus into a significant social leveler for the rest of Israelis, a space where residents from different walks of life were jammed together and forced to meet on equal, inconvenient grounds. Whereas certain cars used by Israelis in high positions were luxurious even by American standards,[130] people who had to waste precious hours in the bus line stared at those private cars racing by with a mixture of "envy and rage."[131] Members of the left wing explicitly drew critical attention to the widening gap between private means of transport and the hard conditions of mass travel.

A cartoon titled "Compare the Lines," shown on page 110, was published in 1951 in a newspaper affiliated with a socialist opposition party, and claimed that the harsh shortage in tires unfairly affected only public transportation.[132]

"Compare the Lines."

Exactly two years earlier, a journalist in the same newspaper scolded Israeli civil and military authorities for wasting needed fuel, and praised the labor leader Yitzhak Ben-Zvi, whom he had seen traveling from Jerusalem to Tel Aviv by bus.[133] In 1953 Ben-Zvi was elected as Israel's second president, but maintained his exemplary modest lifestyle.[134] In a state governed by a labor party and promoting an ethos of simplicity, taking the bus could be conceived as a "reverse" status symbol. In 1954, as the economic situation was starting to improve, a journalist writing for a middle-class men's magazine claimed that many passengers who could perhaps afford a "service" cab (a shared taxi following a regular and definite line) prefer the bus nonetheless. He wrote that Israelis regarded taxicabs as "aristocratic" luxuries, a waste of money, a practice that did not suit their class and ideological stance. He also speculated that people were willing to decline the quiet and comfort of the taxi in favor of the noisy company provided by the bus, where one could talk, joke, or argue.[135]

In her research on Norway during World War II, Kathleen Stokker describes how public trams became central in daily life due to the wartime shortage in fuel. Inside the tram Norwegians of all kinds, including Nazi collaborators, unusually mixed company with Germans, generating an array of positive and negative interactions (e.g., solidarity among anti-Nazis, cold shoulders turned on Germans and collaborators). The tram was therefore depicted in local lore as a microcosm and a metaphor of daily life under occupation.[136] Likewise, the bus was a meeting point for "representatives" of almost all Israeli segments, who seldom met in other circumstances. According to sociologist Dan Horowitz, in the 1950s longtime Israelis and new immigrants, with their mutually alien cultures, were extremely disconnected from each other. The notions of adaptation, integration, absorption, and the melting pot became quite meaningless in these conditions of separation.[137] But the bus was, in this respect, an exceptional space: here the hegemonic ideal of ingathering of the exiles was practiced, not necessarily by choice, but on a daily basis.

Rather than blending harmoniously, as depicted on the ideological level, the actual physical meeting of Israelis from diverse backgrounds and different walks of life enabled passengers to express tensions, suspicions, and hostilities. Perhaps Israelis did not melt into a unified whole, as prescribed by the hegemonic doctrine, but the experience shared by bus passengers could be compared to a pot in which various ingredients are steamed together into a stew: while the ingredients retained some of their original, separate, even antagonistic traits, their combination also produced a particular linking flavor. The main features of the Israeli bus experience — discomfort and informality, intimacy and rudeness — thus mirrored the emerging Israeli culture, which differed considerably from the formal ideal of unity and harmony.

In an autobiographical essay Dan Horowitz writes that demographic change due to unselective mass immigration, alongside the ideological transformation from pioneering voluntarism to institutional centralism, altered Israeli society fundamentally. In these new conditions it was impossible to create an original local culture inspired by the prestate pioneering ethos. Still, writes Horowitz, many longtime Israelis felt uncomfortable with these changes and kept hoping that their prestate culture could be perpetuated.[138] Holding on to their initial notions, longtime Israelis maintained a pure, idealized definition of "proper" Israeli culture, and contrasted it with the actual mishmash that was being practiced in daily life. But should we too adopt these prestate idealized notions when looking back on 1950s Israel? Perhaps rather than label the clear-cut ideal as "Israeli" and then deem the messy historical reality, reflected in the bus, a failure of achieving true Israeliness, one could argue that Israeli culture, as it emerged during the first years of statehood, was from the outset a composite mix. Tensions, suspicions, and hostilities were an integral, essential component of this immigrant culture, rather than an accidental, occasional deviation or side effect. They could become a source of aggression and violence but also a source of vitality and fascination.

Thus, despite its many faults, the indelicate bus ride could provide a sort of entertainment. A Beer Sheva bus driver noticed a child who rode on his bus without getting off at the final stop, over and over again. When investigated by the driver, the boy explained that "Instead of going to the movies, I take a trip on the bus. It's very interesting to watch people and to look out of the window, and it also costs less than a ticket to the movies."[139] Replacing the cinema with destinationless bus rides was probably not a widespread practice, yet in the next chapter we shall see that Israeli moviegoing shared quite a few characteristics with the local bus experience.

Going to the Movies

WHEN SNOW STARTED falling in Tel Aviv in February 1950, children ran into a movie theater and threw snowballs at the screen, thus announcing the exceptional weather event to the audience, some of whom rushed out of the cinema to see the wonder with their own eyes.[1]

Movie theaters were prominent sites in Israeli cities. In addition to their relatively large size, these buildings were often located in central squares and along busy thoroughfares. Their yards provided wide spaces for political rallies and public celebrations, and some theaters' interior halls were used for meetings and other purposes.[2] An indirect indication of movie theaters' familiarity was their frequent use as reference points in advertisements for shops, residential buildings for sale, industrial plants, cafés, and hotels, which were described as being "opposite Mugrabi [cinema]," "near Rama movie theater," "in the vicinity of Ofir," and so on.[3]

In the United States during the economic depression of the 1930s, movies were perceived as a daily necessity rather than a mere luxury,[4] and a similar view held in 1950s Israel. According to a 1952 UNESCO report, Israelis were "the world's most inveterate cinema-goers," attending 120 commercial cinemas, including sixteen open-air establishments, with a seating capacity of 79,500 and 1,200 employees. Another one hundred cinemas, funded or subsidized by the Histadrut, were operating in transit camps and other settlements.[5] From April 1951 until March 1952, when Israel's population was about 1.5 million, 21 million visits were counted in the commercial cinemas, including eight million in Tel Aviv, four million in Haifa, and half a million in Jerusalem. In rural areas each person visited the cinema an average of fourteen times a year, "and the average Tel Avivian goes to the movies 21 times a year."[6] Three years later, when the country's population was almost 1.8 million, 23 million visits were counted in 150 movie theaters, not including agricultural settlements, and the number rose to 26 million in the following year. In 1956, on average, each Israeli frequented the cinema sixteen times a year, a figure surpassed only in Great Britain.[7] The popularity of cinema-going

An Israeli snowman outside the Mugrabi cinema in Tel Aviv, February 1950.
National Photo Collection (Government Press Office), D400-048. Photo by David Eldan.

was not a new phenomenon for most Israeli residents. The pastime was also popular among Jews in their various countries of origin and in Mandate-era Palestine.[8]

There were no cinema chains in Israel, and 75 percent of the movie theaters were in private hands; the remaining one fourth were operated on a cooperative basis.[9] In addition to the cinemas from the Mandate era, new movie theaters were gradually established after the state's founding,[10] some by veteran soldiers.[11] In 1950 one cinema in Tel Aviv started all-day ("non-stop") screenings, and several theaters followed.[12] New air-ventilation systems were installed in some theaters, although they were not always turned on during the shows.[13] The first three-dimensional movie was shown in Haifa in 1953, and several commercial cinemas in Israeli cities offered cinemascope movies.[14]

The Cinema Owners Association campaigned for lower taxes on tickets, which at 50 to 100 percent in Israel dwarfed the claimed 25 percent rate abroad. The price of the ticket included governmental income tax, municipal tax, and a symbolic donation for the Jewish National Fund. In Tel Aviv municipal taxes were particularly high, 20 to 40 percent higher than in peripheral towns.[15] Cinema owners struggled continuously with the Tel Aviv municipality over the issue of taxation. When tickets were stolen from box offices, for instance, the municipality refused to return the tax already paid for these unsold tickets. Cinema owners, for their part, distributed untaxed free tickets to theater workers and all their family members, and held untaxed "special screenings."[16] In Jerusalem, where municipal taxation was lower than in Tel Aviv, cinema owners protested against the constant increases in municipal taxes on cinema tickets by closing down the theaters on Saturday evening, the "night out" portion of the week. When the municipality increased the tax levied on movie posters, cinema owners in Jerusalem protested by ceasing to advertise the movies altogether.[17] Strikes were also occasionally held in Tel Aviv, Haifa, and Jerusalem by cinema workers, who demanded higher salaries and better working conditions from the owners.[18]

The cinema maintained its popular appeal during the recession years, as it was cheaper than other forms of entertainment, such as the theater, the opera, or a concert,[19] and could be afforded by even the poorest members of the population.[20] In Israel's major cities (despite the high municipal taxes), a movie ticket cost as little as one third the price of a ticket in the United States or France, and ticket prices were even cheaper in Israeli peripheral settlements.[21] In addition to reduced-price tickets for soldiers, policemen, and students, cinemas sold "austerity tickets" to 10 to 20 percent of the audience. On Independence Day, municipal authorities were instructed to arrange "austerity tickets" for all moviegoers as part of the national celebrations.[22] Thus, even before the economic recovery, Israeli movie theaters were "always crowded."[23] The cinema in 1950s Israel did not have to compete with television, because local broadcasting was launched only in the late 1960s.[24] The cinema drew all kinds of Israelis: "Young male officers with their girlfriends; young female officers with their boyfriends; members of youth movements in their blue shirts; policemen; soldiers. 'Sabra' Hebrew is mingling with Ladino, Yiddish, German, and French. New immigrants are here as are people who have found a restful corner after a grinding day of work."[25]

Yet the satirist Ephraim Kishon, who immigrated to Israel in 1949 from Hungary, described the Israeli movie theater as "a house of horrors." The Israeli crowd, he wrote, probably wants to identify with the heroes of Hollywood films, who cannot embrace their girl before they get themselves shot, their nose broken, and their teeth smashed out ("only their mouth remains intact for the lusty happy-ending kiss"); similarly, Israelis can't squeeze into the cinema unless they first suffer insults, elbows, sunflower shells spat on the back of their necks, and even occasional blows. Kishon mentioned the faulty Hebrew translation and the inconsiderate behavior of the audience, who talk aloud during the movie, bring along their unmanageable children, smoke and singe their neighbors' clothes and hair.[26]

Much could be learned about Israeli society by analyzing the content and style of locally produced films and newsreels, the work of the National Censorship Committee for Films and Plays, and various cultural effects of the cinema; sadly this wide range cannot be covered properly in a single chapter, and the following pages therefore concentrate only on the actual experience of moviegoing, and then briefly consider the general reception of films among critics and audiences.[27] Movie theaters, like the bus, drew Israelis from all walks of life. Yet while people *had* to use public transport for their daily mobility, frequenting the theater was a choice. While the bus experience was associated, at least partly, with the workday, the cinema experience (with the exception of theater workers) was related to leisure. How did these dissimilarities affect behavioral patterns and social interactions?

In 1950 a resident of Tel Aviv, a new immigrant, wondered why one must wait in line for hours to buy a movie ticket. Why not have the option of buying the ticket in advance, rather than only on the very same day and only starting at 3 p.m.? "Our life is difficult enough," he wrote, but some flaws could be amended easily, and entertainment should be facilitated.[28] "The 'queuing urge' is in our blood," wrote a journalist in the following year. "We cannot give up the line even when it could have made our life easier. Most of the movie theaters in Tel Aviv don't take reservations by phone and prefer long lines to extend at their box office."[29] Tel Aviv residents — who had to spend hours in lines for rationed provisions and for the bus — also had to languish in lines on the way to their favorite pastime. Indeed, according to a 1950 witticism, "our minister of rationing prays that our citizens will possess as much patience in the lines for food as they do in the lines for the movies."[30]

We have seen that uniformed soldiers were privileged with special lines for the cinema and with reduced-price tickets. Many young men, according to the cashiers, would join the priority line, claiming they were soldiers or policemen in civilian clothes who had left their identity cards at home. They thus saved themselves a long wait in the civilian line and purchased cheaper tickets.[31] Other customers, as well as cashiers, became skeptical and suspicious, as a 1952 incident shows:

בכל תור ותור ...
עשנו ראודור

Moviegoing was a popular pastime, and therefore a line for a cinema
box office was chosen in 1950 to illustrate an ad for a locally manufactured
cigarette: "In each and every line smoke Raudor." As we saw in previous
chapters, in the early 1950s Israelis had to wait in many lines, but the line
for the movies probably evoked more desirable associations than the
annoying lines for rationed products or the bus. *Ma'ariv*, March 2, 1950.

A rather indignant crowd collected near a Jerusalem cinema a few days
ago. This particular cinema has surrounded the box-office with an elaborate maze of iron railings to keep queue-jumpers in check, and there was
a general uproar when a lithe and agile young man suddenly vaulted the
railings, ran lightly along the section, and dropped right into the front of
the queue by the ticket window. He was quite unabashed, and explained
that he is a war invalid and as such entitled to get his ticket without queuing. A man who plainly didn't believe in miracles asked to see his dis-
charge book, and there it was, the little green book. All that the athlete was
prepared to say was that he did get hurt in the war, but it wasn't his legs.[32]

The line was frequently slowed down when customers paid with large
bills and the cashiers—who simultaneously had to answer the phone in
their booths—took a while to return the change. Customers' arguments
with the cashiers about the location of the seats ("only in the middle") could
also prolong the wait.[33] When cinema owners were asked about the length
of the lines, the chair of their association replied that lines for concerts, such
as those performed by Yehudi Menuhin (the famed American Jewish vio-
linist first performed in Israel in 1950), were much longer than those for the
movies.[34]

Particularly in Tel Aviv, complaints about lines were often documented.[35] Yet given that attending the cinema was a voluntary leisure activity, the lines were not as tense and antagonistic as those for the bus (and therefore could serve as a friendly locus for a cigarette advertisement, as shown on page 117). Still, similarities existed, such as loud arguments about gate-crushing and collective grumbling.[36] And just as the bus passengers moaned not only about the driver or the bus company but rather about the State of Israel in general, moviegoers also accused the government of not taking steps to bring better order to movie lines.[37] Israel's statism and centralism, then, could be manifested not necessarily in the civic voluntarism aspired for and promoted by Ben-Gurion but often in the public's expectation that the state truly take control of every single facet of daily life, including cinema lines.

Since cinema viewing was the most popular branch of leisure in Israel, claimed a 1951 article in a Mapai-affiliated weekly, it was no longer a private matter but rather a public issue, and so the people and the government should "determine and decide its direction, character, and path."[38] This belief in governmental interference and control covered not just the activity of moviegoing but the content of films as well. As we shall see, writers of various political and cultural affiliations demanded the encouragement of proper movies and the censure of improper ones, although views diverged regarding the definition and criteria for propriety. According to these writers, unsuitable and violent movies might harm youths and new immigrants instead of educating them.[39]

By 1956 thirty-one cinemas operated in Tel Aviv, providing 69.6 seats for every thousand residents, while in Haifa twenty cinemas provided 88.8 seats for every thousand residents.[40] This proportion could partly explain why lines were longer and black marketing much more common in Tel Aviv than in Haifa.[41] However, the high demand in Tel Aviv also stemmed from its thriving outdoor culture, a prominent facet of the city since the prestate era.[42] In Jerusalem there were only thirteen cinemas in 1956, providing 59.7 seats for every thousand residents,[43] and yet demand did not exceed supply, reflecting Jerusalem's less lively nightlife.[44] A resident of Tel Aviv who visited a friend in Jerusalem in 1955 said he now visited the cinema every evening: "It's a pleasure to go to the movies in Jerusalem," he claimed, an opportunity to see a film without having to stand in line or to buy overpriced tickets from profiteers.[45]

Although Jerusalem moviegoers did not have to stand in long lines, they did have to face Haredi protests against cinemas, which opened their box offices and started screening movies on Saturday evenings before the Sabbath

Waiting for the second show at the Eden cinema in Jerusalem in May 1950. Many moviegoers, male and female alike, are wearing white shirts, a typical Israeli "Sabbath" (festive) garment. National Photo Collection (Government Press Office), D207-085. Photo by Teddy Brauner.

was over. A violent demonstration in May 1949 was stopped by the police when the religious demonstrators were about to storm the theater. Cinema owners agreed to start the first Saturday shows at 7:30 p.m. rather than 7:15 p.m. but refused to sell tickets in advance on Fridays. Their reasoning sheds light on Jerusalem's sleepy nightlife: the second show, they explained, cannot start too late because the Jerusalem folk go to bed early and the bus service, connecting the city center to its widely spread neighborhoods, ends early too. Jerusalem moviegoers won't buy tickets in advance, claimed the cinema owners, because they tend to decide about going to the movies only at the last moment, namely on Saturday evenings. Since the division of the city in 1948, the cinema owners explained further, local cinemas had already lost their Christian Arab clientele, who used to flock to the movies on Sundays, and therefore they couldn't afford to screen only one single show on Saturday, the busiest day.[46] Religious Jews complained about similar violation of the Sabbath in other cities as well,[47] but Haredi demonstrations and protests, some resulting in arrests, were unsurprisingly held during the 1950s in the Holy City in particular.[48]

In Tel Aviv in particular, moviegoers had been familiar since the 1940s with the lively illegal commerce by profiteers, who obtained large numbers of the much sought-after tickets, lurked around the theaters, and sold their wares for a gain.[49] By the early 1950s gangs of young profiteers, each directing tens of boys, took control of Tel Aviv cinema's entrances. When cashiers spotted the profiteers and refused to sell them tickets in bulk, the gangs could either intimidate them or, alternatively, place several buyers in the line and thus gradually collect a sufficient number of tickets.[50]

The whole profiteering system was based on the demand for tickets, which exceeded supply.[51] A special committee, founded by the Tel Aviv municipality in order to improve matters in the movie theaters, explained that movie tickets were "a popular necessity" and that while the number of theaters in Tel Aviv had remained almost unchanged, the number of customers had doubled from an average of 350,000 per month in 1949 to an average of 700,000 by 1951.[52] A longtime Israeli connected the problem with mass immigration: he speculated that the movies had become more popular than ever because immigrants who did not know Hebrew, and therefore refrained from attending the theater and lectures, flocked to the cinema instead. The "inferior human material" imported with the mass immigration, he claimed, counted those who abhorred honest labor and preferred profiteering, while inflation enabled customers to pay higher prices for these tickets.[53] Whereas the black market in food supplies and clothes was run behind the scenes, profiteering in movie tickets was conducted in plainer sight.[54]

"Like a malignant cancer in a living body," wrote a journalist in 1954, "a cartel of leeches, composed of hundreds of petty criminals, operates in our midst." He had watched the yard of one central movie theater in Tel Aviv from a nearby balcony, and dramatically reported his findings. Two hours before the movie began, he saw the arrival of an "advance party"—a thirty-year-old man, who sat on the stairs singing "an Eastern tune."[55] During the next half hour, more young men—some as young as sixteen or eighteen—came along, and each took a position in the yard like a sentry. When the yard was filled with customers, the local chief of staff, a man with a gray suit, appeared with two deputies and handed a packet full of tickets to one gang member. At seven o'clock the yard became thick with people craving for the movie, willing to pay any price. The gang recognized this "psychological moment" and used it well: the chief of staff commanded doubling the tickets' formal price, and the order was carried out by all the "agents." Suddenly a thirteen-year-old boy passed among the agents and collected all the tickets:

two policemen came along, and the activity had to be hidden for a while. The same boy served as a "bank" for all the gang's profits until "work" was over. Then the gang members gathered in a corner and waited for their "big boss," a lame man forty years of age, who distributed the earnings and used his stick on a member who dared to complain about his share.[56]

Profiteering was slightly reduced after several new movie theaters had opened in Tel Aviv in 1952, helping satisfy demand,[57] but on Saturdays and holidays, or whenever a blockbuster drew a larger crowd and demand increased once again, profiteers were operating as usual. A reporter who was waiting in line to buy a ticket for "an excellent movie" witnessed "a disgraceful sight." A gang of ruffians violently shoved their way to the head of the line, and one of them even hit and cursed at a woman. A seventeen-year-old, trying to protect his place in the line, was beaten by the gang; the journalist pleaded with the crowd to interfere, but "shamefully no one responded. I alone tried to help the boy and was hit as well." The beaten boy, his nose bleeding, had to leave and seek first aid, and when the writer asked bystanders why they had done nothing to help, they replied that the police, too, feared these hoodlums. In the meantime the box office opened and each profiteer bought six to eight tickets. The cashier, when asked by one of the customers why he had sold many tickets to the profiteers, replied that he had been threatened to comply.[58]

Policemen too were quite helpless:[59] when they managed to confiscate some of the tickets from the profiteers, selling them on the spot for their legal price, these tickets—according to the observing journalist—were sometimes bought back by other profiteers. The police didn't have the manpower to watch all movie theaters in the city, and whenever they arrested offenders, the latter were discharged after paying a small fine.[60] When police arrested profiteers who were not former convicts or petty criminals but rather "respectable" clerks and employees, they informed their workplace about the arrest, hoping to deter them and others by public disgrace. In 1956 the police estimated that about sixty profiteers were operating in Tel Aviv, each employing "subcontractors" in the form of young boys, who went about with only one or two tickets at a time. Whenever these boys were captured by the police, they could claim that they had intended to watch the movie but changed their mind, thereafter selling the tickets for their legal price in the presence of the policeman.[61]

As cinema owners, journalists, and the police mentioned, profiteers could only thrive as long as the public collaborated with their illegal activity and purchased overpriced tickets. Moviegoers in Tel Aviv were willing to pay a double sum not only when legal tickets were sold out at the box office but also in advance, in order to avoid the long line.[62] As we recall, the black market flourished during the years of rationing. Orit Rozin writes that Israelis lacked the sense of obligation that was required to sustain the austerity regime of 1949–1951 in conditions of shortage in food, clothing, soap, and other basic commodities. Driven by feelings of deprivation and injustice, and the notion that the burden was not apportioned equally, most anyone who could afford to buy commodities on the black market did so, even if infrequently.[63] The patterns of cinema-going reveal that Israeli consumers were prepared to break the law before, during, as well as after the years of austerity, and not only when they needed basics such as food, clothing, and soap but also when they wanted to watch a hit movie.

If an arriving bus engendered shoving and pushing among the passengers, the opening of the movie theater doors triggered a similar effect among moviegoers. Stormy entrances into the cinema occurred in Jerusalem as well as in Tel Aviv, despite the shorter lines in Jerusalem. Since the doors opened only shortly before the movie started, customers resorted to pushing in order to avoid looking for their seats in a darkened hall after the movie (or the newsreel) had already begun:[64] "One thousand people squash into a two-meter doorway in fifteen minutes: pushing, panting, swearing."[65]

Using the packed entry as a cover, some children and adults tried to slip into the hall without a ticket. Sneaking into the movies was described using one of two Hebrew terms: when depicted negatively, the act was called "infiltration" (*hisstanenut*), echoing the frequent and threatening Arab infiltration into Israel's territory; but when portrayed forgivingly, as a childish prank, it was labeled "stealing in" (*hitfalkhut*), a slang word associated with the Palmachniks' mischievous lore.[66]

When they finally overcame the challenges of the long line and the insistent profiteers, and after they had managed to squeeze themselves into the theater, spectators faced other trials. Whereas smoking was prohibited in the bus, no law or municipal regulation forbade smoking in the cinema. Smokers, who were asked by their neighbors to refrain from doing so out of mere kindness and consideration, did not necessarily oblige.[67] Why, asked a resident of Tel Aviv, doesn't the municipality outlaw smoking in movies and theater shows, as customary in most countries of the world? If Tel Aviv is considered the most cultural and developed city in the Middle East, then surely policemen could roam the hall and fine the smokers.[68] Yet the special municipal

"Fast ones come first . . .
and the more one pushes
the better": a 1954 cartoon
by Yehoshua Edri in the
Cinema Owners
Association bulletin.
*Yediot hitachdut ba'alei
batei hakolno'a beyisrael,*
February 11, 1954, 9.

committee, which tried to improve Tel Aviv movie theaters and discussed the issue of smoking in 1951, remained undecided on the matter and suggested that it be transferred to the Ministry of Health.[69] Smoking was not subsequently prohibited, and posted signs along with a slide projected before the film requesting, but not requiring, the audience to refrain from smoking failed to deter smokers.[70] The unventilated halls thus stank of tobacco smoke, which mingled with the stench of sweat and dust.[71] No ashtrays were provided, and while most people extinguished their cigarettes on the floor (which was covered with cigarette butts, among other things), many Israelis did so on the back of the seat in front of them, leaving ugly black stains.[72] Along with the occasional cigarette burns on clothing, it was rumored that a fire that broke out in one of Haifa's cinemas was caused by an unextinguished butt.[73]

The habit of eating sunflower seeds and disposing of their shells, as discussed in the context of the bus, was also practiced vigorously by moviegoers. The same municipal committee that was indecisive about smoking did suggest banning the eating of seeds in Tel Aviv movie theaters and forbidding peddlers to sell seeds in the cinema's yard.[74] But the provision was widely ignored. A cartoon from 1951 portrayed three ushers sweeping gigantic piles of shells under the sign "No Seeds Allowed."[75] Despite the signs, movies were watched to the sound of cracking seeds and the occasional shell spat onto one's lap.[76] Another cause of disturbance was crying babies, brought to the cinema by their parents, and the racket made by children who entered the theater unattended by adults.[77] Movies were categorized according to the minimum age of viewers, but the age limit was not enforced.[78]

"שיתפקעו להם ! שלמתי בעדן"

"They can stuff it! I have paid for the ticket!": a 1954 cartoon by Yehoshua Edri in the Cinema Owners Association bulletin. *Yediot hitachdut ba'alei batei hakolno'a beyisrael*, February 11, 1954, 10.

According to frequent complaints, many moviegoers arrived late, after the show had begun, and disturbed those already seated. They came in noisily, stepped on people's feet, and blocked their view. In the dark, arguments erupted when latecomers accused others of sitting in their designated seats, and the ushers had to be called to settle the matter.[79] In 1950 the police arrested two young men who had climbed on their chairs and started booing imperialism when the newsreel presented pictures from the Korean War; then they fought with the ushers who tried to remove them from the theater.[80] Yet most of the whistling and shouting in the cinema had nothing to do with political convictions. That same year, for instance, a particularly shabby and inexpensive Tel Aviv cinema was described as a place where "if you saw a friend or an acquaintance on the other side of the hall, you could climb on your chair and send him a Tarzan call"; if you felt bored, you could shout out a joke or a complaint; when the figures on the screen were in a fight, you could "encourage" them loudly along; and when the couple in the film kissed, you could whistle by putting two fingers in your mouth.[81] During the next years this "mischievous atmosphere" became a norm in many Tel Aviv cinemas, especially whistling and cynical cries during romantic scenes.[82]

The thin line between mischievousness and hooliganism was apparently crossed quite often. In that same shabby, inexpensive Tel Aviv cinema, which also served as a stage theater, the young audience for a children's movie amused itself behind the stage by smashing the props and tearing apart the costumes of a theater company.[83] In another cinema, pranksters poured sewage water into the cashier's booth. There were cases of fires set in cinemas, upholstery cut, seats and windows smashed. The sanitary conditions in many cinemas were poor. In addition to floors littered with cigarette butts, seed shells, sticks from ice cream bars, remains of sandwiches, and the like, "writings of a familiar type" covered the walls of filthy bathrooms, from whence lead pipes were stolen, and people would also urinate in the cinemas' backyards.[84]

When the 1948 film *Louisiana Story* was shown in a Tel Aviv cinema on a Saturday night in 1952, a group of youths demonstrated their boredom and objections by making a violent racket. The show was stopped, the tickets refunded, and the next feature of the movie canceled. Remarkably, the editor of one of the daily newspapers applauded the event as a turning point: the Israeli audience had revolted against the "specialists" — critics and cinema owners — who tried to force-feed it an "indigestible" film.[85] The rival daily, on the other hand, strongly objected: "Yawning is allowed, but breaking seats isn't, and an artistic movie should not be canceled under the terror of uncivilized people." If the police won't put such behavior under control and protect "quiet and disciplined moviegoers," quality films would no longer be imported and screened in Israel.[86] Playwright, translator, and critic Nissim Aloni wrote that the local rejection of an excellent film, which was received enthusiastically in Europe, was a sad testimony to the monopoly of Hollywood films in Israel. He claimed that the youths' belligerence in the cinema was itself an imitation of Hollywood movies, in tandem with their imitation of American dress, manners, and speech.[87] It should be mentioned that in the United States too, even after behavioral norms were consolidated in cinemas during the 1930s and adults thereafter regarded loud talking as a rude disturbance, children and youths still challenged these norms and followed different and noisier conventions.[88]

Back in Israel, cinema workers sometimes had to deal with physical violence, such as when a cashier's window was smashed by an angry customer or when customers pushed or beat the ushers, many of whom were war invalids. The police were occasionally summoned, but they themselves were not immune to beatings.[89] Even when not attacked physically, cinema ushers (each serving 250 customers) could hardly control the stream of pushing and shoving viewers. When moviegoers arrived late, everybody blamed the ushers: those already seated, for having to rise again after the movie had begun, and the latecomers, because the ushers took too long to guide them to their seats in the dark.[90] Cinema owners described the ushers as the gentle victims of rude customers,[91] but Israeli service professionals — as we have already encountered in the example of bus drivers — were not given to politeness. A Warner Brothers executive who visited Israel in 1953 mentioned that the ushers looked unkempt and, along with the cashiers, showed little civility to the customers.[92] That same year a customer complained about a cashier who ate a sandwich while tossing him his ticket and change, and when he asked for a seat in the middle of the hall, the cashier yelled and cursed at him.[93] Hence, when a new cinema was opened in Tel Aviv in 1955, it promised the audience "particularly courteous ushers" as one of its advantages over other cinemas.[94]

In addition to sophisticated equipment, air-ventilation systems, proper acoustics, and an intimate atmosphere, the owners of this new movie theater declared, "The ushers will wear special uniforms, and will behave graciously rather than in the 'typical Israeli' manner. The owners believe that in this way, the audience too will be educated to respect the cinema as a cultural institution."[95] Despite the quotation marks, it is evident that seven years after the founding of the state, "typical Israeli" manners were already consolidated as a recognizable trait. In moviegoing as in other fields, Israeli misbehavior was now and then presented as a side effect of the mass immigration. In 1951 the cinema owners in Tel Aviv wrote to the municipality, "Regrettably, the behavior of the audience has deteriorated lately, and violence has increased. Movie shows cannot be run smoothly without some sort of serious disturbance or other." Cinema workers couldn't control the wild behavior of the audience without new legislation and tighter supervision by the police.[96] The municipal committee that tried to address the problem concluded that the situation had worsened during the "past two years of mass immigration. Today's cinema-goer does not get the impression that he is visiting a cultural institution, among a cultivated audience with fine manners as customary abroad." The situation had become unbearable, agreed the members of the committee: it robbed audiences of the pleasure of moviegoing and "might disgrace our city in the eyes of visitors from abroad."[97]

Until 1953 Hebrew translations did not appear in the film itself; rather, separate handwritten translations were projected alongside the film by a different machine, hand-rolled by a separate operator. Moreover, the employees rolling the translation often either knew no Hebrew or did not know the language of the film (or, as some suspected, were merely negligent). Therefore, the writing did not match the scene, "and the audience witnesses the operator's desperate attempts to correlate the two, as the translation 'jumps' up and down jerkily."[98] This lack of synchronization was a hallmark of Israeli moviegoing in the early 1950s. Understanding the movies' plots could become quite a challenge, and whenever the translation on view did not fit the action on-screen, the audience whistled or shouted the roller into order ("What about the translation?!").[99] Comprehending movies became easier after synchronized translations were printed on the film, but this technique was more expensive than its predecessor and was only adopted by all film distributors after a few years.[100]

The translations themselves were also sometimes deficient. They could include spelling errors and grammar mistakes; foreign terms either left as they were, albeit in Hebrew transliteration, or translated inaccurately; and informal language and local slang used improperly and inappropriately.[101] As early as 1949, the Censorship Committee demanded checking the translation before approving a movie, "due to the faulty Hebrew in some translations." When the committee discovered a translation that was "even more flawed than usual," it sent its comments to the translator. According to the committee, a poor translation not only disrupted comprehension of the film but also might instill mistaken Hebrew among the masses.[102] Involvement by the Censorship Committee extended to the translation of titles, with the committee's aim of achieving precise and correct language often clashing with cinema owners' and film distributors' desire for catchy and appealing titles to draw in the crowds.[103]

When the chair of the Cinema Owners Association enumerated the benefits of moviegoing, he included hearing Hebrew in the narrated local newsreel and reading Hebrew in the films' translations.[104] Moviegoing was supposedly aiding the national mission of spreading Hebrew among new immigrants. However, reading a translation while viewing a film requires sufficient control of the language, not to mention basic literacy, whereas hearing a new language might be easier; therefore dubbing, though more expensive, would probably have been a translation technique friendlier to Israeli new immigrants, as suggested by one municipal education department in 1952.[105] Relatedly, a study conducted in Latin America in the previous decade found that people from higher classes preferred written translations for movies, whereas people from lower classes preferred dubbing—with the study explicitly drawing a link between class and education level.[106] Although no parallel research was conducted in Israel, it is likely that written translations (even when finely executed and synchronized) did not provide a sufficient tool for those Israelis who could neither understand English nor read Hebrew.[107] Most members of Israel's lower classes resided not in the central towns but rather in the country's periphery, where moviegoing was equally popular though less accessible.

In 1952 some entrepreneurs suggested opening new movie theaters in Israeli towns, in line with the demographic impact of mass immigration. In particular, thirteen settlements and immigrant camps with more than four thousand people each had no cinema at all, and twelve more towns and settlements required a second or third movie theater. Providing cinemas for new immigrants was imperative "for our country," wrote the entrepreneurs; the immigrants were fed and dressed, but in times of want, popular entertainment was as important as food and dress, if not more so.[108]

Some of the characteristics of moviegoing, as we have viewed them in the central cities, appeared in various forms in smaller towns too. Every now and then, complained a resident of Beer Sheva, as one enters the cinema, which "today is the only entertainment site in town," one might witness how the violent people enter and grab the seats first. "Anyone who comes in later is told, 'This seat is already taken, pal!' You see a young man, sturdy like a tree, sitting along a whole bench, not allowing anyone else to sit next to him, which naturally leads to arguments and fights." The municipal secretary reassured the complaining lady that the present cinema owners had promised to mark the seats on the tickets and, besides, a new, spacious and sophisticated cinema was being constructed in town.[109] This new theater, with one thousand seats and an air-ventilation system, was advertised as "the grandest cinema in the Negev."[110] Since the Negev was the least populated region in Israel, and since the older movie theater in Beer Sheva resembled — according to witnesses — the shabbiest cinema in Tel Aviv,[111] "the grandest cinema in the Negev" wasn't facing much competition. Like movie theaters in larger and more established cities, Beer Sheva's cinema was used as a local point of reference.[112] In 1952, after the previously mentioned incident over *Louisiana Story* in Tel Aviv, a journalist praised Beer Sheva moviegoers: when the only movie theater in town showed a 1924 Soviet film, which the audience disliked, people left the cinema slowly and quietly, "without whistles and scandals." The film was not shown again and was replaced the next day by an American movie. "The 'civilized' people of Tel Aviv," concluded the writer, could learn how to behave from the residents of the remote Negev.[113]

Moviegoing in the periphery could have its specific problems and unique lore and atmosphere. Commercial cinemas in small towns, numbering three to four hundred seats and conducting only three to five screenings each week, struggled to survive.[114] The "summer clock" (Israeli daylight time) affected the whole country, of course, but smaller towns, where movies were often shown in open-air cinemas, were more affected by the later time of sunset.[115] In the northern town of Nahariya, for example, the single cinema was open-air, operating solely during the summertime. A resident described it as the town's regular Saturday night entertainment. Many attendees brought a cushion to the cinema to pad the hard seats. The lights were turned off only after the latecomers arrived, and there was plenty of time to check out who was there and say hello to acquaintances, as was customary in a small town where many people knew one another. She portrayed a gentleman who translated the whole movie into fluent Yiddish for the sake of his partner, although the man's "fantastical" translation suggested he knew little English. The projector, meanwhile, often broke down, causing interruptions. With the lights turned on, a record played and the audience chatted, along with offering advice to the technician who was trying to fix the projector. Sometimes, when the hitch was serious, the price of the ticket was refunded and the audience returned home.[116]

The Israeli periphery wasn't merely a matter of geographical location but also one of socioeconomic class and status. Thus Jaffa, formally annexed to Tel Aviv in 1948, remained, in fact, a poor town populated by Arabs and new immigrants. Movie theaters in Jaffa and other disadvantaged neighborhoods in Tel Aviv's proximity were therefore called "type B cinemas." They were patronized by new immigrants and the poor, "whose resources are scarce, whose education is limited, and whose social habits completely differ from those of the longtime inhabitants." As a result, the owners of the cinemas in these locations "faced special problems."[117] When a bus arrived in Ramle in late 1949, a reporter heard the following exchange:

> So what do we do tonight, Moshe?
> Tonight? Let's buy some pistachios and go to the movies, right? I'll wait for you near the Ghetto (as the Jews of Ramle call the Arab quarter).[118]

Seven years later the four cinemas of Ramle were portrayed as deficient by a resident who worked as a radio technician: unventilated (a lone ventilator wasn't operated during the shows because it made too much noise), cramped, with very bad acoustics and sound equipment. In two of the cinemas, thirty-six-millimeter projectors were the cause of "at least two breaks" in each movie, and in the cinema that did have a proper projector, the owner also owned the café, and therefore breaks were intentional and particularly long. In one theater the seats squeaked, in the open-air cinema a woman had recently been bitten by a snake, and the third cinema was known as "the flea cinema." In all four cinemas, complained the resident, whenever the

Soldiers at the cinema in Sderot, a development town in the western Negev, in August 1955. National Photo Collection (Government Press Office), D369-056.

translation was not printed in the movie synchronically, the film and the side translation were in a "constant race" with each other.[119] Whereas some of these conditions resembled those in the central cities, others (smaller projectors, the occasional snake) carried a peripheral flavor. The regional health department checked the resident's complaint and replied that all four cinemas in Ramle met legal requirements for both sanitary conditions and security. While objecting to the insult "flea cinema," it consented that many technical and structural conditions were "far from ideal" and that there was room for improvement. Still, things were not too bad "if we take into account Ramle's development in comparison with cinemas in wealthier cities."[120] Rather than adopt a single high standard, the authorities seem to have expected peripheral cinemas to reflect peripheral inferior conditions.

While the radio technician from Ramle was dissatisfied with a thirty-six-millimeter projector, many Israelis had to do with a sixteen-millimeter one. A "mobile cinema" was operated in numerous kibbutzim, new settlements, and transit camps, mostly organized by the Histadrut.[121] Sixteen-millimeter projectors were also used in army camps, as an article titled "The Cinema Comes to the Camp" portrayed humorously in 1949. The camp was swept by excitement when a notice announced the showing of a movie at 8 p.m.

At 7 p.m. soldiers started gathering in the hall, bringing with them chairs from the canteen, crooked benches from the dining hall, and so forth. At 7:30 they were seated, cramped and expectant, and started to crack seeds ("whose shells you could find on the floor but mostly in your collar") and eat dubious canteen sweets. At eight o'clock, with still no signal from the movie opera-tors, the sound of impatient whistles "reached the enemy lines." At 8:30 the tensions peaked when the movie operators arrived with some strange instru-ments, only to realize the amplifier was compromised. At 9:30 the amplifier was fixed and the movie began. Alas, the first two scenes were missing, prob-ably lost sometime during the film's travels "in the past few decades." Then the celluloid tore exactly when the couple was about to kiss, and later the amplifier broke down again. When the celluloid tore for the second and third times, the narrator lost his patience and left the hall.[122]

As we remember, the army performed not only military functions. Israel's southernmost settlement, Eilat, was conquered by the IDF in March 1949, and until 1956 its growth and development as a town were slow. The army pro-vided all the "cultural activity" in Eilat for both soldiers and civilians, includ-ing a couple of movies each week. In 1952, when the army stopped providing these services, "a permanent civil arrangement" was organized instead.[123] Eilat was seen as Israel's ultimate periphery,[124] but even there movies were regarded as a necessity, to be delivered either by military or civilian sources.

Residents of new neighborhoods and settlements with no movie theaters traveled to nearby towns to see a movie,[125] but in some cases cinemas were hard to reach. Then, films were preselected and shown for a minimal price by the Histadrut. In addition to commercial films, new immigrants were shown publicity films about the country or educational films about sanitation. In sites with no electricity, generators were employed, "as long as the immi-grants can enjoy an entertainment that everybody likes."[126] Affiliated with the ruling party, Mapai, the Histadrut used the movies as an educational and indoctrinating tool in the transit camps and in Arab villages.[127] A Histadrut screening in the rapidly growing Arab village of Tamra in July 1956, for exam-ple, included both propaganda for the Workers Union and the State of Israel in Hebrew and then some films in Arabic. These Arabic films included a chil-dren's movie, a local newsreel, a short lecture, a color film about baby care — along with a film in French about Independence Day in Israel — and finally a film about "Djoha and the camel."[128]

By the end of the decade, seven cinemas were operating in the Arab towns, screening mainly films from Egypt (films in foreign languages were not translated to Arabic).[129] Arabic movies also attracted Jews. Three years after the Censorship Committee ruled that Arabic films could be screened only in towns populated by Arabs, cinema owners protested that Jewish Israelis who spoke Arabic composed the majority of the audience for Arabic movies, but had to make long and arduous journeys to the towns where Arabic movies were screened. It would be more sensible, argued the cinema owners, to disallow the screening of Arabic films among the *Arab* Israeli population, who "feed on the Arab nationalism exhibited in these Egyptian movies," whereas the Jewish audience enjoyed the movies' "amusing aspects."[130] The cinema owners were probably concerned mainly about the loss of potential customers, and their wish wasn't granted, but their appeal reflects the widespread craving for Arab culture among Jewish immigrants from Muslim countries.

A war invalid founded a company for screening movies in the transit camps and new settlements in the Jerusalem vicinity, and a depiction of one such event in the Beit Shemesh transit camp underlines the widespread image held by longtime Israelis of Ashkenazi descent of new immigrants from Muslim countries. In the first show the founder couldn't stop residents of the transit camp from streaming into the hall without tickets; the few who did buy tickets shouted and demanded that the movie be screened. When he told his friends in Jerusalem about the incident, a whole group, headed by a friend of his named Jacob, joined him in the transit camp the next evening. Hoping to see yet another movie for free, the camp residents tried to sneak in again. One attempted to use a ticket from the previous night, and when Jacob, performing the roles of usher and guard, found him out, the conniver swore that the ticket was valid, "on the life of my father and mother." Jacob, "who knows the customs of the new immigrants," asked him whether he was willing to swear on the Torah, which the man would not do. The movie started, but unfortunately the generator broke down and the screening stopped. After an hour and a half, with the generator still out of order, the audience started yelling and demanding their money back. Jacob suggested they sing. "We don't want Shiknezi songs!" cried someone ["Shiknezi" being the distorted pronunciation of the word "Ashkenazi" and a derogatory term]. Jacob consented and started singing a well-known Arab song: "Within a second all the audience joined the chorus and even danced the hora to the song's rhythm. One of the transit camp folk said: 'For the life of me, this is better than any movie, to see a Shiknezi singing and dancing like one of us.'"[131]

The hero of the piece, Jacob, was presented as someone whose familiarity with the new immigrants and their culture enabled him to outsmart them.

The immigrants were portrayed as devious, aggressive, primitive, and religiously superstitious. The sketch also illustrates the new immigrants' unwillingness to comply with and adopt the culture of longtime Israelis, as manifested in their songs.[132] Although it ends on a happy note, the evening can be seen to reflect the deep schism that existed between "Shiknezim" and "us."[133]

After reconstructing the conditions of moviegoing in the main cities and in the periphery, we might wonder why, despite its numerous aggravations, Israelis kept flocking to the cinema? The answer is manifold, encompassing the low price of the tickets, the lack of television, and the escapist role of the movie theater and the movies themselves. The chair of the Cinema Owners Association summed up the situation in 1955: For people who cannot afford expensive tickets to the theater, the cinema "is their only entertainment. It is their sole window to the big world" and it provides them with an opportunity to escape "the confinements of a narrow shed."[134] In addition to its cheaper price, the cinema was less demanding than the theater, a lighter diversion that required less formality and effort from the audience.[135]

The negative effect of television broadcasting on the popularity of moviegoing, first in the United States and then in Italy, France, and Great Britain, was well known in Israel, which immediately saw similar results when it finally launched its television broadcasting in 1968.[136] Back in the television-less postwar 1950s Israel, however, cinema played a role similar to that in the pre-TV United States, especially during the Great Depression.[137] Noting this similarity in 1955, a journalist wrote that in a poll of five hundred youths, 90 percent claimed moviegoing was their main form of entertainment, and not necessarily due to any interest in the film itself. Ninety-three percent were embarrassed to host friends at the humble and crowded abodes of their parents, and so "the dark hall [of the movie theater] fed their hunger for intimacy" and allowed them to escape reality.[138] For adult Israelis as well as youths, movies provided a diversion from daily hardships and concerns.[139]

As for the escapist content of the films, the attitude of the critics and the audience differed. During the 1950s dedicated cinema connoisseurs established a national association, the Advocates of Quality Films, with local film clubs in different cities and towns.[140] Their aim was to "nurture quality films and infuse them into the wider public."[141] Small experimental cinemas began to operate in Tel Aviv, and an annual film festival was held in Haifa.[142] Film critics and other members of the cultural elite continuously criticized the low quality of most movies shown in Israeli cinemas; they made a distinction between artistic films (mainly European) and commercial films (mainly from Hollywood) and blamed cinema owners for picking less artistic movies in order to draw larger crowds.[143]

Unlike the critics, cinema owners were unsurprisingly more attuned to public demand. One cinema owner claimed it was the audience, rather than the cinema owners, who determined what was chosen and screened. All the artistic movies, especially those from Europe, were commercial flops and lost money for the theaters (unless they included an attractive actress or sexual content). The owner claimed that cinema owners were not greedy tradesmen, as suggested by the movie critics; they too were advocates of quality films and would have preferred to screen better selections, but economically this was simply unviable.[144]

Indeed, when it came to their favorite leisure activity, many Israelis, who clearly preferred Hollywood-made movies, did not adopt the aesthetic prescriptions of the elite.[145] American movies were not only cheaper to import than European movies,[146] they were also more appealing to the wider Israeli audience. About 80 percent of the movies shown in Israeli cinemas were American, while the rest were imported from Europe (France, Britain, Italy, and the Soviet Union) and some other countries. The preference for Hollywood movies was reflected plainly, for example, in public questionnaires run by local movie magazines.[147]

The choice of seemingly unworthy movies was occasionally explained as related to the unselective nature of the mass immigration. As we recall, the new immigrants were viewed as the main source of unruly behavior in the movie theaters; similarly, they were identified as those requiring low-quality films. When a socialist journalist asked a cinema owner why he showed only bad crime movies, the latter replied, "Our cinema hall is usually filled with new immigrants who can't read Hebrew and do not understand the content of the movie. They should be given something with a policeman chasing a robber and the like." Ignoring the explanation, the journalist announced in his piece that cinema owners should nonetheless choose better movies. "After all," he wrote indignantly, "the cultural demands of the Israeli public differ from those of moviegoers in Jordan, Honolulu or North African countries!" As for moviegoers who can't read Hebrew, the journalist suggested they be introduced to good movies and aided by a plot synopsis, to be distributed in a low-cost program at the theater entrance.[148] As mentioned in the previous chapter, many longtime Israelis maintained an idealized definition of "proper" Israeli culture, and were slow to fully grasp and accept the changes occurring after the founding of the state. Hence, the socialist journalist's suggestion of distributing written programs was impractical, and his assumption regarding the superiority of the "Israeli public" was unfounded in a country absorbing mass immigration from some of the very countries he snubbed. His comments expressed a confused desire to tend to the needy masses and protect them from allegedly exploitative cinema owners, while lacking sensitivity to the actual needs of the masses and showing a strong, though not necessarily conscious, reluctance to acknowledge the cultural changes that had taken place in Israel.

Still, the critics' disregard for widespread preferences was not aimed solely at the new immigrants, nor was it unique to Israel. Israeli journalists and movie experts lamented the failure to disseminate quality films among the wider public, youths in particular, and considered popular Hollywood movies culturally and morally destructive. There is simply no demand, they carped, for movies that do not include "murder, robbery and some erotic enticement."[149] We can find similar rifts between cultural elites in Britain, France, and Italy, who favored artistic films, and the wider popular demand for Hollywood fare. Yet in the European states just mentioned, the struggle also involved protectionist measures to safeguard national films industries vis-à-vis American imports,[150] whereas the Israeli film industry was only taking its fledglings steps, and therefore its anti-Hollywood effort was not justified in economic or patriotic terms. Rather, it was part of the overall hegemonic assumption regarding the educating role of the state, and reflected the cultural elite's attempts to maintain its standards and influence.[151]

Israeli critics slighted American movies and their popularity even as they recognized that the cinema provided an escapist break, whereby the viewer "was transported for two hours into a wondrous world, oblivious to the gray reality of daily life."[152] It should be clarified that while in American English the word *escapist* is associated positively with entertainment, fantasy, and relaxation, its meaning in Hebrew was negative and implied evading action and shunning responsibility.[153] One left-wing writer channeled his pro-Soviet and anti-American political views into a claim that cheap American movies should be forbidden in Israel, given rising rates of crime and the mass immigration from "backward countries." The film industry, he wrote, was a "dream factory," taking advantage of people's yearning for superficial entertainment and star worship. Indeed, the cinema had such a huge appeal because it generously offers the viewer "thrills and illusions, illustrates matters and plots beyond his imagination, allows him during his one hundred and twenty minutes inside the darkened hall to sail away, to watch spectacles and enjoy performances of all sorts, mainly those of an entertaining nature."[154] While acknowledging these powerful effects of the movies, the writer viewed them unfavorably, regarding diversions and distractions as signs of cultural (and perhaps political) weakness that must not be indulged.

Whether driven by left-wing ideologies or mere elitist uprightness, most critics did not condone, and certainly did not sympathize with, the escapist facet of moviegoing, which was so central to 1950s Israel. While the audience simply ignored the cries of the critics and kept quietly consuming "the viewpoints of several people in Hollywood,"[155] explicit antielitist objections were rare. We can view the violent racket during the 1952 screening of *Louisiana Story* in Tel Aviv as an expression of popular discontent. Indeed, as we recall, the editor of one daily described the incident approvingly as a revolt against the enforcement of "indigestible" films by critics and cinema owners.[156] Eight months later the same editor, who had been attacked for "encouraging hooliganism," defended his viewpoint vigorously: the audience has a right to express its opinions, whether the "managers" like this opinion or not. In Italy and Russia, he wrote, which are both cultured countries, audiences often voice their criticism loudly. Only here in Israel the audience receives no respect, regard, or consideration; it is treated as a herd with no rights, apart from the right to obey its uninvited monitors. In any other country, he added, the audience would have torn apart such conceited "preachers," who try to enslave the public's spirit.[157] The feisty editor was a Revisionist, and his words reflected his opposition to Mapai's domination, but beyond partisan considerations, he challenged the widespread hegemonic assumptions regarding the educating duty of the leadership.

A year earlier, in 1951, one of the local movie magazines dared publish a milder criticism of the critics. Rather than presenting a direct attack, the writer treaded cautiously by quoting American critic Edith Lindeman,[158] who claimed that different audiences have different needs. The housewife, for instance, seeks a diversion from her troubles, and the movies should offer her unpretentious perfection. Perhaps, added the local writer gingerly, Israeli critics too should heed Lindeman's advice and remember that different movies might appeal to different audiences, according to their varying needs, tendencies, and expectations.[159]

In 1949, when one critic atypically admitted the escapist pleasure he himself took in a movie, he did so apologetically though feelingly. Reviewing the 1946 Hollywood musical drama *I've Always Loved You*, he mocked the inevi-

table happy ending and criticized the implausible plot and the mediocre act-
ing. However, he wrote, "despite all these flaws, as you sit in the hall you do
not wish to be harsh on this movie." The directing is superb, the colors are
natural, and the music sounds like crystal—"all this blends into something
beautiful and wonderful, delighting the eye and the ear. And how starved are
our eyes and ears!" We live in ugly identical houses, some of us live in sheds,
the streets are dirty, and everything is treated pragmatically. And yet "the
heart craves beauty. The people crave beauty, spectacular colors and eternal
music, which vanquishes, even for a short while, the grayness of our daily
life and gives us the will to live on."[160] Despite his better intellectual judgment, this critic experienced something most Israeli critics, like their European colleagues,[161] ignored or refused to accept: many moviegoers were not
particular about artistic nuance, and Hollywood movies were best suited to
entertain them and divert their minds from reality for a while.[162] As this lone
critic noticed, entertaining diversion could energize viewers and thus could
help them face reality, rather than avoid its responsibilities.[163]

While the critics' displeasure with Hollywood dominated the newspapers
and was rarely challenged openly, even Israelis who accepted the elitist cinematic viewpoint in principle often opted in practice for diverting American
movies.[164] Certainly the goal of the Advocates of Quality Films (to spread
artistic films among the wider public) wasn't achieved. Furthermore, a critical and discerning attitude toward the cinema became an exclusive mark of
distinction for the elite. By 1952 a reporter had already noticed two distinct
types of moviegoers: a short line of people "who look like intellectuals, officials, and professionals" gathers at the cinema showing "refined and classic"
films, whereas the cinemas showing popular films attract much longer lines.
The people in the latter "seem to possess a lighter attitude, a simple joie de
vivre, and less intelligence." They are mostly builders, drivers, tradespeople
and industrialists, as well as "people who would not reveal their occupation."
Predictably, the reporter added his concerns about the fate of quality movies in Israel, because intellectual moviegoers were "a miniscule minority."[165]
And whereas members of the organized youth movements looked down on
American movies as worthless and hedonistic middle-class entertainment,
the salon youths adored Hollywood movies unreservedly and tried to imitate them in their own dress and lifestyles.[166]

Whether they watched artistic or popular films, Western or Egyptian
movies, Israelis went to the cinema to fulfill their aesthetic and emotional
needs, notwithstanding the numerous inconveniences. When he described

"Motkeh Hangs Out
in the City," by Dan.
Publication of Dan's cartoons
in this book are courtesy of
Lotti Gelbert.

מוטקה מבלה בעיר...

the Israeli cinema as "a house of horrors," Kishon concluded sarcastically: "Why, of all places, shouldn't we infuriate and be infuriated in the movie theater?"[167] He thus insinuated that fury was common practice in all other areas of Israeli life. Although attending the cinema was neither as uncomfortable nor as tense as riding the bus, quite a few resemblances nonetheless emerge between the necessary form of transportation and the chosen pastime, ranging from the disorderly long lines to the impatience and impoliteness of workers and customers alike. Living in constant fury and enduring inconvenience, even while whining about it, became an Israeli norm that enveloped both work and leisure. The movies — cheap, at the time unrivaled by television, and delightfully absorbing — were alluring in spite of the accompanying "horrors."

The popularity of moviegoing in Israel did not skip the collective agricultural communities — the kibbutzim.[168] About two hundred kibbutzim were spread all over Israel and along its borders, their entire membership constituting about 5 percent of Israel's population.[169] Due to the kibbutzim's ideological and political centrality and their elevated social status, it would be inaccurate to treat them as "peripheral," despite their small size and modest economic means. Moviegoing in the kibbutzim reflected their socialist communal lifestyle: an elected "cultural committee" was in charge of choosing and renting the movies from the Histadrut with collective funds. The members, who did not pay out-of-pocket for the movie, were free to attend or not. Movies were screened with sixteen-millimeter projectors, as noted before, in public buildings in winter and outdoors on summer nights. Since many screening locations included no seats, kibbutz members had to bring their seats with them, and a procession of people carrying chairs thus became a familiar spectacle on movie nights.[170]

The distinctive style of kibbutz moviegoing is revealed in the cartoon, shown on the opposite page, titled "Motkeh Hangs Out in the City," by Dan Gelbert, a member of Kibbutz Alonim.[171] Motkeh, who could be recognized as a kibbutznik by his clothes, stands in the line for the cinema box office in an Israeli town. Accustomed to the moviegoing practices of the kibbutz and inexperienced in city life, he brings a chair with him. The drawing portrays the kibbutzniks' high self-esteem: Motkeh doesn't mind standing out among the urban moviegoers; on the contrary—he smiles knowingly and confidently, perhaps even defiantly, at the viewer of the cartoon. Yet not all the projecting locations in the kibbutz required members to bring their own chairs: in wintertime kibbutzniks often watched the movies in their communal dining hall, a central building-institution that is the topic of the next chapter.

The Communal Dining Hall

WHEN IT SNOWED all over Israel in February 1950, a *Jerusalem Post* correspondent sent some impressions from the Jordan Valley:

> In town, the "scientific explanations" of the snow can be spread over a large area. In the kibbutzim, they concentrate in the dining halls. Everyone has his own private and personal theory — the Atom — the H-bomb in preparation — American influence over the Panama Canal — political disturbances in the vicinity of the Suez — gulf streams — jet planes — artificial rain — D.D.T. sprayed from the air — the seal who crossed the English Channel — Ingrid Bergman's having a son — the searches for Noah's ark at Ararat — the Mapam [pro-Soviet Israeli party] giving the Russian winter a foothold. Enough of all this. The dining hall was a cosy place to be during the storm — meals were lingered over — and what would one talk about if not to explain — meteorologically speaking — the snow.[1]

Whereas the snow was a singular event in the otherwise warm Jordan Valley, the centrality of the communal dining hall was typical of kibbutz reality.

The kibbutz was a voluntary society: members could leave whenever they wished, and nonmembers could join at any time, provided their candidacy was approved by a stated proportion of the existing membership. The means of production were owned communally, and production was carried out collectively. The first kibbutz was founded in 1909, and during the 1920s and early 1930s the kibbutz movement was firmly established. The 1930s and 1940s saw the movement's most rapid growth, as thousands of Zionists who immigrated to Palestine either joined existing kibbutzim or founded new ones. By 1951 there were 203 kibbutzim with a total population of 65,000.[2]

Kibbutz founders attempted to translate socialist principles into everyday practices and to build a new society based on freedom, equality, mutual help, tolerance, and brotherhood. Their main ideal and motto was Marx's "From each according to his ability, to each according to his needs." Kibbutz mem-

bers were paid no wages, and the kibbutz provided for their basic needs—
education, health care, food, social services, and so on. In the 1950s some
kibbutzim gradually introduced a personal allowance to all members on an
agreed, equitable basis. With a small kibbutz population of tens to hundreds,
all permanent adult residents knew each other personally, enabling kibbutz
society to rely heavily on informal social control. The machinery of kibbutz decision making was based on a network of committees, headed by the
general assembly, an ultimate source of authority that consisted of all adult
members and met regularly.[3]

After the founding of the state, Israeli kibbutzim faced numerous difficulties. Many young immigrants spent the first years of their absorption and
"training" on kibbutzim, but only a few stayed on as permanent members.
Many veteran members, on the other hand, left for the cities in search of
a higher standard of living. In the early 1950s most kibbutz members were
still poorer than the general Israeli population, but kibbutzim received from
the state more lands and subsidized water, and modernized agriculture and
successful industries were making some kibbutzim wealthier. This increased
wealth, and the improved standard of living that came with it, exposed these
kibbutzim to external accusations of neglecting their vanguard Zionist role.
Some kibbutz members, too, defined the change as a betrayal of their original goals and ideals. In prestate Palestine the kibbutzim were regarded by
their members and by the Jewish population at large as embodying the Zionist pioneering ideal, but the general postwar relaxation and dwindling of
the pioneering spirit affected the kibbutzim, which gradually lost their former elevated status. Correspondingly, they no longer received the same government support as they had from prestate Zionist institutions. Ben-Gurion
reacted angrily whenever kibbutzim disagreed with his policies or did not
execute his demands, and he reprimanded them for taking what he considered a puny share in absorbing the mass immigration. In 1951 the main kibbutz movement was divided between the supporters of Ben-Gurion and the
West, on one side, and the supporters of the Mapam opposition party and
the Soviet bloc, on the other. This painful partisan and ideological conflict,
reflecting local politics as well as wider Cold War issues, tore families and entire communities apart.[4]

Despite this crisis, and although demographically a small minority in Israeli society, the kibbutzim still held a relatively dominant political, ideological, military, and cultural status in the state.[5] They were still widely regarded as
the pinnacle of the Zionist enterprise, and kibbutz members, who recruited

themselves to fulfill primary national missions, were viewed as the ultimate achievers of the pioneering ideal and supreme examples of the Zionist new Jew.[6] As the subculture most strongly associated with Israeli hegemonic ideals, the unique kibbutz lifestyle is particularly revealing. In our analysis of daily "strategies" and "tactics," the kibbutz provides a fascinating case study. Given that it was a collective and ideologically committed society, most facets of daily life were highly institutionalized and every practice was supposed to accord with kibbutz ideals. Even so, behavioral patterns continuously corresponded with ideological reasoning, and sometimes revealed complex and subtle changes that occurred within a relatively stable framework.

Just as moviegoing maintained its general popularity but also donned a unique character when carried out in the kibbutz, other daily practices discussed in previous chapters could also reflect the kibbutz's leading national role, on the one hand, and its special attributes as a socialist collective community, on the other. If we look at the linguistic field, for instance, we find that since the Mandate era Hebrew had penetrated much more deeply among the rural population, particularly in collective settlements, than among the urban population. Roberto Bachi mentions that rural localities, as compared to cities and towns, absorbed a larger percentage of young pioneers, who arrived with previous knowledge of Hebrew, and since in rural localities individuals had much contact with the community, the Hebrew environment influenced newcomers rapidly.[7] However, a closer look at some kibbutzim during the 1950s reveals that even members of the founding generation, who were supposed to absorb the new immigrants and "Israelize" them, still now and then used foreign languages, especially German or Yiddish. Whereas reading foreign languages was accepted, and kibbutz libraries contained publications in various tongues alongside Hebrew, *speaking* foreign languages was only tolerated in private; in public, kibbutz members were expected to speak Hebrew alone. Many groups of young new immigrants lived on the kibbutzim for a couple of their teenage years, and it was feared that the use of foreign languages by the kibbutz founders, the venerated long-timers, might be a bad influence on these newcomers as well as on the native children of the kibbutz. In some kibbutzim, even incorrect Hebrew speech and strong foreign (German) pronunciation among longtime members were regarded as defects that should be corrected.[8]

As we saw in the fourth chapter, kibbutzniks borrowed the word *operation* and other military terms when describing nonmilitary missions, including cultural activities and preparation for holidays and festivals.[9] The military presence was particularly strong in the kibbutzim: the renowned Palmach and its commanders were associated with the kibbutzim, and the tenacious fighting of some kibbutzim, when attacked during 1948, became legendary. In the 1950s Nahal units resided and trained in kibbutzim, and native sons of the kibbutzim were overrepresented by far, as compared to their minis-cule percentage in society, in all the leading combat units.[10] Still, when kib-butz members who served as generals and other high-ranking officers came home, they were not exempt from communal duties and performed chores, such as serving in the dining hall, like any other member.[11] Despite the kib-butzim's large share in military action and command, and even though some new kibbutzim were founded on Arab lands conquered in 1948, their mem-bers and leaders sometimes disagreed with the IDF policy, especially regard-ing the military rule over the Arab and Bedouin populations.[12]

Kibbutzim varied by their size, year founded, and founders' countries of origin, and each of the four kibbutz movements[13] highlighted different ideological and political aspects. Yet beyond this diversity, the basic kib-butz creed dictated a certain lifestyle that was shared to a large extent by all kibbutzim.[14] The main features of the kibbutzim were consolidated in the prestate era, among them collective consumer institutions, including a com-munal kitchen and dining hall.[15] As sociologist Georg Simmel notes, the act of eating is particularly primitive as well as selfish, in the sense that the spe-cific eaten portion cannot be shared, and yet this act has been surrounded by complex social public customs of communality.[16]

The communal dining hall was the focal point of the kibbutz and was sometimes referred to as "a secular synagogue." Early kibbutz society viewed itself as a big family, a replacement for the traditional middle-class family.[17] Within this framework the dining hall provided a space for the community's social, political, and cultural existence. It represented the kibbutz internally, for its members, and externally, to guests and visitors. In some kibbutzim the dining hall was significantly called "*ha-bayit*," which in Hebrew means both "the house" and "the home."[18] When a new dining hall was inaugurated in one kibbutz in 1953, for example, it was consecrated with the following words:

This *bayit* symbolizes the strength of the kibbutz; it faithfully expresses the power of our progress: a crown to the kibbutz labor, an adornment to the landscape of the Jezreel Valley. Shall we call this *bayit* "a dining room"? No, for this *bayit* is much more than a place to eat in. This *bayit* is the

Lunch in the dining tent of the recently founded Kibbutz Mefalsim in the northern Negev, 1949. Later that same year the dining hall was relocated to a building. National Photo Collection (Government Press Office), D842-060. Photo from 1949 by Zoltan Kluger.

collective *bayit* of the whole kibbutz, where we shall spend our weekdays and our Sabbath. Where we shall hold our conversations and assemblies, where we shall observe our holidays, where all the matters of our communal life shall be nurtured. It is no dining room, for it is not a room and it is not devoted solely for eating. Let us call the *bayit* by its proper name: the *bayit* of the kibbutz.[19]

Although American utopian communes are often regarded as historical precedents for the kibbutz, it was the Soviet Union that provided an immediate source of inspiration for many kibbutzim. Socialist Zionists, most of them born in Russia and other Eastern European countries, were strongly influenced by Russian and Soviet cultures. Indeed, kibbutz dining halls somewhat resembled the communal food distribution conducted by Soviet revolutionaries. In addition to their emphasis on material necessity, Bolsheviks regarded communal dining as morally superior, while private cooking and private restaurants were depicted as unequal and unjust, and in times of want as irrational as well as inefficient.[20] Although in the beginning many Soviet cafeterias supplied food low in quality and quantity, unprofessionally

Kibbutz Tel Yosef's dining hall in the early 1950s. The building was
planned by the painter and modernist architect Leopold Krakauer in 1933.
Haifa University's Collection of Historical Photographs of the Land of Israel, item 653280.
Courtesy of Daniel Ben-Meir.

prepared and served in squalid conditions, eventually these cafeterias and
collective kitchens improved with the help of special cookbooks. They revolutionized Soviet nutrition and introduced workers and farmers to an en-
riched diet.[21]

At first, when the kibbutz was a new settlement composed of tents, the
dining hall was the "central tent" or a small wooden shack. Permanent buildings, where meals were served three times a day, were erected later on. Beginning in the 1930s some of Jewish Palestine's leading architects designed new
and larger dining halls for the kibbutzim, but they too maintained aesthetic
simplicity to reflect kibbutz ideology.[22] Older kibbutzim gradually designed
their dining halls,[23] and younger kibbutzim could follow their examples and
learn from their experience. However, after the War of Independence, in a
time of recession and shortage, many young kibbutzim couldn't afford grand
expenditures. Therefore, they erected large wooden cabins designed in Europe as part of the postwar rehabilitation effort, and known as "Swedish cabins," to serve as their dining halls.[24]

The food in the kibbutzim was basic, largely supplied from the kibbutz's
agricultural branches and fields (bread was baked locally), and served in

„— — — תמלאו קודם את השולחן!"

Untitled cartoon by Dan.

stark tin dishes. Gradually kitchen facilities improved, new technologies for large-scale cooking were introduced, cooks were sent to professional courses, and some kibbutzim purchased better tableware.[25] Still, the kibbutz diet remained basic, and only those who were either ill or engaged in hard physical labor received additional portions or special diets. From the earliest days of the kibbutz, it became clear that the frugal diet served in the dining hall would not suffice for babies and children, so these youngsters received a different, more nourishing diet.[26] In some kibbutzim children were served in a separate dining hall or in the dining rooms of their communal "children's home," where they lived (e.g., bathed, slept) with other members of their age group.[27] Even in those kibbutzim where children did dine in the communal hall, they sat together within their age group, not with their parents, and were served separately.

As we can see in the above cartoon by kibbutz member Dan Gelbert, the children have already been served and are eating happily at their separate table while the adults have to wait hungrily and impatiently for the grumpy server, who refuses to hand over the food until "you fill in the table!"[28]

The improvement of dining conditions reflected improvements in the kibbutz economic situation, but it did not pass without ideological deliberations: was asceticism merely a result of early kibbutz poverty or had it become a kibbutz principle, one that should be kept even in wealthier kibbutzim? Moving from the shack's long wooden benches to separate chairs in the new dining hall, for instance, stirred many arguments among kibbutz members: whereas chairs were more comfortable, benches (which required cooperation among all sitters) reflected both collectivity and the kibbutz's Spartan spirit.[29] Comparable disagreements could be found in Soviet cookbooks, whose authors did not object to aesthetic decorations, such as flowers on the dining tables and paintings on the cafeteria walls, but who, in some cases, adopted a radical revolutionary viewpoint with regard to food, promoting an ascetic culinary agenda. Other Soviet cookbooks sought to promote the revolution by using simple ingredients in a professional, sophisticated, varied, and pleasuring manner.[30] In revolutionary societies material culture and daily practices are expected to reflect and promote certain ideals; they are therefore constantly checked vis-à-vis the ideological framework. Yet whereas the Soviet Union was a dictatorship, the kibbutz — a much smaller unit — was a direct democracy, where all members could participate in open debates and influence local decisions with their votes.

As mentioned earlier, alongside its main function as a place of communal dining, the hall usually hosted kibbutz gatherings, such as the weekly general assembly and various celebrations. The kibbutz consciously nurtured a new local Hebrew culture and consolidated unique annual festivals.[31] Traditional Jewish holidays assumed new forms and reflected national, agricultural, and socialist ideals. The Seder of the Pesach holiday, for instance, was celebrated communally rather than within the family, and according to a new original Haggadah text.[32] Historian Muki Tsur writes that the size of new dining hall buildings was determined by the standards of one night: that of the Pesach Seder, when the entire kibbutz population gathered with its guests and eating in shifts was impossible.[33] Kibbutz artists put much effort into decorating the dining hall for the Seder and for other annual celebrations.[34]

The Seder in the kibbutz dining hall became a famous Israeli phenomenon. As suggested by a 1950 advertisement for the locally manufactured Blueband margarine, the kibbutz Seder stood for contemporary Israeli life. The Hebrew and English writing in the ad echoed the words of the traditional Haggadah ("In every generation a person is obligated to regard himself as if he had come out of Egypt"), with a commercial twist. The illustration showed the evolution of Pesach through history. The first, upper panel, "And they baked the dough," portrayed the baking of matzot during the exodus from Egypt; the second panel, "Pesach sacrifice in Jerusalem," portrayed Pesach as one of the three annual pilgrimages to the Temple in Jerusalem; the third panel, "Pesach Seder in the Middle Ages," depicted the traditional rabbinic holiday, celebrated within the family; and the bottom and largest panel, representing present-day Pesach, was titled "Pesach Seder in Israel."[35] Although the kibbutz Seder (in this case held in a "Swedish cabin") was actually celebrated in Israel by a demographic minority, its visual portrayal could

A special luncheon celebration in Kibbutz Dan, 1951. To mark the founding of a local nature museum, Beit Ussishkin (eventually opened in 1955), the tables were covered with white tablecloths and kibbutz members wore their festive outfits, although aesthetic simplicity was maintained. JNF Photo Archive, d1355-004.

be easily recognized by potential consumers of Blueband; moreover, it was chosen by the advertiser as an up-to-date and representative model of Israeli authenticity and uniqueness.[36]

The communal Sabbath meal on Friday evenings was a special weekly event in both religious and secular kibbutzim. In the former, unlike the latter, the Sabbath was observed according to Judaic tradition; but in both cases the food was better, tablecloths covered the tables, and a "reception of the Sabbath service" preceded the meal. Members wore their best garments, which were indeed known as "Sabbath clothes."[37] Sabbath meals were the main meals of the week in which all the children ate in the communal hall seated with their families, rather than with their age group[38]; Sabbath meals were thus less revolutionary than other communal repasts, somewhat evoking customs in traditional Jewish families and in middle-class European households.

Events such as bar mitzvahs and weddings, which in summer were held outdoors, were celebrated during winter inside the dining hall. So were dances and shows by kibbutz amateur theaters, along with concerts by visiting musicians and plays by professional theater troupes. Before special reading rooms, libraries, and cultural centers were built, newspapers were brought to the dining hall and read there, and sometimes one corner of the hall served as a library. The kibbutz notice board—a main communication medium between kibbutz institutions and its members—was also located in the dining hall.[39]

But as the kibbutz grew, the multifunctional dining hall became less convenient. In 1950 a kibbutz member suggested building a special cultural center, explaining that the dining hall no longer sufficed for parties, shows, and celebrations. The hall, he wrote, was too small for the entire kibbutz population, even when seated densely: "Last Hanukkah, for instance, there wasn't enough room for all the members and their children, and so instead of the high spirits that this holiday usually evokes, many people felt discontented." In order to prepare the hall for any such event, tables had to be moved to the corners or taken outside, "which surely shortens their life"; a stage couldn't be erected because it would disturb the main function of the hall—dining during mealtimes; and every gathering had to be timed according to the last shift of dining and clearing.[40]

Listening to a concert in the old, stifling dining hall was no pleasure, wrote a member of another kibbutz five years later. "The place lacks festivity, sitting there is uncomfortable, the heat and the flies disturb both artist and listeners."[41] Similar problems faced another kibbutz: shows couldn't begin before work in the communal kitchen ended at 9:30 p.m., "or else the concert is accompanied by the clicking sounds from the adjacent kitchen." During the show members moved the tables and sat on the windowsills while putting their feet on the tables, and the next morning the furniture wasn't back in its proper place, so breakfast couldn't start on time.[42] As mentioned in the previous chapter, moviegoing was particularly popular in the kibbutzim. Yet even as members didn't have to buy tickets, and thus did not have to wait in lines, the small size of some dining halls required either that people arrive early to save a seat or, in some cases, that films be screened twice in order to accommodate all viewers.[43]

While kibbutz dining halls were sometimes treated with elevated reverence, in religious kibbutzim they were actually used for religious purposes as well. Most of the Israeli kibbutzim were secular societies, whereas religious kibbutzim strove to combine Zionism and socialism with Judaism. They followed the values of collectivity and equality championed by the secular kibbutzim but also maintained Judaic tradition in an innovative, liberal manner.[44] Before separate synagogues and schoolrooms were built, prayers and religious learning were conducted in the dining hall.[45] Initially, a sharp separation between holy and secular pursuits was deemed by members of religious kibbutzim as an old-fashioned Diaspora notion. Collective daily life and work in the Land of Israel were viewed as containing some inherent holiness, and therefore conducting religious and nonreligious functions in the same space was not considered a sacrilege.[46] Moreover, the Zionist ideology of manual labor assumed almost devout dimensions in the kibbutzim, and hard work was considered not merely a means to an economic end but an end in itself, a way of connecting man to nature and creation, and the road to national regeneration as well as individual transformation and self-fulfillment.[47]

Nevertheless, the cohabitation of secular and sacred activities in one space proved somewhat problematic. On Sabbath evenings, for instance, members would leave the hall and miss the sermon on the weekly Torah portion when putting their children to bed in the communal child care center; and if they did stay in the dining hall after prayer, it was not necessarily to listen to the detailed homily but rather to save a seat for the Sabbath dinner.[48] Sabbath meals were described as overcrowded and noisy and, owing to the din created by workers and diners, Sabbath hymns couldn't be sung properly. According to the bulletin of a religious kibbutz, "This situation should worry anyone who wishes to educate his children in the spirit of religious collectivity."[49]

In 1952 a member of one religious kibbutz wrote that a synagogue must be built because the dining hall's secular activity always marginalized its role as a prayer house. Sacredness was slighted unintentionally, he claimed, especially regarding the Holy Ark (the ornamental receptacle that contains the Torah scrolls in the synagogue). Since it was placed in the dining hall, it had become part of the place's daily flow, "and its sanctity had been forgotten"; members leaned on the ark while seated at the table or prayed before it with their backs turned, even with their hands in their pockets.[50] Two years earlier a member of another religious kibbutz had expressed his concerns about the multifunctional dining hall: "If a stranger would arrive here during a weekday evening, he might think that he was in a waiting room or a restaurant of any train station in the world." Some people were eating, others were conversing loudly, some were trying to read a newspaper, while still others were playing ping-pong.[51]

In both religious and secular kibbutzim, most workers in the communal kitchen and dining hall were women.[52] Male and female kibbutzniks worked during the day, and all services were conducted by the community intending, among other things, to liberate women from the drudgery of domestic work. However, most workers in kibbutz service branches (such as the communal child care and the communal clothing and laundry institutions) were women. Kibbutz ideology advocated equality between men and women. Indeed, Bachi found that the difference between women's and men's use of Hebrew in the kibbutzim was exceedingly small, as compared to elsewhere in

Meal in the temporary
dining hall (an abandoned
Arab building) in Kibbutz
Ein Tzurim, 1950. The
kibbutz (initially founded
in 1946) was conquered by
Jordan during the war and
rebuilt in a new location
in 1949. JNF Photo Archive,
d36-036. Photo by Verner
Braun. I wish to thank Esther
Rechtschafner for providing
further data on the history of
Ein Tzurim's dining hall.

Israel, where more men than women spoke Hebrew. He concluded that "the
fact that the women take part as full members in the life of the settlement
has brought about complete equality in the use of Hebrew."[53] Nonetheless,
gender equality was never fully achieved in practice, not even during the kibbutzim's most revolutionary era. Since the 1930s, as the number of singles decreased and the number and size of families increased, women were further
marginalized into the (less prestigious) service branches. Even though services were not conducted privately as "housework" but rather communally
and publicly as part of formal and organized branches, their local status was
lower than that of production branches and agricultural fields in particular.[54]
Equal ideology and rhetoric notwithstanding, from the earliest days of collective cooking and dining, women were usually assigned to provide these
services, although some of them were as unqualified for the role as their male
comrades.[55]

Division of labor in the kibbutz became even more gendered in the
1950s.[56] Both male and many female members regarded it as "natural" that
women, rather than men, work in the kibbutz kitchen and dining hall.[57] The
persistence of traditional female roles despite the outward assertion of socialist gender equality could be detected in Soviet society too. The revolution
was supposed to free women from the three Cs — cleaning, cooking, and
child rearing. However, Soviet communal services, including public kitchens and cafeterias, were populated mainly by female workers, and moreover,

these working women kept performing their traditional female roles at home after the workday had ended.[58]

A male member in one kibbutz explained why female members disliked working in the cooking and dining institutions: the work lacked prestige and creativity, it was stressful and wearing, the workers had to deal with petty matters and endure endless criticism from demanding diners. Each member therefore hoped to avoid the unrewarding task and wished someone else would do it.[59] In many kibbutzim serving in the dining hall became a chore taken in turns, rather than a permanent post, which meant that "many servers lack experience."[60] Kibbutz members complained about the servers' inefficient, impolite, and inhospitable behavior. They did not greet the diners; they arranged the tables without noticing missing chairs, which led to noisy chair-dragging from table to table[61]; on Sabbath evenings and special occasions, the servers wore white aprons over their Sabbath outfits,[62] but on weekdays, during long shifts, they could look quite shabby. The serving atmosphere, wrote a kibbutz member, is as important as the food, and it wasn't helped by a server "whose apron is dirty, who hands you the tray with a cigarette in his mouth, and perhaps with some ash on your plate as well."[63] Such a scruffy yet confident dining hall worker was depicted in a cartoon by Dan Gelbert.

Kibbutz members, who became prolific complainers, often criticized other aspects of communal dining as well. In 1949, due to intolerable noise, a kibbutz member suggested conducting an "Operation Silence" in the dining

הוד מעלתו

Dan's cartoon is titled "Bon Appétit!" and the figure is described as "his highness."

Breakfast in the religious kibbutz Bnei Darom, 1953. In the crowded
dining hall, serving with a trolley was regarded as more efficient, as well
as more economical, than buffet-style self-service. Central Zionist Archives,
PHKH\1273675. Photo by Fritz Shlezinger.

hall: Why do members bring their children to the dining hall and let them
run free? Why must they argue and make all their arrangements, not necessarily quietly, during the meals, of all times? Why do they shout across to
each other rather than step closer?[64] A member of another kibbutz wrote
the following year that the racket during mealtimes was so awful that people could converse only by shouting. It was customary to blame the kibbutz
teenagers and temporary residents such as Nahal soldiers for the noise, but
adult members were at fault too. Diners might get used to the nerve-wracking
uproar, but it was no wonder that dining hall servers couldn't keep to their
posts for long, not to mention the bad example that was set for the native
children.[65]

A member who headed the dining hall team in his kibbutz wrote in 1954
that "Our dining hall is also a place of assembly; it is our 'club.' This is where
the members meet and make arrangements for the next day," and thus it becomes a busy employment bureau. He asked all members to use the adjacent
small room, rather than the hall itself, for such arrangements in order to re-
duce the chaos and make things a bit easier for the workers.[66] A member of
another kibbutz had hoped the move to a new dining hall would improve the

„הילדים אינם נכנסים לחדר-האו־
כל אצלנו — אפשר לאכול בשקט!"

"The children don't attend our dining hall and one can eat peacefully": a cartoon by Dan.
Dan Gelbert, *Definitely Internal* (1954), 122.

situation, but a few months after the move he realized sadly that noise during mealtimes had only become aggravated. The larger space was used by children as a racecourse — yet, again, the children, youth immigrants, and Nahal soldiers were not the only culprits: weekday meals, from which the youngsters were absent, were noisy as well. If "the most important public place" in the kibbutz was not made calmer and more pleasant, increasing numbers of members might refrain from dining communally and retreat for meals to their private residences.[67]

While kibbutz society prioritized the welfare and upbringing of children, their presence in the dining hall could be rather disconcerting. They contributed greatly to the general clamor and "turned the dining hall into a playground."[68] In their collective residence the children were watched and disciplined during mealtimes by their caretaker, but when brought to the dining hall by their parents, they imitated their elders' loud behavior, broke away from their parents, scurried around, and disrupted the workers.[69] It wasn't easy to teach children to be neat and quiet during Sabbath meals, wrote a member of a religious kibbutz, "but children will certainly not be quiet when they see the adults conversing loudly during the Sabbath hymns."[70] A member of another religious kibbutz claimed that children follow their parents' example of behavior in public places: "Our children believe that everything that is not allowed in their parents' residence and in the children's home is permitted in the dining hall; this is their no-man's-land, where they can unwind and go wild. They take advantage of the fact that no authority constrains them here — neither parents nor caretaker nor teacher." No kibbutz member, he added, would dare bring a baby or a child younger than two to a synagogue in the city or anywhere else, knowing the child couldn't be hushed and might disturb the prayer; still, members do bring their babies and young children to the prayers and the meals in the dining hall, where they are allowed to behave as they wish. "I am not deluded to think we can create an intimate atmosphere in the dining hall," he wrote, "but we shouldn't accept the present situation, in which every man does that which is right in his own eyes."[71]

Members' behavior was also watched by groups of teenage immigrants who lived on the kibbutz, and in 1955 a kibbutz member wrote that there can be no double standard for longtime older members and younger residents:

> A longtime member goes to the food trolley, takes a few slices of white bread and returns to her seat. A new immigrant then does the very same thing. The former member goes to him and rebukes him for doing so.
>
> Another incident: During breakfast in the dining hall, two older members stand near the steps making an awful racket. When I sat at the table alongside two youngsters, one of them said to the other in a language he thought I couldn't understand, "Why do they tell us to make no noise if they themselves are allowed to do so?" — Explanations are unneeded. Let us remember that we shall reap what we sow.[72]

A member of another kibbutz noticed that people took good care of their private property but disregarded collective property: everyone knew that the furniture in the dining hall had cost a lot of work, effort, and money, and yet this furniture was treated roughly and carelessly by children and adults alike.[73] Another kibbutznik depicted the negligent indifference to collective property shown by some of the members:

> He gets up and leaves the table. Follow him! He walks with his dishes to the trolley. He doesn't throw the leftovers in the bin. He doesn't put the cutlery in the right container. He leaves the cup between the plates and off he goes.
>
> Has he caused some unnecessary trouble [to the dining hall workers]? He doesn't care.
>
> Here comes his friend. Don't-care number 2. He puts his plate on top of the former plate, the leftovers and the cutlery. It hangs loosely, about to tumble down the tower of plates. Someone touches the trolley.
>
> Crash!
>
> Down it fell and smashed; a part of your budget has just been lost in vain. But does he care?[74]

Further damage to the dining hall furniture was caused when the space was used as a movie theater or a concert hall. People dragged around tables, benches, and chairs, sat on the tables, and cracked sunflower seeds and peanuts, leaving shells on the floor.[75] People also "borrowed" tableware from the dining hall, which "were later found, discarded and dirty, near the members' residences."[76] Although kibbutz members were supposed to own basic dishes for their daily needs, still "every member borrows with no hesitation pitchers, plates, vases," and so on from the communal dining hall.[77] Members even "borrowed" from the dining hall cutlery, which was in very short supply. During the years of rationing there was a general deficiency in dishes, and the kibbutzim suffered particularly from a lack of knives. Sometimes a table of six or eight diners had to share one knife. A cartoon by Gelbert shows a member sitting at the table, clasping his hands and praying to find a knife. In another cartoon a knife is tied with a metal chain to the foot of the table, thus securing it from disappearing.[78]

Mistreating furniture and "pinching" dishes from the dining hall had technical and material consequences, whereas other heedless actions harmed a desired aesthetic. Being the central and representative public spaces of the kibbutzim, dining halls were supposed to be clean, tidy, and aesthetically pleasing despite their simplicity. In addition to producing transitory holiday decorations, local artists created permanent internal and external decorations, which portrayed the community and its main ideals.[79] Kibbutzniks expected their dining hall to look appealing especially on Sabbath evening, and complained if it didn't.[80] Here, too, Soviet influence might have been at work. The Soviet aesthetic ideal was supposed to counter perceived bourgeois characteristics, so overstated ornamentation was frowned upon as decadent; laxity, dirt, and inefficiency were also described as typically bourgeois. Soviet style thus hailed functionalism, efficiency, hygiene, and unassuming simple decoration.[81]

Yet aesthetic reality in the kibbutzim's dining halls was affected not only by ideological intentions and actions but also by the daily patterns of informal behavior of workers and diners. Thus, in one kibbutz the staircase ledge in the dining hall was initially supposed to be covered with flowerpots, but in the meantime workers left on the ledge their cleaning tools and mops, trays, plates, and cups, a trivial but ugly habit, wrote one diner, that should be stopped.[82] Diners should push in the seats when they leave the table, wrote another kibbutz member in 1950, not just because it eases the workers' job but also because it looks nicer. The architectural planning of the dining hall, he added sarcastically, does not include putting dishes, clothes, and other artifacts on the windowsills, things that add neither beauty nor grace.[83]

One kibbutz member wrote in 1950 that the notions of individual versus collective responsibility were being blurred and while members were putting a lot of effort into cultivating their private homes, public spaces were being shamelessly neglected. The sorry state of the dining hall served him as an edifying example: while everybody wanted this public place to symbolize and express "the lifestyle which we applaud," in practice each member behaved indifferently.[84] In 1955 a kibbutz member wrote that orderliness in the dining hall depends on self-discipline and giving up one's comfort for the sake of the collectivity.[85] Yet thoughtless acts and negligent treatment of collective property might have reflected gradual changes in kibbutz society. During the 1950s most kibbutzim, especially larger and wealthier ones, were beginning to slowly shift from the extreme communality of the earlier era to a less radical form of collectivity. Decisions concerning private matters, such as the naming of newborns, once settled by the kibbutz general assembly, were now made by individual members. Beginning in the mid-1950s some kibbutzim moved from direct distribution of clothes and shoes to an equally apportioned personal budget, with which members could exercise some free choice. Although the measured move to a personal budget stemmed from practical considerations, it also conveyed the continuous sway to a slightly more privatized, individualized society.[86] As the members of the kibbutzim married, procreated, and aged, the family — once considered by the socialist founders an outdated bourgeois institution — now assumed a greater role in kibbutz society. In addition to the meals taken collectively in the dining hall or the children's home, families started gathering in the parents' residences for an afternoon repast. Tsur regards these "four o'clock meals" as an important step in the kibbutz's transformation into a more familial course,[87] a partial retreat from the revolutionary social structure and a return to a more middle-class lifestyle.

Permanent residences for kibbutz members were being constructed, and although they were small and humble (usually one room and a half and a bathroom with a shower), after years of living in tents and shacks, sharing toilets and bathing in communal showers, kibbutz members regarded these new dwellings as a luxury. Even though the furnishing and decorating of these abodes were restricted by small budgets and formal kibbutz decisions, and although elaborate ornamentation was discouraged because it was associated with bourgeois decadent culture,[88] kibbutz members, especially women, still took great pains to adorn their private residences and give them an individual mark.[89] While the new residences mirrored the increasingly familial structure of the kibbutz, they also reinforced a tendency whereby the more intimate hearth sometimes substituted for communal gatherings and the private residence could occasionally replace the dining hall. In a general assembly meeting in 1949, a kibbutz member said that rather than deal exclusively with the family residence and its furnishing, "members, and especially female members, should take care of the one *bayit* which we all share, the *bayit* in which we spend most of our time — the dining hall and kitchen — and we should add to it the grace and the beauty in which our family residences excel. Let us not flee from the *bayit* that unifies us all to the members' [private] dwellings."[90]

Kibbutz members dreamed of "grand dining rooms in their private homes," wrote a member of another kibbutz in the following year, but since such a dream could not be materialized in the near future, the communal dining hall should meanwhile be improved and upgraded.[91] And just as members didn't hang any odd objects on the walls of their private residence, wrote another, so they shouldn't cover the walls of the dining hall without ample discretion.[92] Once there was a time, wrote a kibbutz member in 1952, when the women took good care of the dining hall, the only public space, where all communal events and socializing took place. But the new private dwellings have revolutionized kibbutz life: kibbutz women now think only about their private abode, "the curtains, the sofa, the chandelier and all the comfort in the room." The nice apartment had a radio, a cooking plate, a kettle, and so forth, freeing the member from her dependency on the communal kitchen. Using the messy dining hall wasn't necessary anymore if everything could be arranged easily and quietly at home, "within the small familial ideal." Some female members wished to return to the familiar path paved by their grandmothers generations ago; some would even like the communal kitchen to be done away with![93] The writer assumed that it had been the "natural" role of female members to nurture the dining hall and kitchen but that the investment of this feminine nature in the private "nest" amounted to a loss and a betrayal of the revolutionary zeal, a regressive retreat to traditional middle-class values.

Growing privatization threatened the role of the dining hall beyond mealtimes: if once it functioned as a communal club and reading room, in the 1950s radio sets were gradually installed and daily newspapers distributed in each family residence. Leisure, even more than mealtimes, was often spent privately rather than communally.[94]

In 1953 a questionnaire about the communal services was conducted in one religious kibbutz. The majority voted for some changes and improvements in the dining hall, but six out of forty respondents agreed that some daily meals should be held privately, while six others checked the option of shutting down the communal dining hall altogether.[95] The dining hall was left open, but the debates persisted, and in the following year a member analyzed the issue in depth. Was the communal dining hall ideologically necessary? Did the principles of equality and sharing *necessitate* communal dining? He himself didn't think so: a communal kitchen was only a practical necessity, and eating in the dining hall was more efficient than leaving work for home during the morning and at noon. Communal institutions were born for functional reasons, but in time people confusedly attributed to them some moral meaning. Under Hassidic influence,[96] some members placed great weight in the socializing facet of communal dining, but such socializing was possible only during breakfast and lunch, when only the adults attended the hall. In the evenings, when the whole family gathered in the dining hall, socializing became impossible. The writer therefore suggested maintaining breakfast and lunch in the dining hall, as dictated by efficiency and as a form of socializing, but enabling members to eat dinner with their children calmly and quietly in the family residence. The only evening dinner that should be left in the communal dining hall, he claimed, was the Sabbath meal, which stood out and held true communal meaning for adults, and especially for children.[97]

Such debates were typical of kibbutz society, in which daily practices were publicly discussed and judged according to whether or not they deviated from kibbutz principles. Members attached to communal dining practical, social, and even moral qualities, but this did not prevent the gradual withdrawal that was occurring from the public to the private space. And although public pressure could be an effective tool in small kibbutz communities, there is evidence that some members opted to eat privately even after being asked to reconsider. This reflected a strong show of resistance against prevailing norms, no small matter in 1950s kibbutzim.[98] Anthropologist Nir Avieli writes that communal dining halls might operate as spheres of coercion, surveillance, and oppression,[99] and perhaps kibbutz members who felt such pressures preferred to eat in private as soon as the option was made available. The kibbutz was a voluntary democratic society, and members couldn't be forced to eat together; but even in the Soviet dictatorship, where pressure was more severe and disobedience risky, a parallel process took place: despite official propaganda urging people to flock to the cooperative cafeterias, and even after the food and the service in these institutions improved, clandestine private restaurants were operating, and most of the Soviet population still depended on the private family kitchen as its main source of nutrition.[100]

The question of Soviet influence on the kibbutzim became particularly explicit in the early 1950s. In some kibbutzim members who supported Mapai, Ben-Gurion's ruling party, and those who supported the pro-Soviet opposition party Mapam became sworn enemies; they wouldn't share the same dining space and took over separate sections of the hall.[101] As mentioned earlier, this internal conflict within the largest kibbutz movement, Hakibbutz Hameuchad, culminated in 1951 with a full-blown rift, and the most prolonged and violent conflict occurred in Kibbutz Ein Harod, the seat of Hakibbutz Hameuchad's leadership. Whereas in other kibbutzim it was agreed that the majority would stay on while the minority would move elsewhere, the Mapam minority in Ein Harod refused to comply. After mounting tensions led to a brawl in the dining hall, the hall's space and the communal kitchen were divided between the warring camps, and even the cutlery was separated and marked. The conflict within Hakibbutz Hameuchad arose during the peak of the Cold War, and was a local reflection of this world conflict. The dividing line in Ein Harod's dining hall was therefore nicknamed "the 38th parallel" after the border between North and South Korea. Yet until Ein Harod was finally separated into two different kibbutzim in 1954, arguments about the fair division of the dining institution's space, facilities, and the quantity of food kept escalating. At some stage sabotage became a daily practice — including throwing garbage, destroying cutlery, and cutting off the cables of the kitchen elevator.[102]

It is no wonder that the dining hall, which served as the kibbutz's core, became a physical battleground when ideological disputes boiled over. A space that initially, and successfully, reflected unity was prone to mirror discord in a way that was just as poignant. In some kibbutzim affiliated with Mapam, for instance, Joseph Stalin's death in March 1953 was mourned and memorial corners with his portrait were erected in the dining halls.[103] Kibbutzim that followed Ben-Gurion and viewed Stalin as a dictator held no such rituals. Indeed, at Ein Harod the warring camps argued, among other things, over the content of slogans hung on the dining hall walls on holidays and special occasions, a sensitive and at times explosive topic for both sides.[104]

Seemingly small matters, such as slogans on the walls or seating arrangements, were all scrutinized in kibbutz society because unlike in classical

Members of Kibbutz Nirim eating in their dining hall in 1955. Nirim was destroyed entirely in the war during a bitter battle with the Egyptian army, and was rebuilt after the war at a nearby site. Located on the border, Kibbutz Nirim had to defend itself from hostile infiltrations, and in May 1955 it was bombed by the Egyptians. Note the rifle leaning on the diner's chair.
National Photo Collection (Government Press Office), D295-047. Photo by Moshe Pridan.

utopias, which are ideals planned for an abstract future, the kibbutz actually attempted to implement its utopian values in the concrete present.[105] The dining hall mirrored the kibbutz's utopian ideals and the difficulties met while trying to realize them.

Kibbutz daily culture was so strongly tied to the community's ideology that relatively little room remained for nonstrategic behavior. Traces of tactics could be detected every now and then, but they too were quickly brought to the surface, discussed directly, either approved of or rejected — but in any case they were institutionalized. Moreover, according to one member, kibbutz society should be entirely controlled by the collective. It was well known, he wrote in 1950, that "in our collective life" no area was to be "exposed" and left to each individual's conscience. "We must try to shape every single matter, big or small, and leave no vacuum within our way of life."[106] Even the aggressive and violent behavior in the Kibbutz Ein Harod dining hall was not of a tactical nature but rather an integral part of the conscious, intentional, ideological strategic struggle.[107] On the kibbutz, strategy was constantly negotiated explicitly on the pages of local bulletins, in various committees, and in the general assembly. Policy was regularly reshaped according to changing circumstances and voiced opinions. Thus, behavioral patterns on the tactical level could be formally turned into strategy, as long as they were regarded as suitable to kibbutz ideology. The conscious public attention paid to every facet of daily life, and the pressure to keep daily life attuned to ideology in all respects, left hardly any leeway for informal appropriation, not to mention challenge and resistance. Still, when a kibbutz member proposed in 1949 that a system of rules be constituted for the dining hall, another member objected that such a constitution would drain the dining hall of its essence: "We have but one constitution—the one in our hearts."[108]

Notwithstanding the strength of public opinion in the kibbutz's small community, this "constitution of the heart" left room for a range of behaviors, and thus strategy was occasionally ignored on the tactical level. Without contesting the importance of the communal dining hall and its central role in the community, kibbutz members often placed their own interests before those of the collectivity, such as when they behaved noisily and rudely. Signs of growing individuality were manifest in the disregard for public property and gradual withdrawal from the communal dining hall to the private residences. The tactical level, then, posed a steady, quiet, accumulating alternative to formal kibbutz strategy. The gradual change in kibbutz lifestyle is described as a reflection and enactment of the decreasing role of ideology,[109] but perhaps ever-growing individualistic daily practices coexisted alongside the collectivist value system and slowly transformed it from within. Rather than view ideological changes as *causing* alterations in kibbutz lifestyle, we can appreciate the subtle effects that daily practices had on the redefinition of kibbutz values.

Thus, even the subculture most strongly associated with Israeli hegemonic ideals was being gradually transformed, slowly yet steadily moving from the principles of early pioneering to a more flexible version of collectivism. The dining hall, both as a site and as an institution, reflected these gradual, subtle changes in kibbutz society.

Informality, Straightforwardness, and Rudeness

BY NOW THE READER must have noticed that Israelis often used casual and familiar forms of social communication. As we saw, informal Hebrew, although still shunned by high and official culture, became a coveted sign of nativity. Informality was apparent even in an institution commonly supposed to be hyperformal — the army. The line between informality and impoliteness was a thin one; Israeli brusqueness could easily become more aggressive, turning into unmistakable rudeness and even occasional violence conveyed, inter alia, in the long lines for rationed products, the bus, and the cinema. When a women's magazine published a pictorial quiz about manners in 1954, the two questions shown on page 164 regarded the cinema and the bus.

"One should not enter the cinema row with one's back turned to the seated audience," admonished the riddle's solution, "and it is also polite to get up and allow the person arriving to have more space." As for the bus scene, "It is extremely impolite for young men to sit comfortably in the bus while a mother carrying her child remains standing."[1] Yet given our close look at the Israeli bus and the Israeli movie theater, such pedantic demands seem rather out of place; behavior in Israeli buses and cinemas was characterized by inconsideration far harsher than turning one's back or not offering one's seat. Daily life in Israel was marked by an animated, unceremonious, noisy, disorderly atmosphere.

It is hard to pinpoint specific "strategies" in this cluster of characteristics, which were usually expressed as part of some other activity or behavior rather than a separate field or an independent entity. The words in this chapter's title are typically used as adjectives (informal, straightforward, and rude) rather than nouns. However, we could regard the Zionist ideal of the "new Jew" (sometimes known as the "new Hebrew" and, after the founding of the state, as the "new Israeli") as a strategic setting, or even as a loosely defined strategic framework.

Reforming the "old Jew," healing and improving him, was not a novel

Detail from a pictorial
quiz on proper manners.
Laisha, July 21, 1954.

project. The exponents of the Haskalah, the Jewish Enlightenment movement, absorbed some of the external, non-Jewish criticism regarding the
Jews, including on their morality and lifestyle, and desired to encourage Jews
to embrace Enlightenment values. These *maskilim* depicted ideal Jews, complete men, revived with the aid of non-Judaic knowledge. Their ideal Jew
maintained his Judaism while also performing his duty as a citizen in his state
and sharing the universal cultural and moral values of Enlightened Europe.[2]
German *maskilim* intentionally attempted to reform the old Jew by increasing and facilitating his contact with non-Jewish society, by replacing Yiddish
with German, and by changing the manner in which Jews dressed, talked,
and interacted. Among other things, the ideal Jew of the Haskalah was supposed to be cleaner and more polite than the old Jew.[3] When the *maskilim*
attempted to spread their ideals in Eastern Europe (the "Half Orient," as
they called it), they depicted German culture and Eastern European Jewish culture as extreme opposites: Whereas civilization was identified solely
with the modern West, Eastern European Jews were portrayed as backward,
primitive, and superstitious. Whereas the *maskilim* had already adopted the
German cultural ideal of self-control, Eastern European Jews lacked sobri-
ety and were in need of serious reform.[4] Similarly, when Eastern European
Jews immigrated to the United States, efforts to Americanize them involved
a "civilizing" process, whereby the Jew had to behave and appear "less Polish and more polished."[5] This process was promoted from the outside by
German-Jewish as well as non-Jewish Americans and, perhaps even more
significantly, embraced by the immigrants themselves.

The Zionist new Jew was thus a national adaptation of an older theme. Zionists were united in their perception of the Diaspora Jew as a degenerated
being (passive and fearful, incapable of resistance or self-help[6]) who had

to be regenerated, even saved, by a national transformation. Still, historian Anita Shapira discusses different models of the Zionist new Jew. The model adopted by most Zionist factions, including socialist Zionists (who created their own specific variant), was the one influenced by Friedrich Nietzsche's ideas. This new Jew was supposed to be active, live close to nature, and be strong, powerful, proud, creative, and emotional, at times violent. According to another model mentioned by Shapira, promoted by Theodor Herzl and others and based on Western middle-class liberalism, the old Jew lacked personal courage, physical grace, tact, and aesthetic sensibility, whereas the new Jew would be brave, graceful, and polite. Although this secular Western model was never fully accepted by Zionist ideological factions, whose activists came mainly from Eastern Europe, it did affect the image of the new Jew promoted by Zeev Jabotinsky, the founder and leader of the Revisionist Zionist movement. Jabotinsky promoted "majesty" as the hallmark of the new Jew, based on the model of the tidy, clean, polite, and decent English gentleman.[7]

The Zionist new Jew was first incarnated in the shape of the pioneer who came from the Diaspora, a place of humiliation and persecution, to build a new national Jewish future. While the exilic Jew represented religiosity and intellectualism, and was depicted as passive and neurotic, the pioneer was seen as an active, artless, physical man of manual labor.[8] The Zionist image of the old Jew was strongly influenced by antisemitic notions, whereas the new Jew assumed traits of simplicity, bravery, and physical strength, traditionally ascribed in Europe to the Jews' antagonists and "opposites," such as the Ukrainian Cossacks.[9] Next to carry the torch of the new Jew was the Sabra, whose nativity supposedly disconnected him from the cumbersome legacy of the Diaspora. As mentioned in the first chapter, the healthful, courageous, active, tough, direct, informal, deeply rooted, spontaneous, and uncomplicated Sabra was perceived as the extreme opposite of the old Jew.[10]

When we move from the strategic, ideological level to the tactical one, we find that the Sabras nurtured a special behavioral style, which partly fulfilled the new Jew ideal in its Nietzschean variant but also included other unprescribed elements. Shapira mentions the Sabras' rough manners, their dislike of bourgeois culture and of expressing emotions, their emphasis on physical elements rather than intellectual ones, their preference for activity over talk, and their strong connection to their native land.[11] As we saw in the fourth chapter, the manly Palmachnik warrior — who epitomized the ultimate Sabra — recoiled from formality and discipline.[12]

Anthropologist Tamar Katriel analyzes a unique Sabra style called "*dugri*." In literal spoken Arabic the word means "straight," but when adopted by spoken Hebrew it assumed the meaning of "direct." In Arabic "to speak *dugri*" means to tell the factual truth, as opposed to a lie, whereas in Hebrew it refers to a stylistic manner of saying things, associated with frankness, honesty, and trustworthiness, as opposed to hypocrisy, dishonesty, and diplomatic parlance. This direct style of speech evolved during the 1930s and 1940s among the first generation of Sabras, especially from families of European decent, and became a prominent element in the cultural style of 1950s Israel. The *dugri* style was not considered by its users as impolite or offensive but rather as expressing important cultural virtues in its unembellished directness.[13]

Katriel describes the *dugri* style as part of the Zionist cultural revolution and the creation of a new Jew in the Land and later the State of Israel. The old exilic Jew was perceived as an unproductive busybody, engaged in ingratiating himself to non-Jews and in Talmudic hairsplitting. *Dugri* speech reflected the Sabra's break from this cultural-mental attitude. It also fed the vision of an equal society, based on mutual trust rather than social hierarchy and its stylistic mannerisms. Israelis were aware that *dugri* speech entailed abruptness, but it was culturally accepted because it enabled daring interpersonal communication. Katriel explains that *dugri* speech was considered assertive: unlike the helpless, passive old Jew who wouldn't speak his mind, the opinionated Sabra was independent and bold enough to voice his thoughts openly. *Dugri* speech was enforced by the value of honesty: direct parlance evoked trust, while indirect style aroused suspicion. A manner of speech correlated to the speaker's inner thoughts and feelings was a source of interpersonal faith and became a mark of worthy individuals and valuable social relationships. *Dugri* speech was also tied to spontaneity. In its stark simplicity it was an "anti-style," reflecting the Sabra's sharp separation between talking and doing. The Sabras didn't regard speech as a social act but rather as an avoidance of action. The less attention one paid to one's speech and style, the more one was perceived as committed to real action. The *dugri* style was therefore terse and matter-of-fact, devoid of decorations and metaphors. It was associated with social solidarity, binding Sabras through its linguistic and cultural inner code.[14]

Israelis were sometimes encouraged to speak *dugri* and praised for doing so.[15] The following anecdote from 1950 is a telling example: "Three-year-old Danny was holding some chocolate in his hand. An [older] boy said to him: 'Such a small boy with such a big chocolate.' [Danny] replied: 'Don't say that

I'm small and the chocolate is big—say directly that you want a piece.'"[16] Despite being younger, Danny reprimanded the older boy for not putting his wish in a straightforward manner. He easily comprehended the insinuation behind the remark, but by the age of three already resented its indirectness. Whereas in some cultures a clear-cut request ("I want a piece of your chocolate") might sound like an uncouth demand, according to the 1950s Sabra code it was the honest way to ask for something. Note that Danny's insistence on rough *dugri* speech went hand in hand with generosity, his reply indicating a willingness to share his chocolate once approached frankly. As we recall, the Sabras were named after the fruit of the common local cactus to indicate their rough and prickly exterior and their sweet interior. Their *dugri* speech, therefore, was not identified with a boorish essence but, to the contrary, and befitting the romantic noble savage, purportedly disclosed their unassuming honorable nature.

While in many respects, as Katriel shows, the Sabra *dugri* style materialized and continued the Zionist new Jew ideal, it could simultaneously be seen as a generational rebellion. The Sabras did not resist the dominant political power and ideology, molded by the founding generation; indeed, they complied obediently with both. However, their *dugri* behavior, and especially their disdain for pompous, long-winded speech, could be read as an assertion of their generation's uniqueness, as a practical daily resistance to the dominant cultural norms of the preceding generation, whose members were still leading the state. While members of the founding generation regarded the Sabras as the realization of the New Jew ideal, they also recoiled from their offspring's roughness and scornful attitude toward ideological rhetoric.[17] In 1953 an Israeli scholar of education described the Sabras' generational rebellion as an understandable reaction. The founding generation *used* their juniors by treating them as the only tool for implementing Zionist ambitions; the sons, he wrote, were expected to accomplish the vision of their fathers. The vision "forced itself" on the youths, who had to put all their strength into its realization. Is it surprising, the scholar asked, if they consider the former generation's ideals as hollow clichés that do not express their own experience? Isn't the younger generation entitled to "add its personal touch to its role and vocation"?[18] *Dugri* style was thus part of the manner in which the Sabras made their own imprint on Zionist reality, their generation's distinctive practical, laconic, antiornamental translation of the new Jew ideal.[19]

We can also find visual manifestations of the Zionist new Jew ideal in people's dress, a topic that has been discussed in detail elsewhere.[20] "In our country," wrote a local journalist in 1954, "the simplicity of dress has reached dimensions unknown in other countries."[21] Indeed, a common style of dress in 1950s Israel was a casual, informal, seemingly careless combination of long or short cotton pants, mainly dark blue or khaki, and a cotton shirt or chemise, with plain double-strapped sandals in summer and flat and solid black or brown shoes in winter. Men who opted for this style typically wore their hair short with a prominent forelock; women either cut their hair to neck or shoulder length, or kept their long hair tied or braided. Israel's Mediterranean climate probably contributed to the informal attitude toward dress, and its widespread popularity in the 1950s was interrelated with the meagerness of resources in postwar Israel while also expressing the ideological values of the national centralist ethos.[22] The simple style of dress upheld the aspiration of creating a new Jew by visually negating the look of the old traditional Diaspora Jew. Rather than covering and hiding the body, loose and bare garments emphasized the body and enabled free movement, unlike the physical restrictions imposed both by the long, thick garments of the traditional old Jew and by the strictly cut contours of the bourgeois suit. This informal style propagated the merits of the new Jews — it exhibited their healthful, upright bodies, intended for active, bold tasks. The simple, informal style became identified as representative of Israeli national dress, particularly for men but also, to some degree, for women. Associated during the prestate era particularly with the pioneers, it had become much more common in Israeli society, even among urbanites and even on "dressy" occasions. It was associated with the Sabras and their native culture and with the brave Palmachniks, and was widely recognized as reflecting Israeli authenticity and quintessence.[23]

Israeli informality, an accepted cultural norm inherited from the prestate era[24] and enhanced by the opinionated, spontaneous attributes of the *dugri* style, was also expressed in disobedient behavior. Whereas disobedience could pose many daily problems (for example, as encountered in previous chapters, noncompliance with policemen's orders), and in certain instances could even endanger lives,[25] it too could be described as an endearing quality, part and parcel of the Sabras' independence. Sports provided an illustration of this angle. Jewish South African immigrants brought with them to Israel unique sporting traditions such as rugby, lawn bowls, and cricket. A sportswriter reporting on the latter "Anglo-Saxon game in Israel" in 1955 was decidedly unenthusiastic. He accurately predicted that cricket would never appeal to Israeli crowds, quoting a taxi driver who was present at the match: "Such a cold game — just like the English." Israelis, the sportswriter added, were used to "hotter" sports and were therefore unlikely to take to this "gentlemen's sport." Moreover, a referee's ruling in cricket was decisive and uncontested — an unheard of idea for Israelis.[26] Six years after the founding of the state, the dominant Israeli "mentality" was sufficiently consolidated to consider certain sports un-Israeli, suitable only for "Anglo-Saxon" minorities. Although the writer used an ironic tone and was probably somewhat judgmental about Israelis' contesting of referees' rulings, he nonetheless seemed to share Israelis "hot" preferences and described them approvingly, even proudly. After all, Israeli disobedience was an exact opposite of the submissiveness that Zionists associated with the exilic old Jew.

Disobedience could stem from Sabra overconfidence, as expressed in a know-it-all attitude, sometimes accompanied by a general sneering dismissal of non-Sabra persons and phenomena.[27] As we recall, Sabras who encountered snow for the first time in 1950 assumed that Israeli snow was the best, and were quick to recover from their surprise and take charge of things.[28] In 1949 a kibbutznik father instructed his Sabra son on how to behave when an expected visitor enters the room. "Say hello nicely and give him your hand," he said, to which the child responded: "What are you teaching me for? I already knew all this when I was a baby."[29] Importantly, this anecdote, in which the cocksure child replies so dismissively and impolitely to his father, was told not as a criticism but rather as an amused boast about the charming "chutzpah" of the Sabras. To members of the founding generation, who tried to create a new Jew in the Land of Israel, there was something gratifying about the self-assurance of their native-born children. One of the stereotypical characteristics of the exilic old Jew, which Zionists abhorred, was his lack of confidence, branching into diffidence, submissive servility, excessive deference toward non-Jews, and self-loathing. Sabras' arrogant confidence was therefore an evident contrast to this hated facet of the old Jew, and seemed to prove that once a Jew was raised in a national context in his own true homeland, his head would naturally be held high.

How did Israeli informality and its accompanying characteristics strike outsiders? George Mikes wrote that he "liked very much the complete absence of pomposity in offices, including the highest offices and ministries," where no one "tried to impress me with the importance of his position." However, he was less appreciative of the Israeli swagger, which he found very annoying. "Every single Israeli is a propagandist and usually a bad one," he wrote, and admiration for Israel's truly great achievements "is almost cancelled out by the irritation caused by this permanent boasting." Mikes also noted that no criticism was taken in good humor: "If something is absolutely and quite obviously indefensible, they will tell you that it is an inheritance from the Mandate and that they have had no time as yet to put it right."[30] A contemporary American tourist went further when portraying Israelis' inability to handle unfavorable comments. He claimed that when Israelis are told that the bathroom in a café is in unacceptable condition, they immediately start boasting of their victorious accomplishments during the War of Independence. . . ."[31] As a consultant in a tourism firm summed up in 1956, "Israeli manners border on sheer bragging and make a bad impression on tourists."[32]

The Sabra's unapologetic loudness, rudeness, and disobedience could be judged unfavorably when measured from the outside. But even in Israel itself, not everyone approved of the *dugri* style of speech and of the Sabras' informal and coarse behavior. The positive word used to describe the likable, but tough, guy was "hevreman." Borrowed from Yiddish, the word literally means "a man of the group" and it indicated someone who was informal and friendly, a "good sport" who accomplished things capably and successfully.[33] In 1951 a writer who viewed the hevreman *un*favorably tried to explain the historical "source of the famous Sabra manners." Members of the founding generation, he argued, were victims of racial hatred and social oppression in the Eastern European small towns and confused "the fair appearance of their enemies and oppressors with the evil content of the latter's hatred." They therefore rebelled against any picturesque expression and replaced the bourgeois tie with short khaki pants, thus creating the hevreman type. This rude and disrespectful Sabra hevreman is nowadays well known "from the street, the bus, the cinema line." Some find this impolite hero charming, and the educators of the young generation maintain and even nurture the features of this type. The hevreman was born out of a wider revolution and was required during a period "when the [Jewish] mind had to overcome its complexes." But now, argued the writer, this type has no place. "It is time to educate our youths properly. We need men of healthful spirits, disciplined, well mannered, and generous, owning Western culture in the beautiful sense of the word."[34] The unnamed writer's notion of the ideal new Israeli suggests the Western liberal model of the Zionist new Jew, fashioned after the perfect gentleman. But as we recall, this model was hardly adopted by actual Zionist factions and remained marginal even on the ideological level. One of the central tenets of this neglected model, notably missing from the dominant Nietzschean new Jew model, was politeness.

Manners are a changing cultural construction.[35] Polite behavior and language have to be acquired; one must learn and be socialized into them.[36] Politeness is usually associated with mutual social cooperation, consideration, and refinement, but sociologists have found different definitions of "politeness" in different national cultures. While Americans, for example, associate politeness with affability, the Japanese do not — preferring closely observed etiquette. The English connect politeness with formality, restraint, regard for the other, discretion, aloofness, and an attempt not to be a burden, while Greeks connect politeness with intimacy, warmth, and friendliness. Russians, too, define politeness as involving warmth and friendliness, as well as avoidance of vulgar speech. Non-Russians, however, often experience Russian manners as too direct,[37] whereas Russians interpret Western European manners as insincere.[38]

Standards and definitions of good manners often differ or conflict among people from various classes, ethnic backgrounds, and age groups. In immigrant societies, such as 1950s Israel, several conventions and norms coexisted simultaneously and, at times, clashed. Shaul Robinson, an expert in education, mentioned in 1953 that "the normal educated civilian is accustomed to the manners of the society in which he lives; but what about a diverse society, in which even the social 'elite' does not share one form of politeness?"[39] The Israeli elite's lack of unified behavioral norms could be observed in a comparison of the state's first two prime ministers. When the writer and editor Shlomo Grodzensky visited Israel in late 1949, he was sitting at the buffet of the Israeli parliament (still located in Tel Aviv, before its move to Jerusalem) and noticed Ben-Gurion, who walked over to him. Grodzensky documented their dialogue, conducted in Hebrew and interspersed with English and Arabic:

I: Shalom, chaver [comrade] Ben Gurion.

He: (looks hard, tries to remember).

I: Grodzensky.

He (angry at himself): Oh, Grodzensky, *cmoovan, bata* for good? [Oh, Grodzensky, of course, have you come for good?] ("for good" was said in English).

I: Well, it's a preface (*hakdama*) to "coming for good."

He: (raising his voice) Ani sonay hakdamot! (I hate prefaces).

I: But, you know it's not so easy. I have a family, two young children . . .

He: In what century are you living? You send a cable to New York, put them on a plane — and *chalas* [that's it] (an end in Arabic!)

Prime Minister Moshe Sharett
visiting David Ben-Gurion in
Kibbutz Sde Boker, 1955.
National Photo Collection
(Government Press Office), D683-030.

Talk to a man like that! But his charm is just overwhelming. Before I said goodbye he told me that he wants to talk to me about something and asked me to get in touch with him.[40]

Grodzensky recorded not only Ben-Gurion's famous impatient directness and total lack of ceremonious formality, which many found charismatic, but also the strong Polish pronunciation that characterized his stark Hebrew speech. Moshe Sharett (1894–1965), Israel's first foreign minister, replaced Ben-Gurion as prime minister when the latter withdrew temporarily from the government and settled in the Negev. Sharett, who mastered eight languages, was also known for his particularly rich and correct Hebrew. His meticulous and formal comportment and dress were sometimes contrasted with the briskness and informality displayed by Ben-Gurion.[41]

Sharett's gentlemanly, tactful reserve was highlighted in an anecdote titled "The Polite Prime Minister," published in a politically unaffiliated newspaper in 1954:

The soldier, who entered the prime minister's car when it stopped to give him a ride on the Tel Aviv–Jerusalem road, did not even bother to greet the prime minister.

Sharett was caught between two passions of his, his politeness on the one hand and his zeal for the Hebrew language on the other, but he succumbed to the former. In order not to insult the impolite soldier, he said to his secretary in Arabic, "[He] doesn't [even] say hello."

Yet the prime minister did not know one thing: the soldier was a new immigrant who understood only Arabic.[42]

Sharett's politeness stood out in Israeli impolite society and distinguished him as the "polite prime minister." Yet the anecdote presented politeness as pointless: all Sharett's efforts led him, ironically, to use the only language that the indecorous soldier knew. Since the final joke was at Sharett's expense, the title "polite prime minister" should be read not as praise but as ridicule. Faced with a polite prime minister after an impolite one, it seems as if some Israelis did not necessarily prefer politeness and did not automatically view courteous civility as the example they should be following.

Yet beyond a generalizing impression of typical impoliteness, we can trace in 1950s Israel a variety of manners, as well as a range of attitudes regarding proper manners, according to differences in ethnicity, class, age, gender, and ideological affiliation. Both overall impoliteness and inner variants were already apparent in the Jewish community of Palestine. That community, too, was described as informal and discourteous, although the definition was subject to the eye and expectations of the observer. Whereas a Jewish Zionist visitor praised 1930s Tel Aviv for its all-Jewish intimacy, which made it possible to start up a conversation with anyone at all,[43] British functionaries usually felt that the Jews in Palestine were unpleasantly "loud, chaotic and aggressive," especially when compared with local Arabs, who impressed them as "picturesque, flattering and sympathetic."[44] The wife of a British officer, for instance, wrote in the late 1930s about the horrible manners of young Jewish natives on the Tel Aviv beach. Incivility, she wrote, was unfortunately characteristic of the entire Jewish community, with the exception of a small number of polite and elegant German-born Jews.[45]

German Jews, who arrived in Palestine after the Nazis came to power, were received by the majority of Eastern European Jews with mixed feelings. Many Yekkes — as the German Jews were called locally — looked down on the local community as an inferior continuation of the Eastern European shtetl, and criticized its lack of order and manners. German Jews stood apart from Eastern European and Middle Eastern Jews not only in their insistent use of German, their higher education credentials, and their Western cultural capital but also in their daily preferences and demeanor, and the great store they put in punctuality and meticulousness, aesthetics and cleanliness.[46] The polished manners of the Yekkes were not welcomed by their Eastern European predecessors, who feared that the former were becoming "a German island" within the Jewish community of Palestine.[47] Jokes were circulated about the Yekkes, targeting their rigidity, their alienation and their inability to master Hebrew properly, their formality and deference. In these corrective jokes, the Yekkes were set against the spontaneous and informal new Jew.[48]

German Jews stood out less noticeably after the founding of the state, due to the growing diversity of Israeli society and the non-European elements in the mass immigration, which seemed more conspicuous to longtime Ashkenazi Israelis and drew more attention. Still, the Yekkes continued to be regarded as the local "champions of etiquette," a quality that appealed to Western tourists and "high society."[49] In 1952 a journalist was taking a taxi with a tourist along one of Tel Aviv's busiest roads during rush hour. Suddenly an ambulance siren was heard, but none of the drivers took any heed and they kept driving uninterrupted, with the exception of one small car, which obediently stopped while its driver signaled the ambulance to pass through. The tourist was horrified that this car alone had made way for the ambulance ("I have never seen anything like this"), to which their taxi driver responded: "Look at the car's driver and you'll see straight away that he's a Yekke. Only the Yekkes are such idiots."[50] When higher education was resumed after the War of Independence, a student from the Technion criticized some of the Yekke professors, who didn't understand "the spirit of the times" and maintained an outdated distance from their students.[51] Yekkes were the rare exception to the Israeli rule, whose bearing met Western standards; but while their manners were not entirely unappreciated locally, they were regarded by other Israelis as too rigid, pedantic, and guileless. In Israeli culture, formal courtesy could be perceived as affected pretentiousness and pompous snobbery.[52]

In 1954 the scholar of Oriental studies Yosef Yoel Rivlin described the clashing norms in Israeli society. Rivlin believed that a mutual cultural blend should take place naturally and gradually, and opposed the attempt to force Israeli society into a unified entity according to the Ashkenazi paradigm. Sephardim and Ashkenazim embrace different concepts regarding social relations, he reasoned. While upholding courtesy, the Sephardi views Ashkenazi "truthfulness" as aggressive crudeness. For his part, the Ashkenazi regards Sephardi politeness as a false deception. The Sephardi is moderate, measured, and composed, whereas the Ashkenazi's temperament is loud and frantic. While Sephardi modesty is considered hypocritical by Ashkenazim, Sephardim view Ashkenazi honesty as impudence.[53] This description does not refer to the new immigrants but rather to the established Sephardi elite who lived in Palestine before the Zionist immigrations. Rivlin, who translated the Quran into Hebrew, descended from a distinguished Jerusalem family and he could assert Sephardi values with scholarly confidence. New immigrants from a lower status, who held less economic and cultural capital than Rivlin, might have found it harder to assert themselves. In the case of many Yemenite Jews, for instance, the older members of immigrant families looked on with horror as their children hurried to adopt Ashkenazi secular norms while neglecting their parents' traditions: "They forsook all the goodness of Yemen without acquiring any new goodness" in Israel. According to the older generation, these youngsters, males and females alike, "were spoiled by excessive freedom" and "some of the girls have become in Israel even more brazen than the boys."[54]

Clashing norms in Israel were not related solely to ethnic backgrounds but also to ideological affiliations. Socialist Zionists, both in the prestate era and after the founding of the state, regarded politeness and detailed formalities as decadent bourgeois hypocrisy. Sabras too associated etiquette with affected bourgeois insincerity, as opposed to the authenticity and straightforwardness of *dugri* style. Israeli discourteousness was thus not a mere *lack* of politeness but often an intentional, ideological discarding of courtesy. Once again we can sense Russian and Soviet influence. Russian manners are proverbially direct, and "genuine" Russian politeness, as we saw, is characterized by warmth, openness, spontaneity, and taking an interest in others.[55] Like French revolutionaries, Russian revolutionaries preferred simple *civilité* over refined politeness. They did not consider old-fashioned politeness a token of worthy culture but rather an obstacle in the way of achieving it. Thus, the 1917 revolution included the abolition of "bourgeois" politeness and language. "Soviet" and "bourgeois" were presented as polar opposites, and many customs, such as fashionable dress and hand kissing, were condemned as "bourgeois."[56] These antibourgeois Soviet notions were adopted by many Israelis, especially by Sabras.

Katriel mentions that a *dugri* conversation could be held without causing offense only if all the participants shared the *dugri* code and the cultural ethos underlying it.[57] Young Sabra directness could clash with older middle-class notions, as depicted in an anecdote from 1951:

Prime Minister Moshe Sharett visiting Kibbutz Nahal Oz in April 1955, after its attack by the Egyptian army. Located on the southern border near Gaza, Nahal Oz was the first Nahal settlement in Israel and became a kibbutz in 1953. Note the visible difference between Sharett's elegant formality and the kibbutz members' Sabra-style dress, as well as their informal postures. National Photo Collection (Government Press Office), D275-061. Photo by Paul Goldman.

A [kibbutznik] boy took the bus. He saw a woman standing, tugged at her sleeve and said: "*Haverah* [Hebrew for both "friend" and "comrade"], sit."
The woman was angry: "I am not your *haverah!*"
He replied: "So stand, if you please, madam."[58]

Like young Danny from the chocolate anecdote, the kibbutznik was able to comprehend and use a polite style of speech ("if you please, madam"), but his initial gallant gesture of offering his seat was rejected by the passenger, because he employed the *dugri* style, as well as making physical contact by tugging at her sleeve. The incident juxtaposed two opposite codes of manners. The kibbutznik boy refrained from stylistic mannerism and intended to perform a concrete act of politeness; the woman, however, could not read the code or recognize the selflessness beneath the rough exterior, for which she was "punished" — that is, the boy referred to her politely, as she had demanded, but withdrew his kind invitation. Told from the *dugri* standpoint, the anecdote contrasted plain speech = true helpfulness with polite speech = selfish inaction.

Politeness could become a location of social struggle over communicational customs.[59] The offended lady in the bus reminds us that not all Israelis admired Soviet directness or adopted *dugri* style. Zeev Jabotinsky spoke of a Zionist ideal that combined citizenship with economic initiative, national values, a republican ethos, and individualism. The Revisionists' ideal of "majesty," referred to earlier, promoted a well-groomed, well-mannered Western European gentleman.[60] However, this ideal was only partly adopted in practice by the activists of the Revisionist movement,[61] and the gentlemanly norm was further marginalized after the founding of the state. Mapai, the leading party, could now use state institutions to enhance its ideology and its ethos and to spread them among wider sectors of the population; the number of Israeli natives was increasing and with it their influence on daily culture; and longtime Israelis, previously divided by political and ideological affiliations, now enjoyed social and economic advantages over the new immigrants and composed a comprehensive dominant layer.[62] Faced with the distinctly different subcultures of Israeli Arabs and new Jewish immigrants from Muslim countries, longtime Ashkenazi Jews might have unconsciously "closed ranks," and despite political disagreements, on the cultural level they gathered around a general, wide, and unified version of "Israeliness."

Still, Western notions of politeness and etiquette were apparent, for instance, among the Yekkes and some urban Polish Jews[63] and occasionally reappeared as instructions aimed at an urban middle-class readership. A leisure magazine in 1954 listed some basic table manners, as "no other routine activity in our daily life accentuates the extent of our manners as much as eating." The list of prohibitions targeted Israeli tendencies (described in other sources too[64]): don't "attack" the food, don't stuff your mouth, don't eat and swallow noisily, never talk with a full mouth, don't insert food into your mouth with a knife, don't smoke during the meal, and so on.[65] Eastern European table manners were considered "barbaric" according to modern Western standards,[66] and nineteenth-century campaigners on behalf of the Haskalah tried to improve the table manners of the Jews.[67] In 1950s Israel new immigrant children from Egypt, Turkey, and Romania were praised for their polite table manners, and children from Iraq and Yemen were praised for being quick learners of such manners.[68] On the other hand, as we shall see, some Israelis regarded table manners as unimportant. Moreover, even while delivering etiquette instructions, various sources discussed manners not as an inseparable part of daily life and something that should become second nature for all but rather as a conscious custom to be implemented by specific segments of society on specific occasions. Thus, a cookbook suggested that the housewife maintain order and aesthetics on her table but that an exact order of tableware and cutlery was maintained only by "sticklers for politeness."[69] Instructions for setting a table clarified that "in our daily life we don't stand on all the customary ceremonial details," but only "when important guests arrive for a festive meal" one should know how to set a table "according to conventions."[70]

Instructions about etiquette were aimed at Israeli women more than men. A women's magazine described the informal and rude behavior of "the modern girl" as unfeminine. It also published the pictorial quiz presented at the opening of this chapter ("test your knowledge in the laws of politeness"). Even though the quiz was addressed to women readers, most items in it actually concerned male courtesy, such as getting up when introduced to a woman, helping a woman put her coat on, opening the door for her, and carrying her heavy luggage.[71] Similarly, a movie magazine instructed young women on polite behavior when going with a young man to the cinema.[72] A newspaper urged women to "learn to be loved" and directed them on how to find favor with their husband through steps such as constant self-grooming and using his favorite perfume: "Last but not least: be humble and modest. Namely, behave properly and do nothing to upset your feminine perfection. Impolite eating, excessively free conduct in society, and wild laughter — all these undermine the woman's magic."[73] The following year the same paper assured its female readers that "every woman can be charming." In England, it related, women take special courses to become socially graceful, and "in our country, which is blessed with so many seminars, we could certainly do with a course to teach the women of Zion good manners."[74]

Impoliteness, as we saw, could in some respects be nicely integrated into the ideal new Israeli, while politeness could be perceived as unmanly and decadently bourgeois. But what about the new Israeli woman? Didn't politeness clash with her ideal? The concept of the pioneer was gendered from the outset and gradually masculinized, and women were marginalized in the myths of the pioneer, the Palmachnik, and the Sabra.[75] Like most national movements, Zionism nurtured the image of a male new Jew while the new Jewess remained vague. The image of the mythical male Sabra was complex and included some unclear elements and contradictions, but the mythical female Sabra was even less distinct and almost insignificant. Her image was based on a couple of stereotypes regarding her physical appearance, a general commitment to contribute to the national mission, and her passive role as the fighter's girlfriend, awaiting his return from the battlefield.[76]

The ideal Sabra girl was depicted as natural and unaffected in her dress and in her manner, a woman who avoids pretentious airs and coquetry. She was supposed to wear neither makeup nor perfume, just as she had to refrain from smoking and drinking alcohol.[77] However, alongside the common ideal of the graceful-but-artless Sabra, 1950s Israeli popular culture enveloped a different feminine ideal, linked with the cosmopolitan urban young woman. And while the ideal female Sabra was expected to show some healthful *dugri* style, it appears that the middle-class urban woman was "allowed," and sometimes even encouraged, to nurture and exhibit good manners. While the ideal new Israeli man was formed and defined more precisely, and toughness was one of his admired traits, the new Israeli woman's image was loosely defined, enabling more diversity. Orit Rozin suggests that women's marginality made them less obligated than men to the centralist ideal.[78] Indeed, since women were less socially and politically central than men, they didn't have to constantly "prove" their commitment to Israeli codes and norms in their behavior. Thus, while all Israeli men were expected to wear simple, casual, and informal clothes, urban women were "permitted" to wear more fashionable, decorated garments. We find comparable sartorial divisions in other historical cases in which men, politically central, were required to dress according to the ruling political ideals whereas women, politically marginal, were less limited and enjoyed a greater "freedom of dress."[79]

Although a closer look reveals the absence of uniformity and a variety of alternatives, by the 1950s Israeli society was already notoriously impolite. In 1950 an American Jewish tourist confessed that he had heard rumors about "Israeli manners and politeness" in the United States but that his visit to Israel showed the situation to be even worse than reported: "When a man is forced to behave politely it turns out badly," because his artificial smile reveals actual contempt and scorn, and it is quite obvious that he doesn't express true embedded courtesy but is only after the tourist's much-needed dollars.[80] As manners are acquired from childhood in one's immediate habitus, fake manners cannot convincingly replace deeply rooted and natural self-regulation.[81] Trying to keep up appearances and pretending to be polite for the sake of foreign eyes wasn't an easy task for Israelis.[82] Yet Israelis craved international recognition, and leaving a bad impression on outsiders was considered a national disgrace. In 1950 a sportswriter claimed that

lessons should be learned from international soccer matches: the local stadium was too small, he wrote, the tickets too expensive, the seats uncomfortable. He suggested hiring more ushers and making sure they behaved politely
toward spectators, "as befits a civilized people." In addition, he wrote, the
games' organizers "must show our guests that we, too, have order and discipline."[83] This desire to present Israel to outsiders as a "civilized" country was
hampered by the general lack of order, discipline, and politeness in Israeli
society.

Following the poor athletic performance of the Israeli national team at
the 1952 Olympic Games in Helsinki, Prime Minister Ben-Gurion established a special committee to investigate the delegation's conduct. While ul-
timately finding no proof of misconduct, the committee nevertheless found
certain organizational faults.[84] On the delegation's deportment, for example, one witness testified that, while several escorts behaved politely, the
Israeli sportsmen lacked "any civility whatsoever." They never thanked the
women from the Helsinki Jewish community who prepared their food, and
displayed bawdy rudeness toward the younger women of the community.
Another witness depicted Israeli behavior more leniently. He assented that
the Israeli guys "showed no respect" when they met members of the Helsinki Jewish community but explained that the delegation was composed "of
average Israeli youths." Before traveling to Helsinki, the Foreign Office gave
them a form with instructions about "customs in the Northern countries,"
and the members of the Israeli team signed it and indeed followed these instructions. However, the witness admitted that "We [Israelis] have no manners compared with the Scandinavian countries." Some of the guys were
ignorant about proper table manners, "because in Israel we take no notice
of such trifles," and they had to be corrected. Israelis disliked the discipline
in the Olympic camp and often grumbled about the rigid lights-out hour
at 11:30 p.m. Israelis also spoke much louder than the Swedes and the Finns
but not louder than the Americans and the Argentines. A third witness described Israelis' loud talk as the only decorum offense he had witnessed but
dismissed it as negligible: "The Jews talk loudly, but so do the Italians and the
French. The English, on the other hand, practically whisper."[85]

Interestingly, the third witness did not attribute loud talk to *Israelis* in particular but to *Jews* in general. Israeli impoliteness was often associated with
the Sabras,[86] but the wild Israeli mentality could also be connected to the old
Jew. Since the days of the Haskalah, Eastern European Jews were depicted
by external observers as impolite, hectic, and loud.[87] The Zionist leader and

physician Max Nordau described the nervousness of Diaspora Jews as part of their cultural degeneration.[88] Psychiatrists — Christian and Jewish alike — described the ghetto Jews, among other things, as hysterical and neurotic.[89] Zionists claimed that the life of the Diaspora Jew had been controlled by "disorder, disorganization, and negligence."[90] So in 1950s Israel a contemporary observer ascribed local bad manners, disrespect, and inconsideration to archetypical Jewish features: Jews, he wrote, tend to be more anxious than other peoples, and despite Jewish bravery during the War of Independence, "a general tendency to panic" still abides in Israel.[91] Another observer likewise argued that local rudeness, hysteria, and bad manners were Jewish characteristics. The hot climate, he added, is not the cause of Israeli tension, as some people claim, because evidently "our Arab neighbors are not plagued by Israeli nervousness."[92] According to this viewpoint, Israeli abruptness was not a novel, Zionist alternative but rather a continuation of old behavioral patterns characteristic of the Eastern European Jewish shtetl.[93] When a journalist praised the well-behaved new immigrants from Iraq, he added that as they stand patiently in the long lines, without complaining or swearing, they seem like Englishmen rather than Jews.[94]

Whereas formal Hebrew culture, molded by the founding generation in the prestate era, negated the Diaspora as a sordid Jewish relic, remnants of exilic Jewish culture were imported by Zionist immigrants and maintained in daily practices, often unconsciously and involuntarily.[95] This importation of Diaspora cultures certainly increased after the founding of Israel with the mass immigration. Furthermore, as historian Israel Bartal argues, the cultural relationship between longtime Israelis from the founding generation and newcomers was not one between a native culture and imported cultures but rather a relationship between different imported cultures.[96]

In a comparative study that includes the Israeli case, Michael Walzer shows that the storm of national liberation passed over both ancient societies and reborn nations "with rather less effect" than the movements' militants expected and hoped for. The radical rejection of the past left too little material for cultural reconstruction, while the old ways, cherished by many, were sustained "under the eyes of the militants but out of their sight."[97] Such informal, often unintentional and inadvertent, cherishing of the old ways characterized some of the Zionist immigrants. As one scholar put it in 1949, Israeli Jews had the homeland on their tongues but exile in their hearts and minds.[98] Moreover, when Israeli natives expressed their authentic total detachment from Diaspora Jewry, its culture, and its traditions, members of the founding generation felt surprised, disappointed, and rather offended.[99] When the Zionist ideal of the new Jew was realized by Sabras in their own extreme, native version, the founding generation suddenly seemed much more Jewish by comparison.[100]

Whether Israeli bad manners were a new phenomenon or remains of the old Jew, those who disapproved of them expected the problem to be solved by some official interference, thus echoing the centralized viewpoint and policy of 1950s Israel. They suggested announcing national politeness competitions and establishing special governmental and municipal committees that would engage in improving local courtesy.[101] And indeed, by the early 1950s, impoliteness and inconsideration had already become the accepted and expected Israeli norm, and hence in order to achieve feats like silence or courtesy local municipalities, firms, and schools had to announce an "Operation Silence" or an "Operation Courtesy" or an "Operation Respect for the Aged."[102] Whether criticized or laughed away fondly, impoliteness was recognized as an Israeli characteristic, while politeness, as the exception to the rule, was often regarded as a redundant trifle and a luxury that had to be pointed out, plainly explained, and officially demanded.[103]

While Israeli impoliteness might have become particularly notorious, Israeli informality was more easily situated within broader developments. The twentieth century witnessed a long-term process of the informalizing of Western manners, which became more lenient and more varied. Since the beginning of the century, the United States had been rising as a leader in this process, because of the relatively early historical development of an American youth culture and the growing influence of Hollywood, and after World War II American manners served even more easily as a model elsewhere.[104] Israel's popular culture was certainly influenced by American trends,[105] but Israeli informality was more extreme and harsher than the friendly American casualness, and it differed from the latter with its heavy emphasis on authenticity and directness. Whereas American ease fit with American comfort, tougher Israeli informality fit with Israeli discomfort. "We have become accustomed to the discomfort caused by other persons," noted an Israeli in 1952. The Israeli way of life, he claimed, lacked decency and good manners. Local discomfort enveloped unsuitable government clerks, who behaved aggressively and rudely, young men who wouldn't offer their seats to pregnant women, and buses that always arrived late.[106] That same year another Israeli described aggressive and offensive speech, disobedience, and unruliness as "stinging whips of violence" that assault you all day long, "when you walk on the street, sit in the public vehicle, or read the daily newspaper."[107]

Inconvenient informality was experienced, inter alia, in impolite service, as we have encountered in the bus and the movie theater. This too was an inheritance from the prestate era and perhaps influenced by Soviet Russia, where the rudeness of service staff became legendary.[108] In addition, in immigrant societies services are often supplied by people whose cultural and educational background presumably qualifies them for higher professions. An asymmetry between original background and present occupation may have rendered Israel a democratic and friendly atmosphere, but this vague social structure also affected the manner in which services were delivered. Rather than behaving submissively and courteously, suppliers of services often expressed indignation, as if insulted by having to serve either their equals or social inferiors. A lack of service consciousness or service culture had emerged in Jewish Palestine, reflecting the amorphous structure of its immigrant society,[109] and this tendency, described in numerous instances, continued and even escalated after the state was founded, when scarcity increased the dependency of consumers and clients on various services.[110] A new immigrant was amazed, for example, when the vendor at a kiosk gave him a dirty glass, unwashed after having been used by the previous customer, and when he dared protest, she yelled at him.[111] A local anecdote related how a tourist waved his cigarette toward a waiter, wishing for him to light it, only to be declined by the waiter, who read the gesture as an offer and replied that he himself didn't smoke.[112] A resident of Jerusalem arrived to pay her taxes at the municipal office, where she was sent upstairs and downstairs and so on. When she finally came to the last office, she recalled, "I waited endlessly and got very tired. I asked the clerk politely whether I could get a chair. He answered very mockingly: 'DO YOU WANT SOME JAZZ TOO?' I thought I did not quite hear well and asked: 'What do you mean?' He said: 'I mean, do you want some music too?'"[113]

The new state apparatus required thousands of new civil servants, some of whom behaved very rudely,[114] and in 1955 the Tel Aviv–Jaffa municipality issued a guide titled "The Civil Servant and the Public," which instructed government clerks about the meaning of democracy, public relations, morality, efficiency, and proper service. Written by the known writer Emanuel Ha-Rusi, the guide explained the complexity of Israeli clientele, which made the clerks' job doubly important. On the one hand, the immigrants from "backward countries" had become used to living on charity (in the immigrant camps) and unaccustomed to democratic liberty and so they interpreted their new freedom in the wrong way. In addition, wrote HaRusi, these immigrants had no roots in the homeland and their lack of Hebrew knowledge alienated them even further. On the other hand, longtime Israelis came mostly from Eastern European countries, so they too were unfamiliar with the proper democratic relationship between the government and its citizens. On top of that, during the prestate era the Jewish community opposed its British rulers, and therefore its members were used to contesting the government rather than cooperating with it. Nonetheless, wrote HaRusi, Israeli civil servants must be patient and courteous; the man of noble spirit "knows how to restrain himself and subdue his primitive impulses," and even when faced with difficult clients, the clerk should be forbearing and let them "get some 'steam' off their chest."[115]

Another inconvenient aspect of Israeli informality was the amount and the nature of local noise. Noise, like manners, is a changing cultural concept,[116] and in 1949 Mikes noted that the quality of the noise in Tel Aviv differs from London noise: "In London everybody is quiet, people do not talk, cars do not hoot, news-vendors do not shout and the cumulative effect of all this silence is the pandemonium of a huge metropolis. Tel Aviv's noise is the result of individual effort. Everybody does his best. Every throat, car-hooter, lorry-engine, anxious mamma and obedient child makes its, his or her contribution."[117]

In attending to other daily sounds in 1949 Tel Aviv, we hear bellowing radios and loud talk, neighbors practicing their musical instruments, amateur "politicians" yelling their arguments in the cafés, young couples and groups shouting in the streets, the deafening conversations of the Dan cooperative drivers in the bus station[118] — all of which were characteristic of Tel Aviv during the prestate era as well.[119] Longtime Israelis of the founding generation looked back nostalgically and tended to relate Israeli shortcomings to the present, to young natives, or to new immigrants, but certain local noisy manners certainly continued uninterrupted from the previous decades.

The animated, unceremonious, noisy, and disorderly atmosphere in 1950s Israel, apparent in material and behavioral facets of daily life, could be experienced as a vital and warm thrill or as an anxious and nerve-wracking overload; but in either case, inconvenience and roughness became embedded in local culture. Whether Israelis complained or joked about these qualities, inconvenience and roughness were present in daily work and leisure activities, reinforced by the style of local speech and manners. Some of their manifes-

Under the title "Quiet Please" and as part of a 1949 "Operation Silence" in Tel Aviv, this notice addresses owners of radio sets: "Your neighbors want to rest!"

Kol hamishmar haezrachi,
September 1949, 13.

tations could be traced back to Eastern European Jewish culture; many were already apparent in the Zionist community of Palestine and would later become an Israeli norm.

The sphere of behavioral conventions and norms was hardly controlled by any precise strategy. The ideal of the new Jew could be viewed merely as an interpretive scaffold, loosely surrounding the tactical level, in which Israeli informality, straightforwardness, and rudeness were practiced on a daily basis. As expected in modern multigenerational societies in general, and immigrant societies in particular, behavioral tactics were constantly negotiated among differing—and sometimes conflicted—sets of norms and conventions. Sabra *dugri* style could be appropriated with nuance. As we saw, women were "allowed" more delicacy than men, and Israelis were expected and asked to tone down their directness and rudeness when they met foreigners. The prevailing Sabra norm was challenged every now and then by rebukes and complaints, made by longtime Israelis from the founding generation. Rather than viewing *dugri* style as the embodiment of the desired new Jew, challengers described it either as a variation of old Jewish nervousness or as an annoying, redundant remnant of a former transitional phase. The Sabra norm was ignored by some Yekkes, Sephardim, and new immigrants, who chose to maintain their original traditional manners rather than assimilate into the prevailing dominant informal culture.

But Sabra style was usually regarded positively as an authentic, quintessential expression of Israeli culture. To a certain degree, it seems as if the strategy followed the tactical level and was molded by justifying and glorifying behavioral daily patterns. Thus, the actual informality, straightforwardness, and rudeness of the Sabras were not necessarily conceived as flaws that should be improved and corrected but rather depicted frequently as an endearing part and parcel of the total whole. They were legitimized after the fact through favorable contrasts with the sordid behavioral patterns attributed to the exilic old Jew. Historian Catriona Kelly maintains that the sharp distinction between "Soviet" and "bourgeois" enabled Soviets to reject comfort and at the same time blur the actual continuation of bourgeois values within Soviet culture.[120] Perhaps the new Jew/old Jew dichotomy was comparably useful in Israeli society? The clarity of the strategic level was never achieved on the tactical one, in which ideals were implemented incompletely and sometimes translated into new, unexpected practices. But by using a dichotomous construction, Israelis could celebrate the newness of their national culture while disregarding the lingering remnants of the old diasporic Jew in Israeli society.[121]

Conclusion

IN EXAMINING THE UNOFFICIAL implementation of hegemonic Israeli ideals in daily life, this book began and ended with two central modes of social interaction. Its first main chapter, following a general discussion of a freak snowfall, was dedicated to linguistic policies and practices, and its last discussed behavioral norms, conventions, and manners. In between we have also covered two issues of public reference and three public spaces. The rationing regime permeated many aspects of daily culture, as we learn from the humor woven around it; comparably, security issues were not confined to the IDF, and cultural militarism could be found in several civilian areas. By reconstructing the experiences of taking the bus and going to the movies, we have studied the common way of transport and the common form of entertainment. We have also visited the communal dining hall, the central public space of the kibbutzim — the Israeli communities most closely associated with the hegemonic ideals of the 1950s. The picture that emerges from this tour of daily public interactions and sensibilities is much more heterogeneous and disordered than that yielded by accounts from studies of the political, ideological, and intellectual spheres. The newness of the state and its "frontier" characteristics are blatantly apparent when we turn our gaze to the practical facets of the everyday. After encountering so many symptoms of raw beginnings and expressions of hectic disarray, we might wonder, by the time we reach the final chapter, why, in such chaos, anyone would even bother about polite manners.[1]

While studying Jewish collective memory in prestate Palestine and Israel, historian Billie Melman challenges the presentation of local culture as a uniform and cohesive entity. She argues that cultural hegemony was not omnipotent and demonstrates that memory, as part of the everyday, was pluralistic and "polyphonic."[2] And indeed, the scholarly focus on Israel's statism and centralism often blurs, and sometimes unintentionally conceals, the messy confusion of daily life. The well-founded conclusion about a successful national hegemony is mistakenly interpreted to show that Israeli society

188 · *BECOMING ISRAELI*

achieved relative homogeneity. And as long as our research is confined only to formal layers (state institutions, political parties and ideologies, "high culture," education, and so forth), findings will usually support and enhance this orderly portrait of decisive hegemonic control, on the one hand, occasionally encountered by conscious political opposition, on the other. And no wonder: formal institutions and set doctrines serve as the agents that promote hegemonic ideals, and they are also the loci at which the same hegemonic ideals can be explicitly contested. The research of these institutions and doctrines certainly produces interesting and convincing results, but these results contain only the clear-cut outlines of formal hegemony and the equally straightforward contours of opposition. Studying hegemony from the angle of mundane daily practices provides a fresh viewpoint, because this informal layer of social interaction does not lie under the political and ideological lamppost. Here we find a wide array of intermediate positions, which are often indefinite and vague. Uncharted by official doctrines, these informal sensitivities, norms, and convictions are enacted in ordinary practices. In order to view the effects of hegemonic ideals on people's actual lives, not only on their conscious ideology, we should avoid limiting our study to narrated principles and formal policies; and as we envelop more daily practices and informal interactions, the picture that surfaces becomes increasingly multifaceted and versatile.

If we wish to understand the workings of Israeli hegemony, a mere distinction between those associated with a hegemonic position and those who remained outside its borders does not suffice. We ought not to presume that while the latter were not always successfully blended in the national melting pot, the former were a unified unit that either fulfilled hegemonic ideals or manipulated them knowingly. Tracing the mechanisms of a successful hegemony requires a closer look at the tangible conduct, rather than the stated doctrines, of the populations who shared, supported, and promoted hegemonic ideals. Thus, directing our attention to the daily practices of longtime Jewish Israelis, mainly members of the European founding generation and their Sabra offspring, has taught us that hegemonic ideals were neither wholly fulfilled nor treated with total cynicism. National ideals were only partly implemented by the dominant Israeli groups and, when so, they were modified in various manners, not always intentionally or even consciously. Indeed, cultural practices can be intentional actions, but they can also be transmitted, reproduced, and transformed even when their participants act with no conscious ideological intent.[3]

The complexity of our case study was further explored by using Michel de Certeau's "strategies" and "tactics" as analytical tools. We know that practices are not deployed in a separate universe but instead are tied intricately to dominant models and norms. And while daily behaviors respond to technologies of power, they also leave their mark on broader political sensibilities and procedures.[4] By focusing on strategies and tactics,[5] even over a short span covering eight years, we have viewed Israeli culture as a dynamic process rather than a fixed entity. Examining the spheres of language, rationing humor, cultural militarism, bus riding, moviegoing, communal dining in the kibbutzim, and regular Israeli manners has revealed a variety of strategic-tactical dynamics.

Some tactics were controlled and dictated by the strategic physical, economic, legal, or political framework. However, strategies were often modified and altered through negotiations with prevailing tactics, as exemplified in the cases of language, transportation, and kibbutz lifestyle. Sometimes tactics appropriated the strategy, when norms were adopted in daily practices but went through processes of adaptation and translation, lending them different characters and meanings; this dynamic was frequently evident in the fields of cultural militarism and daily manners. Israeli culture in the 1950s included exceptional challenging tactics, such as when new immigrants refused to learn Hebrew as part of a wider disposition to acculturate into Israeli society. Yet more often, as we saw in the discussion of moviegoing, strategy was merely ignored by Israelis, who disobeyed the formal elitist norm without necessarily attempting to directly fight or substitute it.

The Israeli case demonstrates that the cultural process cannot be cleanly summarized as a dramatic dichotomous conflict between a technology of power from above and a civic resistance from below. Such a clear-cut bidimensional presentation is naïve and historically inaccurate. As we saw, in daily life dealings between strategies and tactics do not occur solely on the extreme poles of control and resistance but also, and to a large degree, along less specified spectrums through negotiation, appropriation, and disregard. Power, like all elements of social life, is inherently unstable,[6] and we have learned that the strategic level in 1950s Israel was varied and constantly negotiated from within. On the other hand, even when the tactical level did not follow or echo the power structure, it was not necessarily subversive and its relationship with strategy was not always oppositional and disruptive. Cultural practices can involve pragmatic appropriation[7] as well as resistance to power and ideology, socioeconomic circumstances, or dominant cultural norms.[8]

This study reveals that daily practices play an important role in culture not because they unavoidably resist strategies but precisely because they provide such a wide and varied range of behavioral responses. Even in an era known for its institutional statism and ideological centralism, and even within the framework of a successful hegemony, Israeli culture was riddled with clashing differences, unresolved dissonances, surprising collaborations, and prolific negotiations. The finer shades and semishades of historical reality in the first years of statehood should not be artificially forced into an unambiguous theory;[9] rather, as John Fiske argues, practices should "be allowed to expose the incompleteness of theory, to reveal the limits of its adequacy, and specificity should be able to assert the value of that which generalization overlooks or excludes."[10] It is these daily "fruitful tensions between seemingly irreconcilable forces and ideas"[11] that are lacking from the popular images of 1950s Israel, both from the sentimental version of a heroic age and from the condemnatory version of a domineering regime.

While experiencing contradictions and confusion, Israelis found creative ways of coping with and making sense of daily disarray. Hegemonic ideals, even when not implemented in practice to the letter, provided a conceptual framework. In their various appropriations and translations, performances and embodiments, on the conscious level as well as implicitly, these ideals served as a broad orientation and thus helped many ordinary citizens view their daily lives as meaningful. Perhaps this is why, even from within this hectic daily scene, Israelis sometimes could be bothered about manners and presented the topic as a national issue.

Even when not necessarily implementing the pioneering ideal in their own lives, longtime Israelis kept regarding this ideal, with its attributes of dedication and self-sacrifice, as a central motivation for national immigration. They transferred their aspirations from the prestate era onto the new immigrants and found it hard to accept the latter's different motivations and priorities. While new immigrants were often disappointed to find themselves treated with disdain and their lot unimproved in their new country, longtime Israelis felt that their basic ideological ideas were being disregarded.[12] Although the new immigrants were too varied and, at this stage, too weak to create a unified culture that could challenge the hegemony, still longtime Israelis were reluctantly forced to acknowledge that some prestate ideals must be abandoned.[13] The 1950s were thus characterized by messianic rhetoric and sincere high hopes, on the one hand, and a painful mood of broken dreams, on the other. Since realizing national aspirations was accompanied by inevitable disappointments, the difficulties of the present bred nostalgia for the past; new immigrants could direct this nostalgia to their countries of origin, whereas longtime Israelis, both Arabs and Jews, directed it to the prestate era.[14]

Avoiding both nostalgia and judgment, this book offers a messy picture of Israel during its first years of sovereignty. Hopefully the reader will accept this mess as an accurate description of historical reality, rather than attribute it to the shortcomings of the author. The very act of describing practices in retrospect casts them into some linear narrative order. Still, even after charting daily life into words, the depiction that emerges is less dichotomous, less determined, and less elegant than depictions of official institutions and formal activities. Yet when we include some of the messier aspects of social interaction, when we acknowledge dissonance as an inseparable part of human and social life, when we do not impose our desire for clarity on murky historical reality, we can also appreciate the subtle dynamics of hegemony and the various ways in which it affected people's lives. During the early years of statehood, Israeli leaders eloquently described the mammoth economic, social, and security tasks that faced the young state; but it is when we view the 1950s "from the ground" that we can truly appreciate the challenges and perplexities, as well as the thrills, experienced by ordinary Israeli citizens during these first years of statehood.

Notes

Preface

1. Kiryat Anavim bulletin, August 26, 1949—KKAA.
2. Bar-Gil and Schein (2010), 308.
3. Hacohen (1998), 266.
4. Walzer (2007), 133.
5. Shachar (1963), 57–58. Dowty (1995), 41, 43. Yonah and Shenhav (2005), 53.
6. Gramsci (1997), 15. Lears (1985), 571–575. Hall (1979), 332–334. Hebdige (1993), 366.
7. Dowty (1995), 37. Lissak and Cohen (2011), 195. Rozin (2011b), 15.
8. Hebdige (1979), 17. Hebdige (1993), 366–367. Fisk (1998), 376. Brooker (1999), 29–30. Gottdiener (1985), 979–991, 998.
9. Certeau (1984), xi–xv.
10. Certeau (1984), xi, xiii, xix. On the process of producing and consuming culture, also see Hall (2001).
11. Chartier (1995), 83, 86, 88–91, 95–97.
12. The 1948 war is known by different Israeli versus Palestinian names. The one chosen here — the War of Independence — follows common usage in most 1950s Israeli documents.
13. Hadari-Ramage (1995), 355–373. Bar-On (1997), 26. Bar-On (2001), 250–251. Weitz (1998), 241–244. Rosenthal (1997), 192–193. Shalom (1992), 213.
14. Quoted by Moser (1998), 195.
15. As suggested by Herzog (2000), 212–213.
16. On the War of Independence as a break, see Horowitz (1993), 44–45. On the centrality of war and violence in historical discontinuity, see Zerubavel (2003), 82–100.
17. For example, see Douglas (2002), 6.
18. On this "bias towards the political and towards the apparatus of the state," see Melman (2002), 57.
19. Among the latter, Rozin's studies of Israeli housewives during the rationing regime stand out: Rozin (2002a), Rozin (2005a), Rozin (2005b), Rozin (2006), Rozin (2010), Rozin (2011a).
20. The relationship of the human body to the body politic should not be ignored: Fiske (1992), 162.
21. On the integrative approach to history, see Jordanova (2012), 4, 161, 168. On different kinds of information gleaned from archival documents, see Rozin (2011b), 4–5.

22. For more on methodology see Chartier (1988), 1–13, 27–28, 37–48, 109–110. Chartier (1991), 18, 81–83, 197–198.

23. In striking contrast to previous decades, when local daily life was rarely the direct subject of comment and debate. See Helman (2010), 8–9. And compare with the 1950s as the heyday of American sociology and social psychology, when "new forms of living and working presented scholars with all manner of inquiries." See Gundle (2008), 246.

24. Campbell (1997), 47, note 1.

25. I would like to thank Nitza Genut, who suggested the family album parallel at the Institute of Contemporary Jewry's departmental seminar on January 15, 2008.

26. Shavit (1992), 61.

27. Mikes (1950), 41–44. Dankner and Tartakover (1996), 14. The slogan was viewed mockingly by some disappointed longtime Israelis: Horowitz (1993), 44. And see joke in *Dvar hashavu'a*, July 20, 1950.

28. On topics chosen by historians see McKibbin (2000), vi.

29. Ben-Porat (1999), 106–107, 122–123, 129. Gelber (1996), 453. Rozin (2005a), 188. Dowty (2001), 41, 43. Horowitz (1993), 55.

30. Kimmerling (1999), 171. Also see Dowty (2001), 55–56; Enoch (2001), 98.

31. Fiske (1992), 162, 165. Also see Del Negro and Berger (2004).

1. Introducing Israel in White

1. *Davar*, February 10, 1950.

2. Schor (1956), 45–46. See photos by Verner Braun, Fritz Shlezinger, and Rudolph Jonas from 1950 — JNFPA, d179-191, d179-205, d735-267.

3. *Davar*, February 6, 1950, February 8, 1950. Israeli Government (1952), 322–323. Haaretz Annual (1950), 90.

4. For instance, *Davar*, February 9, 1950. *Yediot aharonot*, February 7, 1950. *Yediot aharonot layeled*, February 10, 1950. *Ma'ariv*, February 6, 1950, February 10, 1950. *Hatzofeh*, February 12, 1950. *Haboker*, February 7, 1950. *Herut*, February 10, 1950. *Haaretz*, February 9, 1950. *Jerusalem Post*, February 10, 1950.

5. Horowitz and Lissak (1990), 241. Gat (2002), 191. Shlaim (2004), 658. Bar-On (1997), 26. Bar-On (2001), 250–251. Weitz (1998), 241–244.

6. *Davar*, February 6, 1950. *Yediot aharonot*, February 6, 1950. *Hatzofeh*, February 6, 1950. *Ma'ariv*, February 9, 1950. *Haaretz*, February 7, 1950, February 9, 1950.

7. *Davar*, February 9, 1950. *Yediot aharonot*, February 8, 1950. *Ma'ariv*, February 9, 1950. *Haaretz*, February 9, 1950.

8. Gelber (2001).

9. *Yediot aharonot*, February 8, 1950. And see Geva newsreels from 1951: SA, VT GE 02.

10. See photos of Arab returnees in the Galilee (1949), Acre (1949), and Jerusalem (1950): CZA, 1089223.1, 1088928, 1287330.1. *Palestine Post*, December 19, 1949.

11. *Haboker*, February 10, 1950. *Haaretz*, February 10, 1950.

12. Ozacky-Lazar (2006), 5–21. Greitzer (1997), 151–168. Cohen (2000), 23. Also see Ozacky-Lazar (1996). Boymal (2006), 399–400. Also see Cohen (1951), 131. Schor (1956), 53. On the historiography of the topic, see Haidar (2004).

13. Ozacky-Lazar (1996), v–xx. Ozacky-Lazar (2001), 61–71. Peretz (1991), 100. Dowty (2001), 55–59. Cohen (2000), 116–123. Korn (2008). Boymal (2006), 405.

14. Boymal (2006), 407–408. Sa'adi (1997), 198–199. Amara (2004), 138–139.

15. Gross (1997), 147–149. Giladi (2002), 76–80.

16. Giladi (2002), 76–80. Boymal (2006), 409. Photos by Hugo Mendelson and Fritz Cohen of traditional plowing in Arab villages in 1949, 1955, and 1956: NPC, D298-105, D298-082, D316-050; photos by Ilan Bruner and Fritz Cohen of mechanized plowing in Arab villages in 1954 and 1955: NPC, D299-104, D299-105, D299-099.

17. Shalev (2004), 87. Aharoni and Mishal (2005), 183–184. Abbasi (2012), 412–414. Also see Geva newsreels from 1954: SA, VT GE 05.

18. Schely-Newman (1997), 403. Photo from 1956: NPC, D770-004.

19. Porat (1997), 395–396. Boymal (2006), 399–400. Geva newsreels from 1953–1954: SA, VT GE 01, VT GE 06. Photo from 1950: CZA, 1012066. On the development of the Jewish Negev, see Porat (1993). Also see Shalom (1992), 202.

20. *Ma'ariv*, February 7, 1950; *Haaretz*, February 7, 1950.

21. *Davar*, February 7, 1950, February 8, 1950. *Yediot aharonot*, February 7, 1950. On the "Ein Shemer disaster" also see *Hatzofeh*, February 12, 1950.

22. *Ma'ariv*, February 7, 1950.

23. Lissak (1998), 13. Enoch (2001), 84–87, 90. Sikron (1987), 32, 42. Gat (2002), 193.

24. Enoch (2001), 91–94. Sikron (1987), 35–40.

25. Drori (2006), 247. Sikron (1987), 42.

26. Shapira quoted by Meir-Glitzenstein (2011), 165.

27. Mikes (1950), 150–155. Gat (2002), 196–198. Meir-Glitzenstein (2009), 110. On the geographical spread of the new immigrants, see Sikron (1987), 45–50. The conditions in the camps are documented in Geva newsreels from 1950–1951: SA, VT GE 01, VT GE 02. Also see photos from 1953 and 1954: CZA, 1335137, 13327; and photos by Zoltan Kluger from 1955: CZA, 1281915, 1281924.

28. The subsequent winter was also particularly cold and rainy, and transit camps were flooded. See Israeli Government (1951), 333. Gat (2002), 198. Photos from 1951: CZA, 1281052, 1281054. Also see notice in *Hatzofeh*, January 28, 1952.

29. *Yediot aharonot*, February 6, 1950.

30. *Davar*, February 7, 1950. *Ma'ariv*, February 6, 1950, February 7, 1950. *Hatzofeh*, February 7, 1950. *Herut*, February 9, 1950. Also see tents collapsing under the snow in the Rosh Ha'ayin immigrant camp, photo from February 1950 by David Eldan—NPC, D237-037. In the following, rainy winter, the government announced a special project to provide shelter for children from the camps. While 2,253 children were housed in various state institutions, 1,383 children stayed with families who voluntarily opened their homes—see Sapir (1951).

31. *Ma'ariv*, February 7, 1950. Also see *Davar*, February 7, 1950. *Ma'ariv*, February 7, 1950.

32. *Haboker*, February 9, 1950.

33. *Davar*, February 7, 1950. Also see the medical staff in the Rosh Ha'ayin immigrant camp, photo from February 1950 by David Eldan—NPC, D199-099.

34. *Davar*, February 7, 1950. *Haaretz*, February 7, 1950. *Ma'ariv*, February 6, 1950, February 8, 1950. *Jerusalem Post*, February 8, 1950, February 13, 1950.

35. *Ma'ariv*, February 10, 1950. Also see *Hatzofeh*, February 10, 1950.

36. Cartoon in *Hatzofeh*, February 10, 1950. *Haboker*, February 9, 1950.

37. *Yediot aharonot*, February 6, 1950. *Haboker*, February 9, 1950.

38. *Hatzofeh*, February 8, 1950. This description, which appeared in the religious Zionist newspaper, was followed by a reference to a raging political polemic over the education of children in the transit camps. The journalist voiced his opinion that such wonderful religiosity should not be crushed by secular education.

39. Gat (2002), 201. On Ben-Gurion's mild, noncoercive formula for the melting pot, see Don-Yehiya (2008), 409–411.

40. Guilat (2001). Guilat (2010). Also see Meir-Glitzenstein (2011), 168. Gerber (2013). On the image of the Yemenites among Ashkenazim, also see Ben-Amotz and Hefer (1979), 62, 69, 92–93, 133–134, 194.

41. Enoch (2001), 95–105. Giladi (2002), 10. Rozin (2011a). On ingrained and persistent mutual prejudices between Jews of European, African, and Asian origins, see Sapir (1951), 8, 14, 17, 28.

42. Mikes (1950), 39–40. Also see Meir-Glitzenstein (2009), 121.

43. Rozin (2002b). Rozin (2011a).

44. *Ma'ariv*, February 3, 1950. Also see Halamish (2008). Meir-Glitzenstein (2009), 145.

45. Giladi (2002), 9–16, 25–29. Also see Gross (1995), 231–241. Barkai (2004). Bareli (2007).

46. Haaretz Annual (1950), 60–61. Also see Barkai (2004), 55.

47. *Haaretz*, February 6, 1950, February 9, 1950. *Davar*, February 7, 1950, February 9, 1950. *Ma'ariv*, February 2, 1950, February 6, 1950, February 7, 1950, February 9, 1950.

48. *Ma'ariv*, February 3, 1950, February 5, 1950, February 6, 1950. *Yediot aharonot*, February 7, 1950.

49. Lissak (1998), 41–42, 53–54. On the nostalgic view of the prestate era, see Shapira (1996b), 254. Shavit (1992), 70. Horowitz (1993), 44–45, 53. Bareli (2007).

50. Giladi and Shwartz (2001), 11–15, 73. Golan (1997), 83–102. Geva newsreels from 1954: SA, VT GE 06. Also see photos by Fritz Cohen from 1950: NPC, D401-063, D401-064, D401-065, and photos from 1950 and 1952: CZA, 1333781, 1273986.

51. Ben-Artzi (2002). Schely-Newman (1997), 403. And see Geva newsreels from 1952: SA, VT GE 01.

52. Giladi and Golan (2001), 77–143. Efrat (1997), 103–112. Sikron (1987), 51. Meir-Glitzenstein (2009), 113–128.

53. For instance, *Yediot aharonot*, February 6, 1950. *Ma'ariv*, February 6, 1950, February 8, 1950. *Haaretz*, February 7, 1950.

54. Shalom (1993). Katz and Paz (2004). Mikes (1950), 74. And see photos of war devastation in Jerusalem in 1949, 1950, and 1951: CZA, 1333853, 1333897, 1011867, 1333871, 1012559, 1012560. Photo by Fritz Cohen from 1950: NPC, D543–070.

55. Mikes (1950), 74. On the plight of Jerusalem also see *Gazit*, May–June 1949, 6–7.

Al hamishmar, April 27, 1952. *Hador*, April 2, 1954. *Tavruah* 9, 1956, 3. Letter from May 11, 1955: JCA, 2615.

56. *Yediot aharonot*, February 8, 1950. More details about damage from the snow in Jerusalem are available in *Yediot aharonot*, February 6, 1950, February 7, 1950. *Haaretz*, February 12, 1950.

57. *Herut*, February 9, 1950. Also see *Haaretz*, February 7, 1950, February 8, 1950. *Ma'ariv*, February 7, 1950. Cartoons in *Haboker*, February 10, 1950, and *Haaretz*, February 10, 1950.

58. *Haaretz*, December 20, 1949.

59. *Ma'ariv*, February 6, 1950. Also see *Yediot aharonot*, February 8, 1950. Photo from 1950: CZA, 1333953.

60. *Ma'ariv*, February 9, 1950.

61. *Haaretz*, February 8, 1950. Also see *Herut*, February 8, 1950.

62. *Haboker*, February 10, 1950. Even international soccer matches had to be canceled: see *Yediot aharonot*, February 12, 1950. Telephones were still a luxury item in the early 1950s, and Israeli communication was based on the radio and print media.

63. *Herut*, February 9, 1950.

64. *Herut*, February 8, 1950.

65. Weitz (2001), 5–77. Zachor (1997), 33–35, 38–39. Bareli (2007).

66. On the notion of *mamlakhtiyut*, its origins and development, see Kedar (2002). And compare with notions of nationalism in postwar Britain: Edgerton (2011), 6, 40, 42.

67. Quoted by Lissak (1998), 28–29.

68. Dowty (1995), 36–37. Don-Yehiya (1995), 176, 180. Yanai (1996), 136. Don-Yehiya (2008), 57. Kedar (2002), 129. On the characteristics of the Zionist new Jew, see Shapira (1996a), 427–441. Segev (1984), 277. On the role of *mamlakhtiyut* in unifying the politicized prestate society, see Dowty (1995), 37. Dowty (2001), 5–64. Alatout (2008), 44. Bareli (1999), 25–27, 36–37.

69. Sapir (1951), 19. Eisenstadt (1953), 182, 191. Shtal (1976), 14–17. Shtal (1979), 41, 43. Don-Yehiya (1995), 176, 180. Also see Enoch (2001). Segev (1984), 123, 129–131, 148, 155–160, 167. Lissak (1998), 24–29. Yaar (2007), 74–76. Kimmerling (1999), 172, note 13.

70. Near (1992a), 116–125. Zachor (2007), 137. Also see Drori (2000), 30, 32. Gelber (1996), 450–451. Ben-Avram and Near (1994).

71. Kabalo (2003), 125–126, 152–153. Also see Kedar (2010), 42–43.

72. The prestate pioneering ethos, later idealized by longtime Israelis, was actually practiced by a minority, although it was hailed and admired by the entire community. See Gelber (1996), 450–451. Kabalo (2003), 143. Helman (2010), 89–91.

73. Bareli (1999), 38–39. Zachor (2007), 153–155. Rozin (2005a), 188. Rozin (2011a). Ben-Porat (1999), 113–114. Lissak (1998), 38, 53–54. Giladi (2002), 60. Gelber (1996), 453. Kabalo (2003), 134. Kabalo (2008), 99, 103.

74. On the contradictions within Ben-Gurion's centralism, see Horowitz (1993), 46.

75. See Shavit (1992), 66–68. *Zmanim*, February 12, 1952, October 15, 1954.

76. *Hatzofeh*, February 7, 1950.

77. Cohen (1997), 227–242. Cohen (2001). Don-Yehiya (1984), 55, 93. Bartal (2001), 241–244. Shalmon (1987), 279–283. Segev (1984), 226–227.

78. *Hatzofeh*, February 7, 1950.

79. *Yediot aharonot*, February 6, 1950, February 10, 1950.

80. *Hatzofeh*, February 12, 1950.

81. *Haaretz*, February 7, 1950.

82. Helman (1999), 195–196.

83. Drori (1995). Cohen (2010), 243.

84. *Davar*, February 7, 1950.

85. *Yediot aharonot*, February 7, 1950. *Ma'ariv*, February 7, 1950, February 8, 1950. *Herut*, February 8, 1950.

86. *Davar*, February 6, 1950. *Hatzofeh*, February 12, 1950.

87. *Haaretz*, February 8, 1950.

88. *Davar*, February 9, 1950.

89. *Haaretz*, February 9, 1950.

90. *Yediot aharonot*, February 6, 1950. *Ma'ariv*, February 6, 1950. *Hatzofeh*, February 6, 1950, February 12, 1950. *Herut*, February 7, 1950, February 8, 1950. On a woman whose eye was injured by a snowball, see *Haaretz*, February 10, 1950.

91. *Yediot aharonot*, February 6, 1950. Photo by Herbert Mayerovitch of Moshe Dayan and other soldiers and officers enjoying the snow: CZA, 1025028.

92. For instance, *Davar*, February 6, 1950. *Yediot aharonot*, February 6, 1950. *Hatzofeh*, February 7, 1950. *Ma'ariv*, February 6, 1950. *Jerusalem Post*, February 7, 1950, February 12, 1950. *Yediot aharonot layeled*, February 10, 1950.

93. *Davar*, February 7, 1950. And see children playing in the snow in Haifa, photo from February 1950 by Rudolph Jonas — JNFPA, d735–267.

94. Gelber (1996), 453–454. Also see Sivan (1991).

95. Radai (1956), 78–79. *Dorot*, October 20, 1949, 8–9. For a less idyllic view of the Sabra, see *Zmanim*, September 27, 1954, October 1, 1954, October 6, 1954.

96. Shapira (1996b), 174. Almog (1997). Ben-Rafael (1994), 60–61. Helman (2011), 25–26. On the mythic facets of the Sabra image, see Zerubavel (2002), 116–117.

97. Mikes (1950), 25.

98. Helman (2011), 61–62, 115, 117, 122. Satire in *Haaretz*, June 3, 1951. On the acculturating role of youth movements among new immigrants and the social prestige they provided for longtime Israelis, see Sapir (1951), 28, and Ben-David (1954), 243. On the "salon youths" in later decades, see Heilbronner (2011).

99. *Haaretz*, February 7, 1950. *Yediot aharonot*, February 10, 1950.

100. *Jerusalem Post*, February 12, 1950.

2. *The Language of the Melting Pot*

1. Burla (1954), 89–91.

2. *Zmanim*, June 1, 1955.

3. Safran (1992). Ayturk (2007). Smith (2001).

4. Harshav (1990), 11, 48.

5. Dauber (2005), 46.

6. Sofer (2009), 265–266.

7. Reshef and Helman (2009), 309–310. Rubin (2011), 71–73.

8. Rubinstein and Medina (2005), 336–337.

9. Bachi (1956), 189, 191–192. Also see Morag (2003a), 348.

10. Haaretz Annual (1950), 56. And see Rozin (2011a).

11. Bar-Gil and Schein (2010), 308.

12. Compare, for instance, with the teaching of English among immigrants in the United States: see Stewart (1954), 27–29. According to Israel's 1952 citizenship law, some knowledge of Hebrew is required only from candidates for citizenship who are not included in the "law of return," namely non-Jews: Rubinstein and Medina (2005), 337.

13. *Dvar hashavu'a*, February 1, 1951.

14. *Herut*, January 13, 1956.

15. *Dvar hashavu'a*, February 1, 1951. On the roles of folk songs and dances in local culture, see, for instance, Reshef (2012). Roginsky (2007a). Roginsky (2007b).

16. On the political-partisan facet of linguistic policies, see Kossewska (2010), 176.

17. Photos from seven different ulpanim in 1951–1954: CZA, 1332001, 1332025, 1331976, 1331986, 1332077, 1332029, 1332027, 1332043, 1332089, 1014654, 1015753, 1332129, 1332120. The high social status of the ulpanim's students is also apparent in their dress.

18. Fischler (1987), 145–152. And see Hebrew classes for adults in the camps, photo from 1949 and photo from 1950 by Teddy Brauner — NPC, D197-046, D200-096. Photo from 1951 by Zoltan Kluger: CZA, 1281045.

19. For instance, see *Hedei hanegev*, August 1952, 3–6. Gertz (1956), 121–123. Also see photo from 1950 by Teddy Brauner, photo from 1955 by Fritz Cohen, and photo from 1955 by Moshe Pridan — NPC, D294-108, D264-012, D241-047. Photo from 1950 — JNFPA, d3064-101.

20. Maimon (1953), 28, 34. Bulletin of the Jordan Valley Council, 9, March 12, 1951, 5–6 — NNL. And see photo from 1952 of a young native girl helping elderly new immigrants with their Hebrew homework: CZA, 1332044.

21. Morag (2003b), 167. See photo from 1949 by Teddy Brauner and photo from 1950 by David Eldan of children learning Hebrew in the camps — NPC, D859-097, D200-065. Photos from 1950 and 1954 of youths in immigrants' boarding schools: CZA, 1012434, 1329590.

22. Bar-On (2002), 79–81. Drori (2000), 153–154. Morag (2003b), 167. Fischler (1987), 153. Naor (2009), 37.

23. *Bamachaneh la'oleh*, July 8, 1949, January 15, 1950. *Jerusalem Post*, December 4, 1953. *Omer*, October 5, 1952, May 28, 1954, March 26, 1956. *Alonekh*, December 1950, January 1952, March 1952, May 1954.

24. Correspondence from July–August 1949—NA, 1/10. *Jerusalem Post*, July 6, 1951. *Pnimah*, June 1951. *Dvar hashavu'a*, August 2, 1951, August 9, 1951. *Matzpen*, November 3, 1954. On "Telem," see *Zmanim*, February 15, 1955. *Omer*, March 26, 1956. Maman (2007). Lev-Ari (1987), 221–227.

25. For example, Avivi and Persky (1953), 19.

26. Radai (1956), 68–70, 78–79. Also see Kossewska (2010), 183.

27. Radai (1956), 93–95.

28. Ben-Avram and Near (1995), 22–27, 43. According to Halamish, since the 1930s Zionist immigration was not as selective as claimed: Halamish (2006), 440–448.

29. Schely-Newman (1997), 403.

30. *Pnimah*, June 1951, 56–57.

31. Zameret (1993), 204–210. Also see Segev (1984), 194–195.

32. Shaked (1956). Zameret (1997), 133–134. *Omer*, January 12, 1955. *Yediot hamo'etzah hamekomit ir izrael—Afula* 6, December 1955, 7–8.

33. On the recruiting spirit of the operation, also see *Zmanim*, February 13, 1955.

34. Kimmerling (1999), 190.

35. On tendentious and self-righteous presentations of Israeli history, see Seliktar (2005).

36. Shaked (1956), 156–157. Also see Eisenstadt (1953), 182–183.

37. Shaked (1956), 155.

38. Helman (2011), 21–23.

39. Bachi (1956), 179, 246.

40. *Dvar hashavu'a*, June 8, 1950. Also see *Dvar hashavu'a*, June 7, 1951. Sapir (1951), 21. Photo of Romanian immigrant and his "Sabraizing" son in *Ashmoret*, June 14, 1951.

41. *Dvar hashavu'a*, June 29, 1950.

42. Reshef and Helman (2009), 330.

43. *Dvar hashavu'a*, October 25, 1951.

44. *Omer*, March 26, 1956.

45. Bachi (1956), 202–205, 213–218.

46. Bachi (1956), 202, 207–211, 224, 233–236, 246.

47. Shachar (1963), 158.

48. Bachi (1956), 211–212. Also see *Ashmoret*, August 11, 1949.

49. Bar-Gil and Schein (2010), 299–302, 305–307, 312.

50. *Omer*, October 18, 1954.

51. *Ashmoret*, August 11, 1949.

52. Zur (1997), 67–68. Lissak (1999), 71.

53. Shtal (1979), 43. Morag (2003a), 348. Also see Bachi (1956), 224–225, 229–232.

54. For examples, see *Davar*, February 20, 1953. *Haaretz*, June 3 1955. *Herut*, October 21, 1955. Blanc (1954), 388. Also see *Zmanim*, February 15, 1955. Academy of the Hebrew Language (1955). Photo by Verner Braun from the First World Congress of the Hebrew Language in Jerusalem, 1950: CZA, 1301748. And see Morag (2003a), 349–350.

55. *Kol hamishmar haezrachi*, 8, September 1949, 9. Kibbutz Tirat Zvi bulletin, January 8, 1954—RKMA. *Sport la'am*, April 20, 1952. Israeli Government (1954), 264–268. Drori (2000), 174–175.

56. Articles in *Dorot*, October 20, 1949, December 1, 1949. *Baderekh*, May 18, 1952. *Maavak*, April 10, 1953. Advertisement for courses in *Ma'ariv*, May 22, 1949, *Ha'olam*

hazeh, March 29, 1953. Linguistic quiz in *Yediot aharonot,* January 6, 1950. Also see Morag (2003b), 170–171.

57. *Herut,* January 13, 1956.

58. On Nathan Zach, Yehuda Amichai, and the "Likrat" group, see Shaked (1997), 104–105, 112. Shamir (1999), 53. Bar-Yosef (1991), 129–130, 133–134.

59. Another literary-linguistic direction was explored by the Canaanite movement. See Kurzweil (1965).

60. For examples, see *Hasport haleumi,* December 18, 1949. *Ma'ariv,* April 6, 1956.

61. *Beterem,* May 1, 1952. *Hamodi'a,* September 19, 1952, May 8, 1953, January 28, 1955. *Zmanim,* June 29, 1955. Correspondence from November 1955 — JIA, 1-14/1/6. Mikes (1950), 62.

62. *Davar,* January 11, 1955.

63. Ads in *Ma'ariv,* August 21, 1953, *Beterem,* November 20, 1955. *Omer,* January 24, 1952, October 10, 1952, November 21, 1952. *Yediot aharonot,* July 3, 1955. *Zmanim,* February 13, 1955. Letter from September 1949—NA, 10/1. Protocols from September–October 1951 — ISA, g-5548/4. *Ozer dalim,* 1950, 3–4. *Ozer dalim,* 1951, 6–7.

64. Ad in *Hatzofeh,* January 14, 1949. *Ashmoret,* January 11, 1951. *Dagesh,* January 18, 1951. *Yediot aharonot,* April 30, 1954. Zidon (1952), 119. And see Ben-Amotz and Hefer (1979), 70–71.

65. On the development of this native Hebrew during the Mandate era, see Reshef (2013).

66. Even-Zohar (1996), 737–738. Yet in the 1950s features of the spoken language started to gradually penetrate into the written registers of Hebrew: Reshef (2013) 165.

67. Blanc (1954), 390–391.

68. Listen, for example, to the 1952 performance of the Gadna troupe in Geva newsreels: SA, VT GE 01.

69. Blanc (1954), 190–191. *Dorot,* October 20, 1949. *Ma'ariv,* January 31, 1949, August 4, 1950. *Yediot aharonot,* March 29, 1949. *Al hamishmar,* January 13, 1950. *Hamodi'a,* September 5, 1952. *Dvar hashavu'a,* September 10, 1950, April 26, 1956. *Hadshot hasport,* July 1, 1956. Amos Kenan's satirical column Uzi and Co., published in *Haaretz* in 1950–1952, was particularly famous for its native style — see Kenan (1953). Rosen (1955), 281.

70. Rosen (1955). Blanc (1954). Morag (2003a), 349. Morag (2003b), 169–170.

71. Gelber (1996), 459. Almog (1997), 176–186. Keren (2004), 11–12, 22. On the Palmach and its heritage, also see Horowitz (1993), 48–49. Lissak (2000), 345. Efron (2000), 353. Bar-Or (2010). Also see Geva newsreels from 1952: SA, VT GE 01.

72. *Yediot aharonot,* March 31, 1950. *Dvar hashavu'a,* January 5, 1950. *Hamodi'a,* August 1, 1952. *Bamachaneh,* September 22, 1949, June 7, 1951. Also see Morag (2003a), 351. Ben-Amotz and Hefer (1979), 61, 63, 74, 82, 89–90, 213–214. Bar-On (2006), 476. On the close relation between spoken Hebrew in Israel and military experience, see Morag (2003b), 171.

73. Horowitz (1993), 55. Also see Morag (2003b), 167.

74. Bachi (1956), 199, 212–213.

75. Described by Hila Shalem Baharad in her unpublished MA thesis (The Hebrew University, 2011), 79–80. Also see Bachi (1956), 196, 232. Ben-Rafael (1994), 51–52.

76. *Dvar hashavu'a*, April 28, 1949, July 21, 1949, June 7, 1951.

77. *Sheluchot yotzei teiman*, September 14, 1950. Morag (2003b), 167.

78. Eisenstadt (1952), 34–60. On linguistic acculturation among new immigrants from Poland, see Kossewska (2010), 182, 185.

79. For instance, see *Yediot aharonot*, December 9, 1949. Gan Shmuel bulletin, March 30, 1951 — NNL.

80. Halperin (2011), 383.

81. Morag (2003b), 168.

82. *Omer*, November 21, 1952. Photo by Zoltan Kluger from 1949 — JNFPA, d381–033.

83. Photos from 1950, 1952, 1954, and 1955 — CZA, 1299469, 1337117, 1278167, 1278470.

84. Naor (1997), 219–220.

85. Rojansky (2004). Shalit (2006), 96. Kossewska (2010).

86. In addition to a station that broadcast especially for Jewish communities overseas: *Omer*, July 4, 1951. Also see letter from November 9, 1950: LI, IV208–4967. *Herut*, July 18, 1952. Photos of the radio station "Voice of Zion to the Diaspora" from 1951 and 1952: CZA, 1330399, 1330371, 1330361, 1330368.

87. Lev-Ari (1987), 227. *Yediot aharonot*, January 6, 1950, February 1, 1952. *Hador*, December 17, 1950, May 28, 1954. *Herut*, January 5, 1951, February 18, 1951, October 14, 1955. *Haboker*, February 21, 1951. *Al hamishmar*, June 1, 1951. Ad in *Ma'ariv*, August 30, 1951. Poster from June 12, 1953 — PC, V1967–5.

88. Poster from July 12, 1950 — PC, V1978–1. Poster from September 7, 1951 — PC, V1967–7. Ads in *Ma'ariv*, April 30, 1950, *Haaretz*, December 24, 1950, August 18, 1952.

89. Invitation from December 1952 — NA, 13/3. Poster from March 5, 1950 — PC, V1969–2. *Herut*, August 24, 1955.

90. Photos from Beer Sheva, Jaffa, and Safed, May and July 1949, January 1953 — CZA, 1337146, 1278573, 1280064, 1278603, 1278605, 1278599, 1278601. Photos from 1949 by Zoltan Kluger — NPC, D824–030, D822–083. *Ashmoret*, August 11, 1949. Also see cartoon in *Dvar hashavu'a*, May 3, 1949.

91. Protocol from February 5, 1951 — ISA, gl 3881 mb/15. On Judeo-Arabic see Ben-Rafael (1994), 52–53.

92. For instance, *Yediot aharonot*, December 29, 1950. Uri (1951), 100. Fine (2009), 224.

93. Cohen (1951), 133. Also see protocol from November 30, 1948 — ISA, g-36/717.

94. Correspondence from April–December 1949 and protocol from February 25, 1950 — ISA, g-3/717. Letter from November 11, 1949 — ISA, c-9/717.

95. Protocol from November 2, 1952 — ISA, gl 3881 mb/15.

96. Poster from October 1950 — PC, V1970–5(26). Poster from February 1951 — PC, V1967–7. *Al hamishmar*, January 18, 1949. *Yediot aharonot*, December 29, 1950. *Davar*, October 2, 1950. Memorandum from July 15, 1953 — ISA, gl 3882 mb/40. *Ner*, December 1954–January 1955, 16–18. Neeman (1955).

97. *Al hamishmar*, January 18, 1949.

98. For instance, see Simon (1951). For a different viewpoint see *Ner*, December 1954–January 1955, 16–18.

99. Halperin (2011), 346, 349.

100. Zerubavel (2008), 315, 323, 329, 331, 336.

101. The local identity of the Canaanites, by comparison, was based on pre-Arab history and myths.

102. Zerubavel (2008), 325–326, 334.

103. Arditi (1954). Shtal (1979), 28–29. Lissak (1998), 25–26.

104. Halperin (2011), 177–178, 219, 244, 313–314, 317.

105. *Zmanim*, June 29, 1955.

106. Ads in *Palestine Post*, December 9, 1949, *Haaretz*, December 29, 1950, *Davar*, July 13, 1955. *Dvar hashavu'a*, November 13, 1952. And see Bachi (1956), 196. Note the use of British slang in a security poster from 1949: CZA, 1287066.

107. Article and cartoon in *Dvar hashavu'a*, October 30, 1952. *Herut*, October 28, 1955. *Yediot aharonot*, *Koteret*, May 17, 1956.

108. Anecdotes from *Dvar hashavu'a*, March 9, 1950, February 1, 1951. *Kolno'a*, October 4, 1954.

109. Ads in *Ma'ariv*, October 7, 1949, August 15, 1951, *Omer*, May 28, 1954, *Davar*, September 1, 1955, *Yediot aharonot*, *7 yamim*, July 6, 1956. On the use of foreign languages in ads during the Mandate era, see Halperin (2011), 83.

110. Ads in *Ma'ariv*, May 3, 1949, July 29, 1949, April 30, 1950, May 19, 1950, August 2, 1950, July 25, 1952, December 2, 1952, August 13, 1953, August 20, 1953, *Haaretz*, December 27, 1950, *Hatzofeh*, August 13, 1953, *Ha'olam hazeh*, March 17, 1955, May 25, 1955, July 14, 1955. On ads as indicators of appeal and popularity, see Williams (1993). McFall (2004). Leiss et al. (2005).

111. For instance, see photo from 1949 by David Eldan—NPC, D853-084. Photos from 1950 and 1953—CZA, 1364596, 1278602. Posters from 1949 and 1950—PC, V1970-5(26), V1966-2, V1978-1. Also see Morag (2003a), 350.

112. *Bamachaneh*, June 16, 1949. *Ma'ariv*, May 12, 1950. *Kol yisrael*, April 12, 1951. *Herut*, November 12, 1954. *Hador*, May 20, 1955. *Ha'olam hazeh*, May 13, 1954, November 11, 1955. *Kolno'a*, February 25, 1954. *Davar*, May 13, 1955. *Dvar hashavu'a*, February 9, 1956.

113. Helman (2008b), 112. Compare with Arbena (1996), 222 and 233, note 9.

114. *Dagesh*, June 20, 1950, July 13, 1950. *Lahav: biton dati leumi*, Shvat Tashiab (1952), 7–8. *Herut*, February 1, 1952. *Hatzofeh*, January 19, 1954, November 5, 1954. *Zmanim*, December 31, 1954. *Davar*, September 7, 1955.

115. *Herut*, June 17, 1955, August 24, 1955, October 14, 1955. Also see *Alonekh*, February 1953. *Ha'olam hazeh*, January 5, 1956, June 21, 1956. And compare with Kroes (1996).

116. Helman and Reshef (2007), 73. Helman (2010), 117.

117. Letter from December 28, 1950—ISA, gl 3882 mb/23.

118. Protocol from December 25, 1950. Letters from January 19, 1950, December 18, 1950, and December 28, 1950. Letter from December 14, 1955. Correspondence from April–June 1951. Protocol from February 26, 1951—ISA, gl 3882 mb/23.

119. Decisions from 1949—ISA, gl 3881 mb/12. Letter from August 2, 1949—ISA,

gl 3882 mb/27. Correspondence and protocols from May–November 1951 — ISA, g-9/714. Decisions from 1952 — ISA, gl 3882 mb/23. On the heated debates about reparations from Germany, see Weitz (2001), 117–145. Also see Hirshberg (2006), 512.

120. Letter from August 2, 1949—ISA, gl 3882 mb/27. Also see Helman (2010), 117.

121. Compare with McKibbin (1998), 423, 432, 455–456. Vaughn (1996), 238. Jones (2006), 231. Kroes (1996), 155–156.

122. Letters from December 19, 1950, December 26, 1950 — ISA, gl 3882 mb/23. Also see *Haboker*, December 14, 1952.

123. *Jerusalem Post*, July 5, 1951. Programs, invitations, and postcards from 1955 — NA, 12/2. *Herut*, June 5, 1955. Bachi (1956), 207–208. Helman (2010), 135. Helman (2002), 365.

124. *Ashmoret*, September 8, 1949. *Dvar hashavu'a*, July 13, 1950, September 28, 1950. *Hamodi'a*, March 21, 1952. *Herut*, July 14, 1953. *Jerusalem Post*, December 7, 1950. Ad in *Ma'ariv*, January 23, 1952.

125. *Ma'ariv*, January 23, 1952. *Herut*, December 22, 1950, November 12, 1954. Also see Lev-Ari (1987), 227.

126. Dauber (2005), 46, 48–49. Also see Pelli (2004), 227. Shavit (2009), 25.

127. Rochelson (1988), 400–401. Ben-Rafael (1994), 50–51.

128. Sofer (2009), 264–265. Pilovsky (1980), 163, 166.

129. Helman (2002), 374–377. Pilovsky (1980), 52–54, 154–157, 181. Halperin (2011), 68, 79.

130. On the ambivalent attitudes toward Yiddish among both the prestate Jewish community in Palestine and, later, Israelis, see Pilovsky (1981). Chaver (2004). Bartal (2007), 135–139. Shapira (1996b), 268. Rojansky (2005), 468. On foreign languages that *were* taught at the Hebrew University during the Mandate era, see Trimbur and Jacoby (2009).

131. Bachi (1956), 224.

132. Friedman (1990), 38–41, 52–54, 58.

133. *Hamodi'a*, May 10, 1951.

134. Bachi (1956), 224, 232.

135. On the ideological and partisan composition of religious Israelis, see Don-Yehiya (1984), 55, 93. Bartal (2001), 241–244. Shalmon (1987), 279–283. Segev (1984), 226–227. Dowty (2001), 53. Cohen (1997), 227–242. Cohen (2001).

136. *Lahav: biton dati leumi*, Heshvan Tashiab (1951), 5.

137. Don-Yehiya (1984), 74–75. Fund (1999), 88. Poster from 1955 — PC, V2255. Posters from 1949 and 1955 — PC, V1817. *Hamodi'a*, September 10, 1950. *Dvar hashavu'a*, October 1, 1950. *Omer*, October 5, 1952, October 18, 1954. *Davar*, January 25, 1955. *Haboker*, March 31, 1955. *Beterem*, September 1, 1955, October 1, 1955. Illustrations in *Haisha bamedinah*, December 19, 1949. Cartoon in *Ha'olam hazeh*, February 1, 1951. Cartoons in Tzabar (1951). Geva newsreels, 1954—SA, VT GE 05. Protocols from 1954—JCA, 1751/16, 1853/21–8.

138. *Herut*, February 9, 1950. Bachi (1956), 224.

139. *Dvar hashavu'a*, October 6, 1949.

140. *Dvar hashavu'a*, February 23, 1950. Also see *Dvar hashavu'a*, March 17, 1949, June 16, 1949, September 8, 1949, July 6, 1950.

141. *Yediot aharonot*, January 6, 1950, August 29, 1951. *Herut*, June 17, 1955. *Haaretz*, September 16, 1955. Helman (2002), 374, 377.

142. The issue of the Yiddish theater reached the Israeli Supreme Court. See *Hador*, December 17, 1950. *Herut*, January 5, 1951. *Haboker*, February 21, 1951, July 2, 1951. Also see a cartoon in *Dvar hashavu'a*, January 6, 1949.

143. Letter from August 2, 1949—ISA, gl 3882 mb/27. Protocols from February 5, 1951, March 26, 1951, April 2, 1951 — ISA, gl 3881 mb/15. Protocol from March 17, 1950 — ISA, g-74/716.

144. Protocol from March 13, 1951 — LI, IV-208-6482. *Haboker*, March 14, 1951.

145. For instance, see ad in *Ma'ariv*, August 30, 1951. Posters from September 7, 1951 — PC, V1967-7. Ad in *Haaretz*, August 18, 1952. *Yediot aharonot*, February 1, 1952. *Hador*, May 28, 1954. *Herut*, August 24, 1955, October 14, 1955. *Haboker*, March 5, 1956. On the popularity of Dzigan and Shumacher despite the language controversy, see Efron (2012), 75–79.

146. Protocol from September 21, 1948—ISA, g-8/718. For a more militant stand, see *Haisha bamedinah*, September 1950, 32. For Marc Chagall's oration in Yiddish during his 1951 visit, see Geva newsreels: SA, VT GE 02. On the different attitudes of American Jews and Israelis toward Yiddish, see Howe (1976), 185. Roskies (1999), 49, 57. Rojanski (2007).

147. Rojanski (2004).

148. Rojanski (2005), 467.

149. Gelber (1996), 454.

150. Kurzweil (1965), 289–293.

151. *Yediot aharonot*, December 9, 1949.

152. Bachi (1956), 195–196. Morag (2003b), 168.

153. For instance, *Ma'ariv*, April 27, 1956.

154. *Dvar hashavu'a*, April 28, 1949.

155. *Ashmoret*, September 20, 1950. And see photos from 1949 by Zoltan Kluger of Jewish and Arab dockworkers working and smoking together in the Jaffa port: NPC, D840-025, D840-026, D840-027.

156. For instance, Sapir (1951), 21.

157. Bachi (1956), 246.

158. *Dagesh*, July 13, 1950. On the omnipresence of Israelis in Paris, also see cartoons in *Ashmoret*, November 24, 1949, and Tzabar (1951). On Israeli crooks in Paris see *Yediot aharonot*, November 12, 1956.

159. On the craving for travel abroad, see Rozin (2010), Rozin (2011b).

3. The Humorous Side of Rationing

1. Related to the author by Rachel Brontman on July 18, 2012.

2. Barkai (2004), 42–44. Rozin (2005a), 58. Rozin (2005b), 74. Gross (1997), 138–139. Naor (2009), 63–105.

3. Gross (1995), 232–239. Gross (1997), 140, 142. Giladi (2002), 40–42.

4. Rozin (2005a), 58. Rozin (2005b), 273–290. Rozin (2002a), 107. Rozin (2011a). Also see Ben-Uzi (2008). Barkai (2004), 55. *Hamodi'a*, May 10, 1951. *Dvar hashavu'a*, December 20, 1951. Photo from 1951 — NPC, D720-091. Election poster from 1951 — PC, V2158-7.

5. On the political struggles and the 1952 elections, see Rozin (2011a) and Ben-Uzi (2008).

6. For instance, Mapam poster from August 1950 — PC, V1745-3(11). *Alonekh*, August 1950, 4, October 1950, 5, August 1952, 1. Herut poster from spring 1950: JIA, kh-24/2/7. *Ma'ariv*, August 4, 1950. And compare with Zweiniger-Bargielowska (2002), 3–4, 59, 262–263.

7. Compare Barkai (2004) with Gross (1995) and with Alexander (1992).

8. Rozin (2002a), 87–88. Helman (2011), 30–31.

9. Rozin (2002a), 91. Rozin (2005a), 174. Rozin (2006), 61. And compare with Kynaston (2007), 225. Stitziel (2008), 256, 265, 267. Lewis (2008), 3.

10. Ryan (2004), 164. Lewis (2006), 2–3, 17. Stokker (1995), 206–209.

11. Kerman (1995), 181. Penslar (2007), 175, 185. Oring (1983), 262, 264–268, 271. Hillenbrand (1995), 74–84. Draitser (1998), 120

12. Draitser (1998), 9.

13. Hillenbrand (1995), xv.

14. Townsend (1992), 197.

15. Posters from January 6, 1950, and March 3, 1950 — PC, V1970-4. Also see ad in *Ma'ariv*, March 2, 1950.

16. I am much obliged to John Efron, who sent me this example: see Efron (2012), 71–72.

17. *Haaretz*, August 23, 1951. Similarly, a prizewinning costume in a Purim masquerade depicted half an egg: Gan Shmuel bulletin, March 30, 1951 — NNL.

18. Shavit, Goldstein, and Beer (1983), 252.

19. *Dvar hashavu'a*, July 15, 1949, August 25, 1949, November 10, 1949. *Ma'ariv*, August 4, 1950.

20. *Dvar hashavu'a*, July 15, 1949, August 18, 1949, September 15, 1949, August 10, 1950, November 15, 1951. *Hamodi'a*, September 14, 1951, October 12, 1951. *Ozer dalim*, 1950, front cover. Cartoons in Tzabar (1951). Also see Naor (1987), 101. Weitz (1996), 182–183.

21. *Dvar hashavu'a*, November 17, 1949.

22. *Dvar hashavu'a*, January 4, 1951.

23. Stokker (1995), 142–149. Banc and Dundes (1990), 58–68.

24. Rozin (2005b), 274. Osokina (2001), 198, 200–201. Also see Trentmann (2006), 12.

25. For example, *Dvar hashavu'a*, May 24, 1951, November 15, 1951. Cartoons in *Ma'ariv*, July 15, 1949, *Bamachaneh*, June 2, 1949.

26. *Dvar hashavu'a*, January 4, 1951.

27. *Dvar hashavu'a*, November 9, 1950.

28. Cartoon in *Dvar hashavu'a*, May 24, 1951. Also see *Dvar hashavu'a*, September 19, 1950.

29. *Ashmoret*, October 5, 1950.

30. *Dvar hashavu'a*, March 8, 1951.

31. *Dvar hashavu'a*, August 17, 1950. Also see cartoon in Tzabar (1951).

32. *Dvar hashavu'a*, August 31, 1950.

33. Ibid.

34. *Dvar hashavu'a*, September 19, 1950.

35. *Dvar hashavu'a*, August 24, 1950.

36. *Dvar hashavu'a*, February 22, 1951. Also see *Dvar hashavu'a*, June 7, 1951.

37. *Dvar hashavu'a*, January 4, 1951.

38. *Dvar hashavu'a*, March 30, 1950. Also see *Dvar hashavu'a*, March 23, 1950.

39. For example, see Stokker (1995), 142–149. Banc and Dundes (1990), 58, 68.

40. Draitser (1998), 9, 140.

41. Hillenbrand (1995), 219. Also see Townsend (1992), 191, 206.

42. See cartoons in *Dvar hashavu'a*, June 29, 1950, April 19, 1951. Jokes in *Dvar hashavu'a*, June 29, 1950, March 1, 1951, June 21, 1951, October 8, 1951.

43. Cartoon in *Dvar hashavu'a*, September 6, 1951.

44. *Hamodi'a*, June 15, 1951. *Ma'ariv*, August 17, 1951.

45. *Dvar hashavu'a*, November 29, 1951. Also see jokes in *Omer*, November 11, 1952.

46. *Dvar hashavu'a*, August 24, 1950.

47. *Dvar hashavu'a*, November 24, 1949.

48. *Dvar hashavu'a*, January 4, 1951.

49. *Dvar hashavu'a*, September 20, 1951. Also see anecdote in *Dvar hashavu'a*, February 8, 1951.

50. *Dvar hashavu'a*, October 26, 1950.

51. *Dvar hashavu'a*, October 12, 1950.

52. *Dvar hashavu'a*, April 12, 1951. Also see anecdote in *Dvar hashavu'a*, March 1, 1951.

53. Cartoon in *Dvar hashavu'a*, July 12, 1951.

54. *Dvar hashavu'a*, November 22, 1951. Similar jokes were told in Soviet bloc countries: see Banc and Dundes (1990), 64–65.

55. *Ashmoret*, December 22, 1949. On coffee substitutes and their unpleasant taste, see *Herut*, October 5, 1950. *Omer*, November 14, 1952. *Ma'ariv*, December 8, 1952.

56. *Ashmoret*, September 8, 1949.

57. Rozin (2002). Rozin (2005a). Rozin (2005b). Rozin (2006).

58. *Haboker*, August 10, 1950. Photos from 1950 by Teddy Brauner—NPC, D720-101, D720-102.

59. Cartoon in *Ma'ariv*, August 18, 1950.

60. And see a similar anecdote in *Dvar hashavu'a*, March 1, 1951.

61. Cartoon in *Ma'ariv*, October 11, 1950.

62. On Israeli popular attitudes toward the "Dark Continent," see, for instance, *Yediot aharonot*, December 9, 1949. Helman (2008b), 124, note 111.

63. Cartoon in *Tafrit*, December 1950.

64. For instance, *Yediot aharonot*, March 31, 1950. *Dvar hashavu'a*, March 1, 1951, November 1, 1951.

65. Anecdote and cartoon in *Dvar hashavu'a*, April 5, 1951, May 17, 1951.

66. Cartoons in *Dvar hashavu'a*, September 10, 1950, November 1, 1951. Cartoon in Dosh (1956), 15. Joke in Zidon (1952), 153. On the monotony of the austerity diet, also see cartoon and anecdote in *Dvar hashavu'a*, May 11, 1950, April 30, 1951.

67. *Yediot aharonot*, March 31, 1950.

68. Geva newsreels from 1951: SA, VT GE 02. Also see cartoons in Tzabar (1951).

69. On the deterioration in the quality of locally made clothes, see Helman (2011), 53.

70. Raz (1996), 105–109. On the Utility program in Britain, see Zweiniger-Bargielowska (2002), 50–51, 94–95.

71. Raz (1996), 137. Photo from 1950 by Fritz Cohen — NPC, D720-119. Compare with Stitziel (2005), 56–57, 71, 132. Stitziel (2008), 257.

72. *Dvar hashavu'a*, October 6, 1949. Also see cartoon in *Bamachaneh*, September 7, 1950.

73. Raz (1996), 137.

74. Photos from 1949, 1950, 1951, and 1952 by David Eldan and Hans Pinn — NPC, D221-050, D720-098, D720-090, D720-094, D720-092, D720-090.

75. *Pelota vasca*, or "Basque ball," later developed into the game known as *cesta punta*, or jai alai.

76. *Ma'ariv*, December 1949. Helman (2008b), 103. On humor in advertising see Gulas and Weinberger (2006).

77. *Dvar hashavu'a*, October 12, 1950.

78. *Ashmoret*, August 16, 1951.

79. Compare Geva newsreels from 1951: SA, VT GE 02 with photos by Fritz Cohen from 1951 — NPC, D720-055, D720-055.

80. *Hamodi'a*, October 5, 1951. Also see *Dvar hashavu'a*, October 13, 1949. Geva newsreels from 1952: SA VT GE 01. And compare with Merkel (1998), 292–293.

81. *Dvar hashavu'a*, December 15, 1949.

82. *Dvar hashavu'a*, May 25, 1950.

83. *Dvar hashavu'a*, August 2, 1951.

84. *Dvar hashavu'a*, March 1, 1951.

85. *Dvar hashavu'a*, October 18, 1951.

86. *Dvar hashavu'a*, October 8, 1951.

87. *Dvar hashavu'a*, September 10, 1950.

88. *Dvar hashavu'a*, August 16, 1951.

89. *Dvar hashavu'a*, August 23, 1951.

90. Cartoons in *Dvar hashavu'a*, August 17, 1950, February 15, 1951. *Bamachaneh*, March 6, 1952. Also cartoons in Tzabar (1951).

91. Hagiladi (2011), 248–340.

92. "Rationing," in *Encyclopedia Britannica* (2003). Osokina (2001), 198, 200–201. Trentmann (2006), 12.

93. Zweiniger-Bargielowska (2002), 157, 177, 259. Kynaston (2007), 111.

94. Guenther (2005), 229–232. Also see Stitziel (2008), 264.

95. Rozin (2006), 61–64. Barkai (2004), 54–55. *Ashmoret,* October 5, 1950. Photo in *Dvar hashavu'a,* October 19, 1950.

96. For instance, see *Dvar hashavu'a,* May 11, 1950. *Yediot aharonot,* March 31, 1950. Cartoon from 1951 presented in Rozin (2002a), 91.

97. Cartoon in *Ashmoret,* October 12, 1950. *Dvar hashavu'a,* September 13, 1951. Cartoon in *Dvar hashavu'a,* August 7, 1952. *Haaretz,* November 9, 1951.

98. *Dvar hashavu'a,* June 21, 1951.

99. *Dvar hashavu'a,* March 8, 1951. Also see *Dvar hashavu'a,* November 15, 1951. On Jewish-Arab cooperation in the black market for meat during the 1948 war, see Hagiladi (2011), 213–217.

100. Compare cartoons from *Dvar hashavu'a,* July 6, 1950, March 29, 1951, *Ashmoret,* October 19, 1950, July 12, 1951, with election poster from 1952 — PC, V 1745-53 and with government posters against the black market — ISA, g-26/318, g-23/318, g-9/318, g-7/318, and PC, V 2156-2(14), V 2130-2.

101. Rozin (2005b), 275–278. Barkai (2004), 55. And see photos from 1949 by Fritz Cohen — NPC, D720-064, D720-065, D720-066. *Yediot aharonot,* January 1, 1950. *Alonekh,* December 1950, 6. *Hatzofeh,* August 20, 1952. *Sheluchot yotzei teiman,* November 16, 1952, 4.

102. For example, cartoons in *Ma'ariv,* October 27, 1950, November 2, 1950. *Yediot aharonot,* March 31, 1950. Also see *Ma'ariv,* November 2, 1950. *Haaretz,* August 24, 1951.

103. *Ma'ariv,* October 8, 1950.

104. *Dvar hashavu'a,* May 17, 1951.

105. *Dvar hashavu'a,* August 30, 1951. Also see *Bamachaneh,* September 7, 1950.

106. *Tafrit,* March 1951.

107. *Omer,* October 31, 1952. Also see joke from *Dvar hashavu'a,* January 4, 1951. On Israel's relationship with American Jewry, see, for instance, Sheffer (2010), 34–35, 40–43.

108. *Omer,* January 24, 1952.

109. Compare with humor that solidified Berlin's middle-class consciousness and expressed its superiority: Townsend (1992), 197.

110. Packages also arrived from American Jewish organizations. See photos from 1952 — CZA, 1407297, 1421502, 1421503. Geva newsreels from 1954: SA, VT GE 05. And see cartoon in *Tafrit,* November 1951.

111. Cartoon in *Tafrit,* September 1950.

112. Rozin (2005a), 158–159. Rozin (2006), 52, 56–57. On attitudes toward luxury in the prestate Jewish community in Palestine, see Helman (2010), 91.

113. Letter from December 25, 1949—ISA, 47/c-33/200.

114. Rationing poster, 1950 — CZA: KRA 600.

115. Government poster from 1950 — CZA, KRA 600. Letter from 1950 — ISA, 47/c-3/159. *Haaretz,* August 24, 1950, January 23, 1951. Rozin (2002), 99, 103.

116. Alexander (1992). Lissak (1998), 41–42. Ben-Porat (1999), 121–122.

117. For instance, cartoons in *Dvar hashavu'a,* May 26, 1949, September 6, 1951.

118. Cartoon in *Bamachaneh,* September 7, 1950.

119. Helman (2010), 35.

120. Interestingly, just as it was usually human females who were accused of extravagance and waste during this time of want, the two hedonistic canines, too, were portrayed as females. Also see cartoon in *Dvar hashavu'a,* January 18, 1951. Anecdote in *Yediot aharonot,* April 1, 1949.

121. Stitziel (2008), 254. Stitziel (2005), 69. Also compare with the British case: Zweiniger-Bargielowska (2002), 3–4, 59, 67, 96–98, 257. Kynaston (2007), 300.

122. Rozin (2005b), 285.

123. *Ma'ariv,* August 17, 1951. Letter from 1950 — ISA, 47/c-12/199. And see Rozin (2006), 70–71. Stitziel (2008), 255.

124. Rozin (2005a), 61–64.

125. Helman (2010), 29–30.

126. A persuasive example is provided by Rozin (2011b).

127. Graham (2004), 172–173. Lewis (2008), 4.

128. Ryan (2004), 157.

129. Banc and Dundes (1990), 22–23.

130. For example, see Townsend (1992), 191, 195–196, 200.

131. Hillenbrand (1995), xvi–xvii, 218.

132. On Israeli humor see Alexander (1986), 142–143. Gardosh (1986). And compare with Lewis (2006).

133. Hagiladi (2011), 264 (and cartoons in index volume, 59–60).

134. For example, cartoon in *Ma'ariv,* October 27, 1950. Herut election posters from 1951 — PC, V2158-7.

135. For example, see Lewis (2006), 7.

136. Wood (1994), 270–271.

137. Hillenbrand (1995), xvi, 220.

138. Ibid., 219.

139. Douglas (2002), 5.

140. Draitser (1998), 9.

141. Stokker (1995), 206–209, 213.

142. Gross (1995), 234. Due to its tangible daily effects during 1949–1952, rationing became the "only topic of every conversation": *Hamodi'a,* April 15, 1952.

143. For example, *Dvar hashavu'a,* November 10, 1955. Election poster from 1955 — PC, V2156-2(13).

144. For instance, Rozin (2002a), 88, 118. And compare Israel with the case of 1950s and 1960s East Germany: Merkel (1998), 24, 294.

4. *"A People in Uniform"*

1. Smith (2001), 20.

2. Horowitz and Lissak (1990), 241.

3. Lissak (2000), 327.

4. Horowitz and Lissak (1990), 250, 252, 256. Barak and Sheffer (2010), 33–34. Also

see photo from 1954 by Verner Braun—JNFPA, d216-043. Photo from 1956 by Fritz Cohen and photo from 1955—NPC, D383-093, D369-068.

5. Drori (2000), 31–32. Levy et al. (2010), 147. Cohen (2010), 243. Gat (2002), 191, 194.

6. Horowitz and Lissak (1990), 250. Drori (1995), 609–610. Drori (2000), 65–123. Bar-On (2002), 95–96. Tydor Baumel-Schwartz (2009), 139.

7. Bar-On (1999), 65, 71, 83–84, 89–91. And see article by Itzhak Ziv-Av in *Leket*, 51, March 1952, 2–4, 7, 9–10, 12.

8. IDF (1956), 18. Also see anecdote in *Dvar hashavu'a*, November 3, 1949.

9. Letter from April 4, 1950—IDFA, 526. Letter from February 7, 1956—ISA, gl 3883 mb/79.

10. Horowitz (1993), 48–49. Lissak (2000), 328. Drori (2006), 261, 267–268. Also see Ben-Amotz and Hefer (1979), 42, 124, 172.

11. Drori (1995), 609–610. Drori (2000), 32, 100–176. Gat (2002), 194–195, 200.

12. Bar-On (2002), 77–79. Photos of soldiers voting in the 1951 general elections— NPC, D713-124, D713-125. On the integrative role of mandatory service in democracies, see Barany (2012), 35–36.

13. Drori (2000), 30–32, 130, 175–176. Bar-On (2002), 93–94.

14. Boymal (2006), 400–401. Footage of Druze IDF soldiers in Geva newsreels, 1955: SA, VT GA 07.

15. *Ner*, September 1954, 14–15. Ozacky-Lazar (2006), 47–62. Also see photo from 1949 by Kurt Meirovitz—JNFPA, d345-039. Photos from 1949 and 1950 by Hugo Mendelson and Fritz Cohen—NPC, D363-022, D362-139.

16. Barany (2012), 25, 35.

17. For instance, Kimmerling (1993). Kimmerling (1998). Bar-Or (2010). Levy et al. (2010). Sasson-Levy (2006), 34–35. On the effects of war and militarism on Israeli art and literature, see, for instance, Gertz (1995), 35–66. Feingold (1999). Steinberg (2002), 226–228. And compare with Appy (2001), 81, 87, 90.

18. Lissak (2000), 325.

19. Bar-On (1999), 65.

20. See, for example, the discussion of "cultural militarism" and "cognitive militarism" in Kimmerling (1993), 127–130, and the discussion of "mental militarism" in Horowitz and Lissak (1990), 256.

21. Bar-On (1999), 89–91. Hermann (2010). Cohen (2005). Morris (1996). And compare with Eichler (2012), 4.

22. Bar-On (2002), 88–89. *Ner*, September 1954, 14–15. And see photos from 1949 and 1950—JNFPA, d1220-026, d736-084. Photos from 1956—NPC, D369-022, D369-023. Geva newsreels from 1952: SA, VT GE 01.

23. On the military parade see Azaryahu (1999). Also see photo from 1949: CZA, 1010214. Photos from 1949 and 1951 by Lazar Dinar and Fritz Shlezinger—JNFPA, d1220-032, d330-015. Geva newsreels from 1954: SA, VT GE 06. On the army's entertainment troupes see Shahar (1997). Bar-On (2002), 79–100. Tessler (2007). On the IDF's

cultural involvement see posters from 1949–1950—PC, V1967-7, V1961-18. *Pnimah*, March 1952, 49. *Hedei hanegev*, May 1952, 13. *Bamachaneh*, March 18, 1954.

24. Shalom (1991). Shalom (2002). See photos from 1953 and 1954 by David Eldan and Ilan Brauner and photo from 1955—NPC, D255-042, D255-037, D241-046. Photos from 1949 by A. Malevsky, from 1953 by Zoltan Kluger, and from 1955: CZA, 1273693, 1287524, 1287526, 1016493. Geva newsreels from 1955: SA, VT GE 07.

25. *Hatzofeh*, August 3, 1949. And see description by Beer (2002), 220.

26. *Yediot aharonot*, March 17, 1949, December 2, 1949. Also see *Haaretz*, August 26, 1949.

27. *Ashmoret*, March 30, 1950. Drori (2000), 65–99. Near (1995), 230–231, 255. Drori (2006), 250. Helman (2011), 62, 181. Geva newsreels from 1952 and 1954: SA, VT GE 01, VT GE 06.

28. Bar-On (2002), 95–96. Photos from 1950 by David Eldan—NPC, D200-027, D200-028. Photo from 1950 by Verner Braun—JNFPA, d710-158. Photos from 1950 and 1951: CZA, 1332683, 1012408, 1012595. Geva newsreels from 1951: SA, VT GE 03.

29. *Yediot aharonot*, April 19, 1949.

30. Ad in Lerer (1956), unnumbered page. Ad in *Ma'ariv*, December 13, 1955. And see Dankner and Tartakover (1996), 59.

31. Letter from September 1949—IDFA, 528. *Zmanim*, September 17, 1954.

32. *Ma'ariv*, October 18, 1950.

33. Geva newsreels from 1951–1956: SA, VT GE 01, VT GE 02, VT GE 03, VT GE 05, VT GE 06, VT GE 07, VT GE 08, VT GE 010.

34. Hefer (1956), 66–67. *Yediot aharonot*, April 1, 1949. *Bamachaneh*, May 11, 1950. Cartoon in *Bamachaneh*, May 24, 1951. *Ha'olam hazeh*, July 16, 1953. Photos from 1950 and 1955—NPC, D384-023, D369-055.

35. In the following decades "soldiers' homes" emerged as inexpensive hostels for soldiers. See footage of the raffle conducted by the Committee for the Well-Being of the Soldier on Independence Day 1955 in Geva newsreels: SA, VT GE 08. Also see 1954 poster: CZA, KRA 373. On the committee's work during the war, see Bar-On (2006), 489.

36. *Bamachaneh*, January 25, 1952.

37. Cartoon in Dosh (1956), 21. Cartoon and photos in *Bamachaneh*, September 15, 1949, February 23, 1950. Joke in *Dvar hashavu'a*, September 28, 1950.

38. Letter from May 1948—TAA, 4/1941a. *Herut*, March 31, 1949. Report from May 18, 1952—IDFA, 639. *Olam hakolno'a*, May 29, 1952. Also see cartoon in *Tafrit*, July 1949.

39. *Bamachaneh*, October 20, 1949.

40. *Bamachaneh*, November 15, 1951. Also see cartoon in *Bamachaneh*, March 11, 1954.

41. IDF (1956), 18.

42. Priority was also assigned to veteran soldiers over the civilian population, including new immigrants, in housing and the job market: Naor (2010), 49–50.

43. Bar-On (1999), 84. And see Avneri (1949), 324–326.

44. Sasson-Levy (2006), 35. And compare with changing images of the hero in the postwar United States: Linenthal (1982), 117–136.

45. Eldad and Nedava (1955), 253, 277. Geva newsreels from 1954: SA, VT GE 07.

46. Letter from April 24, 1950 — NA, 2/11. Also see *Hatzofeh*, August 13, 1950.

47. Exhibition guide, October 1950 — NA, 2/11.

48. For instance, see *Ashmoret*, May 10, 1951. *Dvar hashavu'a*, October 23, 1952. *Yediot aharonot*, March 31, 1950.

49. Letter from April 4, 1950: IDFA, 526.

50. Correspondence from May 1951: IDFA, 635.

51. Narration in Geva newsreel of Independence Day 1954: SA, VT GE 06.

52. Cover photos in *Bamachaneh*, April 30, 1952, April 24, 1955.

53. For instance, see the military title and terms used by a voluntary civic organization studied by Kabalo (2008).

54. *Ma'ariv*, September 11, 1950. Also see *Dorot*, October 20, 1949.

55. Hapoel's fifth conference illustrated in *Sport la'am*, April 12, 1952. And see Helman (2008b), 105–107.

56. *Al hamishmar*, January 28, 1953.

57. *Ma'ariv*, February 18, 1949.

58. *Jerusalem Post*, July 29, 1953.

59. Ads in *Haisha bamedinah*, June 1949, 47, *Beterem*, January 1949, 67.

60. *Jerusalem Post*, July 24, 1952.

61. *Ma'ariv*, October 4, 1949.

62. *Hatzofeh*, January 6, 1956. On a seventy-year-old who was arrested for wearing IDF major stripes, see *Haaretz*, August 20, 1951.

63. Bar-On (2002), 256, 260, 266–267. And see photos from 1952 by Zoltan Kluger: CZA, 1287478, 1287483.

64. *Ashmoret*, December 8, 1949.

65. *Bamachaneh*, April 5, 1951. Also see *Zmanim*, January 15, 1954. Cartoon in *Bamachaneh*, January 25, 1952.

66. *Alonekh*, May 1951, 6. On gender roles in the IDF, see Sasson-Levy (2006). Helman (2011), 187–193. Brownfield-Stein (2010). Male soldiers' presumed hypersexuality was also mentioned in *Ma'ariv*, October 28, 1949, February 24, 1950. *Hu vehi*, January 1955. Jokes and cartoons in *Dvar hashavu'a*, April 21, 1949, November 17, 1949, *Bamachaneh*, August 31, 1950, March 11, 1954.

67. *Ma'ariv*, March 17, 1949, March 31, 1949, December 10, 1952. *Yediot aharonot*, March 27, 1949. *Bamachaneh*, September 15, 1949. And see Drori (2006), 255.

68. On the "purity of arms" myth, see Morris (2008), 405–406.

69. *Haaretz*, June 19, 1956.

70. The lexical meaning of the word is "any plan that is implemented," but its main use and association are military — see Even-Shoshan (1966), 1210–1211.

71. *Kol yisrael*, December 14, 1950. Geva newsreels from 1951 and 1954: SA, VT GE 03, VT GE 06.

72. Helman (2008b), 106.

73. *Dvar hapo'elet*, September 1949, 205.

74. The term "Operation Hebrew" was also employed earlier historically: see *Bamachaneh la'oleh*, July 8, 1949.

75. *Pnimah,* June 1951, 56.

76. *Al hamishmar,* December 11, 1953. On cultural activities as "operations" see *Niv histadrut afula,* September 1955, 7–9.

77. *Izmel: alon lemachshavah uvikoret,* Winter 1953 — NNL.

78. *Bamachaneh,* July 17, 1949. *Kol hamishmar haezrachi,* September 1949, 4–5, 12, 16–18, 20.

79. *Ha'olam hazeh,* May 19, 1955.

80. Ad in *Hamodi'a,* December 10, 1954. Letter from March 30, 1956 — JCA, 32.017 / 481-471. Also see ads in *Ma'ariv,* December 26, 1955, December 30, 1955.

81. For other examples see election posters from 1951 — PC, V1745-47, V1745-46. Ad in *Ma'ariv,* August 13, 1951.

82. *Dvar hashavu'a,* March 23, 1950.

83. *Al hamishmar,* January 27, 1953.

84. *Haisha bamedinah,* February 1951, 65–66.

85. *Matzpen,* September 15, 1954.

86. *Herut,* January 20, 1956.

87. *Pnimah,* June 1951, 54.

88. Letter from October 5, 1949—NA, 1/10.

89. *Al hamishmar,* August 9, 1950.

90. *Ha'olam hazeh,* March 11, 1954.

91. *Omer,* July 9, 1951.

92. Zerubavel (2009), 35–36. Helman (2002), 374.

93. On the rapid invention of Hebrew military terms in 1948, see Morag (2003b), 163–164.

94. Compare military style in letters from November 1949, March 1951, and May 1951 — IDFA, 528, 364, 635, with the style in a letter from October 25, 1950 — TAA, 4/3644. *Zmanim,* June 29, 1955. Cartoons in *Dvar hashavu'a,* January 13, 1949, August 25, 1949. Reader's letter in *Dvar hashavu'a,* January 25, 1951. Ad in Haaretz Annual (1952), unnumbered page.

95. Drori (2010), 82, 88–91. Photos from 1955 and 1956 by Moshe Pridan — NPC, D295-035, D259-046.

96. Shefayim bulletin, April 22, 1949, July 15, 1949—YTA. Kiryat Anavim bulletin, July 22, 1949, October 20, 1950 — KKAA.

97. Alonim bulletin, July 22, 1949—KALA. Dorot bulletin, October 25, 1949—YTA. Hazorea bulletin, February 10, 1950, February 13, 1953, May 15, 1953 — KHA. Gan Shmuel bulletin, March 2, 1951, December 14, 1952 — NNL.

98. Gan Shmuel bulletin, February 15, 1956 — NNL. Also see Revivim bulletin, March 5, 1954, April 9, 1954—YTA.

99. For example, *Hamodi'a,* March 2, 1951, March 30, 1951, December 5, 1952. And see Yanai (1996), 135. Friedman (1995), 70.

100. Caplan (2011), 216–217.

101. Friedman (1994), 231–232. Still, the religious parties objected to the IDF's involvement in education, regarding it as a secularizing agent: Gat (2002), 195.

102. *Hamodi'a,* August 8, 1952, March 30, 1951, March 9, 1956.

103. *Hamodi'a,* May 16, 1952.

104. *Hamodi'a,* April 24, 1953.

105. *Hamodi'a,* August 1, 1952.

106. *Hamodi'a,* August 21, 1952, September 12, 1952, November 19, 1954.

107. *Hamodi'a,* October 11, 1954.

108. *Hamodi'a,* March 2, 1956.

109. Helman (2011), 105–106.

110. *Hamodi'a,* November 26, 1954.

111. Unlike the extreme anti-Zionist Haredim: Caplan (2011), 185–186, 216–218.

112. Drori (2000), 65–99. *Ma'ariv,* August 10, 1949. Ad in *Al hamishmar,* January 14, 1949.

113. *Bamachaneh,* September 15, 1949. On the soldiers, "many of whom fancy rather individual forms of dress," also see Shlomo Grodzensky's letter from November 15, 1949—courtesy of Tirza Sandbank and Miriam Talisman.

114. Protocol, letters, and military regulations from 1949, 1950 — IDFA, 7, 528, 630.

115. For instance, Azaryahu (1998) and Shamir (1996).

116. *Yediot aharonot,* April 16, 1949. Notice in *Beterem,* May 1949. Poster from October 1949—PC, V1969-4. Poster from 1949—CZA, KRA 1603. *Bamachaneh,* November 3, 1949. *Haisha bamedinah,* January 1951, 61–62. *Maavak,* April 9, 1952. *Hatzofeh,* January 19, 1954. Cartoons in *Bamachaneh,* May 6, 1954.

117. Feldstein (2009), 267–269. Photos of various sites and events of war commemoration in 1949–1954: CZA, 1327546, 1009861, 1424570, 1011622, 1335351, 1331532, 1277596, 1326181, 1326130.

118. *Pnimah,* June 1951, 56–57. *Omer,* July 1, 1951, February 1, 1952, November 14, 1952, May 8, 1953. *Matzpen,* November 3, 1954. Kossewska (2010), 169.

119. Barany (2012), 36.

5. Taking the Bus

1. *Ashmoret,* August 16, 1951. And see more complaints about the bus service in the *Jerusalem Post,* April 15, 1951, June 25, 1951. *Hamodi'a,* October 12, 1951. *Davar,* November 13, 1952. *Beterem,* November 1, 1955. Haaretz Annual (1953), 117.

2. Cohen (1970), 4. Penslar (1991). Elboim-Dror (1993), 160–166.

3. Compare with Martin (2004), 229, and Friedman (1994). On Israelis' sense of isolation see Rozin (2010), 156. Shlaim (2004), 658. Podeh (1999).

4. Ad in Haaretz Annual (1949), unnumbered page.

5. *Hamodi'a,* May 10, 1951. Zidon (1952), 118. *Hagidu bedan,* December 1951, 28–29. Notice in *Ma'ariv,* May 27, 1949. *Herut,* August 3, 1951. On gradual improvements in bus safety, see *Davar,* January 9, 1955. Also see Geva newsreels from 1951: SA, VT GE 02.

6. *Ashmoret,* February 23, 1950.

7. *Ha'olam hazeh,* June 3, 1954.

8. *Ma'ariv,* July 9, 1954.

9. Certeau (1984), 111–114. Also see Edensor (2013), 191.

10. Burns (1932), 54–55. Bender and Schorske (1994), 81. Harvey (1985), 9, 15. Edensor (2013), 195.

11. Reichman (1971), 55, 58–59, 84.

12. Helman (2006), 627.

13. Giladi (2002), 69. Shlomo Grodzensky's letter from November 13, 1949—courtesy of Tirza Sandbank and Miriam Talisman.

14. Haaretz Annual (1950), 56.

15. Statistical data (issued in January 1955), 4, Table A — ISA, pr-181.

16. Statistical data (issued in January 1955), 4—ISA, pr-181.

17. Schor (1956), 53.

18. Statistical data and map (issued in February 1956), 10 — ISA, pr-341, 14/956/3.

19. Statistical data (issued in January 1955), 4—ISA, pr-181. Statistical data (issued in March 1955), 11 — ISA, pr-341. Map of Tel Aviv, 1950 — MC, Tel Aviv h52. And see *Ma'ariv*, September 9, 1949. Photos from 1951 by Teddy Brauner and Fritz Cohen — NPC, D219-074, D719-064. Developments in Jerusalem's urban and regional transportation were compared unfavorably to those in Tel Aviv: see letter from November 9, 1949—JCA, 32.015/467.

20. Statistical data and map (issued in February 1956), 11 — ISA, pr-341, 14/956/3.

21. Shlomo Grodzensky's letter from November 13, 1949—courtesy of Tirza Sandbank and Miriam Talisman.

22. Haaretz Annual (1953), 334. *Shnaton statisti leyisrael*, 2 (1951), 15. On scuffles between the drivers of rival companies, see *Ma'ariv*, October 7, 1951.

23. Statistical data (issued in January 1955), 4—ISA, pr-181.

24. Transportation map of Israel, 1955 — MC, E12 (1). *Yediot hamo'etzah hamekomit ir izrael — Afula*, 6, December 1955. *Hatzofeh*, January 10, 1949. Photos from 1951 and 1955 — CZA, 1012566, 1278467. Ad in Haaretz Annual (1950), unnumbered page. Ad in *Hedei hanegev*, May 1952, 8.

25. Giladi (2002), 70. *Ma'ariv*, May 25, 1950, August 8, 1950. *Zmanim*, November 12, 1954. On the inadequate train service see *Davar*, July 21, 1950. On the competition between the bus company and the "service" cabs in Tel Aviv, see Shlomo Grodzensky's letter from November 15, 1949—courtesy of Tirza Sandbank and Miriam Talisman. *Smol — shavu'a tov*, February 2, 1955. *Herut*, October 28, 1955. And compare with Gordon (1991), 10–11.

26. *Dvar hashavu'a*, February 24, 1949. And see a similar anecdote in *Dvar hashavu'a*, August 10, 1950.

27. Complaint letter from June 13, 1955 — HMA, a-b/27–4. *Hamodi'a*, May 4, 1951, March 7, 1952, June 20, 1952. Also see Yanai (1996), 135.

28. Mikes (1950), 94. *Ashmoret*, March 15, 1951. *Jerusalem Post*, July 3, 1952. *Herut*, June 3, 1955. For some sectors, like kibbutz members, even the subsidized bus prices were considered a luxury: see Shefayim bulletin, January 12, 1951, October 9, 1953 — YTA.

29. *Hamodi'a*, July 18, 1952, January 2, 1953. *Sport yisrael*, August 24, 1952. Such controversies began in the prestate era: see Helman (2008c).

30. Haaretz Annual (1953), 117–118.

31. Bulletin of the Jordan Valley Council, May 5, 1950, June 21, 1951—NNL. *Maavak*, April 25, 1952. *Carmel hador*, April 13, 1954. *Davar*, April 25, 1955. Photo of May Day parade in 1950 by Fritz Cohen—NPC, D522-137. Geva newsreels from 1955: SA, VT GE 08.

32. Ad from April 1953—KHA, 431. On "winter trips" to the southern city of Eilat, see ad in *Davar*, December 22, 1955.

33. See ads in *Beterem*, October 1950, October 1, 1951. *Ashmoret*, April 9, 1952. *Jerusalem Post*, December 1, 1952. *Ha'olam hazeh*, March 18, 1954, April 15, 1954, August 11, 1955. Haaretz Annual (1953), unnumbered page.

34. *Yediot aharonot*, April 21, 1950.

35. *Ha'olam hazeh*, May 6, 1954.

36. Ad in Haaretz Annual (1952), unnumbered page. Also see Geva newsreels from 1951: SA, VT GE 02.

37. *Gazit*, May–June 1949, 6–7. *Ma'ariv*, July 21, 1950. *Omer*, July 23, 1951. *Hatzofeh*, February 1, 1952. *Ba'ayot beyisrael hatze'irah*, 1, 1951, 3. Even-Chen (1954), 34. Radai (1956), 127. Photo from May 1949 by Zoltan Kluger—NPC, D24-023. Photo in *Bamachaneh*, February 23, 1950. Photos from Tel Aviv and Jaffa, 1951, 1952—CZA, 1176419, 1278581. Photo in *Lagever*, March 17, 1954. Cartoon in *Bamachaneh*, September 15, 1949.

38. *Dvar hashavu'a*, May 18, 1950, November 23, 1950. On the immigration of Iraqi Jews, see Meir-Glitzenstein (2009).

39. *Smol shavu'a tov*, February 27, 1955, 2–3.

40. *Dvar hashavu'a*, November 9, 1950.

41. Naor (1987), 103.

42. Giucci (2012), 130.

43. *Yediot aharonot*, December 14, 1949. *Nivenu—bitonam shel ovdei iriyat heifah*, April 1951, 15. *Hamodi'a*, November 2, 1951. *She'arim*, November 4, 1952. Letter from November 15, 1953—HMA, 1/22-1566/8. And see photo in *Ashmoret*, August 23, 1951.

44. *Jerusalem Post*, September 8, 1952. *Hakol*, September 8, 1952. *Haaretz*, August 21, 1951.

45. Protocol from 1949—JCA, 32.015/467. On three young war invalids who refused to heed a judge's instruction and tried to enter a bus without lining up, see *Jerusalem Post*, September 8, 1952.

46. *Ma'ariv*, July 9, 1954. Also see *Herut*, September 29, 1950.

47. *Ashmoret*, August 16, 1951.

48. *Hamodi'a*, March 21, 1953. *Hagidu bedan*, December 1951, 53.

49. Shlomo Grodzensky's letter from November 13, 1949—courtesy of Tirza Sandbank and Miriam Talisman. Hebrew words originally included by Grodzensky in this letter were translated to English.

50. *Hedei hanegev*, May 1952, 13. See photo in *Bamachaneh*, October 20, 1949.

51. *Ashmoret*, August 16, 1951, August 23, 1951. Also see *Hamodi'a*, August 21, 1952. And see a letter from January 15, 1956—TAA, 4/304.

52. On former Arab towns see Golan (2003).

53. See photos from 1955 — CZA, 1278464, 1278470. Protocols and letters concerning the central bus station, 1955–1956 — TAA, 4/303. Geva newsreels from 1954: SA, VT GE 06.

54. Haaretz Annual (1953), 117.

55. Letter from January 15, 1956 — TAA, 4/304.

56. *Ma'ariv*, July 9, 1954. And see photo by Seymour Katcoff, August 1950 — NPC, D561-002.

57. *Omer*, February 1, 1952.

58. *Omer*, January 11, 1952. Also see *Jerusalem Post*, December 7, 1950.

59. Staged episode in Geva newsreels from 1952: SA, VT GE 01.

60. Kvutzat Yavneh bulletin, December 21, 1955 — RKMA.

61. For instance, *Gazit*, May–June 1949, 6–7. *Hedei hanegev*, May 1952, 13. Letter from November 15, 1953 — HMA, 1/22-1566/8. Photos in *Dvar hashavu'a*, July 11, 1952, *Lagever*, March 17, 1954. Revivim bulletin, January 16, 1953 — YTA. "The bus trip — waiting for it about an hour, standing all the way — is quite an ordeal": Shlomo Grodzensky's letter from November 27, 1949—courtesy of Tirza Sandbank and Miriam Talisman.

62. *Jerusalem Post*, November 24, 1950. Also see *Jerusalem Post*, July 12, 1950. On the creative Palmachnik ways of securing a seat, see Ben-Amotz and Hefer (1979), 141, 160–161, 163.

63. *Bamachaneh*, March 15, 1951. Also see anecdote in *Dvar hashavu'a*, December 7, 1950.

64. Mikes (1950), 93. On the packed buses, also see jokes in *Dvar hashavu'a*, April 6, 1950, November 29, 1951; *Hu vehi*, October 1954, 29. Cartoons in *Bamachaneh*, October 6, 1949; *Yediot aharonot*, October 2, 1950.

65. *Ashmoret*, January 12, 1950, August 16, 1951. *Herut*, November 12, 1954. *Hatzofeh*, July 2, 1954.

66. *Hamodi'a*, November 2, 1951.

67. *Ma'ariv*, July 9, 1954. The article was accompanied by Friedl's cartoon: see the illustration on page 89.

68. *Omer*, February 1, 1952. Compare the standard bus with special air-conditioned sightseeing buses — *Ma'ariv*, December 8, 1952. *Jerusalem Post*, December 28, 1952, October 10, 1955. Photos from 1950 by Fritz Cohen — NPC, D233-104, D446-100.

69. *Tavruah* 9, 1956, 40.

70. *Ma'ariv*, August 24, 1949.

71. *Yediot aharonot*, *Koteret*, June 19, 1951. On the growing of sunflowers see Tirat Zvi bulletin, January 27, 1950 — RKMA.

72. *Kol hamishmar haezrachi*, 8, September 1949, 21–22.

73. *Jerusalem Post*, April 16, 1951.

74. *Jerusalem Post*, August 14, 1950.

75. *Ashmoret*, January 12, 1950, August 23, 1951. *Omer*, February 1, 1952. On the importance of service levels, see Hopkins et al. (1988), 26.

76. *Haaretz*, August 20, 1951. *She'arim*, October 31, 1952. And see photo by Teddy Brauner from 1951 — NPC, D324-094.

77. *Hatzofeh,* May 1, 1950. *Beterem,* April 15, 1952. Notice in Haaretz Annual (1953), unnumbered page.

78. *Hamodi'a,* October 7, 1955. *Davar,* May 4, 1951.

79. *Jerusalem Post,* July 26, 1950.

80. Cartoons in *Omer,* November 11, 1952. *Ma'ariv,* July 9, 1954.

81. Letters from August 24, 1949—JMA, 32.015/467.

82. *Palestine Post,* December 12, 1949.

83. *Yediot aharonot,* June 18, 1950.

84. *Herut,* November 5, 1954.

85. *She'arim,* November 4, 1952.

86. Helman (2006), 630–631.

87. *Dorot,* December 1, 1949.

88. *Ashmoret,* January 12, 1950.

89. *Omer,* February 1, 1952.

90. *Ner,* September 1954, 14. On Hofshi and his ideology see Hermann (2010). Also see Naor (2009), 50. Cohen (2000), 125–126.

91. *Hagidu bedan,* December 1951, 54–55. *Al hamishmar,* August 12, 1949. *Hatzofeh,* May 1, 1950.

92. *Ashmoret,* August 23, 1951. On German, Hungarian, and Hebrew spoken in a Haifa bus, see Shlomo Grodzensky's letter from November 8, 1949—courtesy of Tirza Sandbank and Miriam Talisman.

93. *Hagidu bedan,* December 1951, 16. On police-civilian interactions also see *Hamodi'a,* September 21, 1951. *Haaretz,* August 24, 1951. *Al hamishmar,* January 27, 1953.

94. *Hagidu bedan,* December 1951, 20.

95. *Yediot aharonot,* June 18, 1950. *Ashmoret,* September 20, 1950.

96. *Jerusalem Post,* December 12, 1952. And see photo by Teddy Brauner from 1952 — NPC, D352-059. "Courtesy weeks" were occasionally announced by the Soviet government in an attempt to improve manners: Banc and Dundes (1990), 63.

97. *Lagever,* March 17, 1954. Also see *Hedei hanegev,* Kislev Tashiad (1954), 15.

98. *Hagidu bedan,* December 1951, 53–54. The nostalgic depiction of the fatherly driver of the prestate era was historically inaccurate: Helman (2006), 630–631.

99. Joke in *Hagidu bedan,* December 1951, 80. And see cartoon in *Bamachaneh,* November 22, 1951.

100. *Ashmoret,* August 23, 1951.

101. Quotation from the Kvutzat Yavneh bulletin, December 21, 1955 — RKMA. *Herut,* September 29, 1950. *Ma'ariv,* July 9, 1954.

102. Letter from August 19, 1949—JCA, 32.015/467. *Ashmoret,* January 12, 1950. Cartoon in *Bamachaneh,* May 20, 1954.

103. *Al hamishmar,* January 13, 1950. This too was a custom from the prestate era: see Helman (2006), 631–633.

104. Joke in *Hagidu bedan,* December 1951, 80.

105. *Al hamishmar,* January 13, 1950.

106. *Haboker,* June 21, 1950, March 28, 1951.

107. *Ner*, September 1954, 14. And see Abbasi (2012), 401–406, 412.

108. *Herut*, September 29, 1950. *Ashmoret*, January 12, 1950, August 16, 1951. Cartoon in *Ashmoret*, March 30, 1950. Joke in *Hagidu bedan*, December 1951, 80. On judgmental social attitudes toward the overweight, see Saguy (2013).

109. *Yediot aharonot*, December 9, 1949.

110. Gelber (1996), 453. Lissak (1998), 38, 53–54. Ben-Porat (1999), 113–114. Giladi (2002), 60.

111. And compare with the evocation of the Holocaust by new immigrants from Iraq: Meir-Glitzenstein (2009), 134; and by other Israelis: Rozin (2011b), 4, 14.

112. Eisenstadt (1953), 182–183.

113. Goffman (1963), 16–18, 30.

114. Edensor (2013), 195.

115. Helman (2006), 632–633. And compare a lively conversation on Italian public transportation with the reserved, silent practices in northern Europe: Revivim bulletin, April 3, 1953 — YTA. Certeau (1984), 111–114. Burns (1932), 49–61.

116. *Ashmoret*, January 12, 1950.

117. *Beterem*, April 15, 1952.

118. *Hamodi'a*, February 3, 1956.

119. For instance, *Ashmoret*, August 16, 1951. Anecdote in *Dvar hashavu'a*, May 18, 1950.

120. *Omer*, July 4, 1951.

121. *Yediot aharonot*, August 29, 1951. Also see anecdote in *Dvar hashavu'a*, July 6, 1950.

122. Goode (1992), 22.

123. Naor (1987), 103.

124. *Herut*, September 29, 1950. *Ashmoret*, November 2, 1950. Cartoons in *Dvar hashavu'a*, December 6, 1951, and *Hagidu bedan*, December 1951, 81.

125. *Ashmoret*, August 16, 1951.

126. *Beterem*, July 1, 1952.

127. IDF (1956), 18.

128. *Kol yisrael*, August 31, 1953.

129. For instance, *Herut*, June 17, 1955.

130. Shlomo Grodzensky's letter from November 8, 1949—courtesy of Tirza Sandbank and Miriam Talisman.

131. *Ashmoret*, August 23, 1951.

132. *Al hamishmar*, August 10, 1951. Also see cartoon in Tzabar (1951). Ownership of luxury cars by Mapai leaders was also criticized from the right: for example, see *Herut*, October 5, 1950.

133. *Al hamishmar*, August 12, 1949.

134. Bartov (1997), 321–322, 326.

135. *Lagever*, March 17, 1954. Mikes (1950), 90–93.

136. Stokker (1995), 149–159.

137. Horowitz (1993), 51.

138. Ibid., 43, 45.

139. *Hedei hanegev*, Kislev Tashiad (1954), 15. And see photo from 1953 — CZA, 1178615.

6. Going to the Movies

1. *Hatzofeh*, February 6, 1950.

2. *Kol hamishmar haezrachi*, 8, September 1949, 6, 21–22. *Ma'ariv*, August 28, 1953. Photos from 1949, 1951, 1954—CZA, 1278573, 1176398, 1176360, 1278171, 1278172. Photo from 1949 and photos from 1950 and 1955 by Fritz Cohen—NPC, D219-087, D207-076, D585-027, D726-097.

3. Ads in *Yediot aharonot*, March 16, 1949. *Ma'ariv*, January 12, 1949, December 7, 1949, March 3, 1950, August 10, 1953. *Jerusalem Post*, December 29, 1950, July 20, 1951.

4. Bergman (1970), 1–2. Butsch (2000), 169–170.

5. *Jerusalem Post*, December 1, 1952.

6. Ibid.

7. *Hador* quoted in *Yediot hitachdut ba'alei batei hakolno'a beyisrael*, July 24, 1955, 12. *Haboker*, March 5, 1956. Also see *Davar*, July 9, 1954. Shalit (2006), 93–94. And compare with moviegoing patterns in Britain: McKibbin (1998), 419.

8. Sapir (1951), 21. Thissen (2008), 56. Shalit (2006), 19–26. Helman (2010), 115–120. Helman (2004).

9. *Jerusalem Post*, December 1, 1952. Photo from 1950 by Fritz Cohen—NPC, D235-107. Eldad and Nedava (1955), 252.

10. For instance, letter from March 1949—JIA, 21/5/25. Ads in *Ma'ariv*, February 8, 1949, February 19, 1949, August 28, 1953. *Jerusalem Post*, March 8, 1950. *Haaretz*, March 10, 1950. *Da et irkha, heifa*, November 1952, 6. *Ma'ariv*, February 22, 1954. *Zmanim*, October 30, 1955.

11. Letter from November 11, 1949—NA, 10/1. *Davar*, February 10, 1949. Protocol from April 26, 1954—HMA, 1/22 TZ 32194-1566/8. *Kolno'a*, January 12, 1955. Also see Naor (2010).

12. *Ma'ariv*, March 1, 1950, March 17, 1950. *Yediot aharonot*, March 19, 1950. *Ha'olam hazeh*, April 13, 1950.

13. *Ma'ariv*, June 30, 1950, July 18, 1954. *Yediot aharonot, Koteret*, March 27, 1952. *Davar*, July 7, 1955.

14. *Kolno'a*, December 10, 1953. *Ma'ariv*, December 15, 1954. *Davar*, November 18, 1955. And see Sklar (1994), 283, 285. Dankner and Tartakover (1996), 135.

15. *Ma'ariv*, July 19, 1950. *Jerusalem Post*, December 1, 1952. *Hatzofeh*, November 30, 1952. *Haboker*, November 30, 1952, February 1, 1955. *Herut*, February 1, 1955. Letter from February 19, 1952—ISA, gl 3882 mb/40. Regulation from 1954—ISA, gl 3881 mb/12/2. *Yediot hitachdut ba'alei batei hakolno'a beyisrael*, November 2, 1955, 7. Also see Shalit (2006), 45, 84.

16. *Al hamishmar*, June 12, 1949. *Yediot hitachdut ba'alei batei hakolno'a beyisrael*, September 26, 1952, 5, and May 2, 1954, 6, 12. Letter from October 23, 1955—TAA, 4/629. In one Tel Aviv cinema, every worker received thirty to eighty free tickets: see protocol from July 17, 1951—TAA, 4/628. On the use and abuse of free tickets, see Baram (2004), 56–57.

17. *Yediot aharonot, Koteret*, August 5, 1951. *Haaretz*, November 7, 1955. On inaccurate

reports about cinema owners' income, see correspondence from 1955 and 1956—JCA, 32.017/471–481, 32.017/ASD. On Saturday evenings at the movies, see *Ma'ariv*, July 19, 1950. *Yediot aharonot, Koteret*, March 25, 1951.

18. *Al hamishmar*, June 30, 1949, March 13, 1950. *Ha'olam hazeh*, April 13, 1950. *Yediot hitachdut ba'alei batei hakolno'a beyisrael*, September 30, 1955, 3–9.

19. Letter from June 1949—TAA, 4/1941 A.

20. For instance, see Rieger (1952), 270.

21. *Herut*, November 11, 1955. On reduced-price tickets for soldiers and students, see *Bamachaneh*, October 20, 1949. *Ashmoret*, March 3, 1950. Eldad and Nedava (1955), 253.

22. Letter from April 9, 1952—NA, 13/4. *Yediot hitachdut ba'alei batei hakolno'a beyisrael*, October 18, 1954, 3, 7. On Independence Day movie "treats" see photo from April 1950 by Fritz Cohen—NPC, D725-066. Letters from January 6, 1952, and April 22, 1952—NA, 13/4.

23. *Ha'olam hazeh*, January 7, 1953. *Hador*, April 2, 1954.

24. Shavit (2006), 96. Television was described as a technological and cultural wonder: *Dagesh*, July 13, 1950. *Dvar hashavu'a*, March 8, 1951. *Omer*, January 8, 1954. *Zmanim*, November 12, 1954.

25. *Dorot*, October 20, 1949. On visits to the cinema as romantic dates, see cartoons in *Bamachaneh*, December 7, 1950, March 27, 1952. *Laisha*, May 5, 1954. *Kolno'a*, January 12, 1955. Significantly, the 1950 "Operation Scanning," an attempt to locate young women who tried to avoid military conscription, was conducted in cinemas during screenings—*Ma'ariv*, June 14, 1950.

26. Kishon (1952), 151–157.

27. For example, see Helman (2011), 116–120.

28. Letter from 1950—TAA, 4/3644. Also see *Ma'ariv*, July 19, 1950.

29. *Yediot aharonot, Koteret*, April 19, 1951.

30. *Dvar hashavu'a*, March 23, 1950. Also see cartoon in *Dvar hashavu'a*, October 12, 1950. And see Gelber (1999), 7–8.

31. *Yediot aharonot, Koteret*, April 6, 1952. Also see satire in *Haaretz*, June 4, 1950. Letter from May 18, 1952: IDFA, 639. Cartoon from 1953 in Dosh (1956), 21.

32. *Jerusalem Post*, July 3, 1952. Also see cartoon in *Yediot hitachdut ba'alei batei hakolno'a beyisrael*, February 11, 1954, 20. And see Shalit (2006), 97.

33. *Al hamishmar*, January 11, 1950. *Yediot aharonot, Koteret*, April 6, 1952.

34. *Al hamishmar*, January 11, 1950. On the lines for Menuhin's concerts, see *Al hamishmar, Haaretz, Davar*, April 13, 1950. *Ma'ariv*, August 10, 1951.

35. Photos from 1949 by Fritz Cohen—NPC, D465-034, D465-037. Photo in *Bamachaneh*, February 23, 1950. *Ha'olam hazeh*, January 12, 1950. *Al hamishmar*, May 19, 1950. Protocol from August 31, 1951—TAA, 4/628. *Ozer dalim*, 1951, 8. *Bamachaneh*, February 14, 1952. Letter from March 1, 1956—ISA, gl 3886 mb/51. On lines in Haifa see correspondence from November 1955—HMA, A-B 4-27/1560/8. On feelings of aggression in the line for a theatrical performance, see Kvutzat Yavneh bulletin, December 14, 1951—RKMA.

36. For instance, *Herut*, December 4, 1953.

37. Letter from January 27, 1953 — ISA, gl 3886 mb/51. And compare with grumbling in communist East Germany: Merkel (1998), 294.

38. *Dvar hashavuʻa*, December 6, 1951. Also see *Zmanim*, February 17, 1955. *Al hamishmar*, May 13, 1955.

39. *Ashmoret*, December 8, 1949. *Olam hakolnoʻa*, October 25, 1951. *Yediot aharonot, Koteret*, July 30, 1953. *Haaretz*, August 6, 1953. *Hatzofeh*, November 12, 1953. *Herut*, November 5, 1954. *Al hamishmar*, October 28, 1955. *Kol haʻam*, May 14, 1956. Samet (1954), 82.

40. Statistical reports for 1956/7, 45, table 5 — HMA.

41. *Yediot hitachdut baʻalei batei hakolnoʻa beyisrael*, August 18, 1953, 24.

42. Helman (2010), 106–109, 124–125, 128.

43. Statistical reports for 1956/7, 45, table 5 — HMA.

44. Letter from August 26, 1953 — JCA, 32.017 ASD. *Haaretz*, April 13, 1950.

45. *Haaretz*, November 7, 1955.

46. Segev (1984), 219–222.

47. Letter from May 2, 1949—TAA, 4/1941A. Letter from June 27, 1952 — ISA, g-5/714. Letter from June 13, 1955 — HMA, A-B/4–27-1560/8. Also see *Hamodiʻa*, February 9, 1951.

48. *Yediot aharonot, Koteret*, August 5, 1951. *Hamodiʻa*, August 20, 1954, June 15, 1956. On the founding of the "League for the Prevention of Religious Coercion" in Jerusalem, see Tzur (2001), 210. On Haredi activity in the city, see Friedman (1994) and Caplan (2011).

49. Letters from 1944, 1946, and 1947—TAA, 4/1941A.

50. Letter from April 1950 — TAA, 4/1941A. *Ashmoret*, November 2, 1950. *Yediot aharonot, Koteret*, March 25, 1951. See cartoons of profiteers in *Bamachaneh*, April 5, 1951. *Ashmoret*, March 8, 1951. *Omer*, January 11, 1952. *Yediot hitachdut baʻalei batei hakolnoʻa beyisrael*, February 11, 1954, 27.

51. *Maʻariv*, July 19, 1950. *Yediot aharonot, Koteret*, March 25, 1951. *Yediot hitachdut baʻalei batei hakolnoʻa beyisrael*, November 2, 1955.

52. Protocol from August 31, 1951 — TAA, 4/628.

53. *Dvar hashavuʻa*, December 6, 1951.

54. *Yediot aharonot, Koteret*, March 25, 1951.

55. Could the journalist really hear the tune from the balcony, or was he making ethnic assumptions?

56. Quoted in *Yediot hitachdut baʻalei batei hakolnoʻa beyisrael*, November 2, 1954, 27–28.

57. *Bamachaneh*, February 14, 1952.

58. Quoted in *Yediot hitachdut baʻalei batei hakolnoʻa beyisrael*, May 2, 1954. On profiteering in cinemas showing crowd-drawing films, see *Herut*, November 11, 1955. Also see *Olam hakolnoʻa*, May 29, 1952.

59. Satire in *Haaretz*, June 4, 1950.

60. Quoted in *Yediot hitachdut baʻalei batei hakolnoʻa beyisrael*, November 2, 1954, 27–28. Also see *Herut*, August 3, 1951. *Beterem*, February 15, 1954. *Yediot hitachdut baʻalei batei hakolnoʻa beyisrael*, May 2, 1954, 12.

61. *Haboker,* January 6, 1956. Cartoon in Dosh (1956), 43.

62. *Al hamishmar,* January 11, 1950. *Yediot aharonot, Koteret,* March 25, 1951. *Yediot hitachdut ba'alei batei hakolno'a beyisrael,* May 2, 1954, 12. *Haboker,* January 6, 1956.

63. Rozin (2005b), 287.

64. *Omer,* July 23, 1951.

65. *Yediot aharonot,* March 27, 1952.

66. *Haaretz,* June 6, 1950. *Davar,* July 9, 1954. Letter from August 1955 — ISA, gl 3866 mb/51. Dankner and Tartakover (1996), 12, 31. Shalit (2006), 94. On Palmach pranks see Ben-Amotz and Hefer (1979), 48, 57, 99–114, 137–138, 165.

67. Letter from January 4, 1950 — TAA, 4/1949A. Letter from January 27, 1950 — ISA, gl 3886 mb/51. And see illustration in *Yediot aharonot, Koteret,* March 27, 1952.

68. *Ma'ariv,* April 28, 1950.

69. Protocol from August 31, 1951 — TAA, 4/628.

70. *Yediot aharonot, Koteret,* March 27, 1952. See photo in *Laisha,* September 15, 1954. Shalit (2006), 98–99.

71. *Yediot aharonot, Koteret,* March 27, 1952.

72. *Yediot aharonot, Koteret,* April 4, 1952. Dankner and Tartakover (1996), 124.

73. *Yediot aharonot, Koteret,* March 27, 1952. *Ha'olam hazeh,* January 12, 1950.

74. Protocol from August 31, 1951 — TAA, 4/628. Lemonade, corn on the cob, hot dogs, chewing gum, and pistachios were also sold in the yard — *Ashmoret,* November 2, 1950. *Ha'olam hazeh,* December 3, 1953. And see letter from May 30, 1956 — HMA, A-4-271 TZ 1/1537. Photo from 1956 by Hans Pinn — NPC, D218-070.

75. *Dvar hashavu'a,* June 28, 1951.

76. *Yediot aharonot, Koteret,* June 19, 1952. *Herut,* February 7, 1950. *Omer,* April 23, 1954. Cartoon in *Yediot hitachdut ba'alei batei hakolno'a beyisrael,* February 11, 1954, 22.

77. Letters from June 1950, December 16, 1951, February 25, 1952 — ISA, gl 3882 mb/16. Letter from February 26, 1951 — ISA, gl 3882 mb/23. Photo in *Ashmoret,* November 2, 1950. Protocol from August 31, 1951 — TAA, 4/628.

78. Letter from February 25, 1952 — ISA, gl 3882 mb/16. Letters from 1953–1954 — ISA, gl 3883 mb/70. Letter from August 14, 1956 — ISA, gl 3884 mb/107. *Alonekh,* April 1951, 7. *Zmanim,* February 23, 1955. *Ma'ariv,* January 6, 1956. *Herut,* January 20, 1956. Also see Shalit (2006), 97.

79. *Yediot aharonot, Koteret,* April 6, 1952. *Yediot hitachdut ba'alei batei hakolno'a beyisrael,* January 12, 1956, 11. *Herut,* August 10, 1956.

80. *Haaretz,* August 15, 1950.

81. *Herut,* February 2, 1950.

82. *Yediot aharonot,* April 19, 1951. *Hador,* December 30, 1953. Letter from August 23 — ISA, gl 3883 mb/77. Letter from March 30, 1956 — ISA, gl 3883 mb/51. And compare with Hill (2002), 60.

83. *Hador,* December 13, 1950. Also see Dankner and Tartakover (1996), 31. And compare with Hill (2002), 60.

84. Letters from 1951 — TAA, 4/1941A, 4/628. *Kol ha'am,* June 29, 1951. *Yediot aharonot, Koteret,* March 27, 1952, April 6, 1952. Correspondence from 1953 — ISA, gl 3886

mb/51. Letter from August 20, 1953 — HMA, 1/22-1566/8. *Ma'ariv*, February 22, 1954. Also see ad in *Hatzofeh*, July 29, 1951.

85. *Yediot aharonot, Koteret*, April 20, 1954.

86. *Ma'ariv*, April 25, 1952.

87. *Al hamishmar*, April 25, 1952. And see *Hasseret*, May 8, 1952, 8.

88. Butsch (2000), 171–172.

89. Protocol from July 13, 1951 — TAA, 4/628. Letter from 1951 — TAA, 4/1941A. *Yediot aharonot, Koteret*, April 6, 1952. *Ma'ariv*, December 22, 1955.

90. *Yediot aharonot, Koteret*, March 27, 1952, April 6, 1952.

91. Cartoon in *Yediot hitachdut ba'alei batei hakolno'a beyisrael*, February 11, 1954, 25.

92. *Yediot hitachdut ba'alei batei hakolno'a beyisrael*, August 18, 1953, 26.

93. *Yediot aharonot*, June 11, 1953. Shalit (2006), 96.

94. *Ha'olam hazeh*, December 8, 1955. Also see joke and cartoon in *Bamachaneh*, June 7, 1951.

95. *Zmanim*, October 30, 1955.

96. Letter from 1951 — TAA, 4/1941A.

97. Protocol from 1951 — TAA, 4/1941A. Shalit (2006), 96.

98. *Yediot aharonot*, April 3, 1952.

99. *Ha'olam hazeh*, January 12, 1950. Zidon (1952), 136. Dankner and Tartakover (1996), 204. Baram (2004), 95. Kishon (1952), 152–153. Understanding the films became doubly difficult because cinemas and agents used to "cut" parts of the movie unprofessionally. Articles from April 1952 — ISA, gl 3883 mb/46. Letters from 1956 — ISA, gl 3884 mb/112.

100. Letter from 1953 — JCA, 32.017 ASD. *Yediot hitachdut ba'alei batei hakolno'a beyisrael*, August 18, 1953. Letter from January 17, 1954—ISA, gl 3882 mb/21. Letter from July 23, 1954—ISA, gl 3884 mb/94. *Hador*, July 21, 1954.

101. *Yediot aharonot, Koteret*, April 3, 1952. *Olam hakolno'a*, May 20, 1955.

102. Memorandum from April 7, 1949. Letters from August 3, 1952, February 3, 1955 — ISA, gl 3882/21.

103. *Haboker*, September 14, 1953. *Yediot aharonot, Koteret*, February 3, 1955. Correspondence from January 1956 — ISA, gl 3884 mb/94.

104. *Yediot hitachdut ba'alei batei hakolno'a beyisrael*, November 2, 1955, 6–7. Also see memorandum from April 6, 1952 — ISA, g-23/716.

105. Letter from February 13, 1952 — ISA, gl 3882 mb/21.

106. Handel (1950), 221. On class preferences and moviegoing patterns in Britain and the United States, see McKibbin (1998), 421. Sklar (1994), 269.

107. On moviegoing among new immigrants see Eisenstadt (1952), 50–55.

108. Correspondence from May 1952 — ISA, g-23/716. Also see protocol from August 17, 1952 — ISA, gl 3882 mb/21. Memorandum from April 6, 1952 — ISA, g-23/716.

109. *Hedei hanegev*, May 1952, 14, and August 1952, 13.

110. Ad in *Hedei hanegev*, Kislev Tashiad (1954), 18.

111. *Ashmoret*, August 2, 1951. Also see photo from 1953 — CZA, 1178633.

112. Ad in *Hedei hanegev*, Kislev Tashiad (1954), 12.

113. *Yediot aharonot,* June 6, 1952.

114. *Yediot hitachdut ba'alei batei hakolno'a beyisrael,* September 26, 1952, 9. Also see photo from Safed, 1949: CZA, 1280077.1.

115. *Yediot hitachdut ba'alei batei hakolno'a beyisrael,* August 18, 1953, 23.

116. Quotation from *Jerusalem Post* in *Dvar hashavu'a,* July 26, 1956. Also see letter from January 7, 1952 — NA, 12/2. And compare with parochial cinemas in 1950s Italy: Gundle (2002), 168.

117. *Yediot hitachdut ba'alei batei hakolno'a beyisrael,* January 28, 1955, 33. On the centrality of the movie theater in Kfar Shalem, see Nadad (1956), 7.

118. *Yediot aharonot,* December 9, 1949.

119. Letter from August 1956 — ISA, gl 3886 mb/51.

120. Letter from September 28, 1956 — ISA, gl 3886 mb/51.

121. *Davar,* July 9, 1954. Also see ad in *Al hamishmar,* August 12, 1949. Shalit (2006), 43.

122. *Ma'ariv,* June 17, 1949.

123. *Pnimah,* March 1952, 49.

124. *Dorot,* October 27, 1949. *Jerusalem Post,* July 27, 1951. *Dvar hashavu'a,* October 30, 1952. *Omer,* March 26, 1956. Also see cartoon in *Ashmoret,* January 4, 1951. Geva newsreels from 1956: SA, VT GE 010.

125. For example, *Dvar hapo'elet,* February 1949, 22. And see Shalit (2006), 43.

126. *Tarbut vehasbarah bekerev po'alei heifah,* Kislev-Tevet Tashia (1951), 14–15. And compare with moviegoing in the American countryside: Handel (1950), 111–112.

127. For instance, *Hatzofeh,* February 3, 1953. Also see Segev (1984), 192–193. Fine (2009), 224.

128. Letter from July 10, 1956 — LI, IV-219-133.

129. Shalit (2006), 148–149. *Haaretz,* May 23, 1956.

130. Memorandum from July 15, 1953 — ISA, gl 3882 mb/40.

131. *Yediot aharonot, Koteret,* April 27, 1954.

132. On the centrality of music in the ethnic identity of Israelis, see Amir (2009), 126–153.

133. Also see *Ozer dalim,* 1951, 5.

134. *Yediot hitachdut ba'alei batei hakolno'a beyisrael,* November 2, 1955, 6–7.

135. Compare with Thompson (1977), 94–98.

136. *Kolno'a,* May 25, 1950. *Ashmoret,* May 17, 1951, July 19, 1951. *Rimon,* October 3, 1956. Shalit (2006), 157, 165, 167. On the effects of television see Sklar (1994), 278, 282–283. Oakley (1990), 13–14. Baughman (1997), 74–83. Cullen (1996), 199–225.

137. Bergman (1970), 1–8.

138. Quoted by Shalit (2006), 92.

139. *Dvar hashavu'a,* June 28, 1951.

140. *Ha'olam hazeh,* March 9, 1950. *Hasseret,* May 8, 1952, 1–2, 7–8. Letter from December 3, 1954—TAA, 4/629. *Niv histadrut afula,* February 1956, 9–10. Lia van Leer's 1950s film clubs in Haifa and Jerusalem would later turn into cinematheques.

141. Letter from February 8, 1950 — LI, IV208-4967. Letter from February 21, 1950 — ISA, g-5/714.

142. *Ha'olam hazeh,* April 13, 1950. *Yediot aharonot, Koteret,* May 22, 1952. *Kolno'a,* October 28, 1954. Geva newsreel from 1954: SA, VT GE 07. Poster from 1954: CZA, KRA 1804. Davidon (1955).

143. *Kolno'a,* January 19, 1950, June 1, 1950, October 5, 1950. *Ashmoret,* May 18, 1950. *Olam hakolno'a,* October 14, 1951. *Herut,* July 11, 1952, November 5, 1954. *Dvar hapo'elet,* April 1956, 90. *Ha'olam hazeh,* May 25, 1955, July 5, 1956. Mock trial of the crime film, October 31, 1952 — ISA, gl 3883 nb/60. Also see Shalit (2006), 43.

144. *Olam hakolno'a,* October 25, 1951.

145. *Ashmoret,* December 8, 1949. Also see *Kolno'a,* January 26, 1950. *Haaretz,* June 19, 1953. Notices in *Davar,* July 13, 1955.

146. On the financial arrangement with the American companies, see *Olam hakolno'a,* November 8, 1951. Samet (1954), 80. Shalit (2006), 45–47.

147. *Kolno'a,* March 1, 1951, February 28, 1952. *Jerusalem Post,* December 1, 1952. Haaretz Annual (1954), 112–115. *Yediot hitachdut ba'alei batei hakolno'a beyisrael,* December 15, 1954, 7. Samet (1954), 81.

148. *Al hamishmar,* May 26, 1950. Also see *Omer,* January 8, 1954.

149. *Yediot aharonot, Koteret,* December 30, 1953. Shalit (2006), 43.

150. For instance, Hill (2002), 64. Muscio (2000), 118. Massey (2000), 146–147, 152–153. Kruisel (2000), 218–219. And compare with *Omer,* February 1, 1952.

151. On similar defensive sociocultural motives behind anti-American announcements made by European elites, see Berman (2005), 22–23. Kroes (2002), 311. Hermand (2005), 72. Kruisel (1993), 17, 121. Berghahn (2001), 86, 88. Ellwood (2003), 137.

152. *Yediot aharonot, Koteret,* December 30, 1953. Also see *Hador,* July 1, 1955.

153. Pines (1954), 57.

154. *Al hamishmar,* October 28, 1955. Another critic used the derogatory term "movies for forgetting": *Herut,* June 3, 1955.

155. *Ashmoret,* December 8, 1949.

156. *Yediot aharonot, Koteret,* April 20, 1954.

157. *Yediot aharonot,* December 2, 1952.

158. Edith Elliott Lindeman Calish was the *Richmond Times-Dispatch*'s entertainment critic from 1933 to 1964, as well as a writer of popular songs.

159. *Olam habikoret,* August 23, 1951.

160. *Dorot,* October 20, 1949. And compare with other ambivalent and apologetic reviews of Hollywood movies: *Dvar hashavu'a,* September 29, 1955. *Herut,* November 28, 1954, January 20, 1956.

161. On the different American and European approaches to culture and entertainment, see Bramham et al. (1993). Dyer (2000).

162. Especially as artistic European films offered a stark and sober realism: *Kolno'a,* June 1, 1950. Wagstaff (1998). On selectivity in movies according to class, see Handel (1950), 151, 153–154. On the international appeal of American movies, see Kracauer (1950), 141–146. Sassoon (2002), 123–126. Jones (2006), 231.

163. The latter was often argued by critics: Helman (2004), 77–82. Helman (2011), 119–120.

164. *Lagever,* March 10, 1954.
165. *Ha'olam hazeh,* May 29, 1952.
166. For instance, *Lagever,* February 24, 1954. And see Almog (1997), 329. Shalit (2006), 43–44. Heilbronner (2011), 35, 41.
167. Kishon (1952), 151–157.
168. Helman (2003a).
169. Drori (2010), 82.
170. A child's drawing in *Davar leyeladim,* December 14, 1954.
171. Gelbert (1954), 8.

7. The Communal Dining Hall

1. *Jerusalem Post,* February 13, 1950. And see photos of Kibbutz Ein Harod in snow: CZA, 1011090, 1011083, 1011087.
2. Helman (1992), 169. On the founding of the kibbutzim and their movements, see Near (1992b).
3. Helman (1992), 169–170.
4. Mikes (1950), 138–139. Ben-Rafael (1995), 265–275. Near (1995), 243–259. Near (1997), 171–175, 178–191, 198–222. Near (1992b), 120–121, 126–129. Zachor (2007), 110–112. Giladi and Shwartz (2001), 38–41, 58–72. Weitz (2001), 101–102. Katz (1995), 253–280. Halamish (2010), 36. Golan (2010), 59, 62. Drori (2010), 82. Assaf (2010), 184–191. Pauker (2010), 180. Pauker (2012), 66–67. Ben-Rafael et al. (2000), 41. Cohen-Friedheim (2012), 70, 296–306. Meir-Glitzenstein (2009), 210.
5. Zachor (2007), 108–112, 136. Kochavi-Nehab (2006), 24–25. Drori (2010), 90–91. Schor (1956), 57.
6. Kochavi-Nehab (2006), 24–25. Zachor (2007), 153. And see the founding of a new kibbutz in 1955 in Geva newsreels: SA, VT GE 07.
7. Bachi (1956), 243–244.
8. Dorot bulletin, February 8, 1952, November 6, 1952, July 8, 1955 — NNL. Shefayim bulletin, January 12, 1951, January 1, 1954 — YTA. Hazorea bulletin, July 25, 1952, November 6, 1952, November 4, 1955 — KHA. Kiryat Anavim bulletin, December 28, 1954 — KKAA. Sde Eliyahu bulletin, 23 Nissan Tashai (1950) — RKMA. Revivim bulletin, March 5, 1954 — YTA. Mikes (1950), 142–143. Cohen-Friedheim (2012), 294.
9. Dorot bulletin, October 25, 1949 — YTA. Shefayim bulletin, July 15, 1949 — YTA. Hazorea bulletin, February 10, 1950 — KHA. Gan Shmuel bulletin, March 2, 1951 — NNL. Revivim bulletin, March 5, 1954, April 9, 1954 — YTA.
10. Drori (2010), 90–91. Near (1995), 248. Ben-Rafael et al. (2000), 26–37.
11. Also see Kiryat Anavim bulletin, November 11, 1949 — KKAA. Gan Shmuel bulletin, January 18, 1956 — NNL. Cartoon in Gelbert (1954), 34.
12. For instance, see Revivim bulletin, January 18, 1952 — YTA. Porat (1997), 410–411. Libman (2012), 56–61.
13. Hakibbutz Hameuchad, Ichud Hakvutzot Vehakibbutzim, Hakibbutz Haartzi, and Hakibbutz Hadati.

14. Near (1992b), 191.

15. Near (2010), 19.

16. Simmel (1997). Also see Avieli (2012), 110–111.

17. Shefer and Fogiel-Bijaoui (1992), 13–22. Also see Tal (1994), 134, 137–139. Avieli (2012), 115. In the short-lived Arab Kibbutz, Ahwa, communal eating was one of only three collective institutions: Aharoni and Mishal (2005), 190.

18. Shachnai Ran et al. (2010). Shefayim bulletin, December 29, 1950 — YTA. *Al hamishmar,* January 17, 1950. Photo of the first president and his wife visiting Kibbutz Negba: photo from 1949 by Teddy Brauner — NPC, D671-096. Photos of the second president's wife visiting Kibbutz Bachan, 1956 — JNFPA, d711-226, d711-226. Photo from 1950 — KKAA, 41/14.10. On the communal nature of dining in the hall, also see cartoon in Gelbert (1954), 75.

19. Quoted by Gispan-Greenberg (2010), 152.

20. Borrero (1997), 163–164, 167. On collective kitchens for Zionist workers, see Gofer (2004).

21. Rothstein and Rothstein (1997), 183, 191–192. Poster from 1947 in Snopkov et al. (2010), no. 122.

22. Treiber (2010). Tsur (2020). Tal (1994), 142–150, 160. Compare the dining halls of Kfar Hanassi and Kinneret: photos from 1952 and 1953 by Fritz Cohen — NPC, D271-070, D265-095. And see photo of dining hall in Ein Gedi, 1954 — JNFPA, D296-024.

23. For examples, see photos from 1949 and photo from 1951 by Fritz Shlezinger: CZA, 1010102, 1335167, 1277696.

24. Tsur (2010).

25. Sde Eliyahu bulletin, 15 Heshvan Tashai (1950) — RKMA. Kiryat Anavim bulletin, October 3, 1952 — KKAA. Photos of Degania Alef in 1950: CZA, 1011689, 1335369. Cartoons in Gelbert (1954), 65, 83. Mikes (1950), 148. Near (1995), 245.

26. Tsur (2010). Photo from 1951: CZA, 1329214. Cartoon by Gelbert (1954), 65.

27. For instance, see photo from 1947 of Kibbutz Efal's kindergarten by Zoltan Kluger — NPC, D829-020. Also see cartoon in Gelbert (1954), 130.

28. Cartoon in Gelbert (1954), 73. On the problems of the table-filling system, see Avieli (2012), 116–117.

29. Treiber (2010). Tsur (2010). Dorot bulletin, August 22, 1952 — NNL.

30. Rothstein and Rothstein (1997), 184–185, 189–190.

31. Kochavi-Nehab (2006), 36.

32. Tsur (2007). On the "secular religion" of the kibbutzim until the 1940s, see Soker (1998), 19–23, 26–44, and Shafrut (1988).

33. Tsur (2010).

34. Bar-Or (2010).

35. *Gazit,* January–February 1950, 2.

36. Compare with photos from Kibbutz Sarid and Kibbutz Mizra (1956) in Shachnai Yacobi (2010), unnumbered pages. On Kibbutz Seders as proper representations of authentic Israeli culture, see *Al hamishmar,* June 13, 1955.

37. Helman (2008d), 318–321. Helman (2011), 140–141, 152–153. On the secular Sabbath services see Soker (1998), 51.

38. Photos of Degania Alef in 1950: CZA, 1011689, 1335360.

39. Photo from 1949 by Hugo Mendelson — NPC, D289-084. Dorot bulletin, August 23, 1951, October 2, 1953 — NNL. Revivim bulletin, September 29, 1952 — YTA. Notices from 1954—KKAA, 20.3.7.4. Hazorea bulletin, January 22, 1956 — KHA. Treiber (2010).

40. Gan Shmuel bulletin, 1950 — NNL.

41. Hazorea bulletin, March 22, 1955, April 15, 1955 — KHA.

42. Kiryat Anavim bulletin, January 8, 1955 — KKAA.

43. Dorot bulletin, January 31, 1952 — NNL. Sde Eliyahu bulletin, 24 Shvat Tashai (1950) — RKMA. Photo from 1951 — KKAA, 21/5.63.

44. For instance, see Katz (1995) and Rosenberg-Friedman (2006), 94–95.

45. Beerot Yitzhak bulletin, June 16, 1949. Tirat Zvi bulletin, April 7, 1950, November 30, 1951. Sde Eliyahu bulletin, 5 Heshvan Tashai (1950) — RKMA.

46. Kvutzat Yavneh bulletin, November 2, 1949—RKMA. Also see photo from 1950 by Teddy Brauner — NPC, D294-079.

47. Liebermann (1998), 51. Zakim (2006), 54–55. Dar (2006), 45–47.

48. Kvutzat Yavneh bulletin, November 29, 1950 — RKMA. Also see Sde Eliyahu bulletin, 3 Nissan Tashai (1950) — RKMA.

49. Sde Eliyahu bulletin, 24 Av Tashat (1949) — RKMA.

50. Sde Eliyahu bulletin, 26 Shvat Tashiab (1952) — RKMA.

51. Tirat Zvi bulletin, April 7, 1950 — RKMA.

52. For examples, see photo from 1949 by Fred Chetnik of Kibbutz Yasur and photos of Gan Shmuel, Ein Tzurim, and Shluhot from 1950, 1954, and 1955: CZA, 1277582, 1012372, 1335693, 1334494, 1334495.

53. Bachi (1956), 245.

54. Meimon (1955), 151–155. Efron (2000), 378–379. Fogiel-Bijaoui (2006), 595–615. Ben-Rafael and Weitman (2006), 621. Fogiel-Bijaoui (2010), 150–156. Near (2010), 14. Also see Kafkafi (1999), 204–205. On the labor hierarchy see Talmon-Gerber (2006), 404, 406, 408. Ben-Rafael and Weitman (2006), 617–633. Tehar-Lev (1976), 11–12. Cartoon in Gelbert (1954), 9.

55. Tsur (2010). Dar (2006), 47.

56. Fogiel-Bijaoui (1992), 111.

57. Sde Eliyahu bulletin, 15 Heshvan Tashai (1950) — RKMA. Photo from 1950 — NPC, D263-064. Kiryat Anavim bulletin, December 28, 1954—KKAA. Cartoons by Gelbert (1954), 23, 83.

58. Rothstein and Rothstein (1997), 178–190. Also see Mosse (1985), 185. Evans Clements (1985), 232.

59. Kiryat Anavim bulletin, October 3, 1952, December 28, 1954—KKAA.

60. Hamadiya bulletin, August 1, 1952 — NNL. Photos from 1954 and 1955: CZA, 1277751, 1334498, 1334499.

61. Dorot bulletin, November 7, 1955 — NNL. Sde Eliyahu bulletin, 15 Heshvan Tashai (1950) — RKMA. Kiryat Anavim bulletin, August 26, 1949—KKAA.

62. Photos from 1950 and 1951—KKAA, 45/259, 8/1.181.

63. Dorot bulletin, January 14, 1955—NNL. Also see photo from Kibbutz Gaash in Shachnai Yacobi (2010), unnumbered page.

64. Quoted from Glil-Yam bulletin in *Al hamishmar*, December 8, 1949. Glil-Yam was not the only kibbutz trying to conduct an "Operation Quiet" in the dining hall. See Kiryat Anavim bulletin, August 26, 1949—KKAA; Alonim bulletin, October 8, 1954; and cartoon from April 24, 1949—KALA.

65. Dorot bulletin, August 3, 1950—YTA. On the additional noise made by immigrant youths and Nahal soldiers, see Tirat Zvi bulletin, April 7, 1950—RKMA.

66. Kiryat Anavim bulletin, December 28, 1954—KKAA. Also see Yavneh bulletin, January 19, 1954—RKMA.

67. Sde Eliyahu bulletin, 25 Nissan Tashiag (1953)—RKMA.

68. Dorot bulletin, April 7, 1952—NNL. Alonim bulletin, March 14, 1954—KALA.

69. Kiryat Anavim bulletin, August 26, 1949, December 28, 1954—KKAA. Dorot bulletin, January 14, 1955—NNL.

70. Sde Eliyahu bulletin, 24 Av Tashat (1949)—RKMA.

71. Tirat Zvi bulletin, April 7, 1950—RKMA.

72. Kiryat Anavim bulletin, January 8, 1955—KKAA.

73. Tirat Zvi bulletin, January 26, 1951—RKMA.

74. Hamadiya bulletin, September 23, 1956 (also see September 15, 1956)—NNL.

75. Alonim bulletin, September 11, 1950 (also see June 16, 1950)—KALA. Shefayim bulletin, December 10, 1950, November 16, 1951, April 15, 1955—YTA. Tirat Zvi bulletin, January 26, 1951; Yavneh bulletin, November 24, 1954—RKMA.

76. Dorot bulletin, August 8, 1952—NNL.

77. Kiryat Anavim bulletin, December 28, 1954—KKAA. Also see Dorot bulletin, April 7, 1952. Hamadiya bulletin, August 27, 1956—NNL.

78. Cartoons in Gelbert (1954), 71, 76. Tsur (2010). Kiryat Anavim bulletin, December 28, 1954—KKAA. Dorot bulletin, June 6, 1956—NNL. On the low quality of the tableware, see Near (1995), 245.

79. For example, see photos from 1953 and 1954 in Shachnai Yacobi (2010), unnumbered pages. Photo of Netiv HaLamed Heh in 1954 by Fritz Shlezinger: CZA, 1260864. Also see Gispan-Greenberg (2010).

80. Dorot bulletin, May 23, 1952, June 6, 1952—NNL. Yavneh bulletin, January 19, 1954. Tirat Zvi bulletin, April 7, 1950 (also see March 26, 1956). Sde Eliyahu bulletin, 15 Heshvan Tashai (1950), 3 Nissan Tashai (1950)—RKMA. Also see cartoon in Gelbert (1954), 105. Photo from 1949 by Avraham Malevsky—JNFPA, glass60-047. Photos from 1955: CZA, 1334498, 1334499.

81. Kelly (2001), 288–289. On austere aesthetics also see Jordanova (2012), 99–100.

82. Kiryat Anavim bulletin, August 26, 1949—KKAA.

83. Alonim bulletin, September 11, 1950—KALA.

84. Tirat Zvi bulletin, April 7, 1950—RKMA.

85. Kiryat Anavim bulletin, January 8, 1955—KKAA.

86. Helman (2011), 146–149. Shefer and Fogiel-Bijaoui (1992), 33.

87. Tsur (2010). Shefer and Fogiel-Bijaoui (1992), 23–29, 32.

88. Ornamented dress, for instance, was often regarded as "unsuitable" to kibbutz ideology as well as to its lifestyle: Helman (2011), 150–155. Helman (2008d).

89. Cartoons by Gelbert (1954), 22, 93. Protocol from January 28, 1950 — KAA, 3/ar, General assembly protocols, 1948–1951. Revivim bulletin, February 29, 1950, June 29, 1951, March 27, 1953 — YTA. Hazorea bulletin, November 30, 1951 — KHA. Dorot bulletin, February 6, 1953 — NNL. Shefer and Fogiel-Bijaoui (1992), 31.

90. Kiryat Anavim bulletin, November 11, 1949—KKAA.

91. Sde Eliyahu bulletin, 15 Heshvan Tashai (1950) — RKMA.

92. Tirat Zvi bulletin, April 7, 1950 — RKMA.

93. Kiryat Anavim bulletin, October 3, 1952 — KKAA.

94. Dorot bulletin, August 23, 1951, October 2, 1953 — NNL. *Al hamishmar*, January 17, 1950. Photos from 1953 and 1955 by Fritz Cohen and Moshe Pridan — NPC, D265-111, D295-040. Cartoon in Gelbert (1954), 22.

95. Beerot Itzhak bulletin, June 12, 1953 — RKMA.

96. On the significance of the Sabbath meal in Hassidic tradition, see Nadler (2005).

97. Beerot Itzhak bulletin, November 26, 1954—RKMA.

98. Sde Eliyahu bulletin, 24 Av Tashat (1949), 25 Nissan Tashiag (1953) — RKMA. On gossip and public opinion as informal modes of social supervision in the kibbutzim, see Shefer and Shapira (1992), 44–50.

99. Avieli (2012), 111–112.

100. Borrero (1997), 170–173. Poster from 1954 in Snopkov et al. (2010), no. 153.

101. For example, see Gan Shmuel bulletin, January 7, 1950 — NNL. Kochavi-Nehab (2006), 191. Assaf (2010). Also see cartoon in Dosh (1956), 19.

102. Kafkafi (1993), 435–438. Also see Zachor (2007), 146, 148. Pauker (2012), 74. Photo of Ein Harod in 1951: CZA, 1327095.

103. See photo of Kibbutz Gaash dining hall in Shachnai Yacobi (2010), unnumbered pages. Also see *Al hamishmar*, March 8, 1953. Stalin was particularly admired and mourned in the kibbutzim of the Hakibbutz Haartzi movement: Pauker (2012), 71–80.

104. Kafkafi (1993), 436.

105. Kanari (2003), 18.

106. Tirat Zvi bulletin, April 7, 1950 — RKMA.

107. The amount of violence was discussed and predetermined by each side: Kafkafi (1993), 438.

108. Kiryat Anavim bulletin, November 11, 1949—KKAA.

109. As suggested, for example, by Dar (2006), 47–48.

8. Informality, Straightforwardness, and Rudeness

1. *Laisha*, July 21, 1954.

2. Bor (2001), 48. Feiner (2003), 384.

3. Shavit (2009), 17–18, 20, 25, 27, 29.

4. Gilman (2005), 217, 223. Reifowitz (2008), 2, 8–9.

5. Lederhendler (1991), 331.

6. Walzer (2007), 130.

7. Shapira (1997), 160–165, 174.

8. For instance, Fuchs (1999), 213.

9. Stone Nakhimovsky (2006), 65.

10. On the cinematic portrayal of the Sabra vis-à-vis the Diaspora Jew, see Feldstein (2009), 267–268.

11. Shapira (1997), 174.

12. On the archetypical Sabra-Palmachnik see Ben-Eliezer (1984), 33. Efron (2000), 353.

13. Katriel (1999), 206–207.

14. Ibid., 209–211.

15. For example, see *Ma'ariv*, August 4, 1950. *Yediot aharonot, 7 yamim*, March 12, 1954. *Tevel*, June 2, 1954.

16. *Dvar hashavu'a*, November 9, 1950.

17. Lissak (2000), 323.

18. Robinson (1953), 270–271.

19. Kurzweil (1965), 295.

20. Helman (2011). Helman (2008d).

21. *Lagever*, January 20, 1954.

22. Helman (2011), 21–46.

23. Ibid., 21, 43–44, 181–184, 199–202.

24. Cartoon in *Dvar hashavu'a*, September 1, 1949.

25. On disobeying lifeguards at the seashore, for example, see *Al hamishmar*, August 17, 1953.

26. *Hadshot hasport*, December 11, 1955.

27. *Dagesh*, June 20, 1950, 18–21. Ben-Amotz and Hefer (1979), 140. Ben-Rafael (1994), 61. Mikes described "the average Israeli" — not just the Sabra — as stubbornly opinionated: Mikes (1950), 109.

28. On the tough and unreservedly conceited new Israeli, see Ziv (1986), 31.

29. *Dvar hashavu'a*, August 25, 1949. And compare with a similar anecdote in *Dvar hashavu'a*, May 11, 1949.

30. Mikes (1950), 41–45, 50–51.

31. *Ashmoret*, February 23, 1950.

32. *Dvar hashavu'a*, March 28, 1956.

33. Rosenthal (2006), 129.

34. *Dagesh*, January 18, 1951, 11–12.

35. Wouters (2004), 8. On the gradual construction of the English gentleman and his image, see Berberich (2007).

36. Watts (2007), 9. Also see Lederhendler (1991), 330.

37. Watts (2007), 14–17.

38. Rathmayr (2008), 2.

39. Robinson (1953), 269.

40. Shlomo Grodzensky's letter from November 21, 1949—courtesy of Tirza Sandbank and Miriam Talisman. Translation of the Arabic and Hebrew words was added to the original text in brackets.

41. Bar-Zohar (1980), 363, 397. Helman (2011), 74. *Ma'ariv*, September 3, 2012. See photos by Hans Pinn from 1949: CZA, 1287145, 1287082.1. Photos from 1955 by Moshe Pridan, Fritz Cohen, and Paul Goldman: NPC, D667-019, D667-026, D716-110, D683-029. Even the unceremonious Ben-Gurion would write in 1958 that Israelis lack good manners, politeness, and tolerance: quoted by Kedar (2002), 128.

42. *Yediot aharonot, Koteret*, September 14, 1954.

43. An essay by Marcia Gitlin, 1933 — TAA, 4/3563a.

44. Herbert Samuel quoted by Elboim-Dror (2000), 37. On the Christian notion of Jews as noisy and discordant, see HaCohen (2011), 3, 28–29.

45. Montgomery (1938), 94. *Tesha ba'erev*, June 10, 1937.

46. Shifman and Katz (2005), 847. Lavsky (2012), 266. Compare with the image of the Jewish Eastern European ghetto as dirty: Rochelson (1988), 407.

47. Report from 1933 — LI, IV-104-13-2. Also see Rubin (2011), 71, 96.

48. Shifman and Katz (2005), 849–850, 855. Also see Ben-Amotz and Hefer (1979), 74, 76–77, 128.

49. For example, *Yediot aharonot*, September 13, 1951.

50. Quoted in Sela-Sheffy (2003), 297.

51. *Ashmoret*, September 8, 1949.

52. *Haaretz*, September 16, 1955.

53. Rivlin (1954), 78–79.

54. *Sheluchot yotzei teiman*, April 7, 1952, 3.

55. Rathmayr (2008), 2–5.

56. Kelly (2001), 252–253, 277–278. Rathmayr (2008), 6. The similarity between today's Israeli and Russian manners has been noted by sociologists — see Watts (2007), 16.

57. Katriel (1999), 212. Also see a cartoon in *Dvar hashavu'a*, September 1, 1949.

58. *Dvar hashavu'a*, July 19, 1951. And compare with Ben-Amotz and Hefer (1979), 37.

59. Watts (2007), 17.

60. Liebman and Don-Yehiya (1983), 78. Shavit (1983), 175–176, 180, 200.

61. For instance, Beitar report, June 19, 1934: JIA, B2/24/10. And see Shapira (1997), 62.

62. Lissak (1998), 38, 53–54. Giladi (2002), 60. Gelber (1996), 453. Ben-Porat (1999), 113–114. Horowitz (1993), 50–52.

63. Since the 1920s middle-class Polish Jews, too, nurtured urbane manners and dress, but their cultured self-image notwithstanding, Western European Jews described them as provincial and unsophisticated; for instance, *Haaretz*, June 18, 1926. Also see Helman (2010), 133–134.

64. *Herut*, December 18, 1953. *Hava laisha velaofnah*, January 1955, 18. WIZO (1953), 15.

65. *Hu vehi*, July 1954. Also see *Herut*, December 18, 1953.

66. See Russian example in Kelly (2001), 277–278.

67. Shavit (2009), 34.

68. Sapir (1951), 1932.

69. WIZO (1953), 14–15.

70. *Yediot aharonot, 7 yamim,* December 2, 1955.

71. *Laisha,* July 21, 1954, September 30, 1954.

72. *Kolno'a,* January 12, 1955.

73. *Yediot aharonot, 7 yamim,* February 26, 1954.

74. *Yediot aharonot,* October 7, 1955.

75. Fuchs (1999), 213–214.

76. Horowitz (1993), 81–82. Also see Bernstein (2008), 36–41.

77. *Ha'olam hazeh,* January 19, 1956. And compare with Friedman (1994), 178. Gradskova (2007), 114. Stitziel (2005), 58. Also see *Ha'olam hazeh,* February 18, 1954. Dankner and Tartakover (1996), 42, 79, 130. Almog (1997), 328–332.

78. Rozin (2005a), 188.

79. Helman (2011), 44. And comparably, despite sharing a preference for laconic behavior, women Palmachniks were allowed to express their emotions more than men: Ben-Zeev (2010), 187.

80. *Herut,* August 27, 1950. Also see *Yediot aharonot,* December 16, 1949. *Hamodi'a,* May 8, 1953. American tourists were also warned that Israelis would cheat them financially: *Ma'ariv,* August 21, 1953. On dishonest conduct also see *Herut,* March 26, 1954. Letter from June 29, 1956 — HMA, A-4-271 tz 1537/1.

81. On the unconscious rootedness and the lingering effects of one's original habitus, see Bourdieu (1990), 53–62.

82. Although in certain circumstances they did make an effort: see *Davar,* August 10, 1952.

83. *Hasport haleumi,* January 29, 1950.

84. Helman (2008b), 109.

85. Proceedings, protocols, and reports from 1952–1953 — ISA, g-4/5548, g-3/5548.

86. Cartoon in *Bamachaneh,* September 15, 1949. *Omer,* July 9, 1951. *Dvar hapo'elet,* July 1952, 114–115. Hazorea bulletin, September 1, 1950, December 25, 1952 — KHA. *Hamodi'a,* September 5, 1952, December 12, 1952, October 9, 1953.

87. Shavit (2009), 34. Lederhendler (1991), 332. Haviv (2002), 132.

88. Mosse (1992), 574.

89. Zalashik (2004), 63–64. Efron (1994), 173–174. Efron (2001), 8–9.

90. Naor (2009a), 142.

91. *Beterem,* July 1, 1952, 45–47.

92. *Izmel,* Winter Tashiag (1953). On the heat's negative effects also see *Yediot aharonot, 7 yamim,* March 2, 1956. Bulletin of the Jordan Valley Council, 11, Fall 1952, 6 — NNL.

93. Also note the comparable shtetl/Israeli tendency not to mind one's business: Cala (2004), 134. *Herut,* December 4, 1953.

94. Quoted by Meir-Glitzenstein (2009), 97. Violent behavior in Israeli lines was also compared with quieter lines in Italy: *Beterem,* August 15, 1952. Also see *Hedei hanegev,* August 1952, 13.

95. Helman (2008a).

96. Bartal (2007), 138–139.

97. Walzer (2007), 131, 133–134. Also see Zerubavel (2002), 118.

98. Halperin (2011), 377.

99. A native anti-Diaspora identity was explicitly molded as a radical ideology by the Canaanite movement: see Kurzweil (1965). Also see Arieh Navon's cartoon in *Ashmoret*, September 8, 1949.

100. For instance, see Zerubavel (1991), 203–204.

101. *Haboker*, December 17, 1952. *Izmel*, Winter Tashiag (1953). On improving citizens' behavioral norms as a national task, see Kabalo (2008), 107.

102. Cartoons in *Dvar hashavu'a*, July 15, 1949, August 18, 1949. *Ashmoret*, September 20, 1950. Posters from 1953 — HMA, tz 73808, 21/2471. *Da et irkha, heifa*, December 1952, March 1953. *Haboker*, December 22, 1952. "Operation Cleanliness" too was conducted: *Hamodi'a*, September 6, 1950.

103. *Yediot aharonot*, January 6, 1950. *Yediot aharonot, Koteret*, June 19, 1951. Comic strip in *Omer*, July 4, 1951. Cartoon in *Haaretz*, August 19, 1951. Revivim bulletin, April 3, 1953 — YTA. Ad in *Ha'olam hazeh*, March 18, 1954. *Hatzofeh*, June 25, 1954. Yavneh bulletin, August 29, 1955 — RKMA. IDF (1956), 18.

104. Wouters (2004), 9. Wouters (2007), 13.

105. Helman (2011), 61, 115–122. Geva newsreels from 1955: SA, VT GE 010.

106. *Beterem*, July 1, 1952, 45–47.

107. *Dvar hapo'elet*, July 1952, 114. Indeed, according to Dahan-Kalev the ethnic tensions and crisis that were born in the 1950s "became a prominent component of Israeli social identity": Dahan-Kalev (1996), 190.

108. Rathmayr (2008), 3–4. Banc and Dundes (1990), 63.

109. Helman (2006), 627.

110. Compare with uncivil service in communist East Germany and the USSR: Merkel (1998), 292–293. Rathmayr (2008), 3–4

111. *Omer*, July 23, 1951. On the unfriendliness of vendors also see Migdal Ha'emek bulletin, August 31, 1956 — NNL.

112. *Dvar hashavu'a*, September 22, 1955.

113. Letter from November 26, 1954—JCA, 1853/21-8.

114. For example, see *Beterem*, July 1, 1952, 45–47. *Yediot aharonot*, January 25, 1953. The situation in Israel was compared unfavorably with the efficient civil services in the United States: *Beterem*, August 15, 1952.

115. HaRusi (1955), 10–11, 13. Also see Roth (1950).

116. HaCohen (2011), 1.

117. Mikes (1950), 75.

118. *Kol hamishmar haezrachi*, September 1949, 16–18, 21–22. *Palestine Post*, July 26, 1949. *Bamachaneh*, July 17, 1949. Also see *Hamodi'a*, October 29, 1954.

119. Helman (2010), 30–31. And see a joke about the noise emanating from the Israeli Parliament: *Jerusalem Post*, June 22, 1950.

120. Kelly (2001), 253.

121. As mentioned in the second chapter, the latter were associated particularly with the Haredim: *Ha'olam hazeh*, February 25, 1954. Also see *Omer*, July 9, 1951. *Dvar hashavu'a*, July 31, 1953. And see Friedman (1994), 231, 234, 236. Don-Yehiya (1984), 74–75.

Conclusion

1. I would like to thank Phyllis Deutsch and Sylvia Fuks Fried for posing this question and other helpful points.

2. Melman (2002), 78, 84–85.

3. Auslander (2009), 48. Del Negro and Berger (2004), 7–16.

4. Chartier (1995), 95. Taylor and Trentmann (2011), 240–241.

5. As recommended by Mintz (1986), 14. Also see Bardenstein (2002), 361, note 10.

6. Taylor and Trentmann (2011), 240. On the inherent tension within political ideology, see Cohen (2001), 106.

7. Fascinating examples are provided by Shternshis (2006), 184, and Sparks (1995), 190–193.

8. Guenther (2005), 211–212.

9. Chartier (1995), 96.

10. Fiske (1992), 162, 165. Also see Penfold (2008), 8–9.

11. Landy and Saler (2009), 7. Also see Wilk (2002), 69–70. Taylor and Trentmann (2011), 240.

12. Zur (1997), 74. Shachar (1963), 59.

13. Horowitz (1993), 50–51.

14. On nostalgia for the prestate era, see, for instance, Mikes (1950), 25. Horowitz (1993), 53. Shapira (1996b), 554. On nostalgia for countries of origin, see *Dvar hashavu'a*, January 19, 1956. On nostalgia as a personal and social phenomenon, see Wilson (2005), 24–34. Watson (2006), 49–50.

Bibliography

Archives and Collections

AA	Afula Archive
CZA	Central Zionist Archives
HMA	Haifa Municipal Archives
IDFA	IDF Archives
ISA	Israel State Archives
JCA	Jerusalem City Archive
JIA	Jabotinsky Institute Archive
JNFPA	JNF (KKL) Photo Archive
KAA	Kibbutz Afikim Archive
KALA	Kibbutz Alonim Archive
KHA	Kibbutz Hazorea Archive
KKAA	Kibbutz Kiryat Anavim Archive
LI	Pinhas Lavon Institute for Labor Movement Research
MC	Map Collection of the National Library
NA	Nahariya Archive
NNL	National Library of Israel
NPC	National Photo Collection
PC	Poster Collection in the Manuscript Department of the National Library
RKMA	Religious Kibbutz Movement Archive
SA	Steven Spielberg Jewish Film Archive
TAA	Tel Aviv–Jaffa Municipal Historical Archives
YTA	Yad Tabenkin Archive

Newspapers, Bulletins, and Periodicals

Al hamishmar
Alonekh
Ashmoret
Ba'ayot beyisrael hatze'irah
Baderekh
Bamachaneh
Bamachaneh la'oleh

Beterem
Carmel hador
Da et irkha, heifa
Dagesh
Davar
Davar leyeladim
Dorot

Dvar hapo'elet

Dvar hashavu'a

Gazit

Haaretz

Haboker

Hador

Hadshot hasport

Hagidu bedan: biton pnimi shel havrei
    haagudah

Haisha bamedinah

Hakol

Hamodi'a

Ha'olam hazeh

Hasport haleumi

Hasseret: biton agudat shocharei hasseret
    hatov beyisrael

Hatzofeh

Hedei hanegev

Herut

Hu vehi

Izmel: alon lemachshavah uvikoret

Jerusalem Post

Kol ha'am

Kol hamishmar haezrachi

Kol yisrael

Kolno'a

Lagever

Lahav: biton dati leumi

Laisha

Leket

Ma'ariv

Maavak

Matzpen

Ner

Niv histadrut afula

Nivenu — bitonam shel ovdei iriyat heifah

Olam hakolno'a

Omer

Ozer dalim

Palestine Post

Pnimah

Rimon

She'arim

Sheluchot yotzei teiman

Shnaton statisti leyisrael

Smol — shavu'a tov

Sport la'am

Sport yisrael

Tafrit

Tarbut vehasbarah bekerev po'alei heifah

Tavruah

Tesha ba'erev

Tevel

Yediot aharonot

Yediot aharonot, Koteret

Yediot aharonot layeled

Yediot aharonot, 7 yamim

Yediot hamo'etzah hamekomit ir
    izrael — Afula

Yediot hitachdut ba'alei batei hakolno'a
    beyisrael

Zmanim

Books, Articles, and Dissertations

Abbasi, Mustafa (2012). "A City in Distress: Nazareth under Israeli Military Rule, 1948–1949." *Iyunim Bitkumat Israel* 22: 399–422 [Hebrew].

Academy of the Hebrew Language (1955). *Dictionary for Car Terminology* (Jerusalem: Academy of the Hebrew Language) [Hebrew].

Aharoni, Reuven, and Shaul Mishal (2005). "An Arab Kibbutz: The Rise and Fall of 'Achva.'" *Iyunim Bitkumat Israel* 15: 181–208 [Hebrew].

Alatout, Samer (2008). "Locating the Fragments of the State and Their Limits: Water Policymaking in Israel during the 1950s." *Israel Studies Forum* 23/1: 40–65.

Alexander, David (1986). "Political Satire in Israel: Different Views of Zionism." *Jewish Humor*, edited by Avner Ziv (Tel Aviv: Papyrus), 137–147 [Hebrew].

Alexander, Esther (1992). "Economy and Absorption of Immigrants in the First Decade." *Iyunim Bitkumat Israel* 2: 79–93 [Hebrew].

Almog, Oz (1997). *The Sabra — A Portrait* (Tel Aviv: Am Oved) [Hebrew].

Amara, Mohammad (2004). "The Arab Minority in Israeli Politics: Between Civil Identity and National Identity." *State and Community*, edited by Moshe Naor (Jerusalem: Magnes Press), 136–146 [Hebrew].

Amir, Eli (2009). *Scapegoat* (Tel Aviv: Am Oved) [Hebrew].

Appy, Christian G. (2001). " 'We'll Follow the Old Man': The Strains of Sentimental Militarism in Popular Films of the Fifties." *Rethinking Cold War Culture*, edited by Peter J. Kuznick and James Gilbert (Washington, DC: Smithsonian Institution Press), 74–105.

Arbena, Joseph L. (1996). "Nationalism and Sport in Latin America, 1850–1990: The Paradox of Promoting and Performing 'European' Sport." *Tribal Identities: Nationalism, Europe, Sport*, edited by J. Anthony Mangan (London: Frank Cass), 220–238.

Arditi, Benjamin (1954). "The Main Problem: Discrimination." *Tribe and People: The Problems of Ingathering the Exiles*, edited by David Sitton and Yitzhak A. Abadi (Jerusalem: Israeli Executive of the World Sephardi Federation), 42–47 [Hebrew].

Assaf, Yossi (2010). "Rift and Unification in the Kibbutz Movement." *The Kibbutz: The First 100 Years*, edited by Aviva Halamish and Zvi Zameret (Jerusalem: Yad Ben-Zvi), 183–194 [Hebrew].

Auslander, Laura (2009). "The Boundaries of Jewishness, or When Is a Cultural Practice Jewish?" *Journal of Modern Jewish Studies* 8/1: 47–64.

Avieli, Nir (2012). "The Collective and the Individual in Contemporary Kibbutz Dining Rooms." *Hagar* 10/2, 107–137.

Avivi, Baruch, and Nathan Persky (1953). *One Language: The Book of Learning the Language for Adults* (Part I: Beginners) (Tel Aviv: N. Tabersky) [Hebrew].

Avneri, Uri (1949). *Philistine Fields 1948: Combat Diary* (Tel Aviv: N. Tabersky) [Hebrew].

Ayturk, Ilker (2007). "Attempts at Romanizing the Hebrew Scripts and Their Failure: Nationalism, Religion, and Alphabet Reform in the Yishuv." *Middle Eastern Studies* 43/4: 625–645.

Azaryahu, Maoz (1998). *State Cults: Celebrating Independence and Commemorating the Fallen in Israel, 1948–1956* (Sde Boker: Ben-Gurion Heritage Institute and Ben-Gurion University Press) [Hebrew].

Azaryahu, Maoz (1999). "The Independence Day Military Parade." *The Military and Militarism in Israeli Society*, edited by Edna Lomsky-Feder and Eyal Ben-Ari (Albany, NY: SUNY Press), 89–116.

Bachi, Roberto (1956). "A Statistical Analysis of the Revival of Hebrew in Israel." *Scripta Hierosolymitana*, III: 179–247.

Banc, C., and Alan Dundes (1990). *You Call This Living? A Collection of East European Political Jokes* (Athens: University of Georgia Press).

Bar-Gil, Shlomo, and Ada Schein (2010). *Dwell in Safety: Holocaust Survivors in the Rural Cooperative Settlement* (Jerusalem: Yad Vashem) [Hebrew].

Bar-On, Mordechai (1997). "Israel's Security Policy." *The First Decade, 1948–1958,* edited by Zvi Zameret and Hanna Yablonka (Jerusalem: Yad Ben-Zvi), 11–26 [Hebrew].

Bar-On, Mordechai (1999). "Military Activism and Its Critics, 1949–1967." *The Challenge of Independence,* edited by Mordechai Bar-On (Jerusalem: Yad Ben-Zvi), 62–103 [Hebrew].

Bar-On, Mordechai (2001). "Challenge and Quarrel: The Road to Sinai 1956." *Smoking Borders: Studies in the Early History of the State of Israel, 1948–1967* (Jerusalem and Beer Sheva: Yad Ben-Zvi, Ben-Gurion Research Institute, and Ben-Gurion University of the Negev), 225–251 [Hebrew].

Bar-On, Mordechai (2002). "The IDF, Education and Culture in the Early Years of the Israeli State, 1949–1967." *A Century of Israeli Culture,* edited by Israel Bartal (Jerusalem: Magnes Press), 75–101 [Hebrew].

Bar-On, Mordechai (2006). "Images of the Home Front among the Fighting Units." *Citizens at War: Studies on the Civilian Society during the Israeli War of Independence,* edited by Mordechai Bar-On and Meir Chazan (Jerusalem and Tel Aviv: Yad Ben-Zvi and Tel Aviv University), 467–492 [Hebrew].

Bar-Or, Amir (2010). "The Making of Israel's Political-Security Culture." *Militarism and Israeli Society,* edited by Gabriel Sheffer and Oren Barak (Bloomington: Indiana University Press), 259–279.

Bar-Or, Galia (2010). "Festive Decorations in the Dining Hall." *The Dining Hall as an Allegory* (exhibition catalog), curated by Michal Shachnai Yacobi (Afula: Emek Jezreel Regional Council), unnumbered pages [Hebrew].

Bartov, David (1997). "The First Years of Statehood in the President's Chambers." *The First Decade, 1948–1958,* edited by Zvi Zameret and Hanna Yablonka (Jerusalem: Yad Ben-Zvi), 319–334 [Hebrew].

Bar-Yosef, Hamutal (1991). "New Decadence in Hebrew Literature: 1955–1965 (the Case of Nathan Zach)." *Bikoret uparshanut* 27: 125–152 [Hebrew].

Bar-Zohar, Michael (1980). *Ben-Gurion: A Biography* (Jerusalem: Keter) [Hebrew].

Barak, Oren, and Gabriel Sheffer (2010). "The Study of Civil-Military Relations in Israel: A New Perspective." *Militarism and Israeli Society,* edited by Gabriel Sheffer and Oren Barak (Bloomington: Indiana University Press), 14–41.

Baram, Haim (2004), *Red Yellow Black* (Tel Aviv: Ma'ariv Library) [Hebrew].

Barany, Zoltan (2012). *The Soldier and the Changing State: Building Democratic Armies in Africa, Asia, Europe and the Americas* (Princeton, NJ: Princeton University Press).

Bardenstein, Carol (2002). "Transmissions Interrupted: Reconfiguring Food, Memory, and Gender in the Cookbook-Memoirs of Middle Eastern Exiles." *Signs* 28/1: 353–388

Bareli, Avi (1999). "*Mamlakhtiyut* and the Labor Movement in the Early Fifties." *The*

Challenge of Sovereignty, edited by Mordechai Bar-On (Jerusalem: Yad Ben-Zvi), 23–44 [Hebrew].

Bareli, Avi (2007). *"Mamlakhtiyut,* Capitalism and Socialism during the 1950s in Israel." *Journal of Israeli History* 26/2: 201–227.

Barkai, Haim (2004). "The Foundation of the Monetary System and Macro-Economic Developments, 1948–1954." *Bank of Israel: Fifty Years of Monetary Control*, vol. 1, edited by Nissan Liviatan and Haim Barkai (Jerusalem: Bank of Israel), 39–67 [Hebrew].

Bartal, Israel (2001). "Modern Jewish Nationalism: Religion and Secularism." *A State in the Making: Israeli Society in the First Decades*, edited by Anita Shapira (Jerusalem: Zalman Shazar Center), 239–247 [Hebrew].

Bartal, Israel (2007). *Cossack and Bedouin: Land and People in Jewish Nationalism* (Tel Aviv: Am Oved) [Hebrew].

Baughman, James L. (1997). *The Republic of Mass Culture: Journalism, Filmmaking, and Broadcasting in America since 1941* (Baltimore: Johns Hopkins University Press).

Beer, Haim (2002). *The Pure Element of Time* (Tel Aviv: Am Oved) [Hebrew].

Ben-Amotz, Dan, and Haim Hefer (1979). *The Complete and Unabridged Bag of Lies* (Tel Aviv: Metziuth) [Hebrew].

Ben-Artzi, Yossi (2002). "Kibbutz or *Moshav?* Priority Changes of Settlement Types in Israel, 1949–53." *Israel Affairs* 8/1–2: 163–176.

Ben-Avram, Baruch, and Henry Near (1995). *Studies in the Third Aliyah (1919–1924): Image and Reality* (Jerusalem: Yad Ben-Zvi) [Hebrew].

Ben-David, Joseph (1954). "Membership in Youth Movements and Personal Status." *Megamot* 5/3: 227–247 [Hebrew].

Ben-Eliezer, Uri (1984). "Israel's Native-Born Generation: Social Superiority Conditioned by Political Inferiority." *Medina, Mimshal Vihasim Benleumiyyim* 23: 29–49 [Hebrew].

Ben-Porat, Amir (1999). *Where Are All Those Bourgeoisies? The History of the Israeli Bourgeoisie* (Jerusalem: Magnes Press and Eshkol Institute) [Hebrew].

Ben-Rafael, Eliezer (1994). *Language, Identity, and Social Division: The Case of Israel* (Oxford: Clarendon Press).

Ben-Rafael, Eliezer (1995). "The Kibbutz in the 1950s: A Transformation of Identity." *Israel: The First Decade of Independence*, edited by S. Ilan Troen and Noah Lucas (Albany, NY: SUNY Press), 265–278.

Ben-Rafael, Eliezer, Ephraim Yaar, and Zeev Soker (2000). "The Kibbutz and Israeli Society." *Kibbutz: Continuity and Change* (Tel Aviv: The Open University) [Hebrew].

Ben-Rafael, Eliezer, and Sasha Weitman (2006). "Women and the Reemergence of the Family in the Kibbutz." *A Historical Achievement and Its Evolution*, edited by Abigail Paz-Yeshayahu and Yosef Gorny (Beer Sheva: Ben-Gurion Research Institute), 617–633 [Hebrew].

Ben-Uzi, Yaniv (2008). "The General Zionist Party, 1948–1952." *Cathedra* 127: 141–168 [Hebrew].

Ben-Zeev, Efrat (2010). "Imposed Silences and Self-Censorship: Palmach Soldiers Remember 1948." *Shadows of War: A Social History of Silence in the Twentieth Century*, edited by Efrat Ben-Zeev, Ruth Giano, and Jay Winter (Cambridge: Cambridge University Press), 181–196.

Bender, Thomas, and Carl E. Schorske, eds. (1994). *Budapest and New York: Studies in Metropolitan Transformations, 1870–1930* (New York: Russell Sage Foundation).

Berberich, Christine (2007). *The Image of the English Gentleman in Twentieth-Century Literature: Englishness and Nostalgia* (Aldershot: Ashgate).

Berghahn, Volker R. (2001). *America and Its Intellectual Cold Wars in Europe* (Princeton, NJ: Princeton University Press).

Bergman, Andrew Lawrence (1970). "Depression America and Its Movies" (PhD dissertation, University of Wisconsin, Madison).

Berman, Russell A. (2005). "Anti-Americanism and Americanization." *Americanization and anti-Americanization: The German Encounter with American Culture after 1945*, edited by Alexander Stephan (New York: Berghahn Books), 11–24.

Bernstein, Deborah (2008). *Women on the Margins: Gender and Nationalism in Mandate Tel Aviv* (Jerusalem: Yad Ben-Zvi) [Hebrew].

Blanc, Haim (1954). "The Growth of Israeli Hebrew." *Middle Eastern Affairs* 5/12: 385–392.

Bor, Harris (2001). "Enlightenment Values, Jewish Ethics: The Haskalah's Transformation of the Traditional *Musar* Genre." *New Perspectives on the Haskalah*, edited by Shmuel Feiner and David Sorkin (London: Littman Library of Jewish Civilization), 48–63.

Borrero, Mauricio (1997). "Communal Dining and State Cafeterias in Moscow and Petrograd, 1917–1921." *Food in Russian History and Culture*, edited by Musya Glants and Joyce Toomre (Bloomington: Indiana University Press), 162–176.

Bourdieu, Pierre (1990). "Structure, Habitus, Practices." *The Logic of Practice* (Stanford, CA: Stanford University Press), 52–65.

Boymal, Yair (2006). "The Discrimination Policy toward the Arabs in Israel, 1948–1968." *Iyunim Bitkumat Israel* 16: 391–413 [Hebrew].

Bramham, Peter, et al. (1993). "Introduction." *Leisure Policies in Europe*, edited by Peter Bramham, Ian Henry, Hans Mommaas, and Hugo van der Poel (Wallingford: CAB International), 1–11.

Brooker, Peter (1999). *A Concise Glossary of Cultural Studies* (New York: Oxford University Press).

Brownfield-Stein, Chava (2010). "Visual Representations of IDF Women Soldiers and 'Civil-Militarism' in Israel." *Militarism and Israeli Society*, edited by Gabriel Sheffer and Oren Barak (Bloomington: Indiana University Press), 304–328.

Burla, Yehuda (1954). "From the Secret of the Language." *Tribe and People: The Problems of Ingathering the Exiles*, edited by David Sitton and Yitzhak A. Abadi (Jerusalem: Israeli Executive of the World Sephardi Federation), 89–92 [Hebrew].

Burns, C. Delisle (1932). *Leisure in the Modern World* (London: George Allen & Unwin).

Butsch, Richard (2000). *The Making of American Audiences: From Stage to Television, 1750–1990* (Cambridge: Cambridge University Press).

Cala, Alina (2004). "The Shtetl: Cultural Evolution in a Small Town." *Polin* 17: 133–141.

Campbell, Colin (1997). "The Romantic Ethic and the Spirit of Modern Consumerism: Reflections on the Reception of a Thesis concerning the Origins of the Continuing Desire for Goods." *Experiencing Material Culture in the West*, edited by Susan M. Pearce (London: Ashgate), 36–48.

Caplan, Kimmy (2011). "Developing Circles of Isolation among Extreme Haredim: Amram Blau as a Case Study." *Zion* 76/2: 179–219 [Hebrew].

Certeau, Michel de (1984). *The Practice of Everyday Life* (Berkeley: University of California Press).

Chartier, Roger (1988). *Cultural History: Between Practices and Representations* (Cambridge: Polity Press).

Chartier, Roger (1991). *The Cultural Origins of the French Revolution* (Durham, NC: Duke University Press).

Chartier, Roger (1995). *Forms and Meanings: Texts, Performances, and Audiences from Codex to Computer* (Philadelphia: University of Pennsylvania Press).

Chaver, Yael (2004). *What Must Be Forgotten: The Survival of Yiddish in Zionist Palestine* (Syracuse, NY: Syracuse University Press).

Cohen, Aharon (1951). "Difficulties in the Education of Israel's Arabs." *Megamot* 2/2: 126–137 [Hebrew].

Cohen, Asher (1997). "Religion and State — Secularists, Religious and ultra-Orthodox." *The First Decade, 1948–1958*, edited by Zvi Zameret and Hanna Yablonka (Jerusalem: Yad Ben-Zvi), 227–242 [Hebrew].

Cohen, Asher (2001). "Political Pragmatism in a Modern Religious Movement: Religious Zionism in the First Years of Statehood." *Bar Ilan* 28–29: 105–119 [Hebrew].

Cohen, Eric (1970). *The City in the Zionist Ideology* (Jerusalem: The Hebrew University).

Cohen, Hillel (2000). *The Present Absentees: The Palestinian Refugees in Israel since 1948* (Jerusalem: Institute for Israeli Arab Studies) [Hebrew].

Cohen, Samy (2010). "Civilian Control over the Army in Israel and France." *Militarism and Israeli Society*, edited by Gabriel Sheffer and Oren Barak (Bloomington: Indiana University Press), 238–258.

Cohen, Stuart (2005). "Between the Scroll and the Sword: The Development of Jewish Religious Law respecting the Military and War in Modern Israel, 1948–2004." *Iyunim Bitkumat Israel* 15: 239–274 [Hebrew].

Cohen-Friedheim, Rachel (2012). *The Vanguard That Was Left Behind: Absorption of Immigrants in the Kibbutzim, 1948–1952* (Ramat Gan: Yad Tabenkin) [Hebrew].

Cullen, Jim (1996). *The Art of Democracy: A Concise History of Popular Culture in the United States* (New York: Monthly Review).

Dahan-Kalev, Henriette (1996). "Israeli Identity — Between New Immigrants and 'Old-Timers.'" *Israel in the Great Wave of Immigration*, edited by Dalia Ofer (Jerusalem: Yad Ben-Zvi), 177–190 [Hebrew].

Dankner, Amnon, and David Tartakover (1996). *Where We Were and What We Did: An Israeli Lexicon of the Fifties and Sixties* (Jerusalem: Keter) [Hebrew].

Dar, Yehezkel (2006). "Distributive Justice in Flux: Changing Evaluation of Work in the Kibbutz." *Ofakim Begeografia* 66: 44–64 [Hebrew].

Dauber, Jeremy (2005). "The City, Sacred and Profane: Between Hebrew and Yiddish in the Fiction of the Early Jewish Enlightenment." *Jewish Studies Quarterly* 12/1: 43–60.

Davidon, Yaacov (1955). The Second Film Festival in Israel (Haifa: Cinema Owners Association) [Hebrew].

Del Negro, Giovanna P., and Harris M. Berger (2004). "New Directions in the Study of Everyday Life: Expressive Culture and the Interpretation of Practice." *Identity and Everyday Life: Essays in the Study of Folklore, Music and Popular Culture*, edited by Harris M. Berger and Giovanna P. Del Negro (Middletown, CT: Wesleyan University Press), 3–22.

Don-Yehiya, Eliezer (1984). "Concepts of Zionism in Orthodox Jewish Thought." *Hatzyionut* 9: 55–93 [Hebrew].

Don-Yehiya, Eliezer (1995). "Political Religion in a New State: Ben-Gurion's *Mamlachtiyut*." *Israel: The First Decade of Independence*, edited by S. Ilan Troen and Noah Lucas (Albany, NY: SUNY Press), 171–192.

Don-Yehiya, Eliezer (2008). *Crisis and Change in a New State: Education, Religion, and Politics in the Struggle over the Absorption of Mass Immigration to Israel* (Jerusalem: Yad Ben-Zvi) [Hebrew].

Dosh (1956). *220 Caricatures by Dosh* (Tel Aviv: Karni) [Hebrew].

Douglas, Allen (2002). *War, Memory, and the Politics of Humor: The* Canard Enchaîné *and World War I* (Berkeley: University of California Press).

Dowty, Alan (1995). "Israel's First Decade: Building a Civic State." *Israel: The First Decade of Independence*, edited by S. Ilan Troen and Noah Lucas (Albany, NY: SUNY Press), 31–50.

Dowty, Alan (2001). "State Creation and Nation Building." *Israel in the First Decade*, vol. 1 (Ramat Aviv: The Open University), 5–64 [Hebrew].

Draitser, Emil A. (1998). *Taking Penguins to the Movies: Ethnic Humor in Russia* (Detroit: Wayne State University Press).

Drori, Zeev (1995). "Utopia in Uniform." *Israel: The First Decade of Independence*, edited by S. Ilan Troen and Noah Lucas (Albany NY: SUNY Press), 593–613.

Drori, Zeev (2000). *Utopia in Uniform: The IDF's Contribution to Settlement, Absorption of New Immigrants and Education in the Early Years of the State* (Sde Boker: Ben-Gurion Heritage Institute and Ben-Gurion University Press) [Hebrew].

Drori, Zeev (2006). "Military and Society in Israel during the 1950s." *Iyunim Bitkumat Israel* 16: 243–274 [Hebrew].

Drori, Zeev (2010). "The Kibbutz Movement as a Recruited Elite." *The Kibbutz: The First 100 Years*, edited by Aviva Halamish and Zvi Zameret (Jerusalem: Yad Ben Zvi), 81–102 [Hebrew].

Dunning, Eric (1999). "Soccer Hooliganism as a World Social Problem." *Sport Matters: Sociological Studies of Sport, Violence and Civilization* (London: Routledge), 130–158.

Dyer, Richard (2000). "The Idea of Entertainment." *Only Entertainment* (London: Routledge), 5–9.

Edensor, Tim (2013). "Commuter: Mobility, Rhythm and Commuting." *Geographies of Mobility: Practices, Spaces, Subjects*, edited by Tim Cresswell and Peter Merriman (Farnham: Ashgate), 189–203.

Edgerton, David (2011). "War, Reconstruction, and the Nationalization of Britain, 1939–1951." *Past and Present*, supplement 6: 29–46.

Efrat, Elisha (1997). "The Development Towns." *The First Decade, 1948–1958*, edited by Zvi Zameret and Hanna Yablonka (Jerusalem: Yad Ben-Zvi), 103–112 [Hebrew].

Efron, John M. (1994). *Defenders of the Race: Jewish Doctors and Race Science in Fin-de-Siècle Europe* (New Haven, CT: Yale University Press).

Efron, John M. (2001). *Medicine and German Jews: A History* (New Haven, CT: Yale University Press).

Efron, John (2006). "When Is a Yid Not a Jew? The Strange Case of Supporter Identity at Tottenham Hotspur." *Emancipation through Muscles: Jews and Sports in Europe*, edited by Michael Brenner and Gideon Reuveni (Lincoln: University of Nebraska Press), 235–256.

Efron, John (2012). "From Lodz to Tel Aviv: The Yiddish Political Satire of Shimen Dzigan and Yisroel Shumacher." *Jewish Quarterly Review* 102/1: 50–79.

Efron, Yonit (2000). "Sisters, Fighters and Mothers — The Ethos and Reality of the 1948 Generation." *Iyunim Bitkumat Israel*, 10: 353–380 [Hebrew].

Eichler, Maya (2012). "Introduction: The Personal and Public Politics of Militarizing Men." *Militarizing Men: Gender, Conscription, and War in Post-Soviet Russia* (Stanford, CA: Stanford University Press).

Eisenstadt, Shmuel Noah (1952). *Absorption of the Immigration: A Sociological Study* (Jerusalem: Jewish Agency and the Hebrew University) [Hebrew].

Eisenstadt, Shmuel Noah (1953). "Problems of Leadership among the New Immigrants." *Megamot* 4/2: 182–191 [Hebrew].

Elboim-Dror, Rachel (1993). *Yesterday's Tomorrow*, vol. 1 (Jerusalem: Yad Ben-Zvi) [Hebrew].

Elboim-Dror, Rachel (2000). "British Educational Policies in Palestine." *Middle Eastern Studies* 36/2: 28–47.

Eldad, Israel, and Joseph Nedava (1955). *Ramat Gan Book*, edited by Israel Eldad and Joseph Nedava (Ramat Gan: Ramat Gan Municipality) [Hebrew].

Ellwood, David W. (2003). "American Myth, American Model, and the Quest for a British Modernity." *The American Century in Europe*, edited by R. Laurence Moore and Maurizio Vaudagna (Ithaca, NY: Cornell University Press), 131–150.

Encyclopedia Britannica (2003). Deluxe edition. CD-ROM.

Enoch, Yael (2001). "Immigration and the Absorption of Immigrants: A Sociological Study." *Israel in the First Decade*, vol. 1 (Ramat Aviv: The Open University), 65–128 [Hebrew].

Evans Clements, Barbara (1985). "The Birth of the New Soviet Woman." *Bolshevik Culture: Experiment and Order in the Russian Revolution*, edited by Abbott Gleason, Peter Kenez, and Richard Stites (Bloomington: Indiana University Press), 220–237.

Even-Chen, Aharon (1954). *When We Established Netanya* (Netanya: A Veterans of Netanya Publication) [Hebrew].

Even-Shoshan, Avraham (1966). *The New Dictionary*, vol. 3 (Jerusalem: Kiryat Sefer) [Hebrew].

Even-Zohar, Itamar (1996). "The Emergence of Native Hebrew Culture in Palestine, 1882–1948." *Essential Papers on Zionism*, edited by Jehuda Reinharz and Anita Shapira (New York: New York University Press), 727–744.

Feiner, Shmuel (2003). " 'They Look Like Jews but Dress Like Cossacks': Pre-Zionist Origins of the Jewish Cultural Conflict." *A Hundred Years of Religious Zionism* (*Philosophical Aspects*, vol. 3), edited by Avi Sagi and Dov Schwartz (Ramat Gan: Bar-Ilan University), 375–390 [Hebrew].

Feingold, Ben-Ami (1999). "The War of Independence in Drama, 1948–1949." *The Challenge of Independence*, edited by Mordechai Bar-On (Jerusalem: Yad Ben-Zvi), 307–327 [Hebrew].

Feldstein, Ariel (2009). "Rebirth of the 'Other' in the 1948 War: A Cinematic Expression." *Israel* 16: 251–269 [Hebrew].

Fine, Jonathan (2009). *The Birth of a State: The Establishment of the Israeli Government System, 1947–1951* (Jerusalem: Carmel) [Hebrew].

Fischler, Ben Zion (1987). "The Bestowing of the Language in the Days of Mass Immigration." *Immigrants and Transit Camps, 1948–1952*, edited by Mordechai Naor (Jerusalem: Yad Ben-Zvi), 145–156 [Hebrew].

Fiske, John (1992). "Cultural Studies and the Culture of Everyday Life." *Cultural Studies*, edited by Lawrence Grossberg, Cary Nelson, and Paula Treichler (New York: Routledge), 154–173.

Fiske, John (1998). "Audiencing: Cultural Practices and Cultural Studies." *The Landscape of Qualitative Research: Theories and Issues*, edited by Norman K. Denzin and Yvonna S. Lincoln (Thousand Oaks, CA: Sage), 359–378.

Fogiel-Bijaoui, Sylvie (1992). "From Revolution to Motherhood: The Case of Women in the Kibbutz." *Kibbutz: Continuity and Change* (Tel Aviv: Open University) [Hebrew].

Fogiel-Bijaoui, Sylvie (2006). "Motherhood and Revolution." *A Historical Achievement and Its Evolution*, edited by Abigail Paz-Yeshayahu and Yosef Gorny (Beer Sheva: Ben-Gurion Research Institute), 595–615 [Hebrew].

Fogiel-Bijaoui, Sylvie (2010). "Women in the 100 Years of the Kibbutz." *The Kibbutz: The First 100 Years*, edited by Aviva Halamish and Zvi Zameret (Jerusalem: Yad Ben-Zvi), 147–166 [Hebrew].

Friedman, Jonathan (1994). "The Political Economy of Elegance: An African Cult of Beauty." *Consumption and Identity*, edited by Jonathan Friedman (Chur, Switzerland: Harwood Academic Publishers), 167–187.

Friedman, Menachem (1990). "The State of Israel as a Theological Dilemma." *Alpayim* 3: 24–68 [Hebrew].

Friedman, Menachem (1994). "Neturei-Karta and Shabbat Riots in Jerusalem — 1949–1950." *Divided Jerusalem, 1949–1967*, edited by Avi Bareli (Jerusalem: Yad Ben-Zvi), 224–241 [Hebrew].

Friedman, Menachem (1995). "The Structural Foundation for Religio-Political Accommodation in Israel: Fallacy and Reality." *Israel: The First Decade of Independence*, edited by S. Ilan Troen and Noah Lucas (Albany, NY: SUNY Press), 51–81.

Fuchs, Esther (1999). "The Enemy as Woman: Fictional Women in the Literature of the Palmach." *Israel Studies* 4/1: 212–233.

Fund, Yosef (1999). "The Zionist Facet in Agudat Yisrael's Journalism." *Kesher* 9: 81–89 [Hebrew].

Gardosh, Kariel (1986). "Political Cartoons Reflecting Israel's Development." *Jewish Humor*, edited by Avner Ziv (Tel Aviv: Papyrus), 179–189 [Hebrew].

Gat, Moshe (2002). "The IDF and the Mass Immigration of the Early 1950s: Aid to the Immigrant Camps." *Israeli Politics and Society since 1948: Problems of Collective Identity*, vol. 3: *Israel: The First Hundred Years*, edited by Efraim Karsh (London: Frank Cass), 191–210.

Gelber, Steven M. (1999). *Hobbies: Leisure and Culture of Work in America* (New York: Columbia University Press).

Gelber, Yoav (1996). "The Shaping of the 'New Jew' in Eretz Israel." *Major Changes within the Jewish People in the Wake of the Holocaust*, edited by Yisrael Gutman (Jerusalem: Yad Vashem), 443–461.

Gelber, Yoav (2001). "The Historical Background." *The Palestinian Refugees: Old Problems — New Solutions*, edited by Joseph Ginat and Edward J. Perkins (Brighton: Sussex Academic Press), 17–33.

Gelbert, Dan (1954). *Definitely Internal: Caricatures from Kibbutz Life* (Tel Aviv: Hakibbutz Hameuchad) [Hebrew].

Gerber, Noah S. (2013). *Ourselves or Our Holy Books? The Cultural Discovery of Yemenite Jewry* (Jerusalem: Yad Ben-Zvi) [Hebrew].

Gertz, Aharon (1956). *Emek Hefer: History and Data*, edited by Aharon Gertz (Jerusalem: Emek Hefer Regional Council) [Hebrew].

Gertz, Nurith (1995). *Captive of a Dream: National Myths in Israeli Culture* (Tel Aviv: Am Oved) [Hebrew].

Giladi, Dan (2002). "From Austerity to Economic Growth." *Israel in the First Decade*, vol. 3 (Ramat Aviv: The Open University), 5–84 [Hebrew].

Giladi, Dan, and Arnon Golan (2001). "Urban Planning and Development." *Israel in the First Decade*, vol. 2 (Ramat Aviv: The Open University), 77–143 [Hebrew].

Giladi, Dan, and Moshe Shwartz (2001). "The Agricultural Settlement." *Israel in the First Decade*, vol. 2 (Ramat Aviv: The Open University), 5–75 [Hebrew].

Gilman, Sander (2005). "The Problem with Purim: Jews and Alcohol in the Modern Period." *Leo Baeck Institute Year Book* 50: 215–231.

Gispan-Greenberg, Tamar (2010). "Murals in Dining Halls of Hakibbutz Haartzi, 1950–1967." *Cathedra* 135: 149–180 [Hebrew].

Giucci, Guillermo (2012). *The Cultural Life of the Automobile: Roads to Modernity* (Austin: University of Texas Press).

Gofer, Gilat (2004). "Workers' Cooperative Kitchens in Early 20th Century Palestine." *Israeli Center for Third Sector Research Newsletter* 17: D–F [Hebrew].

Goffman, Erving (1963). *Behavior in Public Places: Notes on the Social Organization of Gathering* (New York: Free Press).

Golan, Arnon (1997). "Settlement in the First Decade of the State of Israel." *The First Decade, 1948–1958*, edited by Zvi Zameret and Hanna Yablonka (Jerusalem: Yad Ben-Zvi), 83–102 [Hebrew].

Golan, Arnon (2003). "Jewish Settlement of Former Arab Towns and Their Incorporation into the Israeli Urban System (1948–50)." *Israel Affairs* 9/1–2: 149–164.

Golan, Arnon (2010). "The Contribution of the Kibbutz to the Settlement Outline." *The Kibbutz: The First 100 Years*, edited by Aviva Halamish and Zvi Zameret (Jerusalem: Yad Ben-Zvi), 51–66 [Hebrew].

Goode, Erich (1992). *Collective Behavior* (Orlando: A Harcourt Brace Jovanovich College).

Gordon, Deborah (1991). *Steering a New Course: Transportation, Energy and the Environment* (Washington, DC: Island Press).

Gottdiener, Mark (1985). "Hegemony and Mass Culture: A Semiotic Approach." *American Journal of Sociology* 90/5: 979–1001

Gradskova, Yulia (2007). *Soviet People with Female Bodies: Performing Beauty and Maternity in Soviet Russia in the mid 1930–1960s* (Stockholm: Acta Universitatis Stockholmiensis, Almqvist & Wiksell International).

Graham, Seth (2004). "Varieties of Reflexivity in the Russo-Soviet *Anekdot*." *Reflective Laughter: Aspects of Humour in Russian Culture*, edited by Lesley Milne (London: Anthem Press), 167–179.

Gramsci, Antonio (1997). "Intellectuals and the Hegemony of Dominant Class in Modern Western Democracies." *Classes and Elites in Democracy and Democratization: A Collection of Readings*, edited by Eva Etzioni-Halevy (New York: Garland), 12–17.

Greitzer, Dina (1997). "Ben-Gurion, Mapai, and the Israeli Arabs." *The First Decade, 1948–1958*, edited by Zvi Zameret and Hanna Yablonka (Jerusalem: Yad Ben-Zvi), 151–168 [Hebrew].

Gross, Nachum T. (1995). "The Economic Regime during Israel's First Decade." *Israel: The First Decade of Independence*, edited by S. Ilan Troen and Noah Lucas (Albany, NY: SUNY Press), 231–241.

Gross, Nachum T. (1997). "Israel's Economy." *The First Decade, 1948–1958*, edited by Zvi Zameret and Hanna Yablonka (Jerusalem: Yad Ben-Zvi), 137–150 [Hebrew].

Guenther, Irene (2005). *Nazi Chic? Fashioning Women in the Third Reich* (Oxford: Berg).

Guilat, Yael (2001). "The Yemenite Ideal in Israeli Culture and Arts." *Israel Studies* 6/3: 26–53.

Guilat, Yael (2010). "Shaping National Culture: The Case of Jewish-Yemenite Crafts in Israel." *Zmanim* 110: 80–91 [Hebrew].

Gulas, Charles S., and Marc G. Weinberger (2006). *Humor in Advertising: A Comprehensive Analysis* (Armonk, NY: M. E. Sharpe).

Gundle, Stephen (2002). "Visions of Prosperity: Consumerism and Popular Culture in Italy from the 1920s to the 1950s." *Three Postwar Eras in Comparison: Western Europe, 1918–1945–1989*, edited by Carl Levy and Mark Roseman (London: Palgrave), 151–172.

Gundle, Stephen (2008). *Glamour: A History* (Oxford: Oxford University Press).

Haaretz Annual (1949). *Haaretz Sheet for the Year Tashai* (Tel Aviv: Haim Publishing) [Hebrew].

Haaretz Annual (1950). *Haaretz Sheet for the Year Tashia* (Tel Aviv: Haim Publishing) [Hebrew].

Haaretz Annual (1952). *Haaretz Sheet for the Year Tashiag* (Tel Aviv: Haim Publishing) [Hebrew].

Haaretz Annual (1953). *Haaretz Sheet for the Year Tashiad* (Tel Aviv: Haim Publishing) [Hebrew].

Haaretz Annual (1954). *Haaretz Sheet for the Year Tashtav* (Tel Aviv: Haim Publishing) [Hebrew].

Hacohen, Dvora (1998). " 'The Battle over the Jewish People': Volunteer Kibbutz and Moshav Members and the Absorption of Immigrants in the First Decade of the State." *Iyunim Bitkumat Israel* 8: 266–297 [Hebrew].

HaCohen, Ruth (2011). *The Music Libel against the Jews* (New Haven, CT: Yale University Press).

Hadari-Ramage, Yona (1995). "War and Religiosity: The Sinai Campaign in Public Thought." *Israel: The First Decade of Independence*, edited by S. Ilan Troen and Noah Lucas (Albany, NY: SUNY Press), 355–373.

Hagiladi, Nimrod (2011). "The Israeli Society and the Black Market from World War II to the Early 1950s" (PhD dissertation, The Hebrew University, Jerusalem) [Hebrew].

Haidar, Aziz (2004). "The Development of Research and Status of the Arab Minority in Israeli Society." *State and Community*, edited by Moshe Naor (Jerusalem: Magnes Press), 116–135 [Hebrew].

Halamish, Aviva (2006). *A Dual Race against Time: Zionist Immigration Policy in the 1930s* (Jerusalem: Yad Ben-Zvi) [Hebrew].

Halamish, Aviva (2008). "Zionist Immigration Put to the Test: Historical Analysis of Israel's Immigration Policy, 1948–1951." *Journal of Modern Jewish Studies* 7/2: 119–134.

Halamish, Aviva (2010). "The Kibbutz and Immigration." *The Kibbutz: The First 100 Years*, edited by Aviva Halamish and Zvi Zameret (Jerusalem: Yad Ben-Zvi), 25–42 [Hebrew].

Hall, Stuart (1979). "Culture, Media and the 'Ideological Effect.'" *Mass Communication and Society*, edited by James Curran, Michael Gurevich, and Janet Wollacott (London: E. Arnold), 315–348.

Hall, Stuart (2001). "Encoding/Decoding." *Media and Cultural Studies: Keyworks*, edited by Meenakshi Gigi Durham and Douglas M. Kellner (Oxford: Blackwell), 166–176.

Halperin, Liora Russman (2011). "Babel in Zion: The Politics of Language Diversity in Jewish Palestine, 1920–1948" (PhD dissertation, University of California, Los Angeles).

Handel, Leo A. (1950). *Hollywood Looks at Its Audience: A Report of Film Audience Research* (Urbana: University of Illinois Press)

Harshav, Benjamin (1990). "Essay on the Revival of the Hebrew Language." *Alpayim* 2: 9–53 [Hebrew].

HaRusi, Emanuel (1955). *The Civil Servant and the Public* (Tel Aviv: Tel Aviv Municipality) [Hebrew].

Harvey, David (1985). *Consciousness and the Urban Experience: Studies in the History and Theory of Capitalist Urbanization* (Baltimore: Johns Hopkins University Press).

Haviv, Zerubavel (2002). *From Eretz Yisrael to Poland in the Name of the Jewish National Fund, 1937* (Jerusalem: JNF Research Institute) [Hebrew].

Hebdige, Dick (1979). *Subculture: The Meaning of Style* (London: Methuen).

Hebdige, Dick (1993). "From Culture to Hegemony." *The Cultural Studies Reader*, edited by Simon During (London: Routledge), 357–367.

Hefer, Haim (1956). *Light Ammunition* (Tel Aviv: Hakkibutz Hameuchad) [Hebrew].

Heilbronner, Oded (2011). "'Resistance through Rituals': Urban Subcultures of Israeli Youth from the Late 1950s to the 1980s." *Israel Studies* 16/3: 28–50.

Helman, Amir (1992). "The Israeli Kibbutz as a Socialist Model." *Journal of Institutional and Theoretical Economics* 148/1: 168–183.

Helman, Anat (2002). "'Even the Dogs in the Streets Bark in Hebrew': National Ideology and Everyday Culture in Tel-Aviv." *Jewish Quarterly Review* 92/3–4: 359–382.

Helman, Anat (2003a). "Hollywood in an Israeli Kibbutz: Going to the Movies in 1950s Afikim." *Historical Journal of Film, Radio and Television* 23/2: 153–163.

Helman, Anat (2004). "Cinema Attendance in the Yishuv and in the Early Years of the State of Israel." *Cinema and Memory: Dangerous Relationship?*, edited by Haim Bresheeth, Shlomo Sand, and Moshe Zimmermann (Jerusalem: Zalman Shazar Center), 73–98 [Hebrew].

Helman, Anat (2006). "Taking the Bus in 1920s and 1930s Tel Aviv." *Middle Eastern Studies* 42/4: 625–640.

Helman, Anat (2008a). "Was There Anything Particularly Jewish about 'the First Hebrew City'?" *The Art of Being Jewish in Modern Times: Essays on Jews and Aesthetic Culture*, edited by Barbara Kirshenblatt-Gimblett and Jonathan Karp (Philadelphia: University of Pennsylvania Press), 116–127.

Helman, Anat (2008b). "Sports in the Young State of Israel." *Jews and the Sporting Life (Studies in Contemporary Jewry*, vol. XXIII), edited by Ezra Mendelsohn (New York: Oxford University Press), 103–127.

Helman, Anat (2008c). "Sport on the Sabbath: Controversy in 1920s and 1930s Jewish Palestine." *International Journal of the History of Sport* 25/1: 41–64.

Helman, Anat (2008d). "Kibbutz Dress in the 1950s: Utopian Equality, Anti Fashion, and Change." *Fashion Theory*, 12/3: 313–340.

Helman, Anat (2010). *Young Tel Aviv: A Tale of Two Cities* (Waltham, MA: Brandeis University Press).

Helman, Anat (2011). *A Coat of Many Colors: Dress Culture in the Young State of Israel* (Boston: Academic Studies Press).

Helman, Anat, and Yael Reshef (2007). " 'The Voice of the First Hebrew City to Its Residents': Municipal Posters in Mandate Era Tel Aviv." *Israel* 11: 61–89 [Hebrew].

Helman, Sara (1999). "Militarism and the Construction of the Life-World of Israeli Males." *The Military and Militarism in Israeli Society*, edited by Edna Lomsky-Feder and Eyal Ben-Ari (Albany, NY: SUNY Press), 191–221.

Hermand, Jost (2005). "Resisting Boogie-Woogie Culture, Abstract Expressionism, and Pop Art: German Highbrow Objections to the Import of 'American' Forms of Culture, 1945–1965." *Americanization and anti-Americanization: The German Encounter with American Culture after 1945*, edited by Alexander Stephan (New York: Berghahn Books), 67–77.

Hermann, Tamar (2010). "Pacifism and anti-Militarism in the Period Surrounding the Birth of the State of Israel." *Israel Studies* 15/2: 127–148.

Herzog, Hanna (2000). "Every Year Could Be Considered as the First Year: Time and Identity Issues in the Debate about the Fifties." *Teoria Uvikoret* 17: 209–216 [Hebrew].

Hill, Jeffrey (2002). "Going to the Pictures: America and Cinema." *Sport, Leisure and Culture in Twentieth-Century Britain* (Basingstoke: Palgrave), 59–75.

Hillenbrand, F. K. M. (1995). *Underground Humour in Nazi Germany, 1933–1945* (London: Routledge).

Hirshberg, Jehoash (2006). "The Tangled Road to Legalization: The Admission of the German Language in Musical Performances in Israel." *Jewish Quarterly Review* 96/4: 510–521.

Hobsbawm, Eric (1989). "Introduction: The Invention of Tradition." *The Invention of Tradition*, edited by Eric Hobsbawm (Cambridge: Cambridge University Press), 1–14.

Hopkin, Jean M., Peter M. Jones, and Gordon Stokes (1988). *Bus Service Levels in Urban Areas: Effects on Bus Use and Travel Behaviour* (Crowthorn Berkshire: Department of Transport).

Horowitz, Dan (1993). *Blue and Dust: The Generation of 1948, a Self-Portrait*, edited by Avi Kazman (Jerusalem: Keter) [Hebrew].

Horowitz, Dan, and Moshe Lissak (1990). *Trouble in Utopia: The Overburdened Polity of Israel* (Tel Aviv: Am Oved) [Hebrew].

Howe, Irving (1976). *World of Our Fathers* (New York: Harcourt).

IDF (1956). *Day by Day: Pocket Book for the Soldier* (Tel Aviv: General Staff) [Hebrew].

Israeli Government (1951). *The Government's Annual Publication* (Jerusalem: Publication of the Israeli Government) [Hebrew].

Israeli Government (1952). *The Government's Annual Publication* (Jerusalem: Publication of the Israeli Government) [Hebrew].

Israeli Government (1954). *The Government's Annual Publication* (Jerusalem: Publication of the Israeli Government) [Hebrew].

Jones, Eric L. (2006). *Cultures Merging: A Historical and Economic Critique of Culture* (Princeton, NJ: Princeton University Press).

Jordanova, Ludmilla (2012). *The Look of the Past: Visual and Material Evidence in Historical Practice* (Cambridge: Cambridge University Press).

Kabalo, Paula (2003). "Teenage Citizens: The Youth Conference in Sheikh Munis — Conflict, Dialogue and Meeting." *Israel* 4: 123–154 [Hebrew].

Kabalo, Paula (2008). "Mediating between Citizens and a New State: The History of Shurat Hamitnadvim." *Israel Studies* 13/2: 97–121.

Kafkafi, Eyal (1993). "The Splitting of Kibbutz Ein Harod." *Iyunim Bitkumat Israel* 3: 427–454 [Hebrew].

Kafkafi, Eyal (1999). "The Psycho-Intellectual Aspect of Gender Inequality in Israel's Labor Movement." *Israel Studies* 4/1: 188–211.

Kanari, Baruch (2003). *Tabenkin in Eretz Israel* (Ramat Efal: Yad Tabenkin and Ben-Gurion University) [Hebrew].

Katriel, Tamar (1999). "Speech Style as Cultural Style." *Keywords: Patterns of Culture and Communication in Israel* (Haifa: University of Haifa Press and Zmora-Bitan), 206–225 [Hebrew].

Katz, Yossi (1995). "The Religious Kibbutz Movement and Its Credo, 1935–1948." *Middle Eastern Studies* 31/2: 253–280.

Katz, Yossi, and Yair Paz (2004). "The Transfer of Government Ministries to Jerusalem, 1948–49: Continuity or Change in the Zionist Attitude to Jerusalem?" *Journal of Israeli History* 23/2: 232–259.

Kedar, Nir (2002). "Ben-Gurion's *Mamlakhtiyut*: Etymological and Theoretical Roots." *Israel Studies* 7/3: 117–33.

Kedar, Nir (2010). "Democracy and Judicial Autonomy in Israel's Early Years." *Israel Studies* 15/1: 25–46.

Kelly, Catriona (2001). *Refining Russia: Advice Literature, Polite Culture, and Gender from Catherine to Yeltsin* (Oxford: Oxford University Press).

Kenan, Amos (1953). *With Whips and Scorpions* (Tel Aviv: Yisrael) [Hebrew].

Keren, Michael (2004). "Commemoration and National Identity: A Comparison between the Making of the Anzac and Palmach Legends." *Israel Studies Forum* 19/3: 9–27.

Kerman, Danny (1995). *Two Jews Took a Train: The Best of Alter Druyanov, Relayed and Illustrated by Danny Kerman* (Tel Aviv: Zmora-Bitan) [Hebrew].

Kimmerling, Baruch (1993). "Militarism in Israeli Society." *Teoria Uvikoret* 4: 123–140 [Hebrew].

Kimmerling, Baruch (1998). "Political Subcultures and Civilian Militarism in a Settler-Immigrant Society." *Security Concerns: Insights from the Israeli Experience*, edited by Daniel Bar-Tal, Dan Jacobson, and Aharon Kleiman (Stamford, CT: Jai Press), 395–416.

Kimmerling, Baruch (1999). "State, Immigration, and the Creation of Hegemony (1948–1951)." *Sotziologia yisraelit* b/1: 167–203 [Hebrew].

Kishon, Ephraim (1952). *The Emerging Émigré* (Tel Aviv: Alexander) [Hebrew].

Kochavi-Nehab, Ronni (2006). *Sites in the Realm of Memory: Kibbutz Jubilee Books* (Jerusalem: Yad Tabenkin and Yad Yeari) [Hebrew].

Korn, Alina (2008). "Good Intentions: The Short History of the Minority Affairs Ministry, 14 May 1948–1 July 1949," *Cathedra* 127: 113–140 [Hebrew].

Kossewska, Elżbieta (2010). "*Nowiny — Hadaszot*: The Absorption of Polish Jews in Israel." *Israel* 17: 167–189 [Hebrew].

Kracauer, Siegfried (1950). "National Types as Hollywood Presents Them." *The Cinema, 1950*, edited by Roger Manvell (Harmondsworth: Penguin Books), 140–169.

Kroes, Rob (1996). *If You've Seen One, You've Seen the Mall: Europeans and American Mass Culture* (Urbana: University of Illinois Press).

Kroes, Rob (2002). "American Empire and Cultural Imperialism: A View from the Receiving End." *Rethinking American History in a Global Age*, edited by Thomas Bender (Berkeley: University of California Press), 295–313.

Kruisel, Richard K. (1993). *Seducing the French: The Dilemma of Americanization* (Berkeley: University of California Press).

Kruisel, Richard K. (2000). "The French Cinema and Hollywood: A Case Study of Americanization." *Transactions, Transgressions, Transformations: American Culture in Western Europe and Japan*, edited by Heide Fehrenbach and Uta G. Poiger (New York: Berghahn Books), 208–223.

Kurzweil, Baruch (1965). "The Essence and Sources of the 'Young Hebrews' ('Canaanite') Movement." *New Hebrew Literature* (Jerusalem: Schocken), 270–300 [Hebrew].

Kynaston, David (2007). *Austerity Britain, 1941–51* (London: Bloomsbury).

Landy, Joshua, and Michael Saler (2009). "Introduction: The Varieties of Modern Enchantment." *The Re-Enchantment of the World: Secular Magic in a Rational Age*, edited by Joshua Landy and Michael Saler (Stanford, CA: Stanford University Press), 1–14.

Lavsky, Hagit (2012). "Then and Now: The Immigration and Absorption of German Jews in Israel between History and Historical Consciousness." *Culture, Memory, and History: Essays in Honor of Anita Shapira*, vol. 2, edited by Meir Chazan and Uri Cohen (Jerusalem: Tel Aviv University and Zalman Shazar Center), 251–274 [Hebrew].

Lears, T. J. Jackson (1985). "The Concept of Cultural Hegemony: Problems and Possibilities." *American Historical Review* 90/3: 567–593.

Lederhendler, Eli (1991). "Guides for the Perplexed: Sex, Manners, and Mores for the Yiddish Reader in America." *Modern Judaism* 11/3: 321–341.

Leiss, William, Stephen Kline, Sut Jhally, and Jacqueline Botterill (2005). *Social Communication in Advertising: Consumption in the Mediated Marketplace* (New York: Routledge).

Lerer, Moshe (1956). *Maccabi Tel Aviv — The Champions! Fiftieth Anniversary of Maccabi Tel Aviv* (Tel Aviv: Sport Publications) [Hebrew].

Lev-Ari, Shimon (1987). "The Mass Immigration and the Israeli Theater." *Immigrants and Transit Camps, 1948–1952*, edited by Mordechai Naor (Jerusalem: Yad Ben-Zvi), 221–234 [Hebrew].

Levy, Yagil, Edna Lomsky-Feder, and Noa Harel (2010). "From 'Obligatory Militarism' to 'Contractual Militarism' — Competing Models of Citizenship." *Militarism and Israeli Society*, edited by Gabriel Sheffer and Oren Barak (Bloomington: Indiana University Press), 145–167.

Lewis, Ben (2008). *Hammer and Tickle: The History of Communism Told through Communist Jokes* (London: Weidenfeld & Nicolson).

Lewis, Paul (2006). *Cracking Up: American Humor in a Time of Conflict* (Chicago: University of Chicago Press).

Libman, Lior (2012). "Hakibbutz Hameuchad's 'State of Shock,' 1948–1954: Textual Expressions." *Iyunim Bitkumat Israel* 22: 25–63 [Hebrew].

Liebermann, Yaacov (1998). "The Work Metaphor in the Kibbutz Change Process." *Kibbutz Trends* 31–32: 50–55.

Liebman, Charles S., and Eliezer Don-Yehiya (1983). *Civil Religion in Israel* (Berkeley: University of California Press).

Linenthal, Edward Tabor (1982). *Changing Images of the Warrior Hero in America: A History of Popular Symbolism* (Lewiston, NY: Mellen).

Lissak, Moshe (1998). "The Demographic-Social Revolution in the Fifties: The Absorption of the Mass Immigration." *Independence: The First Fifty Years*, edited by Anita Shapira (Jerusalem: Zalman Shazar Center), 13–56 [Hebrew].

Lissak, Moshe (1999). *The Mass Immigration in the Fifties: The Failure of the Melting Pot Policy* (Jerusalem: Bialik Institute) [Hebrew].

Lissak, Moshe (2000). "The Palmach in Its Generation and in Historical Perspective." *Palmach: Two Sheaves and a Sword*, edited by Yechiam Weitz (Ramat Efal: Ministry of Defense Press), 319–350 [Hebrew].

Lissak, Moshe, and Uri Cohen (2011). "Scientific Strategists in the Period of *Mamlakhtiyut*: Interaction between the Academic Community and Political Power Centers." *Journal of Israeli History* 30/2: 189–210.

Lomsky-Feder, Edna, and Eyal Ben-Ari (1999). "Epilogue." *The Military and Militarism in Israeli Society*, edited by Edna Lomsky-Feder and Eyal Ben-Ari (Albany, NY: SUNY Press), 301–312.

Maimon, Yaacov (1953). "Volunteer Teachers in the *Ma'abarot*." *Megamot* 4/1: 27–36 [Hebrew].

Maman, Ofir (2007). "Telem, Theater for the Transit Camps: The Emergence of the 'Double Address' in Israeli Theater." *Cathedra* 123: 125–154 [Hebrew].

Martin, Phyllis M. (2004). "Afterward." *Fashioning Africa: Power and the Politics of Dress*, edited by Jean Allman (Bloomington: Indiana University Press), 227–230.

Massey, Anne (2000). *Hollywood beyond the Screen* (Oxford: Berg).

McFall, Liz (2004). *Advertising: A Cultural Economy* (London: Sage).

McKibbin, Ross (1998). *Classes and Cultures: England 1918–1951* (Oxford: Oxford University Press).

Meimon, Ada (1955). *Fifty Years of the Women Workers Movement* (Tel Aviv: Eynot) [Hebrew].

Meir-Glitzenstein, Esther (2009). *Between Baghdad and Ramat Gan: Iraqi Jews in Israel* (Jerusalem: Yad Ben-Zvi) [Hebrew].

Meir-Glitzenstein, Esther (2011). "Operation Magic Carpet: Constructing the Myth of the Magical Immigration of Yemenite Jews to Israel," *Israel Studies* 16/3: 149–173.

Melman, Billie (2002). "The Legend of Sarah: Gender Memory and National Identities (*Eretz Yisrael*/Israel, 1917–90)." *Journal of Israeli History* 21/1–2: 55–92.

Merkel, Ina (1998). "Consumer Culture in the GDR, or How the Struggle for Antimodernity Was Lost on the Battleground of Consumer Culture." *Getting and Spending: European and American Consumer Societies in the Twentieth Century*, edited by Susan Strasser, Charles McGovern, and Matthias Judt (Cambridge: Cambridge University Press), 281–299.

Mikes, George (1950). *Milk and Honey: Israel Explored* (London: Wingate).

Mintz, Sidney W. (1986). *Sweetness and Power: The Place of Sugar in Modern History* (New York: Penguin).

Molcho, Yitzhak Rafael, and Tuvia Ben Hefetz (1951). *Jerusalem Communal Center: The Opening Ceremony*, edited by Yitzhak Rafael Molcho and Tuvia Ben Hefetz (Jerusalem: Achvah) [Hebrew].

Montgomery, Elizabeth (1938). *A Land Divided* (London: Hutchinson).

Morag, Shlomo (2003a). "The Consolidation of Modern Hebrew." In *Studies in Hebrew, Aramaic and Jewish Languages*, edited by Moshe Bar-Asher, Yochanan Breuer, and Aharon Maman (Jerusalem: Magnes Press), 330–352 [Hebrew].

Morag, Shlomo (2003b). "A Decade of Hebrew (1948–1958)." In *Studies in Hebrew*, edited by Moshe Bar-Asher, Yochanan Breuer, and Aharon Maman (Jerusalem: Magnes Press), 160–173 [Hebrew].

Morris, Benny (1996). "The Israeli Press and the Qibya Incident, October–November 1953." *Teoria Uvikoret* 8: 33–46 [Hebrew].

Morris, Benny (2008). *1948: A History of the First Arab-Israeli War* (New Haven, CT: Yale University Press).

Moser, Kurt (1998). "World War I and the Creation of Desire for Automobiles in Germany." *Getting and Spending: European and American Consumer Societies in the Twentieth Century*, edited by Susan Strasser, Charles McGovern, and Matthias Judt (Cambridge: Cambridge University Press), 195–222.

Mosse, George L. (1985). *Nationalism and Sexuality: Respectability and Abnormal Sexuality in Modern Europe* (New York: Howard Fertig).

Mosse, George L. (1992). "Max Nordau, Liberalism and the New Jew." *Journal of Contemporary History* 27/4: 565–581.

Muscio, Giuliana (2000). "Invasion and Counterattack: Italian and American Film

Relations in the Postwar Period." *"Here, There and Everywhere": The Foreign Politics of American Popular Culture*, edited by Reinhold Wagnleitner and Elaine Tyler May (Hanover, NH: University Press of New England), 117–131.

Nadad, Avraham (1956). "Kfar Shalem: Portrait of a Poor Neighborhood." *Megamot* 7/1 (1956): 5–40 [Hebrew].

Nadler, Allan (2005). "Holy Kugel: The Sanctification of Ashkenazic Ethnic Foods in Hasidism." *Food and Judaism*, edited by Leonard J. Greenspoon, Ronald A. Simkins, and Gerald Shapiro (Omaha, NE: Creighton University Press), 193–214.

Naor, Arye (2009a). " 'With Blood and Sweat / Shall Arise a Race': The 'New Jew' according to Zeev Jabotinsky." *Israel* 16: 119–142 [Hebrew].

Naor, Mordechai (1987). "The *Tzena*." *Immigrants and Transit Camps, 1948–1952*, edited by Mordechai Naor (Jerusalem: Yad Ben-Zvi), 97–110 [Hebrew].

Naor, Mordechai (1997). "The Newspapers in the Fifties." *The First Decade, 1948–1958*, edited by Zvi Zameret and Hanna Yablonka (Jerusalem: Yad Ben-Zvi), 215–226 [Hebrew].

Naor, Moshe (2009). *On the Home Front: Tel Aviv and Mobilization of the Yishuv in the War of Independence* (Jerusalem: Yad Ben-Zvi) [Hebrew].

Naor, Moshe (2010). "The 1948 War Veterans and Postwar Reconstruction in Israel." *Journal of Israeli History* 29/1: 47–59

Near, Henry (1992a). "Men and Women Pioneers in the State of Israel, Semantic and Historical Aspects, 1948–1956." *Iyunim Bitkumat Israel* 1: 116–40 [Hebrew].

Near, Henry (1992b). *The Kibbutz Movement: A History*, vol. 1: *Origins and Growth, 1909–1939* (Oxford: Littman and Oxford University Press).

Near, Henry (1995). "The Crisis in the Kibbutz Movement, 1949–1961." *Israel: The First Decade of Independence*, edited by S. Ilan Troen and Noah Lucas (Albany, NY: SUNY Press), 243–263.

Near, Henry (1997). *The Kibbutz Movement: A History*, vol. 2: *Crisis and Achievement, 1939–1995* (London: Littman and Oxford University Press).

Near, Henry (2010). "The Kibbutz' Beginnings: The First Two Decades." *The Kibbutz: The First 100 Years*, edited by Aviva Halamish and Zvi Zameret (Jerusalem: Yad Ben-Zvi), 11–24 [Hebrew].

Neeman, Joseph, trans. (1955). *Selected Arab Poetry* (Jerusalem: Kiryat Sefer) [Hebrew].

Oakley, Ronald J. (1990). *God's Country: America in the Fifties* (New York: Dembner Books).

Oring, Elliott (1983). "The People of the Joke: On the Conceptualization of a Jewish Humor." *Western Folklore* 42/4: 261–271.

Oring, Elliott (2003). *Engaging Humor* (Urbana: University of Illinois Press).

Osokina, Elena (2001). "On Stalinism and the World Experience with State-Regulated Supply." *Our Daily Bread: Socialist Distribution and the Art of Survival in Stalin's Russia, 1927–1941*, edited by Kate Transchel (Armonk, NY: M. E. Sharpe), 195–203.

Ozacky-Lazar, Sara (1996). *Jewish-Arab Relations in the State of Israel's First Decade, 1948–1958* (PhD dissertation, Haifa University, Haifa) [Hebrew].

Ozacky-Lazar, Sara (2001). "Jewish-Arab Relations in the First Decade." *A State in the Making: Israeli Society in the First Decades*, edited by Anita Shapira (Jerusalem: Zalman Shazar Center), 61–71 [Hebrew].

Ozacky-Lazar, Sara (2006). "The Arab Citizens in Israel: The First Decade." *Israel in the First Decade*, vol. 12 (Raanana: The Open University), 3–95 [Hebrew].

Pauker, Alon (2010). "When the Pioneering Kibbutz Met the Centralist State: Difficulties of Self-Image." *The Kibbutz: The First 100 Years*, edited by Aviva Halamish and Zvi Zameret (Jerusalem: Yad Ben-Zvi), 167–182 [Hebrew].

Pauker, Alon (2012). "Hakibbutz Haartzi and the Soviet Union during the First Decade of Israeli Independence." *Iyunim Bitkumat Israel* 22: 64–90 [Hebrew].

Pelli, Moshe (2004). "The German-or-Yiddish Controversy within the Haskalah and the European 'Dialogue of the Dead': Tuvyah Feder's *Kol Mehazezim* versus Mendel Lefin's Translation of the Book of Proverbs." *Leo Baeck Institute Year Book* 49: 227–251.

Penfold, Steve (2006). *The Donut: A Canadian History* (Toronto: University of Toronto Press).

Penslar, Derek (1991). *Zionism and Technocracy: The Engineering of Jewish Settlement in Palestine, 1870–1918* (Bloomington: Indiana University Press).

Penslar, Derek (2007). "The Continuity of Subversion: Hebrew Satire in Mandate Palestine." *Israel in History: The Jewish State in Comparative Perspective* (London: Routledge), 169–186.

Peretz, Don (1991). "Early State Policy towards the Arab Population, 1948–1955." *New Perspectives on Israeli History: The Early Years of the State*, edited by Laurence J. Silberstein (New York: New York University Press), 82–102.

Pilovsky, Arye (1980). *Yiddish and Its Literature in the Land of Israel, 1907–1948* (PhD dissertation, The Hebrew University, Jerusalem) [Hebrew].

Pilovsky, Arye (1981). "Language, Culture, and Nationalism in the New Yishuv: The Public Debate about the Plan of Founding a Yiddish Chair in Jerusalem in Late 1927." *Cathedra* 21: 103–134 [Hebrew].

Pines, Dan (1954). *Dictionary of Foreign Words in Hebrew* (Tel Aviv: Amichai).

Podeh, Eli (1999). "The Desire to Belong Syndrome: Israel and Middle-Eastern Defense, 1948–1954." *Israel Studies* 4/2: 121–144.

Porat, Chanina (1993). "D. Ben-Gurion's Geographic-Settlement Concept and the Development of the Negev, 1948–1952." *Iyunim Bitkumat Israel* 3: 114–143 [Hebrew].

Porat, Chanina (1997). "Settlement and Development Policy and the Negev Bedouins, 1948–1953." *Iyunim Bitkumat Israel* 7: 389–438 [Hebrew].

Radai, Judah (1956). *The First Step: A New Approach for Teaching the Israeli Hebrew Language to Beginners* (Jerusalem: Reuven Mass) [Hebrew].

Raz, Ayala (1996). *Changing of Styles* (Tel Aviv: Yediot Aharonot) [Hebrew].

Reichman, Shalom (1971). "The Evolution of Land Transportation in Palestine, 1920–1947." *Studies in Geography* 2: 55–90.

Reifowitz, Ian (2008). "'Saviour of the People': The Enlightenment and the Depiction of Jews, Poles, and Ukrainians in the Stories of Karl Emil Franzos." *East European Quarterly* 42/1: 1–25.

Reshef, Yael (2012). "From Hebrew Folksong to Israeli Song: Language and Style in Naomi Shemer's Lyrics." *Israel Studies* 17/1: 157–179.

Reshef, Yael (2013). "'The Language That Follows Speech Will Not Be the Same as the One That Preceded It': Spoken Hebrew in the pre-State Period." *Journal of Jewish Studies* 64: 157–186.

Reshef, Yael, and Anat Helman (2009). "Instructing or Recruiting? Language and Style in 1920s and 1930s Tel Aviv Municipal Posters." *Jewish Studies Quarterly* 16/3: 306–332.

Rieger, Hagit (1952). "Difficulties of Assimilation of Yemenite Youths in Israel." *Megamot* 3/3: 259–291 [Hebrew].

Rivlin, Yosef Yoel (1954). "The Tribes of Israel in Historical Perspective." *Tribe and People: The Problems of Ingathering the Exiles*, edited by David Sitton and Yitzhak A. Abadi (Jerusalem: Israeli Executive of the World Sephardi Federation), 61–79 [Hebrew].

Robinson, Shaul (1953). "Education and Training for Social Conduct." *Megamot* 4/3: 266–276 [Hebrew].

Rochelson, Meri-Jane (1988). "Language, Gender, and Ethnic Anxiety in Zangwill's Children of the Ghetto." *English Literature in Transition, 1880–1920* 31/4: 399–412.

Roginsky, Dina (2007a). "Folklore, Folklorism, and Synchronization: Preserved-Created Folklore in Israel." *Journal of Folklore Research* 44/1: 41–66.

Roginsky, Dina (2007b). "The Bureaucratization of Folklore: The Institutionalization of Israeli Folk Dance." *Sadan* 6: 223–268 [Hebrew].

Rojanski, Rachel (2004). "The Status of Yiddish in Israel, 1948–1951: An Overview." *Yiddish after the Holocaust*, edited by Joseph Sherman (Oxford: Boulevard Books), 46–59.

Rojanski, Rachel (2005). "Ben-Gurion's Attitude to Yiddish in the 1950s." *Iyunim Bitkumat Israel* 15: 463–482 [Hebrew].

Rojanski, Rachel (2007). "The Final Chapter in the Struggle for Cultural Autonomy." *Journal of Modern Jewish Studies* 6/2: 185–204.

Rosen, Haim. (1955). *Our Hebrew* (Tel Aviv: Am Oved) [Hebrew].

Rosenberg-Friedman, Lilach (2006). "The Complex Identity of Religious-Zionist Women in pre-State Israel, 1921–1948." *Israel Studies* 11/3: 83–107.

Rosenthal, Ruvik (2006). *Dictionary of Israeli Slang* (Jerusalem: Keter) [Hebrew].

Rosenthal, Yemima (1997). "Israel's Foreign Policy between Security and Diplomacy." *Israel: The First Decade of Independence*, edited by S. Ilan Troen and Noah Lucas (Albany, NY: SUNY Press), 169–196.

Roskies, David G. (1999). "The Shtetl in Jewish Collective Memory." *The Jewish Search for a Usable Past* (Bloomington: Indiana University Press), 41–66.

Roth, Leon (1950). *The Education of the Citizen* (Jerusalem: Magnes Press) [Hebrew].

Rothstein, Halina, and Robert A. Rothstein (1997). "The Beginning of Soviet Culinary Art." *Food in Russian History and Culture*, edited by Musya Glants and Joyce Toomre (Bloomington: Indiana University Press), 177–194.

Rozin, Orit (2002a). "Israeli Housewives and the Austerity Policy." *Israel* 1: 81–118 [Hebrew].

Rozin, Orit (2002b). "Terms of Disgust: Hygiene and Parenthood of Immigrants from Moslem Countries as Viewed by Veteran Israelis in the 1950s." *Iyunim Bitkumat Israel* 12: 195–238 [Hebrew].

Rozin, Orit (2005a). "Food, Femininity and Nation Building in Austerity Israel." *A Full Belly: Rethinking Food and Society in Israel*, edited by Aviad Kleinberg (Jerusalem and Tel Aviv: Keter and Tel Aviv University Press), 155–204 [Hebrew].

Rozin, Orit (2005b). "The Austerity Policy and the Rule of Law: Relations between Government and Public in Fledgling Israel." *Journal of Modern Jewish Studies* 4/3: 273–290.

Rozin, Orit (2006). "Food, Identity and Nation Building in Israel's Formative Years." *Israel Studies Forum* 21/1: 52–80.

Rozin, Orit (2010). "Israel and the Right to Travel Abroad, 1948–1961." *Israel Studies* 15/1: 147–176.

Rozin, Orit (2011a). *The Rise of the Individual in 1950s Israel: A Challenge to Collectivism* (Waltham, MA: Brandeis University Press).

Rozin, Orit (2011b). "Negotiating the Right to Exit the Country in 1950s Israel: Voice, Loyalty, and Citizenship." *Journal of Israeli History* 30/1: 1–22.

Rubin, Adam (2011). "'Turning Goyim into Jews': Aliyah and the Politics of Cultural Anxiety in the Zionist Movement, 1933–1939." *Jewish Quarterly Review* 101/1: 71–96.

Rubinstein, Amnon, and Barak Medina (2005). *The Constitutional Law of the State of Israel* (Jerusalem: Schocken) [Hebrew].

Ryan, Karen (2004). "Laughing at the Hangman: Humorous Portraits of Stalin." *Reflective Laughter: Aspects of Humour in Russian Culture*, edited by Lesley Milne (London: Anthem Press), 157–165.

Sa'adi, Ahmed (1997). "Culture as a Dimension of Political Behavior: The Palestinian Citizens of Israel." *Teoria Uvikoret* 10: 193–202 [Hebrew].

Safran, William (1992). "Language, Ideology, and State-Building: A Comparison of Policies in France, Israel, and the Soviet Union." *International Political Science Review* 13/4: 397–414.

Saguy, Abigail C. (2013). *What's Wrong with Fat?* (Oxford: Oxford University Press).

Samet, Shimon (1954). "Movies." *The Journalists Yearbook for Tashiad* (Tel Aviv: Journalists Association), 80–83 [Hebrew].

Sapir, Rivka (1951). "'Shelter': The Problem of Housing Immigrant Children among Urban Families." *Megamot* 3/1: 8–36 [Hebrew].

Sassoon, Donald (2002). "On Cultural Markets." *New Left Review* 17: 113–126.

Sasson-Levy, Orna (2006). *Identity in Uniform: Masculinities and Femininities in the Israeli Military* (Jerusalem: Magnes Press) [Hebrew].

Schely-Newman, Esther (1997). "Finding One's Place: Locale Narratives in an Israeli Moshav." *Quarterly Journal of Speech* 83/4: 401–415.

Schor, Bar-Kokhba (1956). *Practical Encyclopedia* (Tel Aviv: Yediot Aharonot) [Hebrew].

Segev, Tom (1984). *1949: The First Israelis* (Jerusalem: Domino) [Hebrew].

Sela-Sheffy, Rakefet (2003). "The Yekkes in the Legal Field and Bourgeois Culture in pre-Israel British Palestine." *Iyunim Bitkumat Israel* 13: 295–322 [Hebrew].

Seliktar, Ofira (2005). "Tenured Radicals in Israel: From New Zionism to Political Activism." *Israeli Affairs* 11/4: 717–736.

Shachar, Bezalel (1963). *Culture and Society: The Cultural Work in Israel* (Tel Aviv: Mif'alei Tarbut Vechinukh) [Hebrew].

Shachnai Ran, Idit, and Maayan Natali Smoller (2010). "Kibbutz Time — The Dining Hall as an Allegory." *The Dining Hall as an Allegory* (exhibition catalog), curated by Michal Shachnai Yacobi (Afula: Emek Jezreel Regional Council), unnumbered pages [Hebrew].

Shachnai Yacobi, Michal (2010). *The Dining Hall as an Allegory* (exhibition catalog), curated by Michal Shachnai Yacobi (Afula: Emek Jezreel Regional Council) [Hebrew].

Shafrut, Ezra (1988). "The Bikurim Festival in the Jezreel Valley (1923–1929) in Religious Eyes." *Mehkarey Hag* 1: 91–103 [Hebrew].

Shahar, Natan (1997). "The Military Groups and Their Songs." *The First Decade, 1948–1958*, edited by Zvi Zameret and Hanna Yablonka (Jerusalem: Yad Ben-Zvi), 299–318 [Hebrew].

Shaked, Gershon (1997). "Amichai and the *Likrat* Group: The Early Amichai and His Literary Reference Group." *The Experienced Soul: Studies in Amichai,* edited by Glenda Abramson (Boulder, CO: Westview Press), 93–120.

Shaked, Yosef (1956). "The Operation for Bestowing the Language to the People." *My Homeland: To the Youths and the People* (Jerusalem: Achvah), 154–157 [Hebrew].

Shalev, Michael (2004). "Between Polity and Economy: The Histadrut and the State." *State and Community,* edited by Moshe Naor (Jerusalem: Magnes Press), 82–87 [Hebrew].

Shalit, David (2006). *Projecting Power: The Cinema Houses, the Movies and the Israelis* (Tel Aviv: Resling) [Hebrew].

Shalmon, Yosef (1987). "Religion and State in Modern Jewish Nationality and the State in the Making: Religious Zionism." *Priesthood and Monarchy: Studies in Historical Relationships of Religion and State,* edited by Isaiah Gafni and Gabriel Motzkin (Jerusalem: Zalman Shazar Center), 277–284 [Hebrew].

Shalom, Zaki (1991). "Strategy Debates: Arab Infiltration and Israeli Retaliation Policy in the Early 1950s." *Iyunim Bitkumat Israel* 1: 141–169 [Hebrew].

Shalom, Zaki (1992). "Israel's Rejection of Territorial Demands, 1948–1956." *Iyunim Bitkumat Israel* 2: 197–213 [Hebrew].

Shalom, Zaki (1993). "Israel's Struggle to Thwart UN Resolutions on the Internationalization of Jerusalem in the 1950s." *Iyunim Bitkumat Israel* 3: 75–97 [Hebrew].

Shalom, Zaki (2002). "Strategy in Debate: Arab Infiltration and Israeli Retaliation Policy in the Early 1950s." *Israel Affairs* 8/3: 104–117.

Shamir, Ilana (1996). *Commemoration and Remembrance: Israel's Way of Molding Its Patterns of Collective Memory* (Tel Aviv: Am Oved) [Hebrew].

Shamir, Ziva (1999). "'The Inn of Spirits' Revisited." *Motar* 7: 51–62 [Hebrew].

Shapira, Anita (1996a). "The Fashioning of the 'New Jew' in the Yishuv Society." *Major Changes within the Jewish People in the Wake of the Holocaust*, edited by Yisrael Gutman (Jerusalem: Yad Vashem), 427–441.

Shapira, Anita (1996b). "Elements in the National Ethos in the Transition to Statehood." *Nationalism and Jewish Politics: New Perspectives*, edited by Jehuda Reinharz, Yosef Shalmon, and Gideon Shimoni (Jerusalem: Zalman Shazar Center and Tauber Institute), 253–271 [Hebrew].

Shapira, Anita (1997). "The Myth of the New Jew." *New Jews, Old Jews* (Tel Aviv: Am Oved), 155–174 [Hebrew].

Shavit, Yaacov (1983). *From Majority to State* (Tel Aviv: Hadar) [Hebrew].

Shavit, Yaacov (1992). "Messianism, Utopianism and Pessimism during the 1950s." *Iyunim Bitkumat Israel* 2: 56–78 [Hebrew].

Shavit, Yaacov, Yaacov Goldstein, and Haim Beer, eds. (1983). *Personalities in Eretz Israel, 1799–1948: A Biographical Dictionary* (Tel Aviv: Am Oved) [Hebrew].

Shavit, Zohar (2009). "The Habitus of the 'New Jew' of the Haskalah Movement." *Israel* 16: 11–48 [Hebrew].

Shefer, Israel, and Reuven Shapira (1992). "Individual and Community." *Kibbutz: Continuity and Change* (Tel Aviv: Open University) [Hebrew].

Shefer, Joseph, and Sylvie Fogiel-Bijaoui (1992). "The Family in the Kibbutz." *Kibbutz: Continuity and Change* (Tel Aviv: Open University) [Hebrew].

Sheffer, Gabriel (2010). "Moshe Sharett, the Ministry of Foreign Affairs and the Jewish Diaspora." *Israel Studies* 15/3: 27–46.

Shifman, Limor, and Elihu Katz (2005). "'Just Call Me Adonai': A Case Study of Ethnic Humor and Immigrant Assimilation." *American Sociological Review* 70/5: 843–859.

Shlaim, Avi (2004). "Israel between East and West, 1948–1956." *International Journal of Middle Eastern Studies* 36: 657–673.

Shtal, Avraham (1976). *Cultural Integration in Israel* (Tel Aviv: Am Oved) [Hebrew].

Shtal, Avraham (1979). *Interethnic Tensions in Israel* (Tel Aviv: Am Oved) [Hebrew].

Shternshis, Anna (2006). *Soviet and Kosher: Jewish Popular Culture in the Soviet Union, 1923–1939* (Bloomington: Indiana University Press).

Sikron, Moshe (1987). "The Mass Immigration—Its Dimensions, Characteristics, and Influences on the Structure of the Israeli Population." *Immigrants and Transit Camps, 1948–1952*, edited by Mordechai Naor (Jerusalem: Yad Ben-Zvi), 31–52 [Hebrew].

Simmel, Georg (1997). "Sociology of the Meal." *Simmel on Culture*, edited by David Frisby and Mike Featherstone (London: Sage), 130–135.

Simon, Akiva Ernst (1951). "The Double Meaning of 'Primitivity.'" *Megamot* 2/5: 277–284 [Hebrew].

Sitton, David, and Yitzhak A. Abadi, eds. (1954). *Tribe and People: The Problems of Ingathering the Exiles* (Jerusalem: Israeli Executive of the World Sephardi Federation) [Hebrew].

Sivan, Emmanuel (1991). *The 1948 Generation* (Tel Aviv: Ma'arakhot) [Hebrew].

Sklar, Robert (1994). *Movie-Made America: A Cultural History of American Movies* (New York: Vintage Books).

Smith, Anthony (2001). *Nationalism: Theory, Ideology, History* (Cambridge: Polity).

Snopkov, Aleksandr, et al. (2010). *Classic Russian Posters*, edited by Aleksandr Snopkov, Pavel Sniokov, and Aleksandr Shklyaruk (Moscow: Contact-Culture Publishing House).

Sofer, Oren (2009). "Why Hebrew? A Comparative Analysis of Language Choice in the Early Hebrew Press." *Media History* 15/3: 253–269.

Soker, Zeev (1998). "Kibbutz Culture." *Kibbutz: Continuity and Change* (Tel Aviv: The Open University) [Hebrew].

Sparks, Penny (1995). *As Long as It's Pink: The Sexual Politics of Taste* (London: Pandora).

Steinberg, Shlomit (2002). "The Self-Image of the Israeli Artist: Pioneer, Fighter, Victim." *A Century of Israeli Culture*, edited by Israel Bartal (Jerusalem: Magnes Press), 223–235 [Hebrew].

Stewart, George R. (1954). *American Ways of Life* (New York: Doubleday).

Stitziel, Judd (2005). *Fashioning Socialism: Clothing, Politics, and Consumer Culture in East Germany* (Oxford: Berg).

Stitziel, Judd (2008). "Shopping, Sewing, Networking, Complaining: Consumer Culture and the Relationship between State and Society in the GDR." *Socialist Modern: East German Everyday Culture and Politics*, edited by Katherine Pence and Paul Betts (Ann Arbor: University of Michigan Press), 253–286.

Stokker, Kathleen (1995). *Folklore Fights the Nazis: Humor in Occupied Norway, 1940–1945* (Cranbury, NJ: Associated University Presses).

Stone Nakhimovsky, Alice (2006). "You Are What They Eat: Russian Jews Reclaim Their Foodways." *Shofar* 25/1: 63–77.

Tal, Emanuel (1994). "Architectural Design of Communal Dining Halls in the Early Kibbutz (1926–1935)." *Cathedra* 70: 134–160 [Hebrew].

Talmon-Gerber, Yonina (2006). "Secular Asceticism: Patterns of Ideological Change." *A Historical Achievement and Its Evolution*, edited by Abigail Paz-Yeshayahu and Yosef Gorny (Beer Sheva: Ben-Gurion Research Institute), 401–446 [Hebrew].

Taylor, Vanessa, and Frank Trentmann (2011). "Liquid Politics: Water and Politics of Everyday Life in a Modern City." *Past and Present* 211: 199–241.

Tehar-Lev, Yoram (1976). *Meshek Yagur—A Draft* (Tel Aviv: Hakibbutz Hameuchad) [Hebrew].

Tessler, Shmulik (2007). *Songs in Uniform: The Military Entertainment Troupes of the Israel Defence Forces* (Jerusalem: Yad Ben-Zvi) [Hebrew].

Thissen, Judith (2008). "Film and Vaudeville on New York's Lower East Side." *The Art of Being Jewish in Modern Times: Essays on Jews and Aesthetic Culture*, edited by Barbara Kirshenblatt-Gimblett and Jonathan Karp (Philadelphia: University of Pennsylvania Press), 42–56.

Thompson, David (1977). *America in the Dark: The Impact of Hollywood Films on American Culture* (New York: Morrow).

Townsend, Mary Lee (1992). *Forbidden Laughter: Popular Humor and the Limits of Repression in Nineteenth-Century Prussia* (Ann Arbor: University of Michigan Press).

Treiber, Reuven (2010). "The Kibbutz Dining Hall: Past — Present — Future." *The Dining Hall as an Allegory* (exhibition catalog), curated by Michal Shachnai Yacobi (Afula: Emek Jezreel Regional Council), unnumbered pages [Hebrew].

Trentmann, Frank (2006). "Knowing Consumers — Histories, Identities, Practices." *The Making of the Consumer: Knowledge, Power and Identity in the Modern World*, edited by Frank Trentmann (Oxford: Berg), 1–27.

Trimbur, Dominique, and Danny Jacobi (2009). "The European Powers and the Teaching of Foreign Languages at the Hebrew University during the British Mandate Period." *The History of the Hebrew University of Jerusalem: Academic Progression in a Period of National Struggle*, edited by Hagit Lavsky (Jerusalem: Magnes Press), 134–159 [Hebrew].

Tsur, Muki (2007). "Pesach in the Land of Israel: Kibbutz Haggadot." *Israel Studies* 12/2: 74–103.

Tsur, Muki (2010). "Dining Halls in the Kibbutz." *The Dining Hall as an Allegory* (exhibition catalog), curated by Michal Shachnai Yacobi (Afula: Emek Jezreel Regional Council), unnumbered pages [Hebrew].

Tydor Baumel-Schwartz, Judith (2009). "The Lives and Deaths of Female Military Casualties in Israel during the 1950s." *Israel Studies* 14/2: 134–157.

Tzabar, Shimon (1951). *The Thorn of Tzabar* (Tel Aviv: Tversky) [Hebrew].

Tzur, Eli (2001). " 'To Be a Free People': The History of the 'League for the Prevention of Religious Coercion.' " *A State in the Making: Israeli Society in the First Decades*, edited by Anita Shapira (Jerusalem: Zalman Shazar Center), 205–238 [Hebrew].

Uri, Yaacov (1951). *Roots in the Homeland* (Jerusalem: Reuven Mass) [Hebrew].

Vaughn, Stephen (1996). "Political Censorship during the Cold War." *Movie Censorship and American Culture*, edited by Francis G. Couvares (Washington, DC: Smithsonian Institution Press), 237–257.

Wagstaff, Christopher (1998). "Italian Genre Films in the World Market." *Hollywood in Europe: Economics, Culture, National Identity, 1945–1995*, edited by Geoffrey Nowelle-Smith and Steven Ricci (London: FBI), 74–85.

Walzer, Michael (2007). "Zionism and Judaism: The Paradox of National Liberation." *Journal of Israeli History* 26/2: 125–136.

Watson, Sophie (2006). *City Publics: The (Dis)Enchantment of Urban Encounters* (London: Routledge).

Watts, Richard J. (2007). *Politeness* (Cambridge: Cambridge University Press).

Weitz, Yechiam (1996). "The Debates concerning the Role of Culture in the State's First Years." *Journal of Israeli History* 17/2: 179–191.

Weitz, Yechiam (1998). "The End of the Beginning: Clarifying the Concept of the Starting Point of the State." *Between Vision and Revision — One Hundred Years of Zionist Historiography*, edited by Yechiam Weitz (Jerusalem: Zalman Shazar Center), 235–253 [Hebrew].

Weitz, Yechiam (2001). "General Elections and Governmental Crises." *Israel in the First Decade*, vol. 5 (Ramat Aviv: The Open University), 79–151 [Hebrew].

Wilk, Richard R. (2002). "Food and Nationalism: The Origins of 'Belizean Food.'" *Food Nations: Selling Taste in Consumer Societies*, edited by Warren Belasco and Philip Scranton (New York: Routledge), 67–89.

Williams, Raymond (1993). "Advertising: The Magic System." *The Cultural Studies Reader*, edited by Simon During (London: Routledge), 320–336.

Wilson, Janelle L. (2005). *Nostalgia: Sanctuary of Meaning* (Lewisburg: Bucknell University Press).

WIZO (1953). *This Is How We'll Cook* (Tel Aviv: Ner) [Hebrew].

Wood, Marcus (2004). *Radical Satire and Print Culture, 1790–1822* (Oxford: Clarendon Press).

Wouters, Cas (2004). "Introduction." *Sex and Manners: Female Emancipation in the West, 1890–2000* (London: Sage), 1–13.

Wouters, Cas (2007). "Manners: History and Theory." *Informalization: Manners and Emotions since 1890* (Los Angeles: Sage), 11–34.

Yaar, Efraim (2007). "Continuity and Change in Israeli Society: The Test of the Melting Pot." *Generations, Locations, Identities: Contemporary Perspectives on Society and Culture in Israel*, edited by Hanna Herzog, Tal Kohavi, and Shimshon Zelniker (Tel Aviv: Van Leer Institute and Hakibbutz Hameuchad), 72–104 [Hebrew].

Yanai, Nathan (1996). "The Citizen as Pioneer: Ben-Gurion's Concept of Citizenship." *Israel Studies* 1/1: 127–143.

Yonah, Yossi, and Yehuda Shenhav (2005). *What Is Multiculturalism? On the Politics of Identity in Israel* (Tel Aviv: Babel) [Hebrew].

Zachor, Zeev (1997). "The First Elections and the Political Map." *The First Decade, 1948–1958*, edited by Zvi Zameret and Hanna Yablonka (Jerusalem: Yad Ben-Zvi), 27–40 [Hebrew].

Zachor, Zeev (2007). *The Shaping of the Israeli Ethos* (Tel Aviv: Am Oved) [Hebrew].

Zakim, Eric (2006). *To Build and Be Built: Landscape, Literature, and the Construction of Zionist Identity* (Philadelphia: University of Pennsylvania Press).

Zalashik, Rakefet (2004). "Pioneering Psychiatry: Zionist Newcomers and Jewish Psychiatrists in Palestine in the 1920s." *Israel* 6: 63–82 [Hebrew].

Zameret, Zvi (1993). *The Melting Pot: The Frumkin Commission on the Education of Immigrant Children, 1950* (Beer Sheva: Ben-Gurion Research Institute) [Hebrew].

Zameret, Zvi (1997). "Ten Years of Education." *The First Decade, 1948–1958*, edited by Zvi Zameret and Hanna Yablonka (Jerusalem: Yad Ben-Zvi), 123–136 [Hebrew].

Zerubavel, Eviatar (2003). *Time Maps: Collective Memory and the Social Shape of the Past* (Chicago: University of Chicago Press).

Zerubavel, Yael (1991). "New Beginnings, Old Past: The Collective Memory of Pioneering in Israeli Culture." *New Perspectives on Israeli History: The Early Years of the State*, edited by Laurence J. Silberstein (New York: New York University Press), 193–215.

Zerubavel, Yael (2002). "The 'Mythological Sabra' and Jewish Past: Trauma, Memory, and Contested Identities." *Israel Studies* 7/2: 115–144.

Zerubavel, Yael (2008). "Memory, the Rebirth of the Native, and the 'Hebrew Bedouin' Identity." *Social Research* 75/1: 315–352.

Zerubavel, Yael (2009). "The Conquest of the Desert and the Settlement Ethos." *The Desert Experience in Israel: Communities, Arts, Science, and Education in the Negev*, edited by A. Paul Hare and Gideon M. Kressel (Lanham, MD: University Press of America), 33–44.

Zidon, Asher (1952). *Between Hammer and Pulpit* (Jerusalem: Achiasaf) [Hebrew].

Ziv, Avner (1986). "Psychosocial Aspects of Jewish Humor in Israel and the Diaspora." *Jewish Humor*, edited by Avner Ziv (Tel Aviv: Papyrus), 15–36 [Hebrew].

Zur, Yaron (1997). "The Immigration from Muslim Countries." *The First Decade, 1948–1958*, edited by Zvi Zameret and Hanna Yablonka (Jerusalem: Yad Ben-Zvi), 57–81 [Hebrew].

Zweiniger-Bargielowska, Ina (2002). *Austerity in Britain: Rationing, Controls, and Consumption, 1939–1955* (Oxford: Oxford University Press).

Electronic Sources

Rathmayr, Renate (2008). "Intercultural Aspects of New Russian Politeness." WU Online Papers in International Business Communication, Series 1. Department of Fremdsprachliche Wirtschaftskommunikation, WU Vienna University of Economics and Business, Vienna. http://epub.wu.ac.at/1060/1/document.pdf.

Index

Note: Page numbers in italics refer to the illustrations.